Communication

Communication

Sixth Edition

Larry L. Barker
Auburn University

Deborah A. Barker
Auburn University

PRENTICE HALL, Englewood Cliffs, New Jersey 07632

Library of Congress Cataloging-in-Publication Data

Barker, Larry Lee
    Communication / Larry L. Barker, Deborah A. Barker. — 6th ed.
      p. cm.
    Includes bibliographical references and index.
    ISBN 0-13-155946-X
    1. Communication. I. Barker, Deborah Ann. II. Title.
  P90.B296 1993
  302.2—dc20   92-569
                                          CIP

Editor-in-chief: Charlyce Jones Owen
Acquisitions editor: Stephen Dalphin
Editorial/production supervision: Barbara Reilly
Art director: Anne T. Bonanno
Interior design: Lorraine Mullaney
Cover design: Jerry Votta
Copy editor: Eleanor Walter
Marketing manager: Chris Freitag
Prepress buyer: Kelly Behr
Manufacturing buyer: Mary Ann Gloriande
Photo research: Rhoda Sidney
Photo editor: Lori Morris-Nantz
Supplements editor: Sharon Chambliss
Editorial assistant: Caffie Risher
Cover art: "Petit Pouchet Cafe," 1928, Paris, by Bonnard.
        Collection, Besson. Giroudon/Art Resource.

 © 1993, 1990, 1987, 1984, 1981, 1978 by Prentice-Hall, Inc.
A Paramount Communications Company
Englewood Cliffs, New Jersey 07632

Printed in the United States of America
10 9 8 7 6 5 4 3 2

ISBN 0-13-155946-X

Prentice-Hall International (UK) Limited, *London*
Prentice-Hall of Australia Pty. Limited, *Sydney*
Prentice-Hall Canada Inc., *Toronto*
Prentice-Hall Hispanoamericana, S.A., *Mexico*
Prentice-Hall of India Private Limited, *New Delhi*
Prentice-Hall of Japan, Inc., *Tokyo*
Simon & Schuster Asia Pte. Ltd., *Singapore*
Editora Prentice-Hall do Brasil, Ltda., *Rio de Janeiro*

Contents

Preface   ix

Part 1   Communication Elements

---

1 A Look at Human Communication   1

Key concepts and terms   **1**
Why study human communication?   **2**
Selected perspectives on human communication   **4**
Basic elements of the communication process   **10**
Communication contexts   **16**
Summary   **20**
Exercises   **21**

2 Language, Meaning, and Communication   25

Key concepts and terms   **25**
Functions of language   **27**
Language development   **28**
Meaning   **32**
Language and behavior   **38**
Summary   **43**
Exercises   **44**

3 Listening and Feedback   49
by Kittie W. Watson

Key concepts and terms   **49**
Listening and energy conservation   **50**
Defining listening   **52**
The listening ladder: A five-step approach   **52**
Why listen?   **56**

How to listen   **59**
Feedback   **67**
Giving effective feedback   **72**
Summary   **73**
Exercises   **75**

4   Nonverbal Communication   **79**

Key concepts and terms   **79**
Functions of nonverbal communication   **81**
Types of nonverbal communication   **85**
Awareness of nonverbal communication   **108**
Summary   **110**
Exercises   **111**

Part 2   Intrapersonal, Interpersonal, Small Group, and Organizational Communication

5   Intrapersonal Communication   **119**

Key concepts and terms   **119**
The self   **120**
Self-concept   **125**
The hierarchy of human needs   **129**
The process of intrapersonal communication   **132**
The effects of intrapersonal variables on communication   **137**
Summary   **142**
Exercises   **143**

6   Interpersonal Communication   **147**

Key concepts and terms   **147**
An interpersonal communication model   **148**
Dyadic versus small group communication   **149**
Theories of interpersonal communication   **150**
Variables affecting interpersonal relationships   **155**
Development of dyadic relationships   **161**
Managing interpersonal relationships   **167**
Summary   **171**
Exercises   **172**

7   Small Group Communication   **177**

Key concepts and terms   **177**
Small group communication: An overview   **178**
Definitions   **179**
Some small groups and their functions   **180**
Participating in small groups   **183**

Role structure and status   **187**
The development of a small group   **191**
Leaders and leadership   **192**
Theoretical approaches   **193**
Problem solving through group discussion   **199**
The problem-solving process   **203**
Other factors affecting group performance   **207**
Analyzing small group interaction   **213**
Summary   **216**
Exercises   **217**

8 **Organizational Communication**   **227**

Key concepts and terms   **227**
What is an organization?   **228**
Characteristics of organizations in the 1990s and beyond   **229**
Communication dimensions in organizations   **232**
Networks   **238**
Professionalism and the organization   **240**
Communication situations   **243**
Summary   **248**
Exercises   **249**

Part 3   Public Communication

9 **Ethics, Intentions, and the Speaker-Audience Relationship**   **253**

Key concepts and terms   **253**
Public communication: An overview   **255**
Ethical responsibility and the public speaker   **257**
Purposes of communicating in the public setting   **261**
The speaker and the audience: Audience analysis   **263**
Methods of investigating your audience   **273**
Other audience considerations   **274**
Summary   **282**
Exercises   **284**

10 **Communication Goals: Information Exchange, Persuasion, Entertainment**   **289**

Key concepts and terms   **289**
Information exchange   **290**
Persuasion   **295**
Approaches to persuasion   **296**
Persuasive techniques   **307**
Persuasive situations   **311**
Entertainment, ceremonial, and other special-occasion
    communication   **312**
Summary   **315**
Exercises   **315**

11 Developing and Organizing the Message 321

Key concepts and terms 321
Selecting the topic 323
Narrowing the topic 325
Gathering source materials 326
Parts of the speech 329
Arrangement of the body of the speech 336
Principles of outlining 341
Supporting material 346
Summary 351
Exercises 352

12 Speech Delivery 357

Key concepts and terms 357
Communication apprehension 359
Principles 362
Physical delivery 366
Vocal delivery 372
Style 377
Summary 379
Exercises 380

13 Communication Through the Mass Media 385

Key concepts and terms 385
Mass communication: An overview 386
Characteristics of mass communication 387
Mass communication media 391
Functions of mass communication 394
Advertising 398
Public relations 398
Effects of mass media 399
Appearing on radio and television 406
The future of mass communication 410
Summary 412
Exercises 413

Appendix A: Preparing for a Job Search 417
Appendix B: Sample Speech 434
Appendix C: Sample Student Outlines 440
Glossary 445
Bibliography 457
Photo Credits 463
Index 465

Preface

The first edition of *Communication* was published in 1978. In the 15 years since the publication of that first edition, our world has changed dramatically. International events have changed so rapidly that it's often hard to remember, at times, which nations are our allies and which are our adversaries. Increased international trade has put new pressures on American corporations. Businesses in the U.S. have become more quality oriented and are now realizing, perhaps for the first time, that it's the people in organizations who make the real difference. Business leaders also are beginning to appreciate the importance of accurate and relational communication. Now, more than ever, a person's ability to communicate effectively often determines his or her career success. The 1990s have been labeled the "communication decade." This text serves as a guide to improve vital communication skills in the 1990s and beyond.

The sixth edition of *Communication* is different from the previous ones, in that it is co-authored by a team of two. Given the current information explosion in our shrinking world, it is difficult at this point for one person to keep pace with new trends, research, and theory in the communication discipline. Deborah Barker, the new member of the team, brings fresh insights into many of the content areas in the text. Her training and experience allow her to bring many relevant examples, ideas, and illustrations to both old and new concepts in the book. In addition, her position as director of a basic professional speaking course, serving over 2,000 students each year, has allowed her to field test much of the material in this new edition.

Previous editions of *Communication* contained several features that appealed to a substantial portion of its readers. These included: (1) a complete "minitext" in public speaking within the textbook; (2) an extensive chapter on intrapersonal communication processes; (3) a major emphasis on nonverbal communication throughout the text, accompanied by a fully developed chapter on nonverbal behavior; (4) an emphasis on receiver-oriented communication, reflected by a complete chapter on listening; (5) an integrated set of chapters focused on interpersonal and relational communication; and (6) an emphasis on applied communication, represented by a complete chapter on organizational communication. All of these features have been retained in the sixth edition, and several new features have been added. These include:

1. A completely new chapter on listening and feedback (Chapter 3) written for the text by Dr. Kittie W. Watson of Tulane University. The new treatment of listening reflects the latest research and techniques focusing on listening behavior.

2. An expansion and revision of Chapter 8, Organizational Communication. The revised chapter focuses on new organizational and management trends of the 1990s.

3. Substantial revision and updating of other chapters in this edition, including Chapter 1, A Look at Human Communication; Chapter 2, Language, Meaning, and Communication; Chapter 5, Intrapersonal Communication; Chapter 9, Ethics, Intentions, and the Speaker-Audience Relationship; Chapter 10, Communication Goals: Information Exchange, Persuasion, Entertainment; and Chapter 13, Communication Through the Mass Media.

4. An updated bibliography of all references at the end of the text.

5. An expanded and revised glossary of terms, coded to **boldface** type within each chapter in the text.

6. Numerous new illustrations, examples, and research findings within each chapter.

7. A completely revised instructor's manual. The new manual contains many instructional aids as well as class-tested, item-analyzed examination questions to help instructors prepare tests and quizzes on the text material.

In addition to the new features noted above, the sixth edition also includes (1) numerous visual examples and illustrations, including new photographs, cartoons, and drawings; (2) a new text design for reading ease and student involvement; (3) key concepts and terms at the beginning of chapters to help students identify the most important concepts covered; and (4) complete summaries, activities, discussion questions, and exercises at the end of each chapter.

We hope that this sixth edition of *Communication* will continue to serve the needs of previous users, and grow to serve the needs of those teachers who have not used previous editions. We welcome letters, cards, or calls concerning specific items in the text that you like or dislike, as well as suggestions for improvement in future editions.

ACKNOWLEDGMENTS

During the past 15 years, countless people have contributed to the success of previous editions as well as the present one. Any attempt to acknowledge all those contributors completely and appropriately is bound to be incomplete. We do, however, want to express our thanks and appreciation to all those at Prentice Hall who contributed to the development, creation, and refinement of this and previous editions. Special thanks go to Steve Dalphin for his contribution to this edition.

A special debt of gratitude goes to Kittie Watson not only for her original chapter on listening and feedback, which is featured in the sixth edition, but for her work in helping develop and revise major portions of the text in previous editions. Her time, dedication, and energy are greatly appreciated.

In addition, several friends and students (not mutually exclusive categories) helped with research and development of individual chapters in previous editions. Special thanks to Renee Edwards, Loretta Malandro, Janice Lumpkin, Frances Sayers, Ginger Tubbs, Debbie Smith, Cheryl Fisher, Karen Harris, Sondi Feldmaier, Bob Kibler, Wini Vallely, John Stone, John Garrison, Charles Roberts, Karl Krayer, Frank E.X. Dance, Kathy Wahlers, Mary Helen Brown, and Mary Etta Cook. Thanks to Amy Smith, Kale Hill, Jimmy Thorn, and Gayle E. Houser for their contributions to the sixth edition. Amy helped tremendously in locating recent research findings, Kale helped in manuscript preparation, Jimmy provided moral support, and Gayle contributed significantly in helping revise Chapter 13, Communication Through the Mass Media.

We would also like to express our appreciation for the insightful comments offered by the reviewers of this edition: Kathy J. Wahlers, Barry University; Monte A. Koffler, North Dakota State University; and Charles Roberts, East Tennessee State University.

Finally, thanks to our students during the past two years, who were patient with us while we worked on this revision, and to students over the past 27 years, who helped provide examples for our text.

L. L. Barker, Professor
D. A. Barker, Assistant Professor
Department of Communication
Auburn University

Communication

A Look at Human Communication

KEY CONCEPTS AND TERMS

Communication
Verbal communication
Language
Nonverbal communication
Oral communication
Written communication
Formal communication
Informal communication
Intentional communication
Unintentional communication
Source
Encode
Message
Symbol

Channel
Receiver
Decode
Feedback
Negative feedback
Positive feedback
Ambiguous feedback
Barriers
Context System
Intrapersonal communication
Interpersonal communication
Small group communication
Public communication
Organizational communication
Mass communication

WHY STUDY HUMAN COMMUNICATION?

In a survey of more than 2,000 executives from top American organizations and businesses, one very startling finding emerged. On the average, two-thirds of these executives agreed that 70 percent of graduates from colleges and universities today—including MBAs from some of the finest institutions in the country—are unable to communicate adequately. Specifically, the majority of these executives agreed that:

> 60 to 70 percent of students who graduate from American institutions of higher learning are unable to write well-constructed sentences;
>
> close to 80 or 90 percent of graduates from these schools need instruction on how to write a simple business report; and
>
> less than 20 percent are capable of presenting a concise, clear oral report.

In fact, several top executives reported that the problem has become so far-reaching that their respective companies have set up remedial communication courses for their up-and-coming executives.[1] Others are spending millions of dollars each year on communication training for their executives and managers and are sending their engineers and technicians back to college to improve their communication skills.

Although these statistics are indeed frightening, the fact that you are reading this book and probably are enrolled in a speech communication course right now suggests that you are aware of the importance of maximizing your communication skills. We hope that the previously quoted statistics will underscore for you the importance of these skills and serve as a reminder of their salience throughout your readings.

To help you achieve your fullest potential as a communicator, this text is designed to provide you with the most current information available on human communication theory and research. Additionally, we will present a number of basic communication principles in each chapter to aid you in mastering a variety of social settings and interactions. By increasing your knowledge and understanding of basic communication principles, we hope to accomplish our primary aim: to help you become a more effective and *successful* communicator.

So before you close this book and reenter the fast-paced, ever-changing world of compact discs, high-definition TV, and high-speed computers, take some time to acquaint yourself with the study of human communication. By doing so, you may avoid becoming "just another statistic."

---

[1] J.T. Molloy, *Molloy's Live for Success* (New York: Bantam Books, 1985).

Communication Inventory

Before reading further, take a few minutes to complete Figure 1–1, the Communication Inventory. Use each question to assess your current level of satisfaction regarding your communication behavior.

If you are honest with yourself in answering these questions, you can begin to determine more fully how well you communicate. In addition, by establishing specific communication goals—both here and throughout your readings—you can gauge your progress in these areas along the way. Examples of specific goals that you might have identified include: "I want to be able to organize an oral presentation more effectively" or "I want to be able to express my feelings more completely to my loved ones." Having completed this preliminary assessment, you are now ready to embark on the path to more effective human communication. Let's begin with a working definition of the communication concept.

Defining Communication

If you were asked to define "communication" during an important job interview, where would you begin? You might mention a speaker, a listener, sharing of information, the use of symbols, or a variety of other descriptive terms. However, as you try to define this concept more completely, you may have problems in choosing the right words to express your ideas. You may also find it difficult to answer related questions that the interviewer might ask. The problem is that defining communication is akin to defining the concept of love. Intuitively, we feel we understand it, but it's difficult to put into words.

Interestingly enough, communication experts have never agreed on a single definition of communication. The reason is that it all depends on your perspective. For our purposes, we will define **communication** as a process in which two or more elements of a system interact in order to achieve a desired outcome or goal. Because we view communication as a process, we also perceive it to be dynamic, ever-changing, and unending. In other words, the conversation that you had with a friend yesterday affects you as a communicator today. Additionally, the hundreds of bits of information, ideas, and opinions that you process, evaluate, and store each day also change you to some extent. By tomorrow, you will have changed even more. Fortunately, this process is usually slow and subtle. Otherwise you might be in a constant state of confusion and frustration.

Another important key to understanding communication is to realize that communication events do not occur in isolation from one another. Each interaction that you have affects each one that follows, and not always in a simple, direct manner. For example, your girlfriend (or spouse) tells you without warning that she is seeing someone else. This "bombshell" may result in your lashing out at a friend or co-worker later that day when he reminds you of a project deadline that you must meet. The next day, neither of you is able to communicate with one another as effectively as before because of your preoccupation with the communication event that took place the preceding day. Thus, the process continues.

SELECTED PERSPECTIVES ON HUMAN COMMUNICATION

As you can see, communication is more than one person speaking and another person listening. This section will explain some of the complexities of communication by looking at the dimensions of verbal and nonverbal, oral and written, formal and informal, and intentional and unintentional communication. In addition, we will discuss two indirectly related dimensions—human-computer and animal communication. Finally, we will conclude the chapter with an examination of the basic elements of the communication process and with a look at six primary communication contexts.

1. Circle the response that best represents the degree to which you are comfortable in the following communication settings:

C = Comfortable
SC = Somewhat Comfortable
N = Neutral
SU = Somewhat Uncomfortable
U = Uncomfortable

	C	SC	N	SU	U
a. Asking someone for a lunch date	5	4	3	2	1
b. Facilitating a group discussion	5	4	3	2	1
c. Preparing a written report	5	4	3	2	1
d. Discussing a problem with your boss	5	4	3	2	1
e. Giving an oral presentation	5	4	3	2	1
f. Listening to difficult material	5	4	3	2	1

2. How would you rate your *effectiveness* in each of the following communication settings?

E = Effective
SE = Somewhat Effective
DK = Don't Know
SI = Somewhat Ineffective
I = Ineffective

	E	SE	DK	SI	I
a. Leading a discussion	5	4	3	2	1

b. Promoting yourself to others	5	4	3	2	1
c. Managing difficult people	5	4	3	2	1
d. Creating small talk	5	4	3	2	1
e. Interpreting others' nonverbal behavior	5	4	3	2	1
f. Group problem solving	5	4	3	2	1

3. In which of the following areas do you feel that you could improve? (Place an X beside each response that is appropriate.)

_____ Developing satisfying relationships

_____ Giving dynamic oral presentations

_____ Writing effective reports

_____ Listening responsively

_____ Giving effective feedback to others

_____ Solving complex group problems

_____ Reading nonverbal cues effectively

4. Finally, complete the following sentence by listing three specific goals that you would like to achieve once you have completed studying this text or course.

Upon finishing this text/course in communication, I want to be able to:

a. _____

b. _____

c. _____

FIGURE 1–1
Communication Inventory

Verbal and Nonverbal Communication

When we think of communication, we usually think of spoken messages. However, experts usually divide communication into two primary categories: verbal and nonverbal communication. *Verbal communication* involves the use of symbols that generally have universal meanings for all who are taking part in the process. As such, verbal communication may be spoken or written. These spoken or written verbal symbols are known as *language.* Additionally, verbal communication is highly structured and uses formal rules of grammar. (Chapter 2 covers language in detail.) *Nonverbal communication* involves the use of symbols other than the written or spoken word, such as gestures, eye behavior, tone of voice, use of space, and touch. Although nonverbal symbols have socially shared meanings, they have no formal structure or rules of grammar. (Chapter 4 is devoted solely to nonverbal communication.)

Nonverbal messages usually complement verbal messages. A service-station attendant usually points and uses other gestures while giving directions to a stranger from out of town. At other times, nonverbal symbols completely replace verbal messages. Teachers with cold, fixed stares can

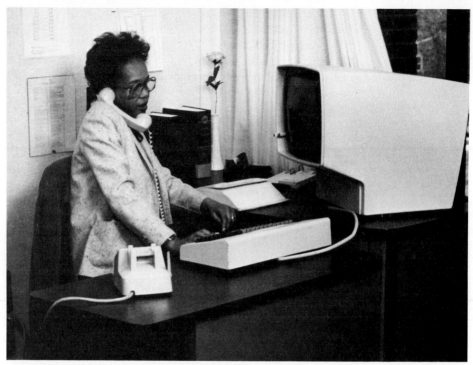

Human-machine communication has become a necessity of everyday life.

easily tell students to be quiet without uttering a word. It is important to note that when nonverbal messages contradict what you say verbally, others usually believe the nonverbal message. For example, when a husband tells his wife verbally that he is interested in hearing about what happened at a political rally as he continues to read the newspaper, he nonverbally communicates uninterest.

Oral and Written Communication

Oral communication refers to messages that are transmitted "out loud." Generally they involve both verbal and nonverbal messages. We participate in oral communication each day either as speakers or listeners when we answer the telephone, listen to a lecture, watch MTV, or talk with a friend.

Written communication is taking place right now as you read this book. Although this type of communication is primarily verbal, it also has a nonverbal dimension. For example, you probably get a different feeling when you receive a personal, hand-written Christmas card than when you are given a mass-produced, printed one from your insurance company.

Both oral and written communication involve the creation and sending of messages. However, they differ in a number of ways. Wallach (1990) argues that these two forms of communication have three primary differences: differences in processing, style, and form.[2]

Processing differences lie in the nature of the two types of messages themselves. Oral messages are continuous, with words and sounds spoken in a connected way. Thus, when we talk, we generally do not focus on individual words or sounds, unless (1) a communication breakdown occurs; (2) the speaker talks with an accent; or (3) the source or receiver stops and asks about a given sound or word. On the other hand, written communication involves the processing of segmented or discrete letter units, marked by boundaries of white space on the page. Thus, when we learn to read, we have to figure out how individual letters and words go together to reflect the continuous sounds we are used to hearing orally. This processing difference is one of the main reasons why we can't read just because we can talk. To read, we must become a linguist of sorts and bring our knowledge of spoken language to the surface in order to analyze and understand written language.[3]

Oral and written communication also differ in form. While oral messages are generally personal, spontaneous, and shared within some context, written messages are less personal and more literate in form. In contrast, oral communication is participant- and situation-oriented, while written communication generally is associated with the public sphere.[4] If you think for a moment about these differences in form, you will understand why humans have difficulty putting their "feelings" on paper. By making the switch from a whispered thought or spoken dialogue to a letter or poem, indeed, we are able to preserve the moment for posterity. In almost every instance, however, the spontaneity and "life" associated with the message will be lost.

Finally, written messages use a more formal style of language, while oral messages are more conversational and informal. Please note, however, that oral and written communication are not mutually exclusive. Many television commercials use written reinforcement of an oral message (for example, when stressing the effectiveness of a new cold capsule).

Formal and Informal Communication

We have all been involved in formal and informal communication situations. In **formal communication,** such as public speaking or mass communication, we pay more attention to both verbal and nonverbal messages. For instance, we use language more precisely and pay more attention to grammar. Additionally, we are more concerned about the image that our dress, posture, and eye contact help convey. Formal communication usually occurs in the

---

[2]G. Wallach, "Magic Buries Celtics: Looking for a Broader Interpretation of Language Learning and Literacy," *Topics in Language Disorders*, 10, no. 2 (1990), 63–80.

[3]Ibid., 65–66.

[4]Ibid., 68–70.

context of status differences. For example, during an appointment with a university dean, a student probably would avoid using slang, sit up straight, dress neatly, and make eye contact.

In *informal communication,* such as interpersonal and small-group communication, people are more at ease and can be themselves. Observers would notice more hesitations and slang in verbal messages and less attention to nonverbal messages such as clothing, posture, and eye contact. When going to a party at a friend's house, you probably wouldn't hesitate to sit on the floor, go to the refrigerator for something to eat, or use the telephone. At a party at your boss's house, however, you probably would be hesitant about taking any of these actions.

Intentional and Unintentional Communication

Most communication has a purpose, but sometimes we take part in communication without realizing it. *Intentional communication* occurs when messages are sent with specific goals in mind. Comedians such as Elayne Boosler and Bobcat Goldthwaite tell jokes to get laughs and entertain audiences. Radio spots are designed to persuade people to vote for local candidates, buy products, or donate time and money.

The use of hand signs is a form of verbal communication.

Other communication takes place ***unintentionally***, without the communicators being aware of it. The greatest number of unintentional messages are nonverbal. Our nonverbal behaviors often speak louder than words. Students or employees who are continually late for class or work might be communicating that they are moonlighting, are irresponsible, or have unreliable alarm clocks.

Intentional communication is sometimes made to appear unintentional. Many lawyers tell their clients how to dress for the courtroom. For example, during her now classic robbery trial, wealthy socialite Patricia Hearst wore conservative, old clothing, which included a large, loosely fitted blouse, under the instruction of her attorney, F. Lee Bailey. The old clothing was used to de-emphasize the fact that she was wealthy, and the large blouse was used to give the impression of weight loss to arouse sympathy among the jurors. (See photo on page 17.)

Additional Communication Forms

Two additional forms of communication that are rapidly becoming of interest to communication scholars are human-computer and animal communication. Indeed, studies of humans and their relationship to computers are of growing concern, given the magnitude of recent advances in computer technology. Studies of animals are and have been important since the dawn of time.

HUMAN–COMPUTER COMMUNICATION.   The growth of human knowledge has escalated beyond belief in modern times. Information that was once conveyed verbally through stories and myths in ancient times is now transmitted through high-tech media such as image retrieval and laser-disc systems. Satellite communication, once a novelty, is now a well-established medium. Once a luxury, personal computers have become a necessity in the average American home. In short, computer technology has established its preeminence in this age of information. What remains to be seen is its impact on future generations.

Although a number of questions may be raised regarding the ultimate impact and effectiveness of various technologies, communication scholars are becoming especially interested in the effects of technology on human communication. For example, to what extent does computer-mediated communication depersonalize interactions and cause a loss of individualization? What effects do computerized conferences have on the group decision-making process? To what extent does computer mediation reduce or increase communication efficiency? Each of these questions ultimately will be addressed by communication scholars in coming years. We, too, will address them more completely in Chapter 13.

ANIMAL COMMUNICATION.   Although the study of animal communication has played a vital role in our understanding of human communication ever since the dawn of time, recent research in this area has revealed a number of striking similarities between animal and human communication.

Specifically, researchers have discovered that animals share with humans a number of characteristics, including those associated with attraction and mating, territoriality, rivalry and play, familial ties, colony organization, division of labor, and a number of other traits that we once assumed were uniquely "human."

For example, the bond between squirrel monkey mothers and infants is not unlike that of humans. When infants are separated from their mothers, they emit loud, easily located, and individually recognizable sounds. In this way, the mother can find her child and serve its needs. Likewise, mother squirrel monkeys have their own form of "motherese," or adult speech that is modified in order to communicate with their infants. This behavior is not unlike the "billing and cooing" of human mothers as they talk with their babies or the simplified speech patterns that we all use to talk with children.[5]

Another similarity between animals and humans lies in the dolphin's ability to avoid dangerous situations. So intelligent are dolphins that they can determine which boats to avoid by "remembering" bad past experiences and by discerning any similarities in approaching boats or ships. In turn, they can signal this information to other dolphins who are swimming nearby.

In short, like humans, animals use a wide variety of communication processes ranging from auditory, visual, and tactile systems to olfactory, thermal, and electrical systems. The primary difference between the two forms of communication seems to lie in humans' ability to use words or symbols—and to string them together into sentences that can build and present abstract ideas or that can tell a story about the past, present, or future. However, as researchers delve more deeply into questions regarding the communication systems of animals, new discoveries regarding their "language patterns" will emerge. Given the vast number of similarities that already have come to light between animal and human communication, it is certain that human communication scholars will be watching.

BASIC ELEMENTS OF THE COMMUNICATION PROCESS

Thus far in your reading you may have formed the impression that communication must be difficult, if not impossible, to study and understand. If it is ongoing, how do we stop it? If it has no beginning or end, how do we get hold of it? Although the task is difficult, it is possible. The communication process is a system that involves an interrelated, interdependent group of elements working together as a whole to achieve a desired outcome or goal.

---

[5]M. Biben, D. Symmes, and D. Bernhards, "Contour Variables in Vocal Communication Between Squirrel Monkey Mothers and Infants," *Developmental Psychobiology*, 22, no. 6 (1989), 617–31.

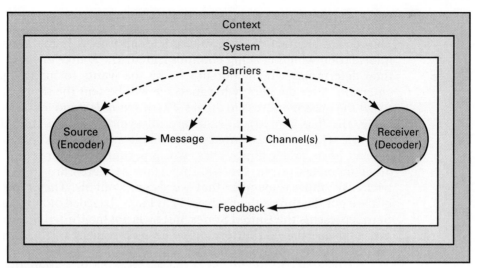

FIGURE 1–2
The Communication Process

We can study communication in much the same way we study biological systems within our own bodies. We can determine the elements involved (circulatory and digestive systems, for example), analyze how those elements affect one another, and thus determine the nature of the process as a whole.

Applying this approach to the communication process, we find eight elements: (1) a source/encoder of communication, which sends (2) a message (3) through a channel(s) to (4) a receiver/decoder, which (5) responds via feedback with (6) possibilities of communication breakdowns in each stage of communication. However, these elements must be understood and analyzed in relation to (7) the situation or context, and (8) the system (such as a relationship), which is created and maintained at some level by the communicators. Figure 1–2 gives us a visual representation of the communication process.

The Source/Encoder

The *source,* or encoder, makes the decision to communicate. The source also determines what the purpose of the message will be: to inform, persuade, or entertain. You may ask how the message gets from the source to the receiver. First, the source must *encode,* or create, a message. That is, the information that the source wishes to convey must be put into a form that can be sent to the receiver. The source generates a message through his or her past experiences, perceptions, thoughts, and feelings. Every ounce of your being may tell you that you are in love, but until you code those feelings into a form that can be sent to the person you love, communication cannot take place.

Message

The second element of the communication process is the **message,** or that information which is being communicated. The source encodes an idea and then determines whether or not he or she wants to inform, persuade, or entertain. After deciding what message will be sent the source uses symbols to get the message across to others. These **symbols** stand for other things. The eagle, the flag, and Uncle Sam are all symbols of the United States, for example. But the most important symbols are words, which can represent objects, ideas, and feelings. These words permit us to share our thoughts with other members of our species. Important as words are to us, they can be tricky. We must remember that words are symbols. They represent things, but are not the things themselves. That lanky, bearded old man we call Uncle Sam represents the United States, but he is *not* the United States—in fact, he doesn't even exist. The letters *a-p-p-l-e p-i-e* represent an all-American pastry, but they are *not* an apple pie.

To increase the likelihood of successful communication, the source must try to encode in a way that the receiver understands, so that the receiver can properly decode (interpret) the message. For example, many American tourists in Paris have discovered that even though their command of French is minimal, it is sometimes easier to communicate in halting French than in English. Some Parisians, despite their fluent knowledge of English, refuse to decode an "inferior" tongue.

Channel

Channels are the means (that is, pathways or devices) by which messages are communicated. Channels may be described and analyzed in two different ways. The first involves the form in which messages are sent to receivers. Forms include both verbal and nonverbal channels of communication. We use our five senses to receive messages from others. We may hear a presidential address over a radio, watch an Olympic gymnast perform a routine on television, smell the aroma of Thanksgiving dinner when opening the door to our grandmother's house, taste the flavors in mint-chocolate-chip ice cream, or hug a friend to congratulate her on her new job.

Channels may also be described according to the manner of presentation employed in communication. The source may speak face-to-face with the receiver, use a public address system to talk with a hundred listeners, or talk over radio or television to millions of receivers. Each of these examples would demand different manners of presentation. Depending on the situation, the source would concentrate on verbal and/or nonverbal channels of communication. If the speaker were on radio, physical appearance wouldn't matter, but if he or she were performing on a cable network program or before a live audience, personal appearance could easily influence the reception of the message. For example, when we go to watch a circus, we expect the clowns to have painted faces and appropriate costumes. If they were dressed in regular street clothes, their performances wouldn't be as effective. Whatever channels of communication are used, the source must learn to adapt the message to make use of the most appropriate channels available for the situation.

Receiver/Decoder

The person (or persons) who attends to the source's message is the **receiver.** The act of interpreting messages is called **decoding.** Receivers decode messages based on past experiences, perceptions, thoughts, and feelings. We receive messages through all our senses, but most often we decode messages by listening or seeing. We first have a physiological reception of stimuli (a noise causes sound waves to hit our eardrum or a movement catches our eye). We then pay attention to both the verbal and nonverbal stimuli and reduce all the stimuli bombarding us to one or two we can cope with more easily. Next, we try to understand the stimuli and interpret them into messages (we decide that the noise is a telephone bell or that the movement is a friend waving to us across campus). Finally, we store this information for later use so that next time we will be able to respond to the stimuli more quickly. It is important to remember that receivers make immediate decisions about what they will respond to in a given situation. During a lecture, an audience member may decide to take a nap. During an argument with your boyfriend or spouse, you may listen only to negative comments. During a crowded party you may watch the nonverbal behaviors of your date (yawning, standing off in a corner alone, and so on) to decide when it's time to leave. As sources of communication, we need to learn to analyze our prospective receivers to determine which communication messages will be most effective.

Of course, all of us are both encoders and decoders; that is, we are capable of both transmitting and receiving messages. When you receive a message, you must interpret it and then encode a response. The response may be silent, noisy, or somewhere in between, depending upon the situation and the existence of any barriers to communication.

Feedback

Another element in the communication process is **feedback.** Each party in an interaction continuously sends messages back to the other. This return process is called feedback. Feedback tells the source how the receiver has interpreted each message. For example, if at the airport you ask your departing friend about his itinerary, and he replies that he didn't pack one, you know your message has not been understood. This kind of feedback, which conveys lack of understanding, is known as **negative feedback.** **Positive feedback,** on the other hand, indicates that the receiver has understood the source's message. It does not necessarily mean that he or she agrees with the source, just that the message was interpreted accurately. Feedback can also be ambiguous, not clearly positive or negative. "I see" and "mm-hmm" can be examples of **ambiguous feedback.** The effective communicator is always sensitive to feedback and constantly modifies his or her messages as a result of the feedback received. After a discreet pause, for example, you might ask your friend not about his "itinerary" but about the cities he plans to visit.

Feedback doesn't have to come from others. We can and do get feedback from our own messages. The fact that we can hear the words we speak and see the sentences we write sometimes lets us correct our own mistakes.

Barriers

The human communication system can be compared with a radio or telephone circuit. Just as in radio transmissions, where distortion can occur at any point along the circuit (channel), there can be similar **barriers** in human communication. The source's information may be insufficient or unclear. (A love-struck hero may think he is ill rather than in love.) Or the message can be ineffectively or inaccurately encoded. (Our hero may know he's in love but can't find the proper words to convey his feelings until it's too late. That is, his signals may not be sent rapidly or accurately enough.) The wrong channel of communication may be used. (He may sing a love song or send flowers when she doesn't like love songs and is allergic to flowers.) The message may not be decoded the way it was encoded. (The object of our hero's love loves him too—like a brother.) Finally, the receiver may not be equipped to handle the decoded message in such a way as to produce the response (feedback) expected by the source. (Our heroine skips town after receiving our hero's impassioned love letter.) Barriers to communication also occur if the sender and receiver are not on the same "wavelength." This is as true in human communication as it is in radio transmission. On the human level, being on the same wavelength involves shared experiences. That is, the source can encode only in terms of the experiences he or she has had. This is why two people from completely different cultures may find it difficult, if not impossible, to communicate. For example, imagine trying to convey the idea of a soap opera like *General Hospital* or *The Young and the Restless* to someone who has never even seen a television set. (In answer to your question, "Yes, such people do exist.") Figure 1–3 shows the necessity for overlapping fields of experience in communication.

Naturally, no two wavelengths can be exactly alike, because each human being's experiences are unique. Communication will be most effective, however, if the boxes that represent the fields of experience of the source and the receiver have a large area in common. If there have been no common experiences (that is, if the boxes don't meet), communication will be impossible.

Context or Situation

Intricately related to the concept of shared field of experience is the concept of **context**, or situation. This element of communication is, perhaps, one of the most important; it affects each of the other elements as well as the

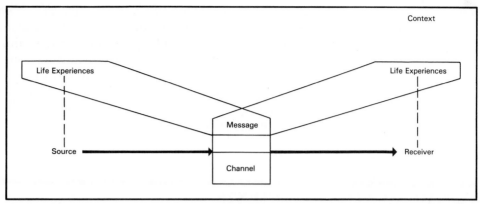

FIGURE 1–3
Interpersonal Communication

communication process as a whole. Look, for example, at the following communicative situation: While working in her office one afternoon, Debbie overhears her office mate Cindy saying to someone in the hall, "Not only do I not have time to see you now; in a hundred years I wouldn't find the time." Had Debbie not peered down the hall in amazement, only to see Cindy smiling and directing this comment to one of the latter's good friends, she probably would have completely misunderstood the message she overheard! With the context supplied, an accurate meaning could be assigned to Cindy's comment.

The System

Finally, the system itself plays a vital role in the communication process. By **system,** we mean that unique entity, bond, or relationship that is created, defined, and ultimately maintained through the process of communication. A system grows, disintegrates, or changes every time a message is exchanged. (At times, the system may be altered even if a message is not exchanged.) In turn, the nature and state of the system have an impact on the messages that are sent *at a given time*, bringing the process full circle. Note our emphasis on the phrase, "at a given time," in the previous sentence. Because the system is constantly in a state of flux due to the process nature of communication, the point in time at which messages are exchanged is significant. If a system, or relationship, is experiencing growth, messages may be exchanged and interpreted in one way. However, if the system is in a state of disintegration, messages may be exchanged and possibly interpreted in another way.

For example, think of the most significant person in your life right now. From its inception, your relationship with this person has grown and developed with each interaction. As it has grown, the relationship in turn has affected what and how you have (and will) communicate at a given moment. When you first met the person about whom you are thinking, no system or relationship existed. As a result, you probably communicated more tentatively, selected your words more carefully, and more closely monitored your nonverbal behavior. However, as the relationship (that is, system) began to develop a "life of its own," you probably grew more comfortable, used less formal language patterns, and felt more at ease regarding your nonverbal behavior. In short, the system, or your relationship with this person, was actually *created* through the process of communication. In turn, the system directs what and how you communicate with your significant other, depending on the state of the system at the time.

COMMUNICATION CONTEXTS

Communication is often thought of as an interaction between two people. However, we participate in several communication contexts each day. These contexts include: (1) intrapersonal, (2) interpersonal, (3) small group, (4) public, (5) organizational, and (6) mass communication. Figure 1–4 describes differences among the contexts of communication. Distinctions generally are made among communication contexts by the number of sensory channels available and immediacy of feedback.

The number of communicators automatically affects the other dimensions of communication. When you watch Arsenio Hall on television, you are observing two contexts or levels of communication: interpersonal and mass

FIGURE 1–4
Distinguishing Characteristics of Human Communication Contexts

CATEGORIES	NUMBER OF COMMUNICATORS	DEGREE OF PHYSICAL PROXIMITY	AVAILABLE SENSORY CHANNELS	IMMEDIACY OF FEEDBACK
	Many	Low	Maximal	Most Delayed
Mass communication				
Organizational communication				
Public communication				
Small group communication				
Interpersonal communication				
Intrapersonal communication				
	One	High	Minimal	Most Immediate

Source: Adapted from G. R. Miller, "The Current Status of Theory and Research in Interpersonal Communication," *Human Communication Research*, 4, no. 2 (Winter 1978), 316–23.

Patty Hearst is shown (left) before her trial, discussed on page 9, and (right) at the Cannes Film Festival in 1988.

communication. As Arsenio interviews one of his guests, he is involved in interpersonal communication. Since the two people are close to one another, all the sensory channels are available to them. They are face-to-face, free to shake hands and touch each other, able to smell cologne or body odors, and so on. They also get immediate feedback such as laughs, facial expressions, or verbal rebukes.

With mass communication, all the situational categories are altered. Instead of being beside Arsenio Hall, you may be in Auburn, Alabama, watching him on television. You become one of millions watching him each evening. Because you are so far from Los Angeles, where the show originates, there are only two sensory channels available: hearing and sight. Reception from these sensory channels is limited because cameras switch back and forth, commercials interrupt, there may be reception difficulties, or you may be watching black-and-white instead of color television. Finally, with mass communication, feedback is delayed. Nielsen ratings don't come out every month, and you cannot be sure that your personal letter will be read by anyone, much less by Arsenio Hall.

As we begin looking at communication, it is important to remember that it is a process. We begin with **intrapersonal communication** and gradually work up the continuum to mass communication. The most basic communication context is intrapersonal communication, which takes place when an individual sends and receives messages internally. For example, if you watch children playing alone, you will often see them singing and talking to themselves. They may be giving themselves directions about how to build a fort with blocks or build the tower of a sandcastle on the beach. Sometimes you probably find yourself in some form of internal argument. Should you study for your test in communication or accept an invitation to that great party you heard about? We also communicate with ourselves at an unconscious level. Usually we don't notice our heart rates, brain activity, or body tension, but they are essential to our survival and tell us about our internal processing (see Chapter 5).

Intrapersonal communication is the foundation on which interpersonal communication is based. Successful communication with others depends first upon effective communication with ourselves. **Interpersonal communication** is usually thought of as occurring between two people. When you call a friend on the phone, go for a job interview, or ask a professor about your last test grade, you are participating in interpersonal communication. The responsibility for successful interaction is shared between two people. The closeness of the communicators places greater attention on the nonverbal responses from others as we monitor feedback (see Chapter 6).

When you and a co-worker are talking and another person joins you, the three of you are involved in **small group communication.** Communication is more complicated with a group of three or more persons. Think about how confusing a meeting can be with everyone talking at once, or about the satisfaction you feel when the combination of individual talents results in an A on a group project. In successful small group communication, each participant has the potential to communicate and adds to the interaction (see Chapter 7).

With **public communication,** one person addresses a group in a lecture or public speech. Few, if any, verbal responses are made by the audience. Remember the last time you spoke before a group? It may have been during "show and tell" in the first grade, giving a toast at a friend's wedding rehearsal, or demonstrating the latest food processor to a group of home-makers. With public communication, a speaker is concerned about personal appearance, delivery, the message, the audience, and their response. Effective speakers adjust their delivery style to the type of audience they address. For example, an architect who shows her plans to a group of executives will be more concerned about her language, reasoning, and appearance than she will be if she is practicing her presentation with her immediate family. The public communicator controls the communication process almost completely (see Chapters 9 through 12).

The area of communication that has gained the greatest amount of attention in recent years is **organizational communication.** Two books—*In Search of Excellence* and *Thriving on Chaos*—are examples of the many books that have addressed the current "management revolution." As a result of growing interest in maximizing communication effectiveness, organizations around the world have begun to seek ways to achieve a number of goals. Some of these goals include improving leadership ability, developing greater responsiveness to clients, creating more efficient work environments, building effective self-management teams, and optimizing the flow of information within organizations themselves and with their publics.

Organizations usually have a chain of command, with one or more top managers making decisions and managing communication. More and more organizations are incorporating management training and development programs that focus on communication skills. Effective communication in organizations ensures greater efficiency for consumers (see Chapter 8).

The communication context with the greatest amount of control for both the sender and the receiver is *mass communication.* By "control" we mean that broadcasters make decisions about information to be sent, generally without input from the mass audience. However, as a receiver, you have maximum control over what you listen to, watch, or read. Types of mass communication include radio, television, newspapers, magazines, telephones, and satellite transmissions.

Mass communication affects every aspect of our daily lives. We wake up to music on the radio, read a newspaper during breakfast, notice signs as we drive to school or work, study textbooks, watch the news and our favorite shows on television or videotape, and go to the local movie theater. The characteristics of mass communication include large audiences, message reproduction, rapid distribution and delivery, and low cost to the consumer (see Chapter 13).

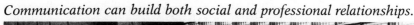

Communication can build both social and professional relationships.

After examining the six contexts of communication, you can see that communication involves more than just two people interacting with one another. Intrapersonal, interpersonal, small group, public, organizational, and mass communication each contain sources, messages, channels, receivers, feedback, barriers, and some form of systems. The interaction of these basic elements within their respective contexts produces what is defined here as "communication."

SUMMARY

Communication is a dynamic, ever-changing, unending process by which people transmit information and feelings to others. Communication plays a major role in all of our lives. By increasing your knowledge and understanding of the principles of communication, you will probably become a more effective communicator.

Eight basic elements of the communication process are the (1) source, (2) receiver, (3) message, (4) channel, (5) feedback, (6) barriers, (7) context or situation, and (8) communication system. The source sends a message comprised of symbols through verbal and nonverbal channels to a receiver. As the receiver decodes the message, he or she responds with feedback. The receiver then becomes the source of the next message that is conveyed. Communication can be hindered by barriers at any point in the process. Two additional elements that affect communication are the context and the overall system itself.

The process of communication has many dimensions and occurs on different levels. Four dimensions of human communication are verbal and nonverbal, oral and written, formal and informal, and intentional and unintentional communication. Human-computer and animal communication are receiving a growing amount of attention from communication researchers at this time.

The six contexts of communication include (1) intrapersonal, (2) interpersonal, (3) small group, (4) public, (5) organizational, and (6) mass communication. In an intrapersonal context, both the sending and the receiving of messages take place within one individual. Interpersonal communication, on the other hand, is characterized by a give-and-take between senders and receivers of messages.

Interaction among three or more communicators is known as small group communication. Small group communication involves a different set of communication roles and functions than those found in two-person communication, primarily because of the increased number of communicators present. Communication is almost entirely one-way in the public communication situation. The public speaker generally holds a distinct advantage in that he or she controls the communication process almost completely.

All communication contexts function within organizations. Differences between small group and organizational communication include a formal structure designed to achieve specific goals through managerial control, leadership, technology, and communication networks. The final context of communication, mass media, has developed communication to its fullest extent, exerting an immensely powerful effect on modern society. Today, more than ever, we are a media society because of audience interest, diversity in messages, rapid distribution, and low cost to the consumer.

The remainder of this book is designed to increase your knowledge and your understanding of communication. Chapter 2 begins by explaining the most basic components of human communication: language and meaning.

EXERCISES

Group Experiences

Breakdowns

DESCRIPTION: The human communication system is a complex process in which breakdowns can occur at any point. In this chapter a simple eight-part model was presented, consisting of a/an (1) source, (2) message, (3) channel, (4) receiver, (5) feedback, (6) barriers, (7) situation or context, and (8) overall system. The purpose of this activity is to identify the barriers that can occur at each stage in the communication process.

PROCEDURE: Think of an important communication you want to make to another person. For example, you may want to tell your parents that you plan to quit school for a semester. Whatever your communication, identify the barriers that could occur at each point in the model.

DISCUSSION: Were you able to identify a potential barrier of communication at each point in the model? By identifying various types of barriers, you should be able to better analyze communication problems that you experience daily. The next time you encounter a communication problem, attempt to determine how the breakdown occurred. Doing so will help you avoid unnecessary barriers to communication in the future.

Walk a Mile in My Shoes

DESCRIPTION: To a large extent, successful communication depends on how well the source encodes his or her message. In any communication interaction, both the source and the receiver have fields of experience that may or may not be shared. When the fields of experience are different for the source and receiver, special attention must be given to sending and receiving messages accurately. One effective method is to "walk a mile in the other person's shoes." This activity is designed to demonstrate (1) the importance of shared fields of experience between the source and receiver and (2) a method for dealing with the different fields of experience of the two parties.

PROCEDURE: There are two stages in this activity. The first stage involves role playing in a situation in which the source and receiver do not share a field of experience. Although a sample situation is provided, you may wish to write your own. A three- to five-minute dialogue should take place between the following characters. Each character should be played in such a way that neither person shares fields of experience nor understands the other's point of view.

> *Source:* A college freshman who wants his parents to sign a permission slip to allow him to live in off-campus housing instead of in a dormitory.
>
> *Receiver:* A parent who never went to college and who considers the purpose of college to be "education," not "socialization."

The second stage of this activity requires that the two role players switch roles. In other words, the college freshman should play the parent, in an attempt to see the world through the eyes of the parent, and the parent should now be playing the college freshman. In this reversed role playing, each person should attempt to understand the other's position based on his or her life experiences.

DISCUSSION: In the first stage of the role-playing situation, the characters had different fields of experience. Communication under these conditions is very difficult, if not impossible. In the role-reversal situation, each character tried to bridge the gap by seeing the world through the eyes of the other person. If you face a similar situation, try to step back and understand how the other person experiences the world.

Responding

DESCRIPTION: Feedback is an important element in the communication process. The three types of feedback include (1) negative feedback, conveying a lack of understanding; (2) positive feedback, indicating that the receiver has understood the source's message; and (3) ambiguous feedback, which is neither clearly positive nor negative. This activity will help you identify the different types of feedback.

PROCEDURE: After reviewing the example given, write a negative, positive, and ambiguous feedback response to each of the following three statements.

> *Statement 1:* I think people from the North weigh more than people from the South—probably because of the climatic differences.
>
> *Statement 2:* If I had my choice, I'd never work for anyone but myself.
>
> *Statement 3:* I hate taking basic course requirements. It seems to me that since I'm paying for my education, I ought to be able to decide what courses to take.

Example

Statement: I would like to go to a private college. I have heard that you can get a better education there.

Positive Feedback: You might check into a private school and see how you feel about its educational program.

Negative Feedback: Private schools have poor athletic programs—why would you want to go there?

Ambiguous Feedback: I see.

DISCUSSION: A good communicator is always sensitive to feedback and constantly modifies his or her messages in response to feedback received. Feedback can be conveyed through both verbal and nonverbal channels.

Personal Experiences

1. Is it true that one cannot *not* communicate? Gather evidence based on logic or personal experience that proves or disproves this statement.
2. Select a person with whom you spend a great deal of time. Observe the type of feedback this person gives you. Is it mostly positive, negative, or ambiguous? Do you tend to like people who give you positive feedback? How do you respond to negative feedback?
3. Are you an effective communicator? Take a day and find out. Determine your awareness of the various elements of communication by observing yourself. Do you listen and respond to both verbal and nonverbal messages?

Discussion Questions

1. What is communication? Identify the basic elements of communication.
2. How does communication today affect communication tomorrow? Discuss the possible effects on the communication process or on you as a communicator.
3. Explain the concept of fields of experience.
4. Identify three different ways in which communication breakdowns occur.
5. How does feedback (negative, positive, and ambiguous) affect the communication process?

Language, Meaning, and Communication

KEY CONCEPTS AND TERMS

Language
Word
Labeling
Interaction
Transmission
Innate
Imitative, learned behavior
Language acquisition device
Infancy
Toddlerhood
Early childhood
Symbolic process
Semantics
Symbol

Sense
Referent
Concrete
Abstract
Ambiguity
Vagueness
Denotation
Connotation
Style
Non-identity
Non-allness
Self-reflexiveness
Semantic or linguistic stereotyping

Randy and Kristie were new to one of the hottest advertising firms in New York City. They had just completed their respective degrees at NYU and Syracuse, and were thrilled to be hired by one of the finest firms in the city. Randy's first assignment was to create a promotional campaign for a client who was marketing a new line of products for salt-water fishing. Kristie was assigned to work with an athletic-wear company on a marketing concept for its newest line of cross-training gear.

As time passed and work with their respective clients became more tedious, Randy and Kristie realized that they had been assigned two of the toughest accounts in town. Although Randy completed his assignment quickly and successfully, he was angry when he learned that his boss deliberately had assigned him to a difficult account. On the other hand, Kristie had a harder time satisfying her client and took several additional months to complete the project. However, she just laughed when she heard through the grapevine that her boss had made the assignment to "see what Kristie was made of."

Over the next two years, Randy worked grudgingly with each assignment and problem that he encountered. Kristie accepted each assignment cheerfully, and when problems arose she responded with her characteristic statement: "No problem. I can handle it." Although Kristie took longer to complete her projects than Randy did, and both were equally successful in working with their clients, Kristie was given the first promotion when a position opened up.

Why did Kristie get the promotion over Randy? Could Kristie's language patterns alone have given her the edge? Whether you are working in a small accounting firm in Laramie, Wyoming, or a Fortune 500 company in New York City, you need to know the organization's "secret words" if you are headed to the top. So says Lois Wyse in her book *Company Manners: An Insider Tells How to Succeed in the Real World of Corporate Protocol and Power Politics.* What "secret words" is she talking about? They are ways in which each company likes to describe itself and think of its products, services, and employees. For example, a company's buzzword one year might be "innovation" and the next year "human resource development." Managers and executives on the rise know the importance of these words to the company and use them accordingly. In addition, these "secret words" include all words or phrases—like "no problem"—that reflect a positive attitude toward work and loyalty to the company.

As you can see, language *can* have an impact on others and on your future career. Thus, an understanding of what language is and how it operates in our daily lives can be useful to you. In this chapter we will focus on a number of topics that will help you better understand how language works. We will begin with a discussion of the functions of language and how people actually develop personal language patterns. We will then address the concept of meaning and some of the features of language that affect our everyday lives, including abstraction and concreteness, ambiguity and vagueness, denotation and connotation, and language style. Finally, we will discuss the relationship between language and behavior. In this section we will address how language is often used to stereotype individuals or their behavior and look at several ways in which we can begin to make our everyday language more effective.

Before we launch headfirst into a discussion of these topics, let's begin with a working definition of language. **Language** is the communication of thoughts and emotions by means of a structured system of symbols. In our language these symbols are known as **words.** The word *innovation*, for example, is just an arbitrary combination of letters that, over time, has come to be accepted as a *symbol* for the introduction of some object or process that is new and exciting. Our ability to use these symbols defines our level of language skill.

FUNCTIONS OF LANGUAGE

Language fulfills three primary functions. We can use it to label, to interact with others, and to transmit information.

Identifying an object, act, or person by name so that she, he, or it can be referred to in communication is known as **labeling.** Once something is named, it takes on all of the characteristics and meanings that we associate with its label. For example, your meaning of the word "success" might include a $120,000-a-year salary and a new Porsche 911, while for someone else "success" may be defined as a $30,000-a-year job and time at night and on weekends to enjoy one's family. The same is true of our respective names. They are badges of our identity and symbols in their own right. That is one reason why we become easily perturbed if someone misspells or (worse yet) makes fun of our names.

The next function of language, **interaction,** focuses on the sharing and communication of ideas and emotions. Through language we can call out an array of emotional responses in others—from sympathy and understanding to anger and confusion. For example, if a friend is in the middle of suggesting an idea for a Saturday retreat, and you believe that you have a "better" plan of action, you can use language more effectively by "holding your fire," letting her finish the idea, and beginning your response in a diplomatic, nonemotional way. For instance, you might say, "That's a great idea. Or we could . . . [your idea]. . . . Let's ask Don and April for their opinions." In this way, language can serve as the basis for a positive rather than a negative interaction.

Through language, information also can be passed on to other individuals. This function of language is referred to as **transmission.** Consider for a moment all of the information that you send and receive daily, from the first "good morning" that you hear until the last sentence you read before turning off the light at night. From books, lectures, and electronic billboards to videodiscs and satellite transmissions, there is no end to the ways through which language can transmit information.

Researchers have argued that transmission of information is perhaps the most important function of language in the history of human civilization.

For example, language connects the past, present, and future. It also ensures the perpetuation of our culture and traditions. Older generations die but, through language, they are able to leave behind their ideas, accomplishments, failures, and plans for the future. Thus, later generations do not have to repeat the trials and errors of their predecessors but can adapt and constantly improve upon the successes of the past. Just think how little of your present knowledge comes from your own experience and how much is based on long-accepted facts. Indeed, language has enabled us to advance intellectually, psychologically, and culturally.

LANGUAGE DEVELOPMENT

Newborn babies have only a few ways to communicate—body movements, facial expressions, and sounds that are generalized to many needs. For example, a cry can mean fear, hunger, pain, or any number of other things. However, as babies grow, they discover language and its importance in ensuring their personal well-being and development.

Babies discover that language is useful for expressing and conveying feelings to others. Their first "mama" or "dada" evokes immediate smiles and caresses. Their later, more sophisticated expressions, such as "I love you" or "Go away," will continue the process of exchanging emotions through language. This aspect of language is quite important in creating psychological balance and adjustment.

During their early years, children also discover the meaning of "yes" and "no." No longer can they do everything they wish and still please others. Through spoken and, later, written symbols, they come to understand their culture and its expectations. Language thus serves as a means of socialization—teaching mores, norms, and accepted behavior.

Theories of Language Development

From childhood to old age, we all use language as a means of broadening our knowledge of ourselves and the world about us. When humans first evolved, they were like newborn children, unable to use this valuable tool. Yet once language developed, the possibilities for humankind's future attainments and cultural growth increased.

Many linguists believe that evolution is responsible for our ability to produce and use language. They claim that our highly evolved brain provides us with an innate language ability not found in lower organisms. Proponents of this *innateness theory,* most notably Eric Lenneberg, say that our potential for language is inborn, but that language itself develops gradually, as a function of the growth of the brain during childhood. Therefore, there are critical biological times for language development—once the growth of the brain is complete (during the early teen years), it is much harder to learn language.

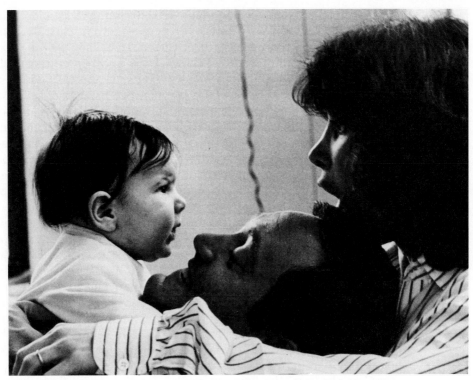

Early interactions between parent and child encourage language and intellectual development.

Current reviews of innateness theory are mixed; however, evidence supporting the existence of some innate abilities is undeniable. Indeed, more and more schools are discovering that foreign languages are best taught in the lower grades. Young children often can learn several languages by being exposed to them, while adults have a much harder time learning another language once the rules of their first language have become embedded.

Although some aspects of language are undeniably innate, language does not develop automatically in a vacuum. Children who have been isolated from other human beings do not possess language. This demonstrates that interaction with other human beings is necessary for proper language development. Some linguists believe that this interaction is more basic to human language acquisition than any innate capacities. These theorists view language as *imitative, learned behavior.* In other words, children learn language from their parents by imitating them. Parents negatively reinforce inexact imitations and positively reinforce more precise imitations, thus gradually shaping their child's language skills.

There are elements of truth in both the innateness and the learning theories of language development. Currently accepted explanations tend to borrow from each viewpoint. Noam Chomsky, for example, says that we are all born with *language acquisition devices* (LAD, for short). This doesn't mean that grammar is somehow innately in our heads, but rather that these

LADs help us sort out the language we hear and understand its grammatical rules. From listening to adults, American children learn, for example, that the usual sentence order is subject-verb-object. They will therefore begin to put words into this order. Children from another culture will learn the grammatical rules of their society. Thus, Chomsky's view suggests an interaction between innate (LAD) and learned aspects of language.

Children who, for one reason or another, have been isolated from speaking humans during the critical periods in which language usually develops find it very difficult, if not impossible, to acquire language abilities. Scientists explain that these children have passed crucial biological times in their neural development, critical periods during which language learning must occur. Once passed, these developmental stages can never be recaptured.[1]

Additionally, the quality of the language environment in which children are reared affects their overall language development. For example, research has shown that children who come to school from homes in which many books and magazines are read, shared, or processed generally make the transition to literacy with greater ease than do children who come from low-print homes.[2] As Geraldine Wallach, one language researcher, has noted, this discrepancy results, in part, from the fact that children from high-print homes talk more like books and have already begun to learn what styles of language are appropriate for various situations. Thus, children who are reared by parents who rely heavily on an oral tradition, rather than on one that emphasizes the importance of reading, will find themselves at a disadvantage when they come to school, because teachers and schools rely almost exclusively on literate or written modes.[3]

As you can see, parents and teachers serve a vital role in language development. Thus, they (and we) must learn to create supportive, stimulating environments that are conducive to language learning. Only in this way can children successfully integrate innate and learned language skills, and become articulate, competent members of society.

The Process of Language Development

From the earliest point in their lives, babies are driven to actively achieve goals: from being fed to having emotional needs satisfied. When internal needs like hunger and thirst are met, babies are able to focus on goals related to the outside world: from discovering and exploring objects to engaging in positive interactions with people. The developmental continuum for a baby's early achievements in language learning and communication may be divided

---

[1]J. N. Bohannon III, B. MacWhinney, and C. Snow, "No Negative Evidence Revisited: Beyond Learnability or Who Has to Prove What to Whom," *Developmental Psychology*, 26, no. 2 (1990), 221–26.

[2]G. Wallach, "Magic Buries Celtics: Looking for a Broader Interpretation of Language Learning and Literacy," *Topics in Language Disorders*, 10, no. 2 (1990), 69.

[3]Ibid., 69.

into three periods of approximate length: infancy (birth through 12 months), toddlerhood (12 to 24 months), and early childhood (24 to 48 months).[4]

According to Prizant and Wetherby, achievements during **infancy** (birth through 12 months) may be classified into four major categories. Although these categories overlap, they generally include: (1) getting the attention of and interacting socially with principal caregivers; (2) participating in "joint activity routines" (for instance, diaper changing, eating, etc.); (3) early vocalizing and gesturing to regulate caregivers' behavior, attract and maintain attention, and share an object or event; and (4) comprehending words in routine interactions.[5]

From birth to nine months, infants' behaviors generally are confined to preverbal gestures and sounds. In fact, research shows that infants not only can make all of the sounds of their own language at this time, but also can produce sounds that constitute all the languages in the world. For example, American infants are able to make the distinct sounds of the French "r" and German "ü."

At nine to ten months, the infant begins to use sounds and gestures to communicate intentionally. Infants can point, use conventional words like "mama" as a general request for objects, mark predictable points in events (for example, say "bye-bye" when the babysitter puts a toy on a shelf), use gaze aversion or thumb sucking to help them cope with stress in the environment, and make decisions about their own behavior based on the facial expressions of caregivers (for example, whether to crawl across the room or put their hand in the toilet).[6]

Toward the end of the first 12 months, infants generally can communicate their intentions and signal for the attention of others. At this point, they generally enter the next stage of language development or **toddlerhood** (approximately 12 to 24 months in age). Toddlerhood is marked by (1) increasing frequency, perseverance, and intentionality in preverbal communication; (2) acquiring symbols to communicate about his or her actions and immediate world; (3) representing past events through internal, symbolic representations (for instance, remembering previous play with a truck, ball, or kitten); and (4) anticipating future events. As toddlers gain these abilities, they begin to reflect and make decisions based on prior experiences. For example, they learn to associate a spanking with pulling the dog's tail and, therefore, begin to make more "informed" decisions.[7]

Around 13 months of age, toddlers begin to form their first words, generally in the form of labels for objects (such as hat, book, or cat). During this "one-word stage," acquiring words is a slow process; however, between 12 and 18 months, children generally increase their rate of sounds and

---

[4]B. M. Prizant and A. M. Wetherby, "Toward an Integrated View of Early Language and Communication Development and Socioemotional Development," *Topics in Language Disorders*, 10, no. 4 (1990), 6.

[5]Ibid., 7.

[6]Ibid., 7–9.

[7]Ibid., 7, 10–11.

coordinating gestures. At 18 months, toddlers begin to show marked improvement in the growth of their vocabulary and produce several new words per day. Finally, between the ages of 18 and 24 months, they begin to use word combinations and to describe states and qualities about people, objects, and events (for example, "Daddy go?"). They also begin to ask for information and bring up events that are associated with other places and time (for instance, "Matthew get ice cream?"). In short, they begin to take part in real conversations.[8]

During *early childhood* (approximately 24 to 48 months in age), a child's achievements normally include (1) an increasing ability to communicate about events and other people's actions; (2) symbolic interactions about past and future events; (3) the ability to comprehend conditional, causal, and other complex relationships; and (4) a basic level of communication competence. For instance, prior to or around 24 months, a child's thoughts may be represented by a single word ("hug" may mean "Daddy, I want a hug") or by several words that are run together (such as "mamagive"). From 24 to 36 months, children begin to grasp sentence grammar, including word and sentence organization. They are able to construct sentences (for example, "Me give mama a hug"), and they experience rapid growth in their vocabularies. They also begin to understand concepts like position, size, and time, and are able to better express their ideas because they can construct more complete and complex sentences. As this period progresses from 36 to 48 months, children start to express their goals, feelings, and thoughts. Additionally, their self-esteem and self-image begin to be significantly affected by their competence in play with other children.[9]

By the time children are six years old, they seem to know all the grammatical rules that enable them to speak correctly. However, the learning process never ceases. With every new experience, their vocabulary can continue to increase as long as they live.

MEANING

Semantics

Our discussion of language thus far has focused on linguistic or language development. Once you have acquired words and grammar, you still must learn to use them effectively to communicate. You gradually learn to combine your words in an infinite variety of ways to transmit an infinite number of messages. Still, transmission of messages is not enough. You also

---

[8]Ibid., 10–12.
[9]Ibid., 7, 12–14.

want them to be received and understood. Commonality of language between speaker and listener is obviously essential for this understanding. What is even more essential is commonality of meaning.

But what is meaning? To provide a starting point for understanding this complex phenomenon, consider the word "jaram." This word *means* nothing. Let's say, though, that you are now shown an object called a "jaram." Hereafter, the word *jaram* will bring to mind a picture of that object. Now the word has meaning for you. The use of words such as *jaram* as symbols representing objects and concepts is known as the **symbolic process.** The study of the relationship between these word symbols and their meanings is called **semantics.**

Semantics is quite a complicated area of study, since many symbols and dimensions of meaning exist. However, researchers generally agree that words have three dimensions of meaning. The **symbol** refers to objects in the real world, and the **sense** to subjective feelings we have about the symbol. The **referent** is the actual object as it exists in reality. Thus, your meaning of the word *football* is a function of the symbol (the word *football*), the sense (pleasant feelings brought on by the thought of last year's winning season), and the referent (an actual football). Of course, this analysis applies only to the linguistic level of meaning. We cannot forget that there are philosophical, psychological, and logical levels of meaning as well.

The quality of children's language environments significantly affects their language development.

Language Features

At a minimum, meaning involves shared understanding or shared agreement regarding a symbol, its sense, and its referent. For example, we probably can all agree that an "office" is a place where business is transacted. However, the word "office" takes on a different dimension of meaning when it describes a large, beautifully decorated corner room with lots of windows— and when the word refers to a 6 × 6 windowless room located near an elevator. What features of language allow the same word to take on such a diverse set of meanings? Although the answer to this question is complex, semanticists have agreed on at least four factors that affect word meanings: (1) the extent to which words are abstract or concrete; (2) the amount of ambiguity and vagueness in a language; (3) the denotative and connotative dimensions of meaning; and (4) language style. Each of these topics will be addressed more completely in the following paragraphs.

ABSTRACTION AND CONCRETENESS. Determining meanings is complicated when the words in question are not concrete. **Concrete** words symbolize objects or events that can be pointed to, touched, or directly experienced. Words like "basketball," "marlin," and "pineapple" are in this category. On the other hand, **abstract** words represent things that we cannot sense directly, such as "freedom," "honesty," "religion," and "politics."

No matter how difficult it may be to define abstractions, they are very important to the communication process. With abstract words, we are able to extend the level of our thoughts and speech beyond the concrete, everyday world. We can talk about the complicated concepts of right and wrong, discuss things that we cannot see, and consider the future as if it existed today.

AMBIGUITY AND VAGUENESS. Two other language variables that affect understanding are ambiguity and vagueness. **Ambiguity** has been defined as the amount of doubtfulness or uncertainty in meanings. Generally, ambiguity arises for the simple reason that human language customarily assigns one symbol to several categories or things. To illustrate, consider the word *heavy*. One can have heavy luggage, a heavy yield of grain, a room heavy with moisture, a heavy odor, heavy gunfire, heavy food, a heavy date, and a heavy book, both in weight and in profundity.

Vagueness can present even greater problems for language users than can ambiguity. A word or phrase is said to be *vague* if it lacks precision or clarity of expression. In other words, vagueness occurs when the language we use is unspecific or imprecise. For example, if you have been asked by your boss to pick up a job candidate whom you have never met, and you are told to look for the tall man at the train station entrance, you may have difficulty locating the person because of imprecision in the description. The definition of "tall" for someone who stands 5'2" may be different for someone who is 6'2" in height.

Vagueness leads to trivial arguments, such as "I say it's green," which is countered by, "Well, I say it's blue." However, vagueness also may lead to more serious concerns, such as "Where does truth end and falsehood begin?" or "Where does business savvy end and corrupt practice begin?"

DENOTATION AND CONNOTATION. Meaning is also affected by the denotation and connotation of particular words. **Denotation** is the objective reference of a word—that is, its factual, concrete meaning. Dictionary definitions present denotations. Some words are primarily denotative, but most words also possess less definable connotations. **Connotation** refers to meanings beyond the objective reference. The word *automobile*, for example, denotes a four-wheeled motor vehicle. Yet it may connote little or nothing to one person, anger to someone who has just been fired from an automobile factory, and pleasure to someone who has just bought a new sports car. Very specific words—*chair, desk, book*, and so forth—are usually without connotation for most people. Other words, such as *obsolete* and *respectable*, can fall either way, depending on context, while words such as *fantastic* and *horrible* are almost totally connotative in nature.

We acquire our connotations from social and personal experiences. The word *farm* means something different to a city dweller than to a country person. The more two people have in common—the more similar their backgrounds, past experiences, attitudes, and outlooks—the better chance they have of attaching the same meaning to a word or concept.

Consider the following situation. Greg is talking with his parents, and all is going well. They are communicating for a change. Then the conversation turns to the subject of drugs. Communication quickly comes to an end. Greg and his parents stop communicating because they have different connotations for the word *drug*. But the word is only a small part of a larger problem. Greg, his mother, and his father have different attitudes about many things, and this difference in attitudes influences the connotations they attach to words. The end result of these differing connotations is often a breakdown in communication.

STYLE. Another factor that influences meaning is **style,** or how we choose, organize, and use those features of the language that are open to individual selection.

The rules of our language dictate the arrangement of words in sentences (subject-verb-object) and frequently determine which forms of words must be used (present or past tense, singular or plural verb). These are not matters of style, but of grammar. Style, on the other hand, refers to an individual's characteristic tendencies to choose particular kinds of words (simple versus multisyllabic, factual versus descriptive), particular sentence constructions (short versus long, complete versus fragmentary), or even particular phrases ("you know," "I mean," or "right on"). For example, some people use more words, phrases, and clauses than do others. Other people use a significantly larger proportion of feeling verbs.

Style is influenced by variables in the speaker as well as in the listener. Have you ever wondered why it seems difficult to talk with some people and easy to talk with others? Think for a minute about blind dates you've had, parties you've attended, or plane trips you've taken. Pleasant interactions are

Words in Wonderland

Lewis Carroll was an English mathematician and logician whose real name was Charles Lutwidge Dodgson. He is remembered, not for his contributions to mathematics or logic, but as the author of *Alice's Adventures in Wonderland* and *Through the Looking-Glass.* These great works are sometimes called "nonsense" literature, but from the excerpts that follow we can see that even in Wonderland Carroll was concerned with the logic of words and how they represent reality.

"Come, we shall have some fun now!" thought Alice. "I'm glad you've begun asking riddles—I believe I can guess that," she added aloud.

"Do you mean that you think you can find out the answer to it?" said the March Hare.

"Exactly so," said Alice.

"Then you should say what you mean," the March Hare went on.

"I do," Alice hastily replied: "at least—at least I mean what I say—that's the same thing, you know."

"Not the same thing a bit!" said the Hatter. "Why, you might just as well say that 'I see what I eat' is the same thing as 'I eat what I see!' "

"You might just as well say," added the March Hare, "that 'I like what I get' is the same thing as 'I get what I like!' "

"You might just as well say," added the Dormouse, which seemed to be talking in its sleep, "that 'I breathe when I sleep' is the same thing as 'I sleep when I breathe!' "

"It *is* the same thing with you," said the Hatter, and here the conversation dropped. . . .

————

Alice's Adventures in Wonderland

"I don't know what you mean by 'glory,' " Alice said.

Humpty Dumpty smiled contemptuously. "Of course you don't—till I tell you. I meant 'there's a nice knock-down argument for you!' "

"But 'glory' doesn't mean 'a nice knock-down argument,' " Alice objected.

"When *I* use a word," Humpty Dumpty said, in rather a scornful tone, "it means just what I choose it to mean—neither more nor less."

"The question is," said Alice, "whether you *can* make words mean so many different things."

"The question is," said Humpty Dumpty, "which is to be master—that's all."

————

Through the Looking-Glass

usually associated with people with whom you hit it off immediately. Even though you may have found commonalities, successful communication was probably based on more than just similar professions or common interests.

Personality differences do exist between communicators, and we tend to make positive and negative judgments based on specific communication styles. We often base first impressions more on how a person says something than on exactly what words he or she uses. This fact of communication life leads to statements like, "She turned me off with her sarcastic attitude," or "He really had a way of making people feel right at home." In fact, the first few minutes of interpersonal interaction often determine whether or not we will continue interaction. These minutes are also often the key to business achievement, social success, family harmony, and sexual satisfaction. Hemming and hawing, overusing profanity, and cutting off another person who is speaking all indicate the influence of personality on a communicator's style.

As you can see, we need to be aware of our own style so that we can communicate more effectively with others. Specifically, when we understand our style of communication, we can adapt to the styles of others. For example, effective communicators tailor their language for a particular audience, or based on the nature and purpose of their messages. For example, a nuclear physicist who uses scientific jargon with colleagues probably should avoid doing so with people outside the profession. Physicians often have a habit of talking with their patients as if the latter were familiar with the latest medical terminology. As a result, patients sometimes feel alienated, especially when Latin terminology seems to change their simple complaint into what sounds like a fatal illness. A considerate physician uses terms that are easily understood by patients.

Korzybski's Laws

As we have seen in the previous discussions, language is a highly complex, yet powerful, phenomenon. However, we can all strive to become more aware of the subtle but powerful influence of words in our lives. Alfred Korzybski, a pioneer in the area of general semantics—the study of the structure and function of speech and resultant behavior—observed that people often falsely identify with words. We sometimes respond to words as if the words themselves were the referent objects they symbolize. In fact, many individuals are tyrannized by words. For example, just hearing the word *spider* may cause someone with a fear of spiders to shiver. The spider itself does not have to be in sight; the symbol, not the referent, causes the response.

This observation led to Korzybski's law of **non-identity**, which says, simply, that a word is *not* the thing it represents. The word *cat* and the animal itself are not one and the same thing. (See Figure 2–1.)

Korzybski's second law, that of **non-allness**, reminds us that a word cannot symbolize *all* of a thing. *Cat* may bring to mind your own pet and the expensive show animal you saw on TV last night. However, *cat* may

FIGURE 2–1
Korzybski's Three Laws

symbolize something quite different for an African who has experienced cats of a larger and more ferocious variety than the string of "Fluffys" you have owned and loved. Neither you nor the African, though, might think of an Egyptian god or a Canadian lynx. Clearly, language never conveys *everything* about *anything*.

Korzybski's third law concerns **self-reflexiveness.** It explains that a word can refer not only to something in the real world but also to itself. The word *cat* not only refers to a kind of four-legged animal in the real world but also to the word formed in English by the letters *c-a-t,* or to the word formed in Italian by the letters *g-a-t-t-o.*

LANGUAGE AND BEHAVIOR

Our discussion of connotation and style revealed the effects of environmental and personal variables on an individual's language usage. It is also important to recognize that our language affects the attitudes and subsequent behaviors of others.

We know, for example, that listeners can accurately identify or estimate, on the basis of speech alone, various characteristics of speakers, including their age, sex, race, socioeconomic status, personality, specific identity, facial and body features, and height and weight. In addition, researchers have found that speech style contributes to a group's or culture's identity and cohesion.[10] One illustration of this language principle was our discussion at the beginning of this chapter regarding organizational buzzwords and their importance. Another example is the use of "secret" rites (and their corresponding language) that groups such as college fraternities and sororities employ.

Language patterns also have an effect on the degree to which people are perceived to be credible or powerful. For example, linguistic patterns typical of women have been found to be less powerful than those associated with men. According to recent research, women make greater use of indirect control strategies, as is reflected in their use of a significantly greater number of questions (for example, "What's next?"). Additionally, women use justifiers ("The reason I say that is . . .") more frequently, apparently perceiving a greater need to provide a rationale for their opinions. Furthermore, they use more intensive adverbs ("I really think X") than do men, perhaps to increase the strength of what they are saying. Finally, women talk more about people than objects, as exemplified in their greater use of pronouns ("We, you, they . . ."), and they employ a more indirect, qualified language style (for example, through the use of adverbs when beginning sentences, such as "Surprisingly, that test was a breeze").[11]

Conversely, men have been found to use a more direct, or overt, control strategy through the production of more interruptions ("Let's move on; we can come back to that point later"). They also have a tendency to use a greater number of directives ("Why don't you finish this report before we talk?") and maintain longer speaking turns through the use of more conjunctions and/or fillers when beginning a sentence ("And another thing we need to consider. . .").[12]

What impact do these language differences have on the attitudes and behavior of other people? One answer seems to lie in the differential language patterns that women and men use when speaking in same-sex as opposed to mixed-sex groups. According to research, when women converse with other women, they are rated higher on sociointellectual status and aesthetic quality than men interacting with other men. In other words, when speaking to other women, females are perceived to be of high social status, rich, white-collar, and literate as compared to men speaking with other men. Additionally, women who interact with other women are perceived to be

[10]A. Maass, D. Salvi, L. Arcuri, and G. Semin, "Language Use in Intergroup Contexts: The Linguistic Intergroup Bias," *Journal of Personality and Social Psychology*, 57, no. 6 (1989), 981–93.

[11]A. Mulac, J. M. Wiemann, S. J. Widenmann, and T. W. Gibson, "Male/Female Language Differences and Effects in Same-Sex and Mixed-Sex Dyads: The Gender-Linked Language Effect," *Communication Monographs*, 55, no. 4 (1988), 315–35.

[12]Ibid., 315–35.

more "beautiful, nice, pleasant, and sweet" than are men when interacting with other men.[13]

However, in mixed-sex groups (men interacting with women and vice versa), language patterns seem to change, and ratings of sociointellectual status begin to increase for men and decrease for women. Additionally, when interacting with men, women are no longer rated more highly than are men on aesthetic quality. Instead, men are perceived to be more "beautiful, nice, pleasant, and sweet" than are women. To their credit, women are perceived to be more dynamic than men when speaking in mixed-sex groups. In other words, women are perceived to be more strong, active, aggressive, and loud than men in mixed-sex communication situations.[14]

Linguistic Stereotyping

Although speech styles have a useful function, as we have seen, they may also serve their users in a negative way. Such a situation usually arises when nonusers of a major style or dialect come into contact with people who are unaware of their function and importance, or who tend to see things and people categorically. Perceptions regarding the Amish people of the Pennsylvania Dutch area illustrate this point. Although the people of this region may share both similar cultures and beliefs, not everyone who speaks with a Pennsylvania Dutch accent prefers old-fashioned clothes and horse-drawn wagons. Assuming such automatic relationships between particular linguistic styles and personal traits is known as *semantic* or *linguistic stereotyping.* For example, many people unfairly underestimate the intellectual ability of people who speak slow and halting English. Conversely, linguistic stereotyping may also produce a perception of intellectual superiority for a speaker with a crisp Oxford accent.

As you may have guessed by now, most semantic stereotypes are negative. They are particularly harmful for individuals who share easily recognizable (yet nonstandard) dialects such as black English or Louisiana creole. Perhaps the greatest damage, however, comes when speakers of the standard or majority dialect of a culture believe that nonspeakers are somehow inferior. In fact, many employers in American businesses and industries are guilty of such perceptions. In turn, such instances of linguistic stereotyping have affected their hiring and firing policies.

The question then becomes: What can we do, given this knowledge concerning linguistic stereotypes? For "native" speakers, the solution seems to reside in concern and awareness—awareness of the information we have presented and a concern for consistency in acting upon it, whether in interpersonal interactions or on the job.

---

[13]Ibid., 331–32.
[14]Ibid.

Awareness and appreciation of different cultures help eliminate linguistic stereotyping.

For non-native speakers, the solution is more complex and will involve a weighing of alternatives and their consequences. To disregard the importance of competence in the standard dialect or style may result in diminished opportunities and rewards. At the same time, individuals should be aware of the importance of their social identities, which are intimately tied to the language they speak.

Perhaps one answer lies in the individual's ability to achieve some degree of linguistic competence in both communities. Although such an attempt would be both difficult and frustrating, it could provide a means by which the "bilingual" or "bidialectical" person may communicate more effectively.

Making Language More Effective

When Clark Gable said "Frankly, my dear, I don't give a damn" in the film *Gone With the Wind* (1939), millions of people were either shocked or titillated. Times have changed. Four-letter words don't offend as they once did. New words come into the language almost daily, as they always have. As the norms and mores of a society change, so does its language. Both society and language reflect the "liberated" spirit of the twentieth century.

Our social identities are inextricably tied to the language we speak.

Unfortunately, liberated language often also means sloppy, imprecise language. Although people seem to be communicating *more* these days, they may be understood even *less*. As a student of communication (and now language!), you should be aware of the trend. You also can become a communication trendsetter by following these tips:

1. Try to speak clearly at all times (that is, use words whose meanings can be understood by those who are listening).
2. Relate to your listeners by being sensitive to their attitudes, beliefs, and experiences.
3. Avoid using slang and jargon (for example, computerese).
4. Minimize the use of regionalisms such as "y'all" or "you guys," especially in the professional world.
5. Converse without using habitual expressions, such as:
   "you know what I mean?"
   "uh-huh" (for yes)
   "uh-uh" (for no)
   "yeah"
   "to be honest"
   "truthfully"

6. Choose language that is appropriate to the purpose of the interaction and the communication setting—your language should be different when you are talking with a friend and when you are giving a presentation.

7. Avoid using vague and ambiguous language—learn to say what you mean and mean what you say.

8. Be careful not to overkill a subject by rambling on and on. Business people especially appreciate others who KISS: "*Keep it simple and short.*"

9. Avoid "I-trouble," or talking too much about you. A conversation of indefinite length about your accomplishments or problems will be perceived as rude and selfish.

10. Finally, be "other-centered"—and learn to be an effective listener. You cannot learn anything new when you are talking.

SUMMARY

Language is our most important tool of communication. It provides us with a means of labeling, or identifying by name, objects, acts, or persons. It is the basis of interaction, the sharing of ideas and emotions, and finally, the means by which we transmit information among ourselves and through the ages from one culture and generation to the next.

There are two major theories of language development: innateness theory and imitative theory. Innateness refers to the inborn ability to speak a language. The imitative theory holds that language is a learned behavior. While these are the two extreme viewpoints, many "middle-ground" theorists like Noam Chomsky draw upon both. Language development itself may be divided into three stages: infancy, toddlerhood, and early childhood.

Meaning is the essential part of any message. Understanding between individuals depends upon similarity of meaning. Semantics is the study of the relationship between our words and their meanings.

Abstraction is the ability to give symbolic meaning to those things that cannot be sensed—concepts, ideals, and so forth. Ambiguity and vagueness arise because one word or symbol can have several meanings, and meaning itself is relative.

Words are also denotative and connotative. They may have concrete and factual meanings, or they may represent something beyond the objective reference.

Meaning is also influenced by style. Each individual has his or her own characteristic way of communicating. Style is influenced by our personalities, our purposes, and our communication settings. In short, these variables and the laws of self-reflexiveness, non-identity, and non-allness (and their use) may drastically affect communication outcomes.

The variables of language also affect our attitudes and behavior. We sometimes assume relationships between linguistic styles and personal or cultural traits. This process is known as linguistic stereotyping and usually has a negative effect upon communication. Linguistic stereotyping plays a large part in racism and causes individuals to react to words and symbols as if they were reality itself. In order to overcome linguistic stereotypes, we must be aware of their existence and concerned with their effects. In addition, each of us should strive to make language more effective. Speaking as clearly as possible, using words that can be understood by others, relating to our listeners, and using language that is appropriate to ourselves and others are only a few of the ways in which we may begin to be more concerned and effective communicators.

EXERCISES

Group Experiences

Meanings Are in People

DESCRIPTION: The fact that a single word is used when referring to many different things (the example *heavy* was used earlier) points to the fact that people attach meaning to symbols; symbols have no meaning in and of themselves. This activity will focus on the multiple meanings we attach to words.

PROCEDURE: Divide into groups of four to six. Each group should list as many different meanings as possible for the words given below. In listing the meanings, a phrase should be used to make clear the specific meaning of the word. Do as many as you can in five minutes. When the time is up, each group should read its list of meanings for each word. If a particular meaning is challenged, a standard dictionary or dictionary of slang should solve the argument.

Word List

cracked	down	black
spirit	high	hot
lid	book	fly
jam		

DISCUSSION: What types of communication problems do multiple word meanings create? Do word meanings change with each generation? How can you use these and similar words in such a way as to make their meaning more explicit?

Do Your Symbols Convey Your Sense?

DESCRIPTION: Alfred Korzybski offers three basic laws, the first of which is the law of non-identity. This law says that a word is not the thing it represents. We often forget how inadequate language is in describing our emotional feelings, for example. This activity will provide you with the opportunity to explore the limitations of language.

PROCEDURE: Divide into groups of four to six. Each group should take the following common phrases and attempt to state them in more precise or explicit language. In other words, you will need to describe what "love" is, for instance. After each group has completed the four phrases, a spokesperson should read the phrases aloud to the rest of the class.

Example	**New Phrase**
I *really like him.*	have a very positive feeling toward him.

I *hate your guts.*
I *love you.*
My head *aches.*
My stomach *is tied in knots.*

DISCUSSION: Do the new phrases sound funny? Are they more explicit than the common phrases? What does the law of non-identity mean to you?

Who's Talking?

DESCRIPTION: How does language affect our behavior? When compared with various languages, English has a distinctive feature. We use the word *I* as a general referent for all the "roles" we play. What "I" do in one situation may not be the same action "I" would take in another situation. Eskimos avoid the direct identification of the term *I* with "self" by using phrases such as "this woman believes" or "this man feels." Eastern philosophy suggests that using phrases such as "I am" or "you are" can be very misleading, for they infer that "you" are the thing, and, moreover, that "you" do not change your basic personality. This activity will provide you with an opportunity to see how often you make use of pronouns such as *I* or *you*.

PROCEDURE: Divide the class into dyads (groups of two) and ask them to converse for ten minutes. At no point during the interaction should they use the following words:

I you he   she they we

Instead, you should replace these words either with formal statements or with an alternative referent. For example:

Normal: I think that . . . (*I* is unacceptable in this activity.)

Formal: It appears that institutions of education are not receiving the necessary financial support.

Alternate: This woman thinks that institutions of education are not receiving the necessary financial support.

In asking a question of your partner, you will also have to take special care with the wording. For example:

Normal: What do you think? (The use of the pronoun *you* is unacceptable in this activity.)

Formal: What are some alternative ways of viewing this situation?

Alternate: What does Dick think? (In this case you would use the name of your partner to replace the personal pronoun *you.*)

DISCUSSION: Did you experience any difficulties during the conversation? Did the "meaning" of the conversation change with the use of your new referents? Did you find the conversation to be more depersonalized when you avoided using pronouns? Was it difficult for you to avoid using the word "I"?

Personal Experiences

1. Sit alone in a quiet room. Very slowly begin saying your name over and over. Do this for ten minutes and see if your name takes on a different meaning. Then consider whether or not you consider your "name" to be "you." Do you believe that a word in any language is not the thing but rather a symbol for it? Is your name simply a symbol for you?

2. Read the poem "The Jabberwocky" from *Through the Looking-Glass.* Then write your interpretation of this poem. Was Lewis Carroll making a comment on language in general? What do the words mean? Where did you find the meanings of the words (dictionary, context of the poem)?

Discussion Questions

1. What are the two main schools of thought on language acquisition in children?

2. Discuss the three stages of language acquisition. How does knowledge of the language development process contribute to an understanding of effective communication?

3. What are the primary advantages and disadvantages of maintaining a nonstandard dialect or style of speaking? In what ways can "standard" users help to increase communication effectiveness between users and nonusers?

Listening and Feedback

Kittie W. Watson[*]

KEY CONCEPTS AND TERMS

Listening energy
Hearing
Listening
Interactive listening
Attending
Perceiving
Interpreting
Assessing
Responding
Listening preferences
Content-oriented listener
Action-oriented listener
People-oriented listener
Social-oriented listener

Thinking–speaking time
  differential
Focusing
Tracking
Reflecting
Digging
Dampening
Redirecting
Feedback
Self-feedback
Listener feedback
Irrelevant responses
Interrupting responses
Tangential responses

[*]Kittie W. Watson is an associate professor at Tulane University. This chapter was written especially for the sixth edition of *Communication*.

With a smile on her face, Liz hung up the phone after talking with her newest client. As president of her own management training and consulting firm, Liz knew the importance of effective communication skills. Although she had placed the call late in the day, and they both had been tired, Liz felt that the conversation had gone off without a hitch. Now she could make the necessary travel arrangements for the training session to be held in Palm Springs within the month.

One week before the trip was to be made, Liz glanced down at her calendar. Phil Sanders had not yet returned her contract for the Palm Springs training program, so she decided to pick up the phone and give him a call. She also needed to reconfirm the name of the person who would be picking her up at the airport. On the fourth ring, Phil picked up the phone, cleared his voice, and said, "Hello."

As the conversation continued, Liz felt her heart slide slowly into her stomach. "Not enough people enrolled . . . session cancelled. . . ," was all that Phil would say. When she politely asked where to send the nonrefundable plane ticket for reimbursement, Phil exploded and said he had no intention of refunding her money. What would she do now? Liz distinctly remembered discussing the possibility of cancellation. Had she only assumed that Phil's company would be responsible for picking up the costs, even if the session were cancelled? Or did they actually discuss the possibility? Unfortunately for both parties, the agreement had been oral. Now it seemed that poor listening on one of their parts was going to cost her company money and jeopardize their newly developed relationship. How could Liz determine where the listening error had actually occurred in order to deal with the situation? How could she avoid a similar listening crisis in the future?

LISTENING AND ENERGY CONSERVATION

Almost daily we read news headlines stressing the need to conserve environmental resources. While we understand that our natural resources are limited, we rarely worry about wasting our communication resources. In fact, few of us have been told how to avoid wasting our most frequently used communication resource: *listening energy.*

One reason we lose listening energy is because we have received little training in how to conserve it. Even though listening skills are usually valued, it is assumed that if people can hear, they can listen. As with other communication skills, however, such as writing, reading, and speaking, without training and practice few people listen well. Unlike the other communication skills, people don't notice when a person fails to listen until it is too late. This is one reason we need to learn to protect our most precious communication resource, listening energy.

KEEP AN EYE ON YOUR LISTENING ENERGY GAUGE. To illustrate what happens to our listening energy, consider Figure 3–1. At the beginning of each day, after a good night's sleep, most of us have a full tank of listening energy. As we enter our day, the process of emptying the tank occurs with little or no awareness. During routine and pleasant morning interactions with roommates or friends, little energy is used. If, however, there is an argument or conflict, we may begin to empty our tanks. Even so, by the time most of us get to class, our tanks are near full. As soon as you enter the classroom, however, listening-energy zappers begin their work. Zappers may include monotone professors, competing outside noises, low lighting, hunger pangs, or attractive people sitting next to you.

By the end of the first class, many students use as much as 50 percent of their listening energy. Attending another class may use 60 percent to 70 percent of the total energy a person starts with. Unless you can discover ways to add some fuel to your listening tanks, you may have little energy to finish the day. And if stress or conflict occurs, you may begin to run on fumes.

All interactions and daily pressures work to deplete listening energy reserves. If we want to improve our listening ability, we must learn to conserve the precious energy we have. To conserve energy we need to make conscious choices about who and what we listen to during the day. This chapter is designed to help you learn more about what depletes your listening energy, information on the listening process, and your personal listening habits. In addition, this chapter will explain the critical role feedback plays in the listening process while providing methods to improve your listening and feedback skills.

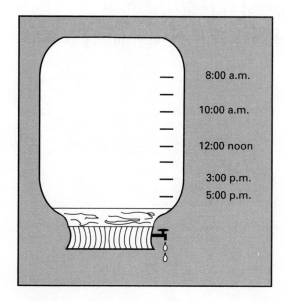

FIGURE 3–1
Listening Energy Tank

DEFINING LISTENING

As described in the communication model in Chapter 1, listeners are not isolated from speakers during the communication process. *Hearing,* which is only one part of the listening process, refers to the physical act of receiving sounds. It is a passive process that occurs even when we're asleep. *Listening,* on the other hand, is hard work and is a dynamic, interactive process involving both speakers and listeners. *Interactive listening,* therefore, is a series of interrelated processes that includes attending, perceiving, interpreting, assessing, and responding. For successful communication to occur, listeners and speakers must take mutual responsibility. In interactive listening, the role of listeners is to plan strategies to help themselves listen more effectively, and the role of speakers is to plan strategies to help others listen more effectively.

THE LISTENING LADDER: A FIVE-STEP APPROACH

One way to help ensure more accurate communication is to examine the challenges and difficulties listeners face at each step of the listening process. Visualize the interactive listening process as a listening stepladder and refer to Figure 3–2 as you read the descriptions for each step along the way. The

Hearing is only one stage of the listening process.

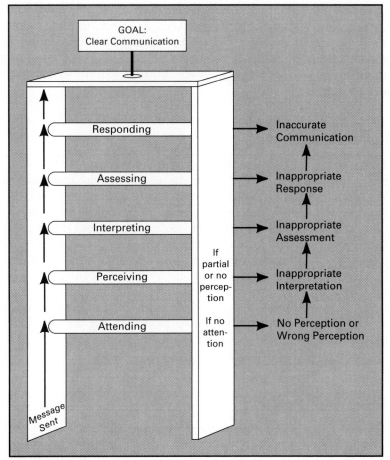

FIGURE 3-2
Listening Ladder

ladder represents the five steps listeners go through when communicating with others. At the top of the ladder is our goal: successful communication. To reach our goal we must make appropriate listening choices at each step. Keep in mind that listening is not easy. Therefore, we frequently miss steps, lose our balance, and/or slip down the ladder.

Attending Level

The initial step of the listening process, which affects the success of all the other steps, is *attending.* At this level we show differing degrees of involvement in verbal and nonverbal environmental stimuli. We demonstrate conscious efforts to listen to others through attending behaviors such as eye contact, forward lean, appropriate facial expressions, and concentration on the message. Unfortunately, many listeners start out with focused attention and find themselves getting distracted. When we get distracted, we unconsciously allow objects, speakers, or events to divert our attention. On many occasions it is our inner voice that hinders our ability to concentrate and to climb steps on the listening ladder. For example, when worrying about being late for class, we often fail to attend to a roommate who makes a request.

Perceiving Level

The next step of the listening process is **perceiving.** At this step, listeners use one or more of their basic senses to receive verbal and nonverbal messages. Mistakes in listening occur when one of the senses does not receive a message or receives one in a distorted fashion. In most cases perception and listening involve hearing, but hearing is only one of the senses involved in the listening process. Although information can be gained from using all of the senses, the primary senses involved in listening are hearing and seeing. It is not unusual for us to miss information when our senses are required to do more than one thing at a time. Friends often miss important bits of information when trying to listen to conversations either in a room with loud music playing or during a football game when the crowd is screaming for the home team. Our perceptions are also influenced by our personal interests, past experiences, knowledge, and skill levels.

Interpreting Level

After you attend to and perceive a message, the next step is to **interpret** what was perceived. Listeners try to understand the meanings of messages at the interpreting level. Unfortunately, because we each differ in our experiences, knowledge, and attitudes, most communication breakdowns occur at this step of the listening process. There are numerous examples that illustrate how this can happen. For example, an American manager worked for a Japanese import firm. One day while discussing a problem with a Japanese accounting manager, the American thought they had come to an agreement and remarked, "It looks like we're thinking on parallel lines." She was surprised two weeks later when the problem surfaced again. She stormed into the accounting manager's office and said, "Didn't we agree we were thinking along parallel lines?" The Japanese manager looked puzzled, held up his hands, and said, "Parallel lines never meet." In essence, he had agreed to disagree. To ensure accurate communication, we must be sure that we interpret each other's messages correctly.

Assessing Level

After we interpret a message, we begin to make judgments about the message and its importance to us. There are two different ways listeners **assess** information. The first deals with the perceived accuracy and credibility of the message. At this level of evaluation, the listener determines whether or not to believe the message, agree with the speaker, and/or retain the information. The second type of assessment occurs when the listener evaluates the relative importance of the individual parts of a message and the message as a whole. These assessments are based on the listener's perceptions of what the speaker believes is important as well as on the listener's personal value system.

Without prior training, most people make hasty evaluations. To ensure accurate communication, it is important to delay our evaluations until the message has been received completely. Probably one of the most dramatic assessing errors that has received national attention occurred with the space shuttle *Challenger* disaster. Engineers warned officials that the O-rings were defective and needed further inspection. Tragically, the information was evaluated as not critical enough to stop the launch. It was not until later that a full investigation discovered that the deaths of Christa McAuliffe and all the professional crew could have been avoided if someone had made a different evaluation.

Responding Level

The last step of the ladder is ***responding.*** Listening is not complete until there has been some kind of response. During this stage, we react to the message and/or sender. The completion of this stage is critical because it is the only step in which responses are actually seen and/or heard. While the responding level is the one most frequently blamed for listening errors, in actuality if listening has been successful up to this point, listening is likely to continue to be successful. When speakers perceive listeners' responses, they can check for understanding and test the accuracy of their interpretations. Even if we don't send verbal responses, we always send nonverbal responses. In fact, a nonverbal response such as the "silent treatment" can actually speak louder than words. (A more detailed discussion about feedback is provided at the end of this chapter.)

The chance for a responding-level error increases when the person listening is not necessarily the person responsible for acting on what was said. You have probably used the drive-thru lane of a fast-food restaurant. Most people have preferences about what goes on their hamburgers or chicken sandwiches. Think of the times you have ordered a sandwich without mayonnaise, had your request repeated back accurately, and then opened the sandwich to find a glob of mayo. In this particular example, chances are that more than one person was involved in responding to your request. When there are intermediaries between the person you communicate with and the person who gives a response, the chances for errors at the responding step increase substantially.

The steps of the listening ladder are hierarchical. Listeners cannot skip steps or proceed effectively to other steps and hope to reach the goal of successful communication. Of course, all these steps may take place in a fraction of a second, so for practical purposes they are not separate or independent. The solid line on the ladder in Figure 3–2 shows the process an effective listener takes in attending to, perceiving, interpreting, assessing, and responding to a message correctly. The dotted line depicts where breakdowns in communication occur on steps of the listening ladder. If listeners fail to attend to messages, there is little or no chance that listeners can progress to other levels. Remember, however, that speakers often don't find out that errors have occurred until it is too late to correct the situation. Therefore, if we want to guarantee accurate communication, we need a reason or incentive to listen.

WHY LISTEN?

One of the questions most often asked by children, teenagers, and adults is: "Why listen?" What they're really asking is: "What's in it for me, if I listen to you?" They're asking their parents, friends, and colleagues to give them incentive to listen. Effective speakers try to provide incentives; however, if listeners expect speakers to motivate them to listen, they may have a long wait. Effective listeners have learned that incentive needs to come from inside themselves rather than from speakers. The focus of this section is to provide you with incentives you can grasp and use to increase your motivation to listen.

Costs of Ineffective Listening

When we fail to listen well we incur *costs*—in loss of time, money, and relationships.

LOST TIME.   Listening errors cost us one of our most valuable resources, our time. How often have you found yourself in the wrong restaurant, classroom, or hotel? Sometimes because of past associations we make assumptions about where we are supposed to meet a friend rather than really listening to what they have to say. Even when we think we are listening carefully, we find ourselves forgetting a number that was just given to us by an operator, or forgetting directions and getting lost in a new city. At other times because of poor listening habits, we make mistakes that cost us both time and money.

LOST MONEY.   One of our greatest motivators is money. We earn it, save it, and spend it. Although most of us have been taught to invest and spend our money wisely, it is estimated that American businesses waste a minimum of $20 billion each year because of avoidable listening mistakes. The invisible or minor listening culprits are the most dangerous ones. Letters have to be retyped, shipments reshipped, orders replaced, and shelves restocked, all because of small listening errors. In addition to wasting time and money, poor listening habits can also hinder relationships.

LOST RELATIONSHIPS. Poor listening creates friction and misunderstanding in both personal and professional relationships. We seek interactions with others that demonstrate we are valued. When someone doesn't pay attention or listen to our requests, concerns, or needs, we often take it personally. It is difficult to believe that others really care when they don't follow instructions in caring for a family pet, forget important dates such as a birthday, or constantly interrupt us when we are talking. When we aren't listened to, we lose trust in the person and the relationship.

As you can see, one listening mistake can have more than one cost associated with it. Not only do we sabotage our relationships, throw away our money, and waste our time, but we also lose our most precious resource, our energy. When we do realize that we have listened ineffectively, many of us have a difficult time accepting the mistake and moving forward. Figure 3–3 provides a simple exercise to enhance your listening effectiveness.

Benefits of Effective Listening

In addition to eliminating the costs associated with ineffective listening, effective listeners can create distinct advantages for themselves.

REDUCED MEETING TIME. Along with the likelihood of improving relationships, saving money, and preserving time, effective listeners can also reduce meeting time. During the estimated 15 million meetings that take place each morning in the United States, think about the amount of time that is wasted due to ineffective listening. Each time information has to be repeated because one person isn't listening, the time of all group members is wasted. In a six-person group, a five-minute review would waste 30 minutes of company time. Listeners who listen effectively decrease time wasted during meetings and may even limit the number of meetings that have to be rescheduled.

INCREASED SALES. Another advantage that effective listeners have over ineffective listeners is better sales records. In fact, reports examining characteristics of the highest-paid salespeople reinforce the value of effective listening. Real estate agents, for example, are much more successful if they really listen to the needs of their potential clients and don't just think about the sales commission. If the agent shows houses out of the buyer's price range, or without consideration for the school system, carport, fenced yard for a dog, or need for an extra bedroom, a prospective home buyer may look for another agent. Effective listeners and sales professionals read between the lines and know when to ask questions, clarify expectations, repeat what was said, and observe what potential customers may be saying nonverbally.

REDUCED STRESS. Good listeners are in demand. Take a moment to list the people you consider to be effective listeners. Most of us probably have rather short lists, since in our society more people prefer to talk than to listen. One reason that good listeners are in demand is that when people feel

To increase your awareness of the listening environment around you, take a few minutes to follow some simple instructions:

1. Set a timer on your watch or microwave for 30 seconds.
2. Close your eyes and just listen with your ears.
3. For these 30 seconds, listen to all the sounds in your environment.
4. After 30 seconds, get a sheet of paper and write down every sound that you heard.
5. Now, put down the book and begin listening for 30 seconds.

Welcome back. You should have been able to list at least five different sounds. Your list may have included air conditioning or furnace fans, outside traffic, a plane overhead, rustling of paper or clothing, footsteps in the hall, doors shutting, elevators dinging, your own breathing, telephones ringing, printers or machinery sounds, voices, music, or birds or crickets chirping.

You probably were not aware of most of these sounds prior to this exercise, but they were there all the time. By focusing your awareness on such sounds, however, you were able to identify them and classify them as important or inconsequential. But let's look more closely for a moment at some of the items on the list of what we heard during the 30 seconds.

While you were taking the above test, were there any other sounds that you may have overlooked? Did you, for example, list your own inner voice? Some of you may have had your voice listed first, but most of us fail to acknowledge the loudest sounds of all—our inner voices. During the day our inner voices never stop talking to us. During the preceding exercise, your inner voice probably made comments such as "This is a long 30 seconds," "Why would the authors ask us to do something like this?" "There are more sounds than I thought," or "I don't hear anything." In actuality your inner voice was and is the loudest sound in your world and does more to hinder your reception of messages than any other interference.

It is our inner voice that:

hinders us from remembering names during first introductions;
causes us to rush to a response ("the great comeback") before people finish their thoughts;
fades in and out of conversations by jumping to other topics and thoughts because of emotional trigger words or associations.

And while it is our inner voice that helps us monitor our interactions with ourselves and others, sometimes our inner voice *screams* when it needs to *whisper, interrupts* when it needs to *wait,* or *argues* when it needs to *reflect.*

FIGURE 3–3
Sounds of Silence

listened to and understood, their stress levels are lowered. In fact, we sometimes forget the need others have to be listened to.

In addition to the benefits already described, effective listening has the potential to reduce paperwork, improve upward communication, and encourage others to participate. As mentioned earlier, we need incentive to listen. Understanding of the costs and benefits of listening should help provide an incentive to improve listening skills.

HOW TO LISTEN

Before changing your listening behavior, it is important to get a picture of yourself as a listener. The goal is to help you see aspects of your listening behaviors and habits. Habits are important to observe because they develop so slowly that you often fail to notice them. The first step toward increasing your awareness is to identify your *listening preferences* and to observe your listening activities and habits in your immediate environment.

Listening Preferences

Listening habits and preferences do not develop in the same ways for all people. Some people prefer to hear from only credible sources, others want to be entertained, some focus on the other person's needs, and others want a speaker to get to the point as quickly as possible. Listening preferences

Habits affect the way that we listen.

develop over a lifetime as a function of socialization and reinforcement patterns.

Based on our preferences, unknowingly, we make judgments and decisions that may hinder our communication effectiveness. Similarly, our own preferences influence how we present information to others. The following paragraphs provide general descriptions of the four listener preferences: content-, action-, people-, and time-oriented.[1]

CONTENT-ORIENTED. *Content-oriented* listeners have a tendency to critically evaluate everything they hear. At times it is as if they are looking under a microscope to determine weaknesses or inconsistencies in information. While they willingly give time to listening, they prefer to listen to experts and highly credible sources. Content-oriented listeners have the ability to see both sides of issues, enjoy listening to challenging or complex information, and elicit high-quality ideas. Because content-oriented listeners carefully question information, in extreme cases, they may intimidate other people. Used in roles of authority, such as parents, teachers, or bosses, this listening style may hinder spontaneous discussions and creative exchanges of ideas.

ACTION-ORIENTED. *Action-oriented* listeners are very time-conscious when listening and encourage others to be time-conscious as well. They often prefer to listen in outline form and find it difficult to listen to speakers who are disorganized. The action-oriented listener is an appreciated member of most meetings because he or she encourages others to stay on task, to keep meeting time to a minimum, and to present information in a logical, organized way. At times, however, because they appear to be in a rush, action-oriented listeners come across as impatient and not very interested in building relationships with others.

PEOPLE-ORIENTED. *People-oriented* listeners are most concerned with how their listening influences their relationships with others. They listen to understand both the content and emotional states of others, willingly take time to listen, and usually remain nonjudgmental. When confronted with personal problems or crises, we seek out people-oriented listeners. Since they are open to all types of people and topics, they can get overly involved with others. In fact, at times people-oriented listeners can lose their objectivity when listening.

TIME-ORIENTED. *Time-oriented* listeners are clock-watchers and encourage others to be the same. They are direct in how they value time and often get impatient with others who waste it. While they encourage efficiency and time management, their self-imposed time constraints can limit

---

[1]K.W. Watson and L.L. Barker, *Personal Listening Preference Profile* (New Orleans, La.: SPECTRA, Inc., 1992).

creativity. Time-oriented listeners must be careful not to interrupt or discount relationships with others.

After reading about these listening preferences, identify your own listening preferences. Think about how it might affect the information you receive and your interactions with others.

Poor Listening Habits

Now that you have identified how you prefer to listen to others, think for a minute about skills you have learned. At first most of us were clumsy at eating with a spoon, walking, learning to ride a bike, or typing a letter. Through practice and trial and error, we learned and reinforced behaviors so that we no longer have to think about what we do.

As with other skills, our listening habits are ones that have been developed and reinforced through the years. Let's turn to some habits that actually affect your ability to listen effectively. While these habits may not be easily observed by others, they do create serious listening problems when they are habitually practiced (see Figure 3–4).

AVOIDING CHALLENGING OR DIFFICULT LISTENING SITUATIONS. Depending on our listening preference, this habit may be more or less severe. The problem with this habit is that improving listening takes practice, and practice needs to take place in realistic and challenging environments. Many of us watch television programs that take little or no effort to absorb rather than watching debates, controversial documentaries, or public lectures. Don't get us wrong—there are time when we can enjoy and actually need to engage in easy listening situations to replenish our listening energy tanks. If, however, you find yourself routinely avoiding challenging listening situations, it may be time for a change.

TOLERATING DISTRACTIONS THAT CAN BE CONTROLLED. We often practice this habit unawares. You may forget that you have the capacity to close doors to cut down on noise. You may neglect to have your secretary hold all calls until an important meeting is completed. You may tolerate noisy office machines that could be sound-dampened, loud radios playing in the car during a conversation, or even traffic noise when you keep the window of your car open. Distractions, for most speakers and listeners alike, decrease the quality of our communication with others. Taking the initiative to control distractions can help save listening energy and make relationships more pleasant and rewarding.

FAKING ATTENTION. Most of us have learned to fake attention so well that we forget we are doing it. In fact, our educational process has often encouraged us to look as if we are listening. We look at the speaker, nod our heads at appropriate times, raise our hands when everyone else does, and even laugh when we hear others laughing. Granted, at times this habit can be useful—and at least make speakers feel that they are appreciated. However,

Instructions: Place an X or check mark in the blank that best describes the extend to which you exhibit these listening behaviors:

	Often	Sometimes	Never
1. Prejudging topics and listening situations as unimportant, dry, or boring	_____	_____	_____
2. Criticizing a speaker's appearance or delivery	_____	_____	_____
3. Getting ego-involved with subjects and letting your emotions take control	_____	_____	_____
4. Listening only for facts (while overlooking intent, purpose, or structure of a message)	_____	_____	_____
5. Trying to outline everything when taking notes	_____	_____	_____
6. Faking attention to the speaker	_____	_____	_____
7. Tolerating or creating distractions during communication activities (e.g., turning on the television while talking at the dinner table or turning your desk to see what is happening in a hallway outside your office)	_____	_____	_____
8. Avoiding messages that are difficult to understand	_____	_____	_____
9. Reacting to specific words rather than the broader concept in a message (for instance, words like "abortion" that trigger word reactions)	_____	_____	_____
10. Letting your mind wander when you can somewhat follow what a speaker is saying	_____	_____	_____

FIGURE 3–4
Your Listening IQ

when you get caught faking, relationships are damaged and valuable information can be lost. Being aware of this habit is the first step toward overcoming it in critical listening situations. Make a commitment to concentrate your listening energy on the speaker in important settings in order to overcome the habit of faking attention.

CRITICIZING A SPEAKER'S SPEAKING STYLE OR PERSONAL MAN-NERISMS.   In a class where a professor used the sound "uh" some 20 times during the first five minutes of class, students could hardly help keeping count. The problem was that the professor didn't test the class on his "uh's," and many students didn't pass the test on the lecture. Of course it's easy to blame speakers for their sins. As effective listeners, however, we can't afford to let such mannerisms keep us from selfishly getting important points from the message. Focusing on the important elements in the communication setting rather than on the speaker's mannerisms is a much more profitable expenditure of listening energy.

CONCENTRATING ONLY ON EASY-TO-REMEMBER FACTS AND MISSING THE BOTTOM LINE.   At times we half-heartedly make efforts to remember facts that stand out, and completely miss the speaker's main points. This habit has also been referred to as "majoring in minors." Unless we listen with an intent to understand the essence of the message, we may fall into the habit of picking and choosing only selected tidbits to process and remember. When we put these bits together at the end of the presentation or conversation, we may find that we have a totally incorrect perception of what the speaker was trying to get across.

WASTING THE *THINKING–SPEAKING TIME DIFFERENTIAL*.   You may have seen the Federal Express commercial that featured John "Mighty Mouth" Moschitta speaking at a rate of 500 words per minute. For a limited period of time, we can muster enough energy to listen and comprehend information at these fast rates. However, since most speakers in conversation use 125 to 145 words per minute, we can listen at a much faster rate than others can speak. When a person speaks too slowly, we may get in the habit of daydreaming or doodling rather than using the time to internally anticipate, summarize, evaluate, and review what we have heard. In these cases, we run the risk of missing valuable information.

Skill Building to Improve Listening Habits: Climbing the Listening Ladder

Our listening habits usually go unnoticed until something goes wrong. It is only when we are reminded that we missed an important meeting or forgot to return a call that we realize that a change in our listening habits is necessary. Even so, when our friends and family members confront us about our poor listening habits it is often human nature to make excuses. If we want to reach our goal of successful communication, however, then we must take responsibility for the process.

Just as a speaker's role is to connect with and help the listener, the listener's job is to reach out to the speaker. As a person climbs the listening ladder, he or she must have confidence that each progressive step of the ladder will hold and that the next step will be as steady as the first. At times, listeners must test for the sturdiness and stability of the ladder to ensure successful communication. The following examples and suggestions are designed to help listeners climb the listening ladder successfully.[2]

FOCUSING. If we want to get the most from a listening situation, we must prepare ourselves to listen by *focusing*. Effective listeners make sure that they have an adequate energy supply and use the energy to concentrate on what a speaker is saying. Paying attention to others requires effort, but most listeners have not practiced the skills necessary to stay involved when others are talking. It does little good to attend to others as listeners if the message doesn't have a chance of getting through. The following suggestions provide a basic foundation for taking responsibility for the success of communication and for getting ourselves ready to listen.

1. Remove or reduce distractions by turning off TVs, closing drapes or blinds.
2. Sit or move closer to the speaker.
3. Minimize interruptions by unplugging the phone and closing the door.
4. Ask the speaker to speak louder.
5. Focus attention and concentrate.
6. Prepare for the speaker, topic, and situation in advance.
7. Look at the speaker.
8. Be rested.

TRACKING. Most of us have been guilty of interrupting or discouraging others from talking. The *tracking* strategy encourages others to keep talking and you to keep listening. Especially when we listen to a person who has a different point of view, it is easy to begin evaluating their message before they finish talking. We all have been guilty of "planning the great comeback" or "rehearsing a response." Rather than jumping to conclusions, it would be best to mentally note or jot down points you'd like to clarify—and keep listening. The following suggestions should help us in following what others have to say.

1. Avoid interrupting.
2. Withhold or defer judgment.
3. Remain objective with minimum bias.
4. Be aware of the speaker's biases.
5. Show nonverbal encouragement through head nods, eye contact, etc.
6. Ask about priorities of requested actions.

---

[2]L.L. Barker, P.M. Johnson, and K.W. Watson, "The Role of Listening in Managing Interpersonal and Group Conflict," in *Listening in Everyday Life,* ed. D. Borisoff and M. Purdy (New York: University Press of America, 1991), 139–62.

REFLECTING. Listeners may need to test their understanding. Listeners can clarify messages by *reflecting*—using such questions as, "So are you suggesting that we wait until next week to go to the mountains?" or "Do you want me to come to the meeting at 9:00 or 9:30?" Remember, listeners are put at a disadvantage if they fail to get involved with the speaker throughout the communication interaction. Listeners need to ask questions or to take control of the communication situation to make sure that they have interpreted messages correctly. When listening:

1. Summarize key points.
2. Describe the emotional state of the speaker.
3. Repeat ideas or paraphrase to the speaker.
4. Identify words with multiple meanings.
5. Analyze and adapt to the speaker's point of view.

DIGGING. Identify a time when you have tried to hide what you were thinking or feeling from someone else. Perhaps you didn't want to hurt someone's feelings or were afraid of what another person would think of you. Keeping our thoughts and feelings hidden interferes with accurate communication. Thus, before making important decisions, most of us would like to know more about what is going on within a person. *Digging* is a strategy to help listeners discover underlying issues and concerns. Digging clarifies verbal and nonverbal messages by reflecting on the emotions and thoughts of speakers. To get additional information:

1. Ask open-ended questions that require more than a yes or no answer.
2. Ask for examples.
3. Ask clarification questions.
4. Use preliminary closes to check for feelings.
5. Ask for additional evidence or supporting material.

DAMPENING. In some listening situations the needs of one person to talk are so great that the appropriate way to listen is to say little or nothing. The person may be angry, depressed, excited, or happy. *Dampening* is a listening strategy to use to calm a person when he or she is in a negative emotional state. When a person is angry, for example, he or she may begin to take the anger out on others. As listeners we can choose to "punch back" or to "take the blow." If we respond in anger or punch back, we usually intensify negative emotions. If, however, we choose to become a pillow and take the punch, the person usually begins to calm down and may begin to respond less emotionally. When trying to calm the speaker:

1. Refrain from rehearsing a response.
2. Use encouraging remarks to keep the other person talking.

3. Use empathetic responses to demonstrate understanding.
4. Avoid interrupting the speaker.
5. Summarize the speaker's feelings to show understanding.

REDIRECTING. It is not unusual for speakers to get sidetracked during meetings or conversations. While digressions can be appropriate, many are not; as a listener you may need to get the person back to the topic or task at hand. When diversions occur, the listener's *redirecting* helps the speaker get back on track by using comments such as: "Now that we've discussed . . . , how can we use the information to. . . ?" or "Since this topic wasn't on the agenda, why don't we table this until our next meeting?" To get a person back on the subject:

1. Restate the original topic or issue.
2. Make statements that clarify the message.
3. Ask questions to get the person back on track.
4. Summarize what has been said to provide feedback.
5. Explain how the topic changed direction.

To sum up, you can improve your listening behavior by being aware of your listening energy and habits. Even before reading this chapter, chances are that you already knew many ways to be a better listener. The trick is to actually behave appropriately in actual listening situations. Some of the more desirable listening behaviors are listed in Table 3–1. These "effective listening habits" constitute ten tips for overcoming some of the worst listening habits listed in Figure 3–4.

TABLE 3–1
Tips for Effective Listening

1. When listening to "uninteresting" subject matter, look for benefits and opportunities by asking, "What's in it for me?"
2. Judge content—not the appearance or delivery of a speaker.
3. To avoid getting overstimulated by some part of a message, hold your fire: Avoid making a judgment until the message is complete.
4. Avoid listening only for facts by listening for central themes and ideas.
5. Be flexible when taking notes; take fewer notes and use different systems of notetaking depending on the speaker.
6. Overcome the temptation to fake attention by working hard to listen and assuming an active listening stance (for example, lean forward, make eye contact with speaker).
7. Resist distractions by fighting or avoiding them; learn how to concentrate.
8. Seek out difficult material rather than avoid it; use "heavy" material as an exercise for the mind.
9. Keep an open mind when confronted with an emotional word with which you are uncomfortable. Work to interpret color words rather than to get hung up on them.
10. Capitalize on the fact that thought is faster than speech: Use the thinking–speaking time differential to summarize mentally, weigh evidence, and listen "between the lines."

Source: Adapted from L. K. Steil, L. L. Barker, and K. W. Watson, *Effective Listening: Key to Your Success* (Reading, Mass.: Addison-Wesley, 1983), 72–73.

FEEDBACK

Communication is a circular process. As a message is transmitted from sender to receiver, a return message, known as **feedback,** is transmitted in the opposite direction. Feedback is a message that indicates the level of understanding or agreement between two or more people in communication in response to an original message. Feedback represents a listener's verbal or nonverbal commentary on the message being communicated.

Feedback is an ongoing process that usually begins as a reaction to various aspects of the initial message. For example, a definite response is being fed back to the speaker when we shake our heads affirmatively or look quizzically at the speaker. Feedback plays an essential role in helping us to determine whether or not our message has been understood; whether it is being received positively or negatively; and whether our audience is open or defensive, self-controlled or bored. Feedback can warn us that we must alter our communication to achieve the desired effect. If we are not aware of feedback or don't pay any attention to it, there is a strong possibility that our efforts at communicating will be completely ineffective.

To emphasize the importance of the feedback mechanism in communication, you need only imagine yourself growing up for the last 18 years or so, never having received any feedback. No one has praised you as you learned to walk or ride a bike. No one has warned you not to chase a ball into the street or to put your hand on a hot stove. No one has shared your tears or laughter. You probably would not function well at all. How would you appraise your self-concept? What values or morals would you possess? While such an existence is impossible, since a certain amount of feedback comes from you yourself as well as from others in the environment, this example does suggest the various functions and effects of feedback in the communication process.

Nothing that man possesses is more precious than his awareness.

ROBERT DE ROPP

Types of Feedback

There are two types of feedback: self-feedback and listener feedback (see Figure 3–5).

Self-feedback applies to the words and actions that are fed back into your central nervous system as you perceive your own muscular movements and hear yourself speak. Feeling your tongue twist as you mispronounce a word or, in a library, suddenly realizing that you are speaking too loudly are examples of self-feedback. Another example would be hearing yourself use a word incorrectly, or reversing sounds—for example, asking, "Were you sappy or had?" instead of "happy or sad."

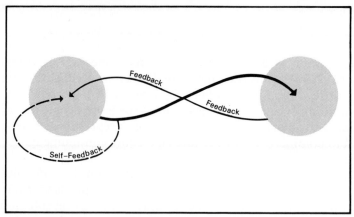

FIGURE 3–5
Self-Feedback and Listener Feedback

Research indicates that self-feedback plays an important role in the nature and form of our judgmental processes, especially when listener feedback is absent. For example, Hagafors and Brehmer have found that our judgments become more consistent when we are required to justify them to others and when no other form of listener feedback is present. In addition, under these conditions our judgments seem to become more analytical and less intuitive. It seems that self-feedback in the form of justification alters the nature and form of our overall judgmental process.[3]

The other major type of feedback, ***listener feedback,*** involves verbal and nonverbal responses. Verbal feedback may take the form of questions or comments. A listener may, for instance, ask a speaker to explain the last point or give praise for making the story so interesting. Nonverbal feedback may be transmitted by applause or laughter, to indicate approval, or by a blank stare, which might indicate disinterest or confusion. Even silence can act as feedback. If a teacher asks a question and no one answers, the silence may indicate lack of knowledge, misunderstanding, or perhaps dislike of the teacher. If a father asks his son if he has finished his homework and the son doesn't reply, that silence is meaningful.

Functions of Feedback

Feedback serves various functions in the communication process. The first of these functions is to evaluate what is right or wrong about a particular communication. If you give a speech to the class, your teacher will offer criticism and suggestions for improving your delivery. If someone is

---

[3]R. Hagafors and B. Brehmer, "Does Having to Justify One's Judgment Change the Nature of the Judgment Process?" *Organizational Behavior and Human Performance*, 31 (1983), 223–32.

watching you hang a painting, he or she will give you feedback as you try various positions, to help you find the right place for it. As will be discussed in Chapter 4, nonverbal feedback, in the form of nods and hand movements, helps to regulate turn taking in conversation.

Secondly, feedback can serve to stimulate change. For example, a popular soft-drink company, after changing its century-old formula, received so much mixed feedback in the form of letters and phone calls that the company not only retained the new formula but brought back the original formula and placed both on grocery-store shelves.

A third function of feedback is to reinforce, to give reward or punishment. A father says, "I'm proud of you, son," or "Jim, can't you ever keep quiet!" When used in this way, rewarding feedback encourages certain behaviors, while punishing feedback is intended to discourage certain behaviors. Comedians rely on positive reinforcement from their audience in the form of laughter; their performance may improve if they sense that the audience feedback is positive.

Effects of Feedback

If you have ever made a phone call and unexpectedly found yourself talking to an answering machine, or prepared and sent a tape to a friend overseas, you may have felt somewhat uncomfortable, or even foolish. It is difficult to sound conversational when there is no one on the other end to respond. This example suggests that feedback is an essential part of the communication process. We can see this through the effects of feedback.

Probably the most important effect of feedback on the communication process is in improving the accuracy of understanding. For example, a teacher seeing only blank stares during a complicated lecture might make a conscious effort to repeat and clarify certain points until the audience shows signs of nodding in agreement. As this example indicates, feedback may increase the amount of time necessary for a communication interaction to be completed. Nonetheless, it ensures a more thoroughly and clearly transmitted message.

In terms of intrapersonal and interpersonal communication, the most significant effect of feedback, and one that is often long-range, is its impact on self-concept. Surely you know people who have poor self-images and little feeling of self-worth. It is probable that such individuals have based this self-image on punishing feedback received from family and peers during crucial periods of identity development. On the other hand, an individual who has had considerable rewarding feedback from family and friends is likely to develop a favorable self-concept.

Feedback also affects performance. As organizational psychologists Fay Walther and Susan Taylor have noted, feedback is essential to maintaining satisfaction and increased task performance. Because we often do not recognize our problems and deficiencies, we may feel justified in continuing a given level of performance. Through increased feedback (if it is timely and

Feedback serves to stimulate change.

consistent), task performance may be improved. As a result, overall well-being and job satisfaction may be maximized.[4]

Feedback can work in two directions, however. For example, a beginning tennis player who has been praised for her skill at the sport (rewarding feedback) will probably perceive it to be an easier game than will a player who performs equally well but who has received harsh criticism (punishing feedback). Similarly, a student who fails a test (punishing feedback) may aim for just passing the next one instead of working for an *A*. Thus, we can see that feedback also affects performance expectations.

Another important effect of feedback on performance concerns task behavior, particularly in small groups. When people find themselves in small group situations in which they don't know the other members of the group, they often suffer from feelings of rejection and hostility. Those negative feelings can keep the group from performing any type of cooperative work. Positive reinforcement from group members, as well as from outside observers, will help the group interact better and will ultimately improve performance. For example, a group of quarrelsome young children compli-

---

[4]F. Walther and S. Taylor, "An Active Feedback Program Can Spark Performance," *Personnel Administrator*, 28 (1983), 107, 109, 111, 147, 149.

mented on how well they are cleaning up their play area may continue the task with renewed enthusiasm.

Feedback can also affect your attitude toward your own messages or toward the messages of others. There is an extensive body of research on this aspect of feedback. Basically, the findings indicate that "we respond with positive motivation to feedback that is consistent and timely, and includes some positive information."[5] In addition, Taylor and Walther have also found that we do not generally experience adverse reactions to negative feedback as long as the information is perceived as accurate.[6]

We have all had experiences that, though less controlled than research studies, help to clarify the findings of these feedback studies. Perhaps you remember a time when you were in a theater, watching a comedy that you and the rest of the audience did not find amusing. No one was laughing. Yet when several members of the audience later began to laugh loudly, your reaction somehow became more favorable. Soon you were laughing, too. This is the reason for using laugh tracks in television situation comedies.

INAPPROPRIATE FEEDBACK RESPONSES. Sending and receiving feedback is a continuous process. Although we cannot stop giving feedback, we can learn to modify our feedback responses. Think about how you prefer to be listened to. Have you ever had a negative reaction to responses such as "I know how you feel," "You shouldn't feel that way," or "I told you so"? Responses like these occur when we don't think about what we are saying. We should try to avoid the following ineffective responses: irrelevant, interrupting, and tangential.

Irrelevant responses do not apply to the situation that is being discussed. A person may hear only part of a message and respond as though he or she heard it all. A person who arrives late to dinner, for example, may ask questions that have already been answered or tell stories that have already been told without knowing what has already been discussed. *Interrupting responses* break into the words and thoughts of another person. Interruptions are frustrating because they cause others to lose their train of thought or refrain from participation in future conversations. Men usually interrupt interactions more frequently than women, unless the women are highly educated.[7] *Tangential responses* sidetrack a conversation. When this happens it may be difficult to get back to the original discussion. When one person feels compelled to tell about an automobile accident he or she witnessed, for example, and another person responds by talking about his or her automobile insurance policy after an accident, the interaction gets off track. These feedback responses do not encourage effective communication or demonstrate concern for the needs of the speaker.

---

[5]Ibid., 107.

[6]M. Taylor and F. Walther, "The Relationship of Feedback Dimensions to Work Attitudes and Behavior: Process and Practical Implications" (paper presented at the Midwestern Academy of Management, April 1981).

[7]L.R. Smeltzer and K.W. Watson, "Gender Differences in Verbal Communication During Negotiations," *Communication Research Reports* (1986), 74–79.

Feedback is often so spontaneous that you are unaware of giving or receiving it. Nevertheless, there are ways to consciously make your feedback more effective. One method is to focus on observations rather than inferences. For example, consider the following situation: A young woman passes a friend whom she had dated several times. She says hello, but her friend walks right on by. The next time she sees him, she asks, "Hey, are you mad at me? You ignored me the other day when I saw you downtown." She has assumed a negative motive for the man's action, although he may simply have been preoccupied. The woman's feedback to her friend would have been more productive if she had relayed the facts, and only the facts, as she understood them: "Hey, I saw you the other day and called to you, but you didn't answer." This would permit the man to make an honest response, rather than a defensive one.

Another method for increasing the effectiveness of your feedback is to use description rather than judgment. The captain of a basketball team would be more helpful in coaching her players if she said, "You're not running for the ball, and you're moving too slowly," as opposed to, "You're really getting lazy."

It is also important to give immediate feedback. We often delay our responses to problems and conflicts and wait for emotions to die down. It is better to deal with anger or hurt when it occurs, when you are in touch with your reactions. Feedback at the time is more specific and accurate than it can be, say, two months later. Yet sometimes extreme emotions make you overreact or respond in ways you later regret. Again, your feedback should be appropriate to the situation, and controlled to the extent possible.

Limiting feedback is another means of increasing its effectiveness, particularly in a one-to-one situation in which you are the listener. Constantly nodding or interjecting comments in such situations is interfering, at best, and may show superficiality and insincerity, at worst. Thus, it is necessary to guard against overresponding. A smile or nod of agreement to particularly significant statements does more to show that you understand than continuous "uh-huhs."

The act of using conscious feedback techniques may sometimes seem unnatural. It is important to remember, however, that effective feedback does improve the communication process. While feedback that is entirely calculated tends to be stilted, awareness of the feedback mechanism and the messages you are transmitting is an asset to communication.

Changing Habits: A Three-Step Approach

Most of us have known for a long time that we aren't very good at listening or giving feedback, but somehow we never did anything about it. If you want to make the effort to change your habits at this point in your life, there's no time like the present. Listening and feedback behaviors are habits, pure and simple. You have developed most of your habits through accident or trial and error, and some aren't as effective as they could be. Since listening is a skill, it can be learned.

Based on personal experience, we'd suggest taking a three-step approach toward changing listening habits. The first step involves making an inventory of your energy zappers. Since energy zappers need to be decreased or eliminated systematically, the only way to do this is to make specific goals (preferably in writing) to avoid or reduce such energy drains. Next, make a specific plan to conserve and renew energy necessary for effective listening. Review the strategies and make plans to implement them at once. Pick only one or two strategies initially. They should be easy to implement and practice.

The second step is to make a conscious decision to improve your listening skills *in general* with one person you'd like to listen to more effectively. In other words, make a firm commitment to begin trying to become a better listener with that person in as many ways as possible. At this point you will need all of the energy you can muster. If you've ever tried to change habits before, such as stopping smoking or going on a diet, you know how important it is to begin your quest with a lot of positive energy. Select one person with whom you interact frequently to begin your general improvement goal. The stimulus of the person in your presence should help remind you of the general desire you have to improve yourself as a listener. If appropriate, it is also a good idea to discuss your listening improvement plan with the person to whom you will try to listen more effectively. As you become more entrenched in new effective listening patterns, you can broaden this step to include a second, third, or fourth person. The key here is to let the person's presence remind you of your need to listen more efficiently and effectively to him or her.

The third step is to begin working on one specific listening or response habit across all listening situations. Think of the skills, techniques, and strategies you can use to modify existing habits or to create new or more appropriate ones. The key here is to fully understand the strategies available, feel motivated to use them when appropriate, and plan to implement them whenever possible. Try to keep the habit you want to change firmly in mind in most communication settings and work on the habit each time the opportunity presents itself.

SUMMARY

Despite the importance of listening in the communication process, studies have shown that many of us are poor listeners. We often take listening for granted and place little, if any, importance on developing good listening skills. In addition, few people have realized the importance of conserving listening energy and making conscious choices about who and what they listen to during the day.

Listening is an interactive process involving five distinct steps: attending, perceiving, interpreting, assessing, and responding. The steps of the process are hierarchical. For successful communication to take place, listeners and speakers must take mutual responsibility for the outcome. When listeners fail to listen, the costs include lost time, lost money, and lost relationships. Effective listeners, on the other hand, receive benefits of reduced meeting time, increased sales, and reduced stress.

Listening habits are important to observe because they develop slowly over time. One habit involves the preferences that individuals have in the ways that they listen to others. The four listening preferences are content-, action-, people-, and social-oriented. Many people have developed and reinforced poor listening habits, such as avoiding challenging or difficult listening situations, tolerating distractions, faking attention, criticizing a speaker's speaking style, concentrating only on facts, and wasting the thinking–speaking time differential. Listening skills can be improved. Six important strategies to use to improve listening include focusing, tracking, reflecting, digging, dampening, and redirecting.

One of the most important responsibilities of the listener is to transmit effective feedback to the speaker. Simply stated, feedback is a reaction to various aspects of a particular message. It may be communicated through verbal comments or nonverbal gestures. While feedback is usually identified with reactions of the listener, there is also a certain amount of self-feedback, which takes place inside the communicator.

Both self-feedback and listener feedback function to regulate performance in communication processes, to stimulate change in listeners, and to reinforce selected behavior patterns. Feedback ensures greater accuracy in interpreting messages. On a psychological level, feedback affects our self-concept. If the information is consistent and timely, rewarding feedback tends to improve self-concept, task performance, and satisfaction. Negative feedback is effective if we perceive the information to be accurate. In addition, feedback in groups can help to improve performance of the assigned tasks. Finally, feedback can produce changes in a communicator's attitude toward his or her own messages or toward the messages transmitted by others.

While most feedback is communicated without your full awareness, it is possible to adopt conscious strategies to make your feedback more effective. These strategies focus on observations rather than inferences and on description rather than judgment. In addition, they stress immediate but controlled feedback. Remembering such strategies in everyday feedback situations ensures more effective communication and listening.

One way to change habits is to use the three-step approach to improving listening and feedback.

EXERCISES

Group Experiences

Do You Really Understand What I Am Saying?

DESCRIPTION: We use the word *understand* very loosely. Most of the time we mean that we are "hearing" something and translating it into the way we perceive the world—and then we call this phenomenon "understanding." The following experience is an opportunity to see how well you understand another person and how well he or she understands you.

PROCEDURE: Divide into groups of three. Persons A and B should discuss an issue they find controversial. Person C should observe the interaction and report on it after the exercise is completed. After each communication between Person A and Person B, the listening partner should attempt to paraphrase the speaker's position until the speaker accepts the paraphrase. An example of this interaction would be as follows:

Person A: I think that war is a waste in general. On the other hand, George Kennan claims that war can clear the path for a new form of government to emerge.

Person B: What I heard you say is that war isn't bad as long as it serves to clear the way for better forms of government.

Person A: I will not accept your paraphrase.

This process will continue until Person B provides an acceptable paraphrase for Person A. The person doing the paraphrasing should try to use different words than those of the speaker. The interaction should take from 15 to 20 minutes. At the end of that time, Person C should offer an appraisal of what occurred.

DISCUSSION: When you have completed this activity, ask yourself these questions: How long did it take you to provide accurate paraphrases for your partner? How long did it take your partner to provide accurate paraphrases of your position? Was your verbal message clear? What are the implications of this activity? Does it suggest that most of the time we do not truly understand what another person is saying?

Did You See What I Saw?

DESCRIPTION: Our psychological makeup causes us to attend selectively to different stimuli, but we do not necessarily select the same stimuli as another person. We truly see the world through our own set of filters. The following activity demonstrates this idea.

PROCEDURE: Have one person arrange approximately 30 different items on a tray, such as a can opener, a lipstick, a pen, a paperclip, and so on. Include (1) items that most people would not know the name of, such as a special tool; (2) items that are typically used by one sex as opposed to the other (pipe, lipstick); and (3) items that are "taboo," such as underwear, a sanitary napkin, and so on.

Each individual may take 20 seconds to look at (not touch) the items on the tray. Immediately after you view the tray, try to list everything you saw. (Afterwards you may wish to check your list against a complete list of the items on the tray.)

DISCUSSION: The most obvious finding of this experiment is that people will remember different things. Were the first five items you remembered different from the first five items others remembered? Did you remember the "male" items? the "female" items? Did you attempt to describe the items for which you did not have a particular name? By comparison, did you remember more, less, or the same number of items as other people did? Do you selectively attend in listening as well as in seeing?

Silence Is Golden

DESCRIPTION: Most of us are poor listeners. We are usually thinking about what we want to say rather than about what the other person is saying. Try the following experiment, and check out your own listening behavior.

PROCEDURE: Divide into dyads (groups of two). Person A should begin the conversation by describing a peak experience—a high point in his or her life. Person A should talk in short stretches, no more than 30 seconds at a time.

Person B must then wait ten seconds before continuing the conversation. Person B should either respond to A or describe a peak experience of his or her own. The same guideline of length applies to Person B.

This process continues with each person waiting ten seconds before speaking.

DISCUSSION: Does it feel awkward to wait before talking? At which point in listening do you begin to think about what you are going to say? Do you usually try to avoid these silent spaces? By the way, are you a good listener?

Personal Experiences

1. Change the type of feedback you normally give people. For example, listen to a person in a one-to-one interaction without giving any verbal or nonverbal feedback. Make sure that you are not unconsciously

nodding your head or shifting your position. Observe the person's reactions to the absence of feedback. After the conversation is over, ask how the person felt—if he or she noticed anything peculiar during the course of the interaction.

2. Take a ride with a friend in a car, on a bus, or on a bicycle. Ride for about 20 minutes and then discuss what each of you observed about your physical surroundings during the ride. Did you notice different things, people, places? Why did you observe different things? Do you tend to associate with people who select the same "stimuli" in the world as you do?

3. Observe yourself during a class of your choice—particularly one in which there is a lecture presentation. Watch the number of times your attention wanders—and for how long.

4. Sit in a public area, such as a library, a town square, or a park, and close your eyes for ten minutes. Listen to the different sounds around you and try to determine what you are hearing. Would you normally be hearing these sounds if you had your eyes open? How aware are you of different sounds? Do you selectively listen during everyday activities?

Discussion Questions

1. How do we distinguish *listening* from *hearing?*
2. What qualities does a good listener possess?
3. What effective methods of verbal and nonverbal feedback can you use as a good listener?
4. How does the type of feedback provided by a listener affect the communicator?

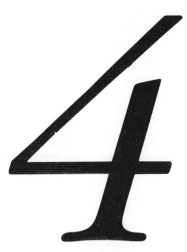

Nonverbal Communication

KEY CONCEPTS AND TERMS

Repeating
Substituting
Complementing
Regulating
Turn-yielding cues
Turn-requesting cues
Turn-maintaining cues
Turn-denying cues
Accenting
Deception cues
Leakage
Kinesics
Emblems
Illustrators
Regulators
Affect displays
Body manipulators

Proxemics
Intimate distance
Personal distance
Social distance
Public distance
Territoriality
Paralanguage
Pitch
Resonance
Tempo
Voice quality

*C*orporate etiquette is one of the hot buzzwords in international business today. As more and more organizations enter the international marketplace, their executives and managers are rediscovering the importance of "minding their manners" and are turning to etiquette experts for refresher courses.

Why has corporate etiquette become such a hot topic in boardrooms across the nation? According to Letitia Baldrige, America's first lady of etiquette, good manners are "cost-effective" because they:

> increase the quality of life in the workplace,
>
> contribute to optimum employee morale,
>
> embellish the company image, and
>
> play a major role in generating profit.[1]

As a result of the importance of these variables to success in any organization, Baldrige and other experts have been jetting across America and consulting with corporate moguls on topics ranging from the etiquette of giving out business cards to seating arrangements at high-level dinners.

Interestingly enough, these two topics—and the hundreds of others that etiquette consultants are addressing in their seminars each day—have long been the purview of nonverbal communication experts as well. In short, the overriding message of both groups is this: *How* we say something to others is often more important than *what* we say.

Although this chapter does not address the topic of corporate etiquette per se, it does address several related areas of interest—for example, the messages that we send to others through our facial expressions, eye behavior, body movements, gestures, clothing, and personal appearance. In addition, the chapter discusses the importance of touch, space, paralanguage, smell and taste, and environmental factors to communication. Because we acquire nonverbal behavior patterns early in life, we seldom have reason to think about them consciously. However, as Letitia Baldrige would agree, a great deal of information is communicated and can be learned from nonverbal expressions—both your own as well as those of people around you.

Before we continue, it is important to emphasize one point. No element of nonverbal behavior—be it a wink, a slouch, a tone of voice, or a gesture—can be interpreted in isolation. Verbal and nonverbal behavior are complementary; neither is really complete without the other. In addition, if we are to fully understand the nature of the nonverbal communication process, we must also consider the context, or the overall situation in which nonverbal behavior occurs, and its relationship to an individual's entire verbal and nonverbal behavior patterns.

---

[1]S. Gelles-Cole, ed., *Letitia Baldrige's Complete Guide to Executive Manners* (New York: Rawson Associates, 1985), 3.

FUNCTIONS OF NONVERBAL COMMUNICATION

Nonverbal communication plays a vital role in every communication event. From the clothes we wear during an important interview to the music we select to set the stage for a romantic evening, nonverbal cues send messages that are frequently more compelling and eloquent than any verbal statement. (*Note:* This statement assumes that each of you has worried—at least once—about "how you look" for an important date.) Although we are all aware to some degree of the impact of nonverbal communication, you may not be cognizant of the extent to which nonverbal messages function in our everyday lives. Specifically, nonverbal communication serves to repeat, substitute, complement, regulate, or accent our verbal messages. In addition, nonverbal cues often serve as a means for deception.

Repeating

"Me?" said Danny, with wide, innocent eyes, pointing his index finger to his chest. "I'd never do something like that!"

When we communicate with one another, we use words and their nonverbal equivalents at the same time. For example, verbal statements of agreement or disagreement ("Right, right," "No way," "Are you kidding?") are often accompanied by a nod or shake of the head to indicate positive or negative feelings. We call these nonverbal gestures *repeating* messages because they convey the same meaning as the verbal message. Of course, either the words or the nods by themselves would be enough—but repeating messages are done almost without thinking. They are a very basic part of language behavior, occurring naturally, without conscious thought or intent.

Substituting

They did not say a word, but we knew exactly how they felt by looking at their faces.

When hearing or speaking is impossible, nonverbal communication often replaces verbal messages. In such instances nonverbal messages are called *substitutes,* because they take the place of words. Thus, someone directing you into a tight parking space might substitute gestures for words when the car's noisy engine prohibits speaking. Another kind of substitution is made when someone with whom you've had an argument attacks you with "looks that could kill."

For nonverbal communication to act as a substitute, it must be recognized and, more importantly, interpreted in the same way by most of the people in a specific group, subculture, or culture. For example, people in the United States interpret the "thumbs down" sign to mean "no." Such well-known substitutes are so universal that they have been recorded in dictionaries of American gestures. Misunderstandings may occur, however, when we try to use our culture's nonverbal substitutes in another culture. Thus, Americans who say "I" by pointing to their chests would not be understood in Japan, where "I" is symbolized by pointing to one's nose.

Complementing

"You don't believe it hurt, huh? Well, just let me shove you the way that idiot shoved me. You'll see!"

We also use nonverbal language to complement, complete, or accent explanations of how to do something or in descriptions of specific sizes or shapes. To understand how important these *complementing* actions can be, just try the following without using nonverbal behavior: Teach a new dance step, explain how to tie a slip knot, or describe the shape of an hourglass.

Complementing behaviors are also used to emphasize emotional feelings or attitudes. The same complementing gesture can accompany quite different emotions, however:

The gold, silver, and bronze medal winners skated out onto the ice and up to the podium to receive their medals. When the bronze medalist was announced, the silver and gold medalists applauded enthusiastically. When the gold medalist was finally announced, the silver medalist applauded, but as she did, a tear ran silently down her cheek.

In this example, the complementing gesture of applause was used in two instances, first to express a positive response (happiness) and then to accompany a negative one (disappointment).

Regulating

Lily knew her father wanted to talk. She could feel his steady gaze upon her. As she turned and looked at him, he said, "Lily. . . ."

One of the most common purposes of nonverbal communication is *regulating.* Let's say that you and a friend are discussing a movie you saw the other night. Without regulating messages, you might sound something like this:

"Hey, did you catch the movie at the Plaza the other night? O.K., I'm finished talking for the moment. You can speak."

"Thank you. I wanted to answer your question. Yeah. Great. Especially that scene in the woods. . . ."

"Can I talk?"

"You want to talk again? Sure."

"Thanks. I just wanted to say that I let out the biggest scream during that part!"

Fortunately, typical conversations don't require this kind of verbal permission to speak or respond. Instead, nonverbal cues keep the conversation flowing through our use of a conversational turn-taking system, or the rules of interaction that we learned early in life. This system is comprised of four major sets of nonverbal cues: (1) turn-yielding, (2) turn-requesting, (3) turn-maintaining, and (4) turn-denying cues.

Turn-yielding cues tell our listener that we no longer wish to speak for the moment and want him or her to take a conversational turn. Turn-yielding cues include ending a turn with a question (such as, "What do you think?"), slowing our speech rate, and increasing our eye contact with the listener. On the other hand, we give *turn-requesting cues* when we want to take a conversational turn. For example, we may lean forward, take an audible breath, nod our head more rapidly, fill our pauses more often (for instance, "umm-hmm," "yeah"), or raise an index finger, as if to say, "I would like to take a turn."

Conversations also are regulated by turn-maintaining and turn-denying cues. We use *turn-maintaining cues* when we are speaking and do not wish to yield the floor to the listener. Cues that help us maintain the floor include increased speech rate, a raised hand, a touch on the listener's arm that says, "I'm not quite through talking yet," and averting our gaze away from the listener's eyes. *Turn-denying cues* are useful when we are listening, the speaker wants us to take a turn, and we do not wish to speak at that time. If we want to deny (avoid) a turn, we generally will remain silent, exhibit a more relaxed posture, lean slightly backward, and gaze directly into the speaker's eyes, as if to say, "Please continue." Or we may actually say, "Please go on. I would like to hear more."

Accenting

> Sally slammed the book shut. "Oh, what's the use! There's no way I'll learn all this by tomorrow!"

Another function of nonverbal communication is *accenting,* the use of gestures, such as nods, blinks, squints, and shrugs, to help emphasize or punctuate spoken words:

> Adrienne's cocker spaniel just won first prize in the dog show. As she leads him out of the ring, friends and family congratulate both Adrienne and the dog with warm words, but also with pats on the back.

Accenting can also be achieved by changing the pitch or stress on a word or group of words. In fact, our entire meaning often depends on which words are accented:

> *I* want to dance with him.
> I want to dance with *him.*
> I want to *dance* with him.

Deceiving/Revealing

"I'll see you and raise you five bucks," Kelly said with his usual poker face.

Sometimes we purposely deceive others or supply them with false information. You may not like a friend's new haircut, for example, but still say, "Your hair looks great!" to avoid hurting his feelings. At the same time that you are saying this and staring convincingly into your friend's eyes, you may be nervously pulling at your coat buttons. If your friend is sensitive to nonverbal behavior, he may pick up this contradictory message.

Deception cues (such as an overly exaggerated smile or a frown that is too severe) suggest possible falsehood but do not tell what information is being withheld or falsified. **Leakage,** on the other hand, implies "spilling the beans" about the withheld information. For example, biting a fingernail can leak nervousness, or a clenched fist can leak the desire to fight.

Research on deception has demonstrated a relationship between the message-sending ability of the body and the deception and leakage cues that the body reveals. Research by Paul Ekman, one of the pioneers of nonverbal communication, has shown that the face, voice, and hands betray us the most. Specifically, Ekman found that two kinds of smiling help to differentiate honesty from deception as well as the leakage of negative information. "Duchenne's smile" is a smile that involves both the muscle around the eye as well as the muscle that pulls up the corner of the lip. This type of smile is believed to be a sign of true enjoyment. Conversely, a "masked smile" is one that involves the muscles associated with the lip, but also includes small muscular traces of disgust, anger, fear, sadness, or contempt. The latter type of smile is associated with concealing negative feelings and discriminates between deception and enjoyment or honesty.[2]

Another cue that indicates deception is a change in pitch. Whenever we are attempting to conceal or mask the truth, our pitch usually changes in an upward direction. We have all seen movies in which a character's voice actually squeaks when he or she attempts to lie. This humorous behavior associated with lying on television or in movies is actually not far from the truth. When facial and pitch measures were combined in Ekman's research, people who took part in his study were able to accurately detect deception 84 percent of the time.[3]

Finally, deception seems to be associated with a decreased number of illustrators, or gestures that we use to accent or emphasize our spoken words. Specifically, Ekman argues that we generally decrease the number of gestures we use when we are thinking harder about what to say or inventing a story. Additionally, we seem to use fewer gestures when we are talking about negative emotions. In either event, the number of illustrators we use indeed tends to indicate the presence or absence of deception.[4]

---

[2]P. Ekman, "Lying and Nonverbal Behavior: Theoretical Issues and New Findings," *Journal of Nonverbal Behavior*, 12, no. 3 (Fall 1988), 170.
[3]Ibid., 170.
[4]Ibid., 170–71.

As you can see, unconscious movements of our bodies often are dead giveaways of our thoughts. Remember this fact the next time you want to know what someone is thinking. Listen to the words, look at the smile, listen to the voice, and watch the hands. Somewhere in the person's body movements, the truth prevails.

TYPES OF NONVERBAL COMMUNICATION

Many people, because of popularized reading, consider body language to be the only form of nonverbal communication. However, nonverbal communication includes body language and much, much more. Each day we nonverbally signal our moods, attitudes, and values to others. Have you ever dressed up for a job interview, hugged a friend, been late for an appointment, wanted to sit in a certain seat in a class, or used your hands while talking? If so, you were communicating to others nonverbally. We are often unaware of our nonverbal behaviors. In our attempt to increase sensitivity to different types of our nonverbal behavior, we will examine facial expressions, eye behavior, kinesics and body movement, personal appearance and clothing, touching, proxemics, paralanguage, smell and taste, and environmental factors.

Facial Expressions

The face is perhaps the most obvious vehicle for nonverbal communication. It is a constant source of information to those around us. For example, a neuromuscular therapist uses nonverbal cues from a client's face to gauge the existence and subsequent release of "trigger points," or muscular tissue in which a great deal of tension has built up. Likewise, attorneys specializing in criminal law pay close attention to the face and eyes of future clients for clues to the latter's possible guilt or innocence.

How does the face send such nonverbal cues? When something makes you happy or sad (or produces any other emotion), your nerves immediately send a message to the face, which causes the muscles to contract or relax. The feedback you get from these muscle movements is one of the cues that tells you what emotional feeling you are having. This process is a form of internal self-feedback in intrapersonal communication, which will be discussed in the following chapter.

*Faces tell us a lot about
the emotions of others.*

Think of all the things your face can say about you without your saying a word. Things such as wrinkles, baldness, and coloring comment not only on your age but also on the kind of life you lead. For example, we suspect that people with dark tans spend a considerable amount of time outdoors. The length and style of your hair and the amount of makeup you wear suggest your economic status, interest in fashion, and sometimes even your politics. All of these things, plus the facial expressions that reveal emotion, can speak for you before you ever open your mouth.

Charles Darwin first argued that many of our facial expressions evolved from lower animals, and scientists are still debating this issue. On one side of the debate, some research has yielded support for Darwin's theory about universal behaviors. For example, Paul Ekman and his colleagues have identified seven emotions that can be discerned universally from facial expressions: happiness, fear, sadness, anger, disgust, contempt, and surprise.[5] Identification of these emotions was based on a number of studies that demonstrated the recognition of emotions by adults across a number of cultures.

However, contradictory results have emerged in several cross-cultural studies, particularly those in which descriptions of situations have been

---

[5]P. Ekman and W.V. Friesen, *Unmasking the Face* (Englewood Cliffs, N.J.: Prentice Hall, 1975).

supplied to individuals who are making judgments. For instance, using photographs that were identical to those used by Ekman in one of his studies, Niit and Valsiner conducted an experiment with Estonian and Kirghiz university students in the Soviet Union. Subjects were asked to describe the emotion that an individual in a photograph was attempting to convey— either with or without an accompanying description of the situation in which the emotional expression might occur. Results of their study revealed differences in students' recognition of the emotions when situational cues were supplied, while no differences from prior research emerged when situational descriptions were not provided.[6] Studies such as these support an alternative theory of facial expressions and their origins: It is the context of the event that supplies the meanings for facial expressions. Thus, one's culture is responsible for the ways in which its members encode and decode facial expressions.

Although the debate concerning the origin of facial expression continues, some agreement exists regarding the universal ability of humans to encode and decode emotions via facial expressions. However, this "agreement" is qualified by the argument that cultures do differ in their uses of facial expressions and, hence, have a profound effect on how emotions are encoded and decoded.

It also is important to note that cultural rules and societal pressures often inhibit spontaneous facial expressions. At early ages children learn which expressions are acceptable and which are unacceptable by hearing things like, "If you keep frowning, your face will grow like that" or "A shot is nothing to be afraid of; you've got to act like a big boy now." We also learn how to adapt our facial expressions to meet the expectations of others. How many times have you smiled politely when receiving an unwanted gift, held back tears after a bitter disappointment, or avoided laughing when watching someone trip over a curb? We all adjust many of our natural facial expressions to those considered to be more appropriate.

Eye Behavior

For centuries poets and painters have paid tribute to our expressive eyes. Modern-day researchers, too, have been intrigued by the eyes and the many nonverbal messages they convey. Specifically, research has shown that eye behavior functions to:

1. provide information,
2. regulate interactions,
3. exercise social control,
4. express intimacy, and
5. facilitate goal achievement.[7]

---

[6]T. Niit and J. Valsiner, "Recognition of Facial Expressions: An Experimental Investigation of Ekman's Model," *Tartu Riikliku Ulikooli Toimetised: Trudy po Psikhologii*, 429 (1977), 85–107.

[7]C. L. Kleinke, "Gaze and Eye Contact: A Research Review," *Psychological Bulletin*, 100, no. 1 (1986), 78–100.

Certain eye behaviors are associated with definite moods, reactions, and attitudes. In this way they provide us with information about people with whom we interact. For example, consider the common, negative traits that we associate with "small, beady eyes." For people who have the misfortune of being born with such eyes, they are often associated with cheating, lying, and general negativity. We also have certain beliefs and feelings about eye pupil size. Indeed, research indicates that our pupils dilate (grow larger) when we are presented with a pleasant stimulus (such as a picture of someone we love) and constrict when we are subjected to a negative stimulus (such as a grating noise or an unfamiliar touch).[8] Additionally, people with large pupils are perceived to be happier and attractive, while those with small pupils are perceived to be angry or unattractive.[9] However, it is important to realize that pupil variations occur in the context of other facial features. Thus, the child with eyes that have naturally large pupils and who seems to be innocent and sincere can be "caught" in deception if we attend to other nonverbal cues, such as his or her facial expressions.

Eye contact is another significant behavior that provides us with information. For example, public speakers who never look up from their notes while speaking send a message that they are nervous or highly formal. Speakers who do look at their audience during a speech are perceived to be more friendly, sincere, and relaxed. Likewise, listeners who do not look at a speaker send a message that they are distracted, are bored, or have little regard for the speaker. Perhaps this is why angry teachers or parents command, "Look at me when I'm talking to you." While you may not be angered personally when others avoid eye contact while you are speaking, this eye behavior on a receiver's part may indicate a lack of interest in what you are saying.

As we stated earlier, eye behavior also serves to regulate interactions. To substantiate this claim, one need look no further than the public speaking setting. When public speakers catch the eyes of listeners, they significantly increase the chances of catching the audience's attention as well. Effective public speakers use periodic "eye checks" to ensure that their listeners are still there and being attentive. Moving toward the audience (away from the lectern) and using more direct eye contact is an excellent strategy to use if you ever think you are "losing" an audience. In interpersonal communication, the principle is the same. Eye contact allows you not only to gain the attention of others, but also to direct the conversational turn-taking system overall.

Although we have pointed out certain commonalities in human eye behavior thus far, individual differences also exist when we converse with others. Depending on the speaker, gaze directed at other people can range in

---

[8]R.H. Chaney, C.A. Givens, M.F. Aoki, and M.L. Gombiner, "Pupillary Responses in Recognizing Awareness in Persons with Profound Mental Retardation," *Perceptual and Motor Skills*, 69 (1989), 523–28.

[9]E. H. Hess, "Attitude and Pupil Size," *Scientific American*, 212, no. 4 (1965), 54.

duration from 10 percent to more than 70 percent of the time. Such differences are often associated with social control, the third function of nonverbal behavior. For example, research has shown that eye behavior is associated with patterns of dominance and submissiveness. Specifically, dominant and poised communicators tend to look more at others during conversations than do submissive, uneasy individuals, especially when they assume the speaking role.

Eye behavior also allows us to express intimacy, or our inner feelings to others, especially our interpersonal attitudes and the level of intimacy we are experiencing. Think for a moment about the last time you gazed into the eyes of someone whom you love. If he or she responded in kind, you probably felt the "connection" associated with mutual gaze. If the person diverted his or her gaze to somewhere else in the room or to the floor, you probably felt that something was amiss. This communicative/monitoring function of eye behavior allows us not only to collect information but also to regulate the level of interpersonal intimacy that we are experiencing. In short, the eyes, indeed, may be viewed as "the window of the soul." Through them we can communicate additional—and often more "meaningful"—information not in the verbal exchange.

The fifth function of eye behavior is facilitation of goals. This function is associated with our use of eye behavior to accomplish some action; for example, our use of gaze to encourage or discourage behavior on the part of others. We are all familiar with the ability of respected teachers to stop someone from talking with a simple, straightforward glare. Conversely, we also are able to encourage others when we offer a warm glance and an encouraging smile.

Kinesics and Body Movement

The human body is so incredibly versatile that it can send thousands of nonverbal messages. In fact, it is hard to know just how to classify all of these nonverbal communications. Ray Birdwhistell, a pioneer in the field of nonverbal communication, coined the word **kinesics** to describe the study of body movement. Early researchers categorized body expressions according to the part of the body involved—facial expression, trunk movements, hand gestures, and so forth.

Birdwhistell viewed body expressions as a language that, like French or Russian, could be studied, learned, and understood. Recent specialists such as Paul Ekman and Wallace Friesen have focused on the general functions of nonverbal communication discussed previously and have come up with five classes of specific body expressions: emblems, illustrators, regulators, affect displays, and body manipulators.[10]

---

[10]P. Ekman and W. V. Friesen, "The Repertoire of Non-Verbal Behavior: Categories, Origins, Usage, and Coding," *Semiotica*, 1, no. 1 (1969), 49–98.

EMBLEMS. *Emblems* are commonly recognized signs that communicate a message that generally is unrelated to an ongoing conversation. They usually take the form of gestures. For example, if you and a co-worker suddenly realized that your animated conversation was disturbing an officemate, you might hold an index finger to your lips. This indication to talk more quietly serves to reduce the volume of your conversation without interrupting its flow. We learn such emblems early in life through imitation and continue to use them throughout our lives (see Figure 4–1).

Beware of the man whose belly does not move when he laughs.

CHINESE PROVERB

ILLUSTRATORS. These body expressions illustrate the verbal language they accompany. *Illustrators* may accent or add emphasis to a phrase; show the direction of thought; point to an object or place; depict spatial

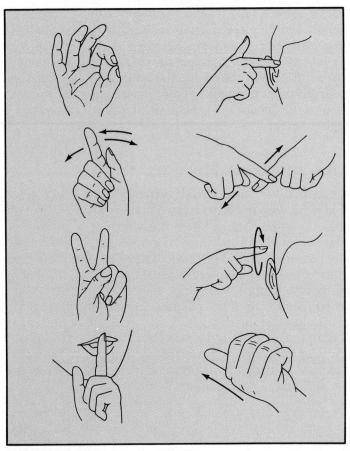

FIGURE 4–1
Can you identify these emblems?

relationships, rhythms, or bodily actions; or demonstrate shape. You are using an illustrator when you point to someone across the room while shouting his or her name, or when you use your hands to estimate the length of the fish that got away.

REGULATORS.   As we explained in the previous section, *regulators* control verbal communication. Regulators such as gazes, nods, and raised eyebrows assist in the exchange of listening and speaking roles among participants in a communication setting. They provide smooth transitions in conversations.

AFFECT DISPLAYS.   Body changes that convey our internal emotional states are *affect displays.* These emotional displays can involve facial expressions, such as angry stares or wide-eyed fear, or body movements, such as trembling hands or knocking knees. Affect displays are not always strictly tied to what we are saying at the time. For example, a ticket agent may be surprised by the deep sadness that lines the face of a man who has just asked for a ticket for the next plane to Pittsburgh, unaware that the passenger is going home to attend the funeral of a loved one. Because facial affect displays are easily simulated, they often can be used in deception. For example, we have all heard the expression, she was "smiling on the outside but crying on the inside."

BODY MANIPULATORS.   *Body manipulators* are movements that were originally associated with body functioning (such as rubbing the eyes when one is tired), that have come to be used unconsciously and independently of bodily needs. For example, twirling your hair during a test, rubbing your

Our bodies convey our emotional states.

chin while you are thinking, and rocking yourself in the fetal position when you are upset are examples of body manipulators as we are defining them here. Other body manipulators involve touching an object or another person. Drawing "doodles" on a pad with a pencil while you are talking on the phone provides an example of an object-focused body manipulator. Patting someone's hand while you are communicating with them is an example of an other-focused body manipulator.

All body movements that involve contact with some body part are not necessarily classed as body manipulators, however. Some of these movements may be emblems or illustrators, depending on their nature and purpose. For instance, placing a forefinger against your temple may act as an emblem for "thought." Likewise, tapping the top of your wrist may serve as an illustrator if you are asking someone for the correct time.

BODY MOVEMENT AND POSTURE. Body movements fall into one of several categories. For instance, how you walk is often a strong indicator of how you feel. When you have a problem, you may walk very slowly with your head down and your hands clasped behind your back. You may even pause to kick a rock on the ground. On the other hand, when you feel especially proud and happy, you may walk with your chin raised, your arms swinging freely, and your legs somewhat stiff—with a bounce in your step.

We all know how to "read" such obvious nonverbal cues, but conscious and sustained effort can help you pick up even more subtle expressions of the nonverbal language. For example, you sometimes use your body parts to show that you are or are not associated with the people near you. Thus, crossing your legs in the same way the person next to you crosses hers may

We use our bodies to transmit messages about degrees of association and agreement.

indicate identification with that person. Or, if you are standing and arguing with three other people, you may soon find yourself assuming the body posture of the person with whom you agree—both of you standing with your hands on your hips, for instance, while your two opponents may also assume like postures.

Other movements and gestures show openness and honesty. Holding the hands open while talking indicates sincerity; hands clenched into fists reflect the opposite. Similarly, if someone unbuttons or even takes off his or her coat in your presence, this conveys openness and friendliness toward you.

In contrast to these gestures of openness are those that indicate defensiveness. The crossed-arm-on-chest position is perhaps the best-known defensive gesture. Charles Darwin argued that this stance is universal in all societies and that it strongly influences anyone who is observing. In fact, communication often comes to a complete halt when someone assumes this position, which says, in effect, "I have now withdrawn from this conversation." Of course, this is not true every time someone crosses his or her arms. However, if it happens during a conversation, you might examine what you have just said or done that would have prompted a withdrawal.

Even the way you sit communicates information. Someone who is speaking while his or her legs dangle over the arm of a chair might be saying, "I am not feeling cooperative. In fact, I am unconcerned or hostile to your feelings or needs." Similarly, people who sit backwards on chairs or put their feet up on a desk may be signaling their feelings of superiority, saying, "I am the dominant person here."

Such reflections of dominance seem to perpetuate sex role stereotypes. Men, for example, characteristically express dominance by taking up more space in a bed than a woman; crossing their legs at the thighs (which takes up a considerable amount of room); and looking into a woman's eyes while talking to her. Women, on the other hand, often use submissive gestures when they are with men: compressing their bodies into a small space in bed; crossing their legs at the ankles or sitting with uncrossed legs held tightly together (which takes up very little space); and looking down when talking to men. We shall explore such spatial relationships later in the chapter.

Personal Appearance

Each year Americans spend millions of dollars on cosmetics, weight control, and plastic surgery to increase their physical attractiveness. To become beautiful people, we starve ourselves to lose weight, spend countless hours in front of mirrors styling our hair and applying makeup, use special conditioners to halt thinning hair, and wear clothing to accent a bulge here and minimize a bulge there. We have been told that inner beauty is what counts in relationships, but research on first impressions suggests that physical attractiveness affects interpersonal outcomes. Physical appearance influences job interviews, blind dates, consumer buying behavior, grades in school, and even courtroom decisions.

Although the face usually determines beauty, we are also judged by our body shapes, skin color, and hair. Every time television sets are turned on, advertisements are stereotyping people according to their physical attributes. Can you remember ever seeing an overweight, unkempt, scar-faced doctor recommend a leading aspirin? Advertisers usually hire neat, clean, attractive models to sell their products. Unattractive individuals are usually used only in advertisements that feature before-and-after sequences, such as when methods for increasing bust size or achieving younger-looking skin are being advertised. To look just right, we are encouraged to change our skin color and texture by applying makeup and medications, getting a golden tan, or using special skin softeners. Society also influences our views on hair. Men want to keep their hair because it is masculine to have hairy chests, beards, and mustaches. Women, however, are constantly finding ways to get rid of their hair. By electrolysis, depilation, and shaving, women eliminate unsightly hair under arms, on legs, over lips, and on eyebrows. Certainly, the way we look is important to ourselves and others. We manipulate our physical appearance so that we will be perceived as attractive rather than unattractive.

Clothing

It is often said that clothes make a person, but it may be more true to say that clothes *are* the person. Your clothes provide visual clues to your interests, age, personality, and attitudes. Even status information is gained from the clothes' age, condition, and fashion. Some of us are interested in clothing as a means of keeping up with the latest social changes. Others use clothing as a form of decoration and self-expression. T-shirt designs, for example, are a communication channel between the wearer and the world.

By a man's fingernails, by his coat-sleeve, by his boots, by his trouser-knees, by the callosities of his forefinger and thumb, by his expression, by his shirt cuffs—by each of these things a man's calling is plainly revealed. That all united should fail to enlighten the competent inquirer in any case is almost inconceivable.

SHERLOCK HOLMES

In the previously mentioned *Letitia Baldrige's Complete Guide to Executive Manners*, Ms. Baldrige emphasizes the importance of clothing in the business community.[11] She suggests that clothing determines a person's job success. Thus, dress is an influential variable in the total system of nonverbal communication. It can fulfill functions ranging from protection, sexual attraction, and self-assertion to self-denial, concealment, group identification, and the display of status and role. To illustrate, have you ever thought of the impact that clothing color can have on evaluations of job

---

[11]S. Gelles-Cole, ed., *Letitia Baldrige's Complete Guide to Executive Manners* (New York: Rawson Associates, 1985), 130–31.

applicants? Research indicates that both facial expressions and clothing color (light vs. dark) significantly affect evaluations of competence, power, character, and sociability in female job applicants.

For example, Damhorst and Pinaire Reed asked male and female executives from 158 organizations in two major Texas cities to judge photographs of six female job applicants wearing either dark or light colors and exhibiting either a smiling or serious facial expression. Results of the study indicated that, overall, smiling models were perceived to be more powerful and competent than nonsmiling models. Additionally, male subjects rated models who wore dark colors as more powerful and competent than those who wore light, pastel colors. When rating models on character and sociability, males again rated women in dark jackets more positively, but only when the models were placed in nonsmiling poses.[12]

Conversely, female raters did not base judgments of power and competence on color of clothing. Additionally, female executives rated those models who wore dark clothing and were not smiling more negatively on character and sociability factors. The researchers concluded that socialization factors may have been the root of the differences that emerged in the study. Since men have been socialized to perceive the dark business suit as a symbol of corporate achievement and power, they viewed female applicants in dark colors as more competent and powerful than those wearing pastel colors. Conversely, since women generally have not been socialized to pursue corporate careers, they have not yet developed strong norms and expectations for women's business attire. Likewise, women have been allowed to experiment more freely with clothing colors and, consequently, do not perceive specific colors to be a symbol of business credibility.[13]

Touching

Do you often reach out to touch other people? Although ours is not a "high-contact" culture, touching is nonetheless the most basic form of nonverbal communication.

We all use touch at times. To emphasize a point or to interrupt another person, for instance, we may grab the speaker's elbow and interrupt with, "But you don't understand." Touching can be used as a calming gesture, too. We frequently try to comfort someone with a pat on the back and a "there, there." In other situations, touching provides reassurance. Not only do we reach out to reassure ourselves of the presence of people we are fond of, but we sometimes do the same with objects—stroking the smooth leather of our gloves, for instance.

These behaviors suggest the importance of touching to human beings. In fact, physical contact with other humans is vital to healthy development.

---

[12]M. L. Damhorst and J. A. Pinaire Reed, "Clothing Color Value and Facial Expression: Effects on Evaluations of Female Job Applicants," *Social Behavior and Personality*, 14, no. 1 (1986), 89–98.

[13]Ibid.

Lack of such contact in childhood may contribute to physical and psychological problems later in life. To understand the significance of this statement, consider how parents touch and teach their children about touch. A child who is reared in a high-contact family will have a high touch orientation. As a result, he or she generally will see and share touch in different ways than a child who is reared in a low-contact family. If parents teach their children through words or deeds that touch is something to be given generously, in turn, their children will see and give touch in this way. Conversely, children who are taught that touch is "dirty"—or, at best, should be minimized—will grow up to view touch as their parents did, unless a "significant other" later in their life helps them to see touch in a more positive and loving way.

Touch is vital to healthy development.

Proxemics

Just as we communicate with words, gestures, and facial expressions, we also can send messages by placing ourselves in certain spatial relationships with other people and objects. The study of these spatial factors is called *proxemics;* it focuses on how we react to space around us, how we use that space, and how our use of space communicates certain information. For example, the amount of space in which a person must live or work communicates a message about the status of that individual. Consider a typical North American family comprised of two parents and three sons, but whose house has only two bedrooms for the children. In recognition of the eldest son's status, chances are that he will have a room to himself, while the two younger children share the second bedroom.

SPATIAL ZONES. Edward T. Hall, a pioneer in the study of proxemics, specified four spatial zones of interpersonal communication: intimate distance, personal distance, social distance, and public distance.

Intimate distance stretches from actual contact to 18 inches. A parent and child, two intimate friends, or other close pairs would have contact in this zone. Of course, even strangers can be thrown into this zone (such as on a crowded elevator). However, such forced closeness is usually countered by silence, averted glances, and other nonverbal messages that say, "O.K., this is fine for now, but it's only going to last for a minute, because I don't really know you."

Personal distance, from 1½ to 4 feet, is the zone we use for casual interactions. You would probably assume this distance when talking with a friend at a cocktail party. In contrast, *social distance,* from 4 to 12 feet, is used by people meeting for the first time or by people conducting business. *Public distance,* from 12 to over 25 feet, is most often used in formal address; for example, by a teacher lecturing students or by a politician speaking at a rally.

We also adapt our behavior when forced to interact in a different zone. For example, when even close friends are farther than 12 feet apart (public distance), they often speak in more formal phrases. On the other hand, casual acquaintances placed in an intimate distance usually whisper and use small, rather than expansive, gestures. Compare the gestures you use when sitting next to a friend with those used to shout a greeting to your neighbor across the street.

Also consider how people will talk before they enter a crowded elevator, but will stop abruptly once the doors close. The reactions that you receive are interesting if you do choose to continue a conversation after the elevator begins to move. Others who are in the elevator cannot help but overhear the conversation, but they will often turn away or lower their heads and pretend not to listen. It is even more interesting (despite the risk of some strange looks) to watch the response of others when you laugh out loud to yourself in this quiet atmosphere.

Intimate distance.

It is important to note that these spatial zones, though common for white, middle-class Americans, are by no means universal. Each culture has its own spatial needs. Thus, Arabs stand so close to each other while talking that they can easily touch and perceive body odors and heat—very different from the "non-contact" culture that characterizes the majority in the United States.

TERRITORIALITY. Scientists have long observed the territorial habits of animals but have only recently begun to understand that humans exhibit similar territorial needs and controls. In fact, all of us carry our own personal space around with us. This *territoriality*—the need to call space *our* space—is another facet of proxemics.

Territoriality implies a desire to possess or give up space or objects around us. For example, different body parts permit us to claim temporary possession of an object. Thus, we often use our hands to reach out and grab an object (as in straightening someone's tie or holding another person's hand). Or, we employ our whole bodies as spatial indicators. Standing with hands on hips and elbows extended, for instance, claims all of the space around our bodies and says, "Don't come any closer to me than my elbows, or else!" On the other hand, when we are kissing, we close our eyes, perhaps

Personal distance.

to break down spatial barriers. "It's okay," we imply. "Your closeness is not infringing on my territory." We also use objects to define our territory. Have you ever used books, paper, pencils, sweaters, and other objects to stake out your space at a library table? Such markers say, "This area is mine."

SEATING ARRANGEMENTS. Did your father always sit at the head of the table in your house? The person who sits at the head of a table will usually be designated the "leader," whether or not that designation is appropriate. Have you ever avoided taking a chair at the head of a table for this very reason? The two ends of a table and the middle seats on the sides are "hot seats" in which people either do, or at least are expected to, talk more.

These examples illustrate the effects of seating arrangements on interpersonal interactions. Some spatial arrangements, such as a round table, encourage us to face each other and to communicate. Other arrangements—for example, a row of chairs in a theater or classroom—force us to face away from one another. These arrangements naturally produce less interaction.

Thus, different seating arrangements are desirable for different types of interactions. If two people are having a friendly conversation, they might prefer seats at the corner of a rectangular table. When working together on a task, they might sit side by side. During competition (playing cards, for example) they would prefer to sit across from one another, thereby making it more difficult to see each other's hand and easier to establish strong eye contact.

Similarly, spatial relationships in the classroom can influence student-teacher interactions. The three most popular ways to arrange classrooms are in rectangular, horseshoe, and modular arrangements (see Figures 4–2, 4–3, and 4–4). Most classrooms in America are rectangular, with desks arranged in straight rows. This arrangement is best for information dissemination or straight lectures. Horseshoe and modular arrangements are frequently used with smaller classes. Courses in disciplines such as home economics, architecture, horticulture, and speech communication would be likely to use these arrangements. Both the horseshoe and modular arrangements increase student participation. The grouping of the modular design allows for maximum interaction and is especially effective for teachers who need to work with groups and individual students.

Most of us also have preferences about where we sit in classes. Have you ever been disappointed, on the first day of class, to find that you couldn't sit in the back row, in front of the teacher, or by the blackboard? A variety of factors, such as wanting to sit by the best-looking student, or wanting to be able to see the board, determine seating preferences. Investigations of seating arrangement and interactions in classrooms indicate that students who sit in

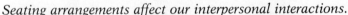

Seating arrangements affect our interpersonal interactions.

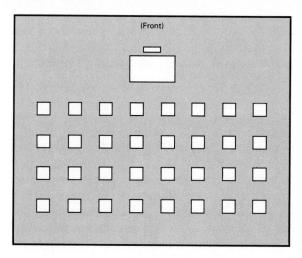

FIGURE 4–2
Rectangular Seating Arrangement

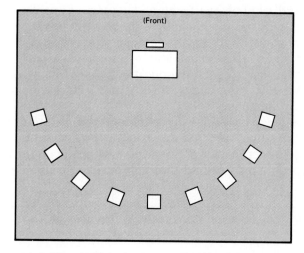

FIGURE 4–3
Horseshoe Seating Arrangement

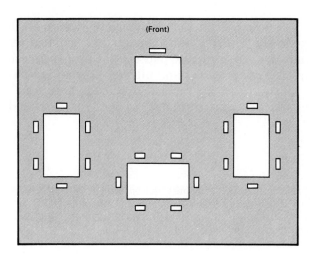

FIGURE 4–4
Modular Seating Arrangement

front rows may actually receive higher grades than those who sit farther back.[14] Additionally, proximity or closeness to the teacher is related to student enjoyment, motivation, interest, and feelings of inclusion.[15]

Paralanguage

The next time you turn on the TV, close your eyes and listen to the actors' voices. What emotions are they portraying? Are the speakers male or female, British or American? How old are they? Try the same experiment while listening to a radio talk show. Is the caller nervous, tired, angry? **Paralanguage,** or variations in the voice, allows us to answer these questions. Paralanguage is "a language alongside of language" and includes vocal characteristics such as pitch, range, resonance, tempo, and quality, and various vocal sounds such as grunts, groans, and clearing of the throat.

Although paralanguage is closely tied to verbal expression, it is quite unlike the signs and symbols we know as language. Consider voice **pitch.** Some people use a wide variety of changes in their pitch while others make few pitch changes or even talk in a monotone. For instance, we generally drop our voices (pitch) at the end of a statement and raise our pitch level at the end of a question. Ask yourself the question, "May I have some water?" and notice how your voice rises on the word "water." Pitch changes like these are part of your paralanguage.

Other paralanguage cues relate to **resonance,** the variations from a thin and quiet voice to a loud and booming voice. For example, shyness or embarrassment can affect the voice. Have you ever begun an introduction to a large group of people only to find that nervousness has made your voice fade to a mere whisper?

I understand the fury in your words but not the words.

WILLIAM SHAKESPEARE

Some people speak so quickly that it is hard to pick up all their words; others speak very slowly. This paralanguage quality is called **tempo.** Good public speakers know that the ability to pause at the proper time and to draw out words for emphasis creates color and interest in what is being said. The nervous orator's short, choppy phrases and monotonous style are a real giveaway to the audience that the speaker is ill at ease and probably inexperienced.

---

[14]W. B. Holliman and H. N. Anderson, "Proximity and Student Density as Ecological Variables in a College Classroom," *Teaching of Psychology*, 13, no. 4 (1986), 200–203.
[15]R. J. Millard and D. V. Stimpson, "Enjoyment and Productivity as a Function of Classroom Seating Location," *Perceptual Motor Skills*, 50 (April 1980), 439–44.

Paralanguage cues are also revealed by the **quality** of a speaker's voice. Voice quality is most often associated with variations of harshness and breathiness in the voice. Quality also involves smoothness of delivery and other similar factors.

Although paralanguage, as we have described the concept so far, may seem to focus only on subtle nuances, paralinguistic expressions need not be subtle. For example, sounds such as sneezing, coughing, or crying all serve well-recognized purposes. Similarly, if you walk into a room in which two of your friends are deeply involved in a conversation, rather than standing there until one of them notices you, you might clear your throat. This simple noise communicates your presence and says, "Hey, look at me. I'm here."

Paralanguage conveys information about age, sex, emotional states, personality variables, and other common attributes. Thus, it should not surprise you to learn that words in themselves account for only 7 percent of the communication of feelings. More important, researchers have found, are vocal cues, which account for 38 percent, and facial expressions, which account for 55 percent. To understand how true this finding is, consider a typical conversation. The speakers start out quite friendly but slowly build to a heated argument. As anger increases, voices become louder (intensity), the range of voices increases (pitch), and the speed of the exchange quickens (tempo). Even if you couldn't understand the speakers' angry words, their paralanguage would immediately tell you that the two people were quarreling.

Environmental factors influence our behavior.

Smell and Taste

Every day we use our senses of smell and taste to receive information about the world around us. However, we also use the mediums of smell and taste to send out such information about ourselves. Think, for example, about the last time you were getting ready to go out with a very special person. After getting out of the bathtub, where you showered with deodorant soap and washed your hair with scented shampoo, you probably put on deodorant or antiperspirant and adorned yourself with after-shave lotion or perfume. You then proceeded to brush your teeth with a fresh-tasting toothpaste and, perhaps, gargled with a "germ-killing" mouthwash. Finally, you put on fresh-smelling clothes and odor-free shoes, the former having been washed in a freshly scented detergent and rinsed in a fabric softener, and the latter "freshened" with "odor-eating" talcum powder or foot pads.

A North American's perceptions of smells and tastes differ, however, from the perceptions of members of other cultures. For example, many North Americans have been conditioned to be ashamed of natural body odors. Have you ever kept your distance from someone for fear that the garlic on your breath would be offensive? Such a feeling of self-consciousness concerning a potential message such as this is only one example of how our culture differs from other cultures. Members of several cultures would feel quite insulted if you deprived them of your breath!

The sense of smell, however, is not the only "silent" sense that sends and receives messages. Our sense of taste allows us to receive messages of pleasure as well as warning and has the ability both to influence and to reflect our physical needs as well as preferences and attitudes. Do some smells and tastes make you happy, depressed, or nostalgic? If you do not believe in the communicative power of these two senses, be aware of them the next time you smell the cologne or perfume of your "significant other" before he or she enters the room, or taste a metallic flavor the next time you feel ill. You may open yourself up to an increasing awareness of two additional and viable channels of communication.

Environmental Factors

ARCHITECTURE AND OBJECTS.   Have you ever walked into a room and immediately felt at home, calm and relaxed? Or avoided a building that made you feel nervous and insecure? Nonverbal messages from architectural structures and other objects around us indeed can influence our behavior. For this reason dentists have comfortable chairs and pleasant decors in their waiting rooms—all to make us worry a little less. Nightclub, bar, and restaurant owners have also learned that interiors can greatly influence their customers. They realize that dim lighting, a quiet atmosphere, and soft music lead to greater intimacy, which encourages their patrons to stay longer.

These informal observations are supported by scientific studies. One classic experiment, for example, used three rooms: an "ugly" room, designed

TABLE 4–1

Association of Moods and Colors

MOOD	COLOR
Exciting, stimulating	Red
Secure, comfortable	Blue
Distressed, disturbed, upset	Orange
Tender, soothing	Blue
Protective, defending	Red, brown, blue, purple, black
Despondent, dejected, unhappy, melancholy	Black, brown
Calm, peaceful, serene	Blue, green
Dignified, stately	Purple
Cheerful, jovial, joyful	Yellow
Defiant, contrary, hostile	Red, orange, black
Powerful, strong, masterful	Black

From L. B. Wexner, "The Degree to Which Colors (Hues) Are Associated with Mood-Tones," *Journal of Applied Psychology*, 38(1954), 432–35.

like a janitor's storeroom; a "beautiful" room, with carpeting, draperies, and other decorations; and an "average" room, decorated like a professor's office. While located in these different rooms, subjects were asked to rate a series of photographs of faces. Those in the beautiful room gave higher ratings to the faces than did those in the ugly room. While the beautiful room was found to stimulate feelings of pleasure, comfort, enjoyment, and the desire to continue the activity, the ugly room caused fatigue, headaches, discontent, sleepiness, irritability, and hostility. Subsequent measures of recall and problem solving in these rooms showed better performance in the beautiful surroundings.[16]

COLORS.   We all recognize clichés of color and emotion—"tickled pink," "feeling blue," "green with envy," and "seeing red," to name a few. It is well known that specific colors are associated with particular human moods. As one early study demonstrated (see Table 4–1), we tend to describe some moods in terms of a specific color, while other moods are associated with two or more colors. Additionally, research on achievement motivation has shown that highly motivated people prefer cool or somber colors and tend to be in a hurry, while people who are less motivated prefer warm or brighter colors, like red and yellow, and are generally less time-conscious. To support these earlier findings, Charles and Carlota Salter investigated automobile color as a predictor of driving behavior. Specifically, they focused on color of car and propensity of the driver to speed at great velocities and to run red lights and stop signs. Results of their study revealed that drivers of cars with higher-achievement colors (such as blue and black) tended to speed at higher

---

[16]A. H. Maslow and N. L. Mintz, "Effects of Esthetic Surroundings: I. Initial Effects of Three Esthetic Conditions upon Perceiving 'Energy' and 'Well-Being' in Faces," *Journal of Psychology*, 41 (1956), 247–54.

"We want it done in tattletale gray."

rates and to run red lights more often than drivers of cars with low-achievement colors (such as red or yellow). However, they did not tend to run stop signs more often.[17]

The difficulty with such research, of course, is in discerning whether people pick colors that are truly associated with specific moods or whether their choices actually reflect learned stereotypes. Do you respond to different colors in different ways? What colors are you wearing at this moment? Do they reflect the mood you were in when you dressed? Answering these questions may give you some interesting insights into your reactions to particular colors. What about color combinations? Are there certain color combinations, say orange and red, that you would *never* wear? Why not? What nonverbal messages do you think you send by wearing such combinations?

TIME.   Americans are preoccupied with time. Just observe the many timepieces around us—clocks in our homes, schools, and workplaces; church bells chiming every quarter-hour; banks lighting up the time, second by second; radio stations announcing the time after every commercial; and almost everyone wearing a wristwatch (some of them even with alarms!). Time also plays an important part in our everyday oral discourse. We "kill time," "waste time," and "use time" wisely, depending on the situation. We also use expressions like "it's high time," "time is of the essence," and "now is the time to. . . ."

---

[17]C. A. Salter and C. D. Salter, "Automobile Color as a Predictor of Driving Behavior," *Perceptual and Motor Skills*, 55 (1982), 383–86.

Time is significant in nonverbal communication as well. Time is a valued commodity. Time is money—we are paid for the time we spend at work. Time is power—the more time someone gives you, the more important you are. Time is status—we are more punctual for an important business meeting than for a casual get-together. In short, we are compulsive clock-watchers—bound to our watches, time clocks, agendas, and timetables. Time keeps running on . . . running us.

Scientists have discovered that perceptions of time provide important nonverbal cues, cues that vary from culture to culture. Western industrialized cultures, for example, think of time in linear-spatial terms related to past, present, and future. Thus, Americans think of moving "through" time, with the present as the intermediate point between past and future. In contrast, other cultures stress "felt time," the "now" of living for each day and not for the past or future. Greeks, for instance, see themselves as stationary. Time comes up behind them, overtakes them, and then becomes the past. Many American Indians have the same concept. Indeed, the Sioux have no words for "time," "late," or "waiting."

We also make certain assumptions about other people based on their time-consciousness. Those on time for appointments are considered most sociable and composed; those who are early are seen as least dynamic; and latecomers are usually viewed as least sociable, composed, and competent. Bringing time closer to home, consider how someone else's time conceptions affect you. If you discover that your boss or professor is very time-conscious—keeps track of tardiness, absenteeism, and so forth—how might you modify your behavior? How would use of time affect such a boss or instructor?

MUSIC. Have you ever put on soft music to set the mood for a special date or wondered why some restaurants play classical music and others play top 40? Maybe you haven't thought about the reasons behind the music selections, but whether you know it or not, music affects us and our interactions with others. Muzak Corporation, the largest producer of music for businesses, corporations, and industries, has provided evidence that music increases production and reduces errors, tension, and absenteeism. In addition, music influences our ability to learn, attention span, mental imagery, and creative ability. Additionally, music facilitates our learning, performance level, and overall state of peacefulness.[18]

Music also plays a major role in our society. Americans spend more money on CDs and cassettes than they do on textbooks for schools. The power of the music industry can be attributed to its diversity. With more than 8,000 radio stations, we have the freedom to tune into anything from rap to jazz to acid rock. Tastes in music communicate information about others. Person-

[18]T. Caspy, E. Peleg, D. Schlam, and J. Goldberg, "Sedative and Stimulative Music Effects: Differential Effects on Performance Impairment Following Frustration," *Motivation and Emotion*, 12, no. 2 (1988), 123–38.

ality characteristics are often associated with the types of music to which people listen. However, to assume that intellectuals listen to classical music, truck drivers enjoy country-and-western music, and long-haired liberals get into hard rock is to engage in dangerous generalizations. Just as there is diversity in the sounds of music, there is diversity in what people appreciate and like to listen to in music.

AWARENESS OF NONVERBAL COMMUNICATION

The previous sections have described some of the meanings attached to specific gestures, body language, expressions, and environmental stimuli. Again, we must assert that these nonverbal messages cannot be viewed in simple, black-and-white terms. Like words, nonverbal communication has connotations as well as denotations. Just as each of us responds differently to a given word, term, or concept because of our different experiences, attitudes, and beliefs, so too do we respond differently to nonverbal messages.

Awareness of your own nonverbal behavior and that of others can increase your sensitivity in social interactions. We are usually attentive to nonverbal stimuli—we purposely wear clothes that evoke a particular response (positive or negative), and we reach out and touch a friend who is unhappy to let him or her know that we are there. At other times, we overlook or misread nonverbal cues that might enrich our understanding of interpersonal communication. Similarly, just as we may misinterpret the nonverbal behavior of others, they may do the same with us. Thus, you should consider questions such as, "I know what my beard means to me, but what does it mean to my parents?" "Does my being overweight influence her feelings about me?" and "I wonder if they think I'm unfriendly because I don't go over and join them."

In the following section we will discuss the factors that affect our interpretation of nonverbal messages.

Context

Context influences our own nonverbal communication as well as our responses to other people's nonverbal messages. For example, when you are at home watching a movie on television, you probably prop your feet up on the coffee table or curl them under you on the sofa. You might noisily dig to the bottom of the potato chip bag, ignoring the crumbs that miss your mouth and fall to your chest. And, if the beer or soda you've been drinking should make you burp—so what? But what if you were watching the same movie in a crowded theater? Your behavior might differ considerably. Even if you wanted to slouch, the stiff theater seats might prevent it. If you insisted on potato chips rather than a less noisy snack, you would probably be more careful not to rattle the bag or scatter the crumbs. And, if the soda had the same effect on you it has at home, you would probably suppress the burp or let nature have its way—discreetly.

We learn appropriate context behaviors by negative reinforcement during childhood. How many times were you told as a child, "Don't put your feet on that table! You're not at home now!" Or, did you ever get stern looks because you talked too loudly in a movie theater or popped your gum in a library? After much scolding and some praise, we learn to vary our nonverbal behaviors according to whom we are with, where we are, and whether or not the situation is defined as formal or informal.

Just as context modifies your own nonverbal behavior, so too it affects your response to nonverbal messages in your environment. For example, a simple gesture can have several different meanings, depending on the context in which it occurs. Let's say you are driving your car down the road and you spot someone hitchhiking. In a matter of seconds, you must decide whether to stop. What you do is based on contextual variables—first, consider your mood. Are you feeling helpful, or do you want to be bothered? Are you in a hurry or on a leisurely drive? Are you afraid of all hitchhikers, never pick them up, or do you usually give them a lift? And what about the environment? Would it make a difference to you if it were daytime or night? On a crowded highway or on a country road? In the summer or during a snowstorm? What about the person himself . . . or herself? Would it matter to you if the hitchhiker were a man or a woman? Or perhaps a man *and* a woman—or a man with his pet German shepherd?

Would the hitchhiker's age and weight influence you? Or clothing, hairstyle, and other gestures? Finally, if and when you do pull over, would you take a few more seconds to change your mind after studying facial expressions, voice, and general demeanor?

Stereotypes

As you can see, the same gesture—"Hey, I need a ride. Please pick me up."—can be interpreted in many different ways, depending on the context and, of course, your stereotypes.

Like it or not, most of us do have stereotypes about people and the way they act. These stereotypes play a large part in first impressions. Whether or not the stereotypes bear any resemblance to reality, they do exist and must be considered when analyzing interpersonal behavior.

As our hitchhiking example demonstrated, we often make judgments about the personality and behavior of individuals just by observing their physical appearance or superficial actions. In fact, we sometimes make important decisions based on voice alone: "I didn't like the sound of his voice, so I. . . ." or, "As soon as she started to talk, I knew I could trust her." Researchers have verified this reliance on voice characteristics. In one experiment, students listened to two tape recordings of the same speaker. On one recording the speaker used a conversational delivery pattern—that is, a smaller range of inflections, a greater consistency of rate and pitch, less volume, and generally lower pitch than in the second recording, in which the speaker used a more dynamic delivery pattern. The students in this study did not realize that they were hearing the same speaker with two different vocal approaches. Instead, they rated the speaker who used the conversational delivery as honest and person-oriented, while the dynamic delivery elicited descriptions of tough-minded, task-oriented, self-assured, and assertive.[19]

Of course, we all have stereotypes about many aspects of behavior other than voice. Do you have certain beliefs about the way people should or shouldn't walk, smile, sit, stand, eat, laugh, sneeze, or cry? Ask yourself *why* the next time you jump to a conclusion based solely on some aspect of another person's behavior. Chances are your conclusion doesn't reflect the facts of the situation. Herein lies the danger of stereotypes: Too often they turn out to be assumptions completely unrelated to objective facts.

However, the main point of this chapter is awareness: You cannot eliminate your stereotyped response to nonverbal messages, but you cannot disregard those stereotypes either. Thus, if you know, for example, that someone has a negative stereotype about blue jeans, either you will not wear them when you are with that person or you will not be surprised or offended by the person's behavior when you do. In short, awareness improves understanding, and understanding improves communication—be it verbal or nonverbal.

---

[19]W. B. Pearce and F. Conklin, "Nonverbal Vocalic Communication and Perceptions of a Speaker," *Speech Monographs*, 38 (1971), 235–41.

SUMMARY

In addition to our spoken and written language, all of us communicate on the nonverbal level of body movements, gestures, facial expressions, tone of voice, and other related signs. Our interpretation of such nonverbal messages is a function of both their context and their relationship to the sum of the communicator's verbal and nonverbal behavior patterns.

The six basic functions of nonverbal communication are repeating, substituting, complementing, deceiving, regulating, and accenting. The body expressions that serve these functions are limitless. The language of facial expressions, eye adjustments, and related movements is responsible for a significant part of all human communication. In addition, specialists have organized body expressions into classes such as kinesics and body movement.

Classes of body expressions include emblems, illustrators, regulators, affect displays, and body manipulators. These expressions and the functions they serve are the subject of the scientific discipline known as kinesics, or body language.

In addition to kinesic messages, we communicate through our personal appearance and our choice of clothing. Likewise, touch, the most basic form of non-verbal communication, is an important part of our communication system and contributes to our overall sense of well-being.

In addition to these forms of nonverbal behavior, we communicate by our relationship to the space about us and our use of that space. Proxemics, the study of these spatial factors, specifies several distinct zones of interpersonal communication that are affected by our territoriality.

The last three areas of nonverbal communication we discussed are paralanguage, our senses of taste and smell, and environmental factors that surround us.

It is important to become aware of these factors and of the context in which nonverbal messages occur. In addition, we must recognize the perceptual stereotypes that always affect our interpretation of both verbal and nonverbal messages. This heightened awareness can help ensure understanding of others and improve communication on all levels.

EXERCISES

Group Experiences

How's Your Sign Language?

DESCRIPTION: As children, we used nonverbal communication as our direct statement of what we wanted, while verbal communication was the complement. As we grew older, this process became reversed, so that our nonverbal communication no longer served as a direct statement but as a complement to what we said verbally. Children depend a great deal on sign language (gestures that replace words, numbers, and punctuation). Research shows that children are easily able to send and interpret 12 frequently used gestures. Try this activity and see if your sign language is as good as a child's.

PROCEDURE: Divide into groups of four to six members. Each member should try to send a short phrase nonverbally. The following list of phrases is offered only as a beginning—these are the phrases mentioned above that children are able to use quite easily.

Go away	Be quiet	Shape (round or square)
Come here	Give me attention	I don't know
Yes	How many	Goodbye
No	How big	Hi

The first person to accurately guess the message becomes the next sender. This process continues until all members have had the opportunity to create at least two messages.

DISCUSSION: How well do you send and interpret nonverbal messages? Consider this question in light of the activity you have just completed. If you have trouble sending messages nonverbally, you may need to work to improve your communication. On the other hand, if you have trouble interpreting messages, you may be misinterpreting people. Problems with either sending or interpreting nonverbal messages may lead to communication breakdowns on an interpersonal or group level.

How Others Stereotype You

DESCRIPTION: Are you aware of how others stereotype you on the basis of your behavior and personal appearance? Not many people are. This activity will provide you with information about how others view you and should also help you understand your own nonverbal behavior.

PROCEDURE: Divide into groups of four to six members. Each member should make a list of everyone in the group and put his or her name on the top of the list. Across the top of the paper, three categories should be written: books, dogs, and adjectives. Starting with yourself, select one choice from each category that most closely reflects you or the person for whom you are making the choice. When you are selecting, try to determine the specific behaviors that cause you to view a person in a particular stereotyped way.

Category A. Which book would you most likely find *(insert name)* reading?

a. *How Managers Make Things Happen*
b. *How to Read the Stars*
c. *The Wild, Wild West*
d. *One Hundred Ways to Improve Your Golf Swing*
e. *The Koran*
f. *How to Eat Better and Spend Less*
g. *How to Be Your Own Best Friend*

Category B. What type of dog does *(insert name)* remind you of?

a. Poodle
b. German shepherd
c. Sheepdog
d. Cocker spaniel
e. Dachshund
f. St. Bernard
g. Chihuahua

Category C. Which group of adjectives most closely describes *(insert name)*?

a. Open, optimistic, energetic
b. Meticulous, nervous, punctual
c. Soft-hearted, good-natured, loving
d. Competitive, dominant, authoritative
e. Closed, pessimistic, quiet
f. Fun-loving, ambitious, talkative
g. Introspective, spiritual, analytical

DISCUSSION: There are two ways to assess the results of this activity. Either start with a category and discuss each group member in the category, or start with a particular group member and discuss him or her in each of the three categories. Whichever method you choose, keep in mind that meanings are in people, not in words. Try to provide information on *why* you made a particular selection. Focus on the personal appearance of the person and consider whether you stereotyped hairstyle or clothing in a particular way. If you find that the impressions others have of you are inconsistent with the way you view yourself, then observe your own behavior and personal appearance to understand what you are nonverbally conveying to others. The expansion of nonverbal awareness begins with understanding how you project impressions to others.

It's Not What You Say, It's How You Say It!

DESCRIPTION: This activity can be conducted either in small groups of four to six members or as a demonstration activity in which the majority of the class serves as an audience while four or five individuals play roles in selected situations. Two partners will be needed for each role-playing scene. Two scenes are offered as examples of the type of drama that can be reenacted to illustrate the effects of pitch, rhythm, intonation, intensity, and other vocal qualities. The purpose of this activity is to clearly demonstrate that it's not *what* you say, but *how* you say it!

PROCEDURE: Two partners will be needed for each role-playing activity. Each team can either invent a scene they would like to portray or use one from the following list. In each scene only numbers are to be used—absolutely no words are permitted. For example, practice by reading the following numbers tenderly, angrily, and sadly: 42, 567, 3, 356, 8. Once you get a feel for this, try one of the following scenes. After a team plays a scene, the group should discuss the emotions and feelings that were being conveyed.

Scene 1: Husband and Wife

The wife comes home from work and the husband is irritable after spending the day watching the children and cooking. He displays his irritability the moment she walks through the door. The wife at first tries to be supportive, but then fights openly with her husband.

Scene 2: A Couple

In this scene the couple has been dating for a long time. Finally, after waiting for months, he pops the question. The scene is tender and romantic.

DISCUSSION: Are you aware of the subtle nonverbal cues that are sent through the voice? Consider how, even if the words are identical, a change in pitch, intensity, or even pause rate can dramatically alter the meaning of a message. After participating in this activity, you should be able to listen to your own vocal characteristics to see how you alter messages. Also consider the extent to which the vocal characteristics of others influence your interpretation of their messages. In other words, is it *what* they say or *how* they say it that counts?

Body Expressions

DESCRIPTION: The body and the face convey many emotional meanings in both speaking and listening. Most of us learn to convey emotions through our facial expressions but have difficulty conveying emotions with other parts of our bodies. The following activity will provide you with an opportunity to determine how well you send and interpret the nonverbal display of emotions through the use of facial expressions and body movement.

PROCEDURE: Write each of the following body areas and emotions on separate cards.

Body Areas	Emotions
Whole face	Hate
Whole body	Love
Hands only	Anger
Face only	Surprise
Mouth only	Happiness
Eyes and eyebrows only	Distrust
Feet only	Disgust
Dyad (whole body with another person)	Contentment

Divide into groups of six to eight members. (Each group needs one set of cards.) The first person should select one card from the "body area" category and one card from the "emotion" category. The person should then try to portray the selected emotion with *only* the body area designated on the card. The rest of the group has three guesses to determine both the correct body area and the emotion. If the group guesses correctly, the person receives one point. If the group does not guess correctly, the person loses one point. After the first person has finished, the cards should be returned to the appropriate deck. Go around the group until each participant has had three turns. The number of turns may be modified depending on the number of participants in the group and the amount of time available for the activity.

DISCUSSION: As a group, identify which emotions were most difficult to convey and which were easiest. Identify which body areas most accurately sent the emotional states and which least accurately. Which was more difficult—the creation of nonverbal messages or the interpretation of them?

Conversation and Space

DESCRIPTION: Particular spatial arrangements may either aid or inhibit interactions. We are constantly readjusting our distance from other people and objects to match the nature of our conversations. The following activity provides you with the opportunity to experience the relationship between conversational topic and distance.

PROCEDURE: Divide into dyads. The members of the dyad should stand directly opposite one another at a distance of ten feet. Engage in a conversation on any topic you choose, but while you are talking, maintain the distance of ten feet between you and your partner for three minutes. After three minutes reduce the distance to five feet and continue to talk. You may change topics as many times as you wish. After another three minutes reduce the distance to two feet, then 12 inches, and finally six inches. Each distance should be maintained for a minimum of three minutes.

DISCUSSION: Discuss your reactions to the various conversational distances you maintained with your partner. Did the topic of the conversation or the intensity with which you discussed the topic vary with the different distances? Did certain topics seem inappropriate at particular distances? What types of topics do you consider to be appropriate at the following distances: ten feet, five feet, two feet, one foot, six inches?

Personal Experiences

1. Strike up a conversation with a stranger while you are waiting in line, sitting in a bus, or walking on campus. After a couple of minutes, ask if he or she would be willing to participate in an experiment requiring no more than a few minutes. If the person is willing, ask him or her to relate the first impression of you. Stress the need for an honest appraisal of your personal appearance, nonverbal behaviors, and conversational qualities. Is the impression accurate? What was your reaction to the description of you? How aware are you of the nonverbal impression you create?

2. Select a person in one of your classes for observation. Watch your subject over a period of several days and see if you can classify his or her nonverbal behaviors as (a) regulators, (b) illustrators, (c) emblems,

(d) affect displays, or (e) adaptors. What does this classification tell you about the person? For example, does the absence of the use of regulating nonverbal behavior suggest that the person may not provide adequate listening response for a speaker?

3. Watch television with a friend, but at separate locations. Have your friend watch the same program so that you can compare notes later. When you watch the program, however, turn off the sound completely. Watch the body movements and facial expressions very carefully and try to understand the story line. After the program, tell your friend what happened—describe the emotions, the drama, and the interaction between characters in the program. Then listen to your friend's description. What were the major differences in your descriptions? Did the absence of sound produce more information on the nonverbal level while reducing the content of the information, which is obtained through the verbal medium?

4. The next time you have a telephone conversation with someone you have never seen (a telephone operator, a salesperson), try to determine information about that person on the basis of vocal cues. For example, try to guess age, height, weight, race, sex, and the area of the country he or she is from. After you have made some tentative guesses, check your results by asking your telephone partner to verify the information. Try this several times and see how vocal cues help, hinder, or do not affect the identification of background and personality characteristics of an individual.

5. Observe yourself for a day to determine how you see "time." Record the number of times you look at a clock, ask for the time, or refer to time in any manner. Next, go a step further and determine whether you live in present time, future time, past time, or linear time (no past, present, or future). How well can you relate to people who have a different time orientation?

6. Pick a task that takes approximately two hours to complete. Work on the task for one hour in an "ugly" room and one hour in a "beautiful" room. What effect did the difference in environment have on your productivity? Did you experience different physical feelings in each room? Are you sensitive to your environment?

Discussion Questions

1. What is the difference between nonverbal communication and nonverbal behavior?
2. What are some of the ways (functions) in which we use nonverbal communication?
3. How is the formation of first impressions related to stereotyping?
4. Can you describe your nonverbal behaviors during speaking and listening?

5. What nonverbal behaviors do you use to defend your territory and personal space?

6. To what extent do nonverbal behaviors reflect our attitudes or emotions?

7. Do cultural norms regarding the use of space tell us anything about a given society?

8. How important do you consider paralinguistic cues to be in verbal communication?

Intrapersonal Communication

KEY CONCEPTS AND TERMS

Physical self
Instinctive component
Moving component
Automatic processing
Effortful processing
Body image
Emotional self
Intellectual self
Habit
Unity principle
Self-concept
Self-fulfilling prophecy
Reference group
Role
Ascribed role
Achieved role
Gender role
Social role
Hierarchy of human
  needs
Physiological needs
Safety needs
Need for love
Esteem needs
Self-actualization

Stimuli
Internal stimuli
External stimuli
Overt stimuli
Covert stimuli
Threshold of
  consciousness
Reception
Selective perception
Intensity
Cognitive processing
Memory
Sensory storage
Short-term memory
Long-term memory
Retrieval
Recognition
Recall
Sorting
Assimilation
Emotional processing
Physiological
  processing
Gestalt
Biofeedback

Transmission
Self-feedback
External self-feedback
Internal self-feedback
Interference
Value
Attitude
Belief
Opinion
Prejudice
Trait
Locus of control
Manipulation
Dogmatism
Tolerance of
  ambiguity
Self-esteem
Maturity
Defense mechanism
Rationalization
Projection
Insulation
Reaction formation
Identification
Repression

*F*ourteen years after Dr. James Black began the highly experimental project, little did the Welwyn Research Institute in England know that their chief of pharmacology would eventually bring to market the most successful drug in history. The drug that was developed at Welwyn for Smith, Kline and French Laboratories (SK&F) is called Tagamet, a wonder drug that heals ulcers quickly and painlessly. Tagamet became the first billion-dollar drug in pharmaceutical history and changed the course of SK&F from "the senior citizen of the drug business" into one of the world's foremost pharmaceutical research and development firms. However, the drug probably never would have emerged had it not been for Black's vision, scientific persistence, and defiance of the institutions for whom he worked. As a result of his argument that pharmaceutical researchers could move away from blending chemicals "like medieval herbalists" and could actually solve problems by designing combinations of atoms, Smith and a handful of SK&F "baton carriers" eventually introduced Tagamet to the world and ultimately moved pharmaceutical research into the twentieth century.[1]

How does this story relate to intrapersonal communication? Intrapersonal communication takes place whenever we evaluate and react to internal and external stimuli—and involves messages that are sent and received within ourselves. Thus, intrapersonal communication involves not only our intellect but also our physical and emotional sensations. To work 14 years on a single project required more of Dr. Black than his creativity, especially when he was fighting an uphill battle with the very institutions that supported him. To see his vision through to the end, Black had to deal with trillions of stimuli—from frustrations that must have mounted as he worked on the project, to physical fatigue, to outside input regarding his success or failure, to name just a few.

As you can see, intrapersonal communication is more far-reaching than just "talking to yourself." As you will read in the following pages, intrapersonal messages reflect your physical, emotional, intellectual, and social selves. They also reflect your habits, self-concept, self-related roles, and your attitudes, values, and beliefs. However, intrapersonal communication does not require 14 years to emerge during a person's lifetime. This form of communication takes place every moment that we live.

THE SELF

The study of intrapersonal communication begins with knowing yourself. As soon as you begin to examine *the* self, however, you discover that you are, in fact, *many* selves.

---

[1]P. Ranganath Nayak and J. M. Ketteringham, "Tagamet: Repairing Ulcers Without Surgery," *Breakthroughs: How the Vision and Drive of Innovators in Sixteen Companies Created Commercial Breakthroughs That Swept the World* (New York: Rawson Associates, 1986), 102, 129.

The Physical Self

The **physical self** may be divided into three primary categories of behavior: the instinctive component, the moving component, and the body concept.

The **instinctive component** of the physical self consists primarily of internal bodily functions, including digestion, breathing, blood circulation, pupil dilation, the building of new cells, the elimination of bodily wastes, and all other physiological processes that are capable of functioning below our level of consciousness. Additionally, the five senses (sight, smell, taste, hearing, and touch), sensations of weight and temperature, and all reflexes like laughter and yawning belong to our body's internal functions.[2] We have all experienced messages from each of these areas of the body and responded to them accordingly. For example, if our stomach growls, we head straight for the refrigerator; if we are warm, we adjust the thermostat on the air conditioner.

The **moving component** consists of automatic and effortful processing of information and the behavior that results. Most of our behaviors each day are highly **automatic,** particularly in terms of the depth of processing that is required in order to complete them. These behaviors are designated as automatic because we have learned and rehearsed them to the point that we no longer have to think about performing them. We use automatic processing when we wash our faces, brush our teeth, drive our cars, and write a letter or paper. If you question whether these behaviors are really automatic, try using the hand opposite the one that you usually use to write your name or brush your hair. If you are not ambidextrous, you will find that doing so will require more conscious effort on your part than when you use your primary hand to complete the same task. This difficulty is due to the necessity to use more effortful processing.[3]

The easiest person to deceive is one's own self.

EDWARD BULWER-LYTTON

Effortful processing also plays a role in the functioning of our physical selves. Effortful processing takes place whenever we have to process information consciously in order to complete an act.[4] For example, when was the last time that you were asked to do something that you have never done before, such as ice skate, rollerblade, or prepare a meal from a recipe you have never used before? Chances are you had to "stay awake" the whole time in order to complete the task without risking disaster. You probably were

---

[2] P. D. Ouspensky, *The Psychology of Man's Possible Evolution*, 2d ed. (New York: Vintage Books, 1974), 26–28.

[3] D. R. Barker, L. L. Barker, and M. Fitch-Hauser, "Origins, Evolution, and Development of a Systems-Based Model of Intrapersonal Processes: A Holistic View of Man as Information Processor," in B. D. Ruben, ed., *Information and Behavior*, vol. 2 (New Brunswick, N.J.: Transaction Books, 1988), 207–8.

[4] Ibid., 206–7.

unable to complete the task mechanically, but instead had to concentrate on every move.

As infants, we do not recognize ourselves as being separate from the environment. Such physical recognition usually develops at around 18 months of age, as we acquire more accurate perceptions of our bodies. Such bodily concepts—better known as body image—are vital for normal mental and emotional development.

Body image is defined as a person's perception of his or her physical self. While this perception remains fairly constant in a normal individual, it is subject to change at times. If you feel hurt or depressed, you may actually feel smaller, more vulnerable. The reverse is true, too—a dieter may have a distorted body image each time he or she gains a pound or two. For the most part, however, a person with a fairly healthy personality will have a fairly healthy body image.

The Emotional Self

Another self is the **emotional self.** Emotions are conscious feelings that are accompanied by physiological changes, such as rapid heartbeat, tensed muscles, or raised blood sugar level. We are usually all too aware of the stimuli that prompt our emotional responses. Barely missing the car that darts out in front of you from a side street can tie your stomach in knots long

The first step toward effective communication with others is successful communication with yourself.

after the stimulus is gone. At other times, before we realize it, our emotional selves take over. Crying for no reason at all, yelling at your best friend, or laughing out loud while others just smile are all examples of our emotions taking control.

The Intellectual Self

Your *intellectual self,* or the self associated with your mental processes, involves mental actions or behaviors such as concept and word formation, use of comparison and contrast, use of logic and reasoning, and the process by which we solve problems and make decisions. At this very moment your intellectual self is functioning as you read this text (that is, if your mind is not wandering to that upcoming weekend). In short, our intellectual self is our mental self—a self that we will learn more about in the following sections.

Habits

Each of us possesses *habits,* or repetitious behaviors, that become so automatic that we are hardly aware of them. You may have a habit of biting your nails or stroking your chin while you are thinking, even though you do not consciously choose to do so.

In contrast to these harmless habits, other unconscious behaviors have more serious consequences. Some individuals, for example, always fall in love with the wrong people. Psychologists say that this happens not by accident but because there is some conflict within the individual that encourages this type of relationship. Such habitual behavior patterns usually continue as long as they fulfill certain needs within the individual.

Some of these behaviors directly affect our communication. Do you know people who constantly pepper their communication with misused words, or who have the knack of always saying the wrong thing at the wrong time? The characters of Rose and Sophia on television's *The Golden Girls* are perfect examples. Rose constantly interprets events through the eyes of innocence and Sophia through the eyes of a 70-year-old skeptic. Both end up making hilarious and often embarrassing remarks to Dorothy and Blanche.

The Unity Principle

At this point you may be asking, "If, in fact, I am a product of all of these selves, why am I not more aware of it?" The answer to this question lies first in our need to maintain a *unified* conceptual system,[5] as evidenced by our ability to process information that is inconsistent with our values, attitudes, and beliefs. Valerie, for example, loves to wake early in the morning, read *The Wall Street Journal,* and have several cups of coffee to start her day. As she

---

[5] M. Nicoll, *Psychological Commentaries on the Teaching of Gurdjieff and Ouspensky,* vol. 3 (Boulder, Colo.: Shambhala, 1984), 882, 1203.

rushes her way through a busy week in the office, she also likes to take time to sit, have several more cups of coffee, and talk with her supervisors about both problems and progress in their respective departments. Despite the large amounts of coffee Valerie consumes, what is the probability that a special program on the effects of caffeine on the human system would cause a behavioral change in Valerie's habits? Depending on several factors, there probably would be little or no change. She probably would not even believe that the program could apply to her, and the information either would be lost in memory or would never be processed at all.

In addition to the impact that our need for perceptual unity has on our perceptions of the self, several other factors contribute to our illusions of a unified self. These include the use of words such as *I*, *me*, and *mine*, which also reflect unity; our sensations of having one body and one name associated with our bodies (both of which usually remain the same over time, once we reach adulthood); and our observations of the regularly recurring patterns of behavior that we associate with ourselves. Each of these contributes to the illusion of oneness.

Along with the innate function of our conceptual systems to maintain a unified and happy self, we can also consciously work toward a unified self by increasing our awareness of who we are—our many selves. One such method of increasing awareness is through the use of the Johari Window, a concept that focuses on increasing awareness of the private self and the public self.

Awareness and You

The distinction between our private and our public selves is well illustrated by the Johari Window, shown in Figure 5–1. Designed by Joseph Luft and Harrington Ingham, the Johari Window compares aspects of open (public) versus closed (private) communication relationships.[6]

The "open" section in the diagram represents self-knowledge that you are aware of and are willing to share with others. The "hidden" section represents what you are aware of but are not willing to share. The "blind" section represents information of which you yourself are unaware but which is known to others. The "unknown" section represents what is unknown both to you and to others.

Although each section of the Johari Window is conceptually the same size in Figure 5–1, in "real-life" situations different proportions would be drawn for each relationship that we are in, depending on the amount of information that we share with that individual. In a close relationship, for example, our open area might be considerably larger than the hidden area. When communicating with a casual acquaintance, our hidden area would be the largest part of the window.

Let us see how this window applies to a particular communication situation:

---

[6]J. Luft, *Of Human Interaction* (Palo Alto, Calif.: National Press Books, 1969).

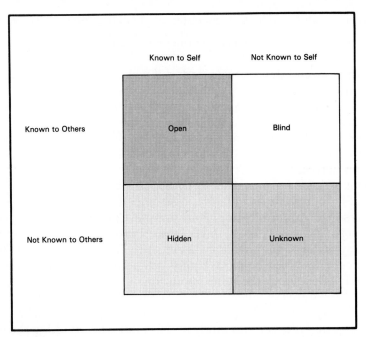

	Known to Self	Not Known to Self
Known to Others	Open	Blind
Not Known to Others	Hidden	Unknown

FIGURE 5–1
The Johari Window

Linda and Tony are reunited after a two-month separation. Linda lets Tony know how much she missed him (open), but does not tell him that she has started to date someone new (hidden). Tony senses that Linda is upset, although she claims that she is fine (blind). The unknown in this situation is a whole range of feelings that are not clear to either of them. For example, both individuals are probably unsure about Linda's feelings toward Tony.

Again, you can use the concept of the Johari Window to increase your self-awareness. This, in turn, should improve your communication with others. As you strive to shrink the blind and unknown segments, you may begin to discover a self you only partially knew before, a self that may or may not resemble the concept you've always had about that person you call "me." The more information you can bring into the open from the hidden, blind, and unknown areas, the better your interpersonal communication will be.

SELF-CONCEPT

Before we begin a discussion of self-concept, take out a piece of paper. Quickly jot down the many roles that you play, using nouns that describe the most important aspects of who you are. The list might look something like this:

Joanie: woman, athlete, competitor, student, daughter, friend, animal lover

Jerry: man, student, fiancé, gourmet cook, tennis player, lover, poet

What special descriptive words did you use? How varied were the roles that best describe you?

The first purpose we had in mind when asking you to develop this composite was to illustrate the highly complex and elaborate nature of our self-perceptions. Indeed, one need look no further than the number and variety of the terms to see that our composites reflect a host of ideas we have about ourselves.

Our second purpose was to demonstrate that this picture we have of ourselves—our **self-concept**—has a strong effect on both intrapersonal and interpersonal communication. For example, Crystal, who thinks of herself as a footloose and fancy-free swinger, would probably enjoy being asked on a cruise by a new man whom she recently met. However, Cindy, whose self-concept includes being a highly religious person, would probably be extremely offended by the same invitation. A good communicator is sensitive to the self-concepts of others and knows that their values and attitudes affect how they respond (that is, the effective communicator would be sensitive and respond quite differently to Cindy and Crystal when inviting the two women on such a cruise).

At this point you may be wondering how our self-concept came to exist. Self-concept is not inborn; rather, it is developed through interaction with people and the environment. Specifically, it develops as a function of three primary sets of variables: our past experiences, the reference groups with which we identify, and the roles that we play in our lives. The interaction between ourselves and these three variables has affected and will continue to affect our self-concept.

Past Experiences

Your past shapes the way you feel about yourself and the way you react to others. A small child may stop thinking of himself as Superman after falling down and finding that he is not indestructible. Sometimes past experiences shape your self-concept without your awareness. A child who is constantly criticized at home and made to feel worthless may develop a negative self-concept without realizing the reasons behind it.

Other early experiences can also color your self-concept. A child's school experiences are particularly important. The child who achieves success in the early grades will probably have a better self-concept than a child who has had constant academic failure. In turn, these positive or negative past experiences sometimes create a **self-fulfilling prophecy.** Children who see themselves as inferior or dull may perform below their actual abilities. Similarly, children with highly positive self-concepts may prove to be overachievers. Self-fulfilling prophecies can also reinforce self-concept. If a teacher is told that John is a discipline problem, the teacher expects John to misbehave. Sensing this expectation, John may very well cause the trouble that is expected of him. John's self-concept of being "bad" is thus reinforced.

Self-concept is particularly influenced by the socializing and dating experiences of adolescence. The boy who succeeds in getting a date with every girl he asks may come to view himself as a real ladies' man. On the other hand, frequent rejections might cause him to think of himself as a failure. Self-concept is often so shaky during adolescence that many boys ask someone out only when they are sure that the answer will be yes. Girls, too, are frequently unsure of themselves during adolescence, when changing bodies and social expectations can greatly influence self-concept.

Reference Groups

Groups that give you a sense of identity and help you establish your attitudes and values are known as *reference groups.* Reference groups contribute to your self-concept. Especially during adolescence, when a person's self-concept is so changeable, groups provide a certain amount of stability.

The adolescent group, like all groups, is characterized by a structure that defines the roles of group members in relation to other members and to those outside the group. The group also provides a set of values or group norms that are common to all the members and distinct from the values they share with outsiders. Thus, group membership enables a member to identify

Unique among the masses—you!

with an established whole. This identification is extremely important because individuals incorporate into their own self-concepts many of the ideas, attitudes, and values of the people with whom they identify.

Roles

Whatever your self-concept, your behavior is strongly affected by the people with whom you interact. Typically, you assume different behavior patterns, or *roles,* in different social settings. In fact, the setting often dictates the roles other people are playing and to which you then respond.

ASCRIBED AND ACHIEVED ROLES.   Some roles are *ascribed* to you and are thus out of your control. They are based primarily on gender, age, kinship, and general place in society. For example, infants are expected to act in a certain way and grandparents in another. In recent years our understanding of ascribed gender roles has undergone striking transformations. Whereas our society once felt that being a female meant being gentle and passive, today many women reject these attributes as artificial and limiting and in no way necessary to being a woman.

Unlike ascribed roles, *achieved* roles are earned through individual accomplishment. We all possess different capabilities, and society recognizes these differences. A union steward, an athlete, and a company president all occupy their positions at least to some extent because of their abilities and drive.

GENDER ROLES.   As we mentioned previously, *gender roles* are usually ascribed, defined, and encouraged by each culture. They are a product of the cues children pick up from their surroundings and from same-sex models in the community. In addition, gender-role identity is shaped by children's relations with parents and their relations with one another, the sexual taboos that exist in the culture, and the social class to which the children belong. Obviously, these biologically and socially determined roles are extremely important to the development of self-concept.

SOCIAL ROLES.   Each of us also assumes a number of *social* roles, defined by our environment. Sometimes an entire structure or organization is based on separate but complementary social roles. In the army, for instance, the roles of the enlisted personnel, the officers, the cooks, the military police, the medics, and so on are clearly defined and join together to form a working unit. Each role has its own duties, skills, and established set of norms. If someone steps out of role, that person is subject to criticism and sometimes to punishment.

It is the combined interaction of your self-concept with these social, gender ascribed, and achieved roles that determines your communication behavior in any given situation.

The ideas and attitudes of others strongly influence our overall self-concepts.

THE HIERARCHY OF HUMAN NEEDS

Before special holidays (Christmas, birthdays, and so on) many people make lists of all the things they want. If you were to make a list right now, it might include money, jewelry, clothes, a car, airline tickets, roller blades, or a mountain bike. These are items some of us want, but what would you include if you had to make a list of your *needs?* Your list would probably look quite different. If you haven't thought recently about what you really need, take a few minutes to do so right now.

Some of our wants and needs are similar because we are driven by common internal motivations. Abraham Maslow, a well-known psychologist, examined hundreds of people and discovered five basic human drives. Each

Self-actualization—being and doing all that we are capable of.

of us has physiological, safety, love, esteem, and self-actualization needs. These needs, or drives, are known as the **hierarchy of human needs.**[7]

PHYSIOLOGICAL.   Before we attend to other drives, we first have to satisfy our **physiological needs**—desires for things such as food, water, shelter, and sex. If you are hungry after not eating all day, it is difficult to think about studying or playing tennis before you've given yourself some nourishment. If you've pulled two all-nighters in a row, you're probably not interested in going out to have a beer with your friends until you've had some sleep.

SAFETY.   After we have met all our physiological needs, our next concern is for **safety.** We like to feel secure, stable, and in control. Many people work hard all their lives and save in every way so that they will be free from fear and anxiety about money when they retire. All of us think of ways to protect ourselves from danger by doing things such as investing in life insurance, putting locks on doors, or installing smoke detectors.

[7]A. H. Maslow, *Motivation and Personality*, 2d ed. (New York: Harper & Row, 1970), 35–46.

LOVE.   Many people would put *love* as their most important human need, but physiological and safety needs are usually met first or in combination with other needs. Some people feel insecure unless they are dating or married. In this case security and love may be taken care of simultaneously. Love involves another person and is not a one-way street. Only through giving and receiving affection, care, and concern can we gain approval and acceptance from others. To increase our sense of belonging, many of us get involved in various types of group activities, but generally we satisfy the love need through relationships with family, friends, and lovers.

ESTEEM.   After we feel loved and accepted, we look for *esteem.* Usually we must first acquire self-esteem or worth before others will attribute esteem to us. Esteem is a desire for dignity, achievement, competency, and status. Some people get graduate degrees, others master difficult skills in sports, and still others do no more than be themselves to gain admiration and respect from their peers.

SELF-ACTUALIZATION.   Our last basic human need is for *self-actualization,* or striving for all that we are capable of being. Self-actualization includes long-range goals for using our full potential and developing ourselves in all areas. Self-improvement is one form of self-actualization. Throughout our lives we meet small challenges such as winning a marathon (or just completing it), getting an *A* in physics, writing a novel, or sailing around the world. Our ultimate goal, however, is being and doing all that we are capable of—for personal satisfaction.

Self-esteem involves a readiness to accept the views of others.

Intrapersonal communication is the foundation upon which interpersonal communication rests. Therefore, it is necessary to understand how you communicate with yourself before you approach the process of communicating with others. Figure 5–2 can help you visualize the intrapersonal communication process. The elements that set the process in motion are called *stimuli.*

Internal Stimuli

The brain is made aware of the state of the body by nerve impulses, ***internal stimuli*** that can prompt you to respond by communicating. Let's say you have the flu. Your muscles ache, your fever is high, and you are depressed. Such a miserable state may prompt you to call a doctor to relieve your physical ills and a friend to relieve your depression. The internal stimuli in this situation have resulted in communication.

External Stimuli

External stimuli are, of course, those stimuli that originate in the environment outside of your body. There are two kinds of external stimuli. ***Overt stimuli*** are received on the conscious level. They are picked up by the sensory

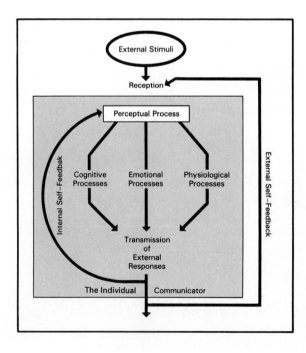

FIGURE 5–2
Intrapersonal Communication

organs and then sent to the brain. More than one overt stimulus usually affects a person at any given moment. For example, the pizza being advertised on TV and the sounds and aromas coming from the kitchen can prompt an eager, "What's for dinner?"

Covert stimuli are external stimuli that are received on the subconscious level. Let's say you are getting dressed for work. One of your favorite songs comes on the radio, so you turn the volume up. The song ends and the news begins, just as you discover a gaping hole in your sock. You find another pair and finish dressing, but you are running late. Is it too cold for your lightweight jacket? You suddenly realize that the weather report has just ended, but you have no idea what was said, despite the blaring volume.

The stimulus of the weather report was received and stored in your brain, but it was below the **threshold of consciousness.** Thus, you were not consciously aware of *what* was said, even though you recognized that you were hearing the weather report. Such covert stimuli have been shown to affect behavior and communication. Split-second presentations of the words, "Drink Smith's Beer" can indeed make a viewer feel thirsty.

You do not need to leave your room. Remain sitting at your table and listen. Do not even listen, simply wait. Do not even wait, be quite still and solitary. The world will freely offer itself to you to be unmasked, it has no choice, it will roll in ecstasy at your feet.

FRANZ KAFKA

Reception

The process by which the body receives stimuli is called **reception.** In intrapersonal communication, both external and internal receptors send information to the central nervous system. External receptors for the five senses—sight, sound, smell, taste, and touch—receive stimuli that are changed into nerve impulses and then sent to the brain. These external receptors are located on or near the body's surface and react to physical, chemical, and mechanical stimuli to provide you with information about the environment. Internal receptors such as nerve endings, on the other hand, convey information about your interior state—the dryness of your mouth or the fullness of your stomach, for example.

Although your body receives every stimulus present in a particular communication setting, you could not possibly communicate in response to every one of them. The process that helps you to cope with this jumble of stimuli is called **selective perception,** the screening out of a huge number of stimuli present in your environment, which permits attention to just a few. What determines which stimuli we do perceive? The main factor is **intensity:** Loud sounds, bright colors, sharp smells, and so forth are often perceived when less intense stimuli are not.

Processing

Processing of internal and external communication occurs at three levels: cognitive, emotional, and physiological. At each level of processing, some stimuli receive more conscious attention than others. This attention is a function of the particular stimulus and of the context in which it is presented. Some stimuli are perceived with full awareness (traffic lights, sirens, TV programs), while others may not be consciously noticed (background noise during a lecture, the hum of fluorescent lights in a room). Stimuli that are perceived consciously, or at least with some awareness, are the first to be processed. Stimuli that are perceived subconsciously are usually "stored" in your memory for later processing.

COGNITIVE PROCESSING. *Cognitive processes* are associated with the intellectual self and include the storage, retrieval, sorting, and assimilation of information. We don't know exactly how such processing occurs; our goal here is simply to describe these processes on both the conscious and subconscious cognitive levels.

Memory: The storage of information that we choose to remember is called *memory.* There are three forms of memory: (1) sensory storage, in which the information is held for only an instant; (2) short-term memory, in which the information is stored for several seconds; and (3) long-term memory, in which the information is stored indefinitely. *Sensory storage* refers to our ability to hold some information for a fraction of a second after the stimulus disappears. For example, you are not aware of the gaps between frames when you watch a movie because each frame is held in sensory storage until the next appears. The major difference between sensory storage and *short-term memory* is that in the latter, data are analyzed, identified, and simplified so that they can be conveniently stored and handled. Short-term memory is a kind of "holding device" in which you keep information until you are ready to use or discard it. If such information seems useful, you may transfer it to the permanent storage of *long-term memory* for future reference.

Retrieval: Information is stored so that it can be used to help establish the meaning of later incoming stimuli. However, stored information is relatively useless unless it can be retrieved from memory. Such *retrieval* takes the form of either recognition or recall. *Recognition* involves awareness that certain information is familiar, having been experienced previously. *Recall* is more difficult, in that it requires reconstruction of the information that has been stored. For example, while we may recognize a certain word whose meaning we looked up last week, we may be unable to recall its definition.

Sorting: Your mind contains countless bits and pieces of information. In any particular processing situation, you must first select or *sort* the most relevant information from your entire storehouse of knowledge. Here again we know very little about the actual workings of our individual selection systems. We do know, however, that such selection processes occur. For example, when we read, we sort the letters until we are able to make words of them.

Assimilation: Cognitive processing is not simply the sum of memory storage, retrieval, and sorting functions. Rather, it involves **assimilation,** the process of incorporating some aspect of the environment into the whole set of mental functionings in order to make sense out of what goes on around us. To continue our reading example, your ability to read was first learned, then stored in long-term memory. Whenever you open a book, you retrieve this information, use it to sort the letters on the page into words, and then assimilate the words into sentences and ideas that have meaning for you.

EMOTIONAL PROCESSING. As mentioned at the beginning of this chapter, intrapersonal processing also involves **emotional processing,** or the nonlogical response of an organism to a stimulus. Later in this chapter we will take a closer look at the different variables that operate in emotional processing. However, it is important to mention here that variables, ranging from attitudes, beliefs, and opinions at the subconscious level to emotions at the conscious level, all interact to determine our response to any particular communication.

PHYSIOLOGICAL PROCESSING. The third type of processing occurs at the physiological level and is associated with the physical self. Although **physiological processing** is of obvious importance in staying alive, its significance to intrapersonal communication is only beginning to be recognized. As we said earlier, some of the subconscious variables in this process are heart rate, brain activity, muscle tension, blood pressure, and body temperature.

Brain wave activity has been given considerable attention lately as an aid in determining information processing. Have you ever wondered what parts of your brain process certain types of information? Research with an electroencephalograph (EEG) suggests that we alternate between our right- and left-brain hemispheres to process stimuli.[8] Generally, if you are balancing your checking account, reading a textbook, or writing a term paper, you will be using your left hemisphere. The left hemisphere processes information logically and is concerned with speech and with mathematical and analytical tasks. The right hemisphere, in contrast, processes information abstractly and is involved with imagery and with spatial, musical, and *gestalt* (viewing an object or event as a whole rather than looking at its individual components) tasks. When you listen to your favorite album, imagine how you will look in a new outfit, or sketch a picture, you are using your right-brain hemisphere.

Monitoring physiological variables makes it possible to control internal processes. First, we must be aware of what our states are. Awareness is much

---

[8]D. E. Sellers and D. W. Stacks, "Toward a Hemispheric Processing Approach to Communication Competence," *Journal of Social Behavior and Personality*, 5, no. 2 (1990), 45–59.

more developed in some people than in others. For most people, conscious physiological awareness is limited to sensations of pleasure, pain, tension, and relaxation. Some people use **biofeedback,** a form of external self-feedback, to help themselves become more aware of their physiological processing. Subjects are attached to instruments that provide information about physiological parameters such as pulse rate, muscle tension, and skin temperature. In some manner, this information helps individuals to alter these levels. For example, biofeedback has been used to teach control of bodily functions such as heart rate, blood pressure, and seizures. In addition, through the power of positive imagining, biofeedback has been shown to create confidence, increase self-control, and establish enhanced and peak performance in athletic, educational, and psychophysiological endeavors.[9]

Transmission

The process by which messages are sent from a source to a receiver is called **transmission.** In intrapersonal communication the source and the receiver are the same person. Thus, transmission takes place through nerve impulses in the brain rather than through sound waves in the air or words written on a page. The intrapersonal communication cycle is completed when the brain reacts to these nerve impulses by transmitting a message to smooth muscles, which regulate the movements of the body. As we described at the start of this chapter, putting a hand on a hot pan causes the individual's touch receptors to send a neural transmission to the brain, saying, "It's hot," which causes the brain to transmit a message to the muscles in the hand, ordering, "Move away from the pan immediately."

Feedback

We usually think of feedback as information from another person. In intrapersonal communication, however, there are two kinds of **self-feedback**—external and internal.

External self-feedback is the part of your message that you hear yourself. This kind of feedback enables you to correct your own mistakes. For example, you would surely backtrack if you heard yourself say something like "external felf-seedback."

Internal self-feedback is usually picked up through bone conduction, nerve endings, or muscular movement. For example, you might perceive an awkward facial gesture without actually seeing it—simply by feeling the muscle tension in your face. Again, perceiving this information enables you to correct yourself.

---

[9]P. Norris, "Biofeedback, Voluntary Control, and Human Potential," *Biofeedback and Self-Regulation,* 11, no. 1 (1986), 1–20.

"It looks OK to me."

Interference

Interference is another important variable in the communication process. **Interference** refers to any factor that negatively affects communication. It can occur at any point along the communication network and at any level of communication. For example, the blast of your neighbor's stereo or a splitting headache might make it impossible for you to read.

A special form of interference occurs intrapersonally when stimuli are processed at one level, although another level is better suited to dealing with them. For example, many people react emotionally to information that should be processed on a cognitive level. Have you ever started crying or gotten angry in response to a bad test score, when if you had remained calm, you might have been able to analyze and profit from the bad news? On the other hand, some individuals insist on processing information on the cognitive level when an emotional response would actually be more helpful. Often a good cry can relieve the pressure of a bad day better than a careful rehash of the day's events.

THE EFFECTS OF INTRAPERSONAL VARIABLES ON COMMUNICATION

Even though a particular communication may focus on the here and now, your personality and past experience influence your interpretation of it. Thus, it is important to consider the intrapersonal factors that influence the communicators. For example, the experiences of someone who has recently lost a mate will no doubt affect that person's communication on the subject of death.

Personal Orientation

The way you react to the following situation will be determined by your personal orientation.

> Warren and Jerry are interviewing for the job of advertising copywriter in a large advertising agency. Neither of them has had any experience, but both come to the interview prepared to show samples of the kind of work they are capable of producing. Jerry's samples represent many hours of hard work and a little talent, while Warren's show much talent but very little effort—he lifted them almost word for word from a textbook.

How do you feel about Jerry and Warren? Do you respect Jerry for his honesty and hard work, or do you appreciate Warren's craftiness in trying to get the kind of job he wants? Your reaction to this situation reflects the values, attitudes, beliefs, and opinions that make up your personal orientation.

VALUES. Each of us maintains a set of *values*—moral or ethical judgments of things we consider important. Values can be a source of conflict within an individual as well as a barrier between people of opposing standards. Fearing a malpractice suit, for instance, a doctor who comes upon an accident victim may be reluctant to offer assistance. His or her values will determine what action is taken. Sometimes an individual will voice one set of values and be guided by another. For example, parents may scold their children for dishonesty but think nothing of cheating on their income tax.

ATTITUDES. An *attitude* is a learned tendency to react positively or negatively to an object or situation. It implies a positive or negative evaluation of someone or something. Attitudes operate at three different levels: (1) cognitive, (2) affective, and (3) instrumental. The cognitive level involves a particular belief, the affective level involves a particular feeling, and the instrumental level involves overt behavior or action.

Let's examine a specific situation. Carlotta Ramirez, a member of the state board of higher education, is a strong opponent of free tuition. Her negative attitude toward the topic can be broken down in this way:

1. *Cognitive (belief):* People who value a college education should be willing to pay for it, even if it means going to work to get enough money for tuition.
2. *Affective (feeling):* People who try to get something for nothing make me angry.
3. *Instrumental (action):* I vote no on the proposal for free tuition at state universities.

BELIEFS, OPINIONS, AND PREJUDICES. We have already used the term *belief.* A belief is anything accepted as true. Note that this definition does not imply either a positive or negative judgment. For example, you may believe that there is life on other planets, yet this belief does not indicate a positive or negative attitude toward that idea. However, if you were to take your belief one step further to say that since you believe there is life on other planets, it would be in our best interests to increase space exploration programs, you would then be voicing an *opinion.* An opinion lies somewhere between an attitude and a belief. It implies a positive or negative reaction.

Not all our beliefs and opinions are well founded. Sometimes they are based on preconceived ideas and not on our own actual experiences. In this case they are, in fact, *prejudices*—preformed judgments about a particular person, group, or thing. None of us is free from prejudice, but certain prejudices are more harmful than others. Think for a moment about your own experiences with prejudice, when you were either guilty of prejudice or were its victim. Or consider this example of how foolish our prejudices can be:

> Although it was against her principles, Ruth had agreed to help a good friend out of a tight spot by accepting a blind date with the friend's uncle from Louisiana. Ruth, who had never been south of Philadelphia, just knew that an evening spent with this hick was going to be one of the most boring of her life.
>
> He arrived, and, sure enough, his accent was unlike anything Ruth had ever heard. By evening's end, however, she had changed her mind. Full of admiration for the most interesting and beautifully mannered man she had ever met, Ruth eagerly awaited their next date.
>
> He never called again. A few weeks later, Ruth learned from her friend that he had returned to New Orleans and, before leaving, had announced: "All Yankee women are alike—hard to please!"

Think about the groups toward which you may be prejudiced. Does this example suggest ways in which you may be oversimplifying to the point of prejudice?

Personality Traits

Another way the self affects our communication is through personality variables known as *traits.* Personality traits are those qualities that distinguish one personality from another. As the following examples indicate, some personality traits aid communication, but many are barriers to communication.

LOCUS OF CONTROL. One important personality variable that affects the communication process is *locus of control,* or the degree to which we perceive reinforcement either as contingent upon our own efforts or actions (internal locus of control) or as a result of forces beyond our control and due to chance, fate, or situational contingencies (external locus of control).[10] A difference in communication patterns emerges for those who believe that they control events and those who believe that their desired outcomes will accrue as a function of the degree to which they fit in with the beliefs, desires, or attitudes of people who have power over them. The former person, with a more internal locus of control, would be more straightforward upon presenting new plans to an upper-level supervisor, while the latter person's communication (the person with an external locus of control) would be more indirect, vague, and ambiguous.

MANIPULATION.   Related to the locus of control that a person exhibits is the degree to which he or she attempts to manipulate others. People vary with regard to the characteristic of *manipulation,* or the degree to which they attempt to achieve goals by dominating and controlling others. However, research has shown that people who have an external locus of control (that is, who believe that the world is ordered and controlled by others) often desire that control for themselves and tend to exhibit greater manipulative behaviors than do people who have an internal locus of control. Given that the latter believe that they control their own fates, they do not generally manifest excessive degrees of manipulation.

DOGMATISM.   One of the most difficult personality traits encountered in a communication situation is *dogmatism.* Dogmatic individuals have closed minds and are reluctant to accept new ideas and opinions. Yet they may accept without question the word of certain authorities and expect the same kind of blind acceptance from those they consider their inferiors. Dogmatic individuals often remain steadfast to ideas or opinions in spite of contradictory evidence.

TOLERANCE OF AMBIGUITY.   While some people can live with shades of gray, others insist on things being clearly defined and unambiguous. This varying *tolerance of ambiguity* frequently affects the communication process. Consider the following example:

> Phil and Max go to see a movie. After the movie both agree that the film was extremely well done. However, Max is bothered by several inconsistencies that Phil didn't seem to notice. Max points out three areas in the film that he thought were ambiguous. When he asks Phil for clarification, Phil admits that he can't explain the confusing segments of the film.

Phil's tolerance of ambiguity is greater than Max's. Phil was able to ignore the ambiguities, while Max found them troublesome. Perhaps you have experienced a similar situation when reading a complex book or when trying to analyze a particular communication interaction.

---

[10]D. J. Canary, E. M. Cunningham, and M. J. Cody, "Goal Types, Gender, and Locus of Control in Managing Interpersonal Conflict," *Communication Research,* 15, no. 4 (August 1988), 430.

SELF-ESTEEM. Communication is also affected by the self-esteem of the sender and the receiver. *Self-esteem,* which is your enduring evaluation of yourself, often determines your confidence in what you are saying and your readiness to accept the view of others. Therefore, in the communication process, it is important to use your perception of another person's self-esteem as a means of evaluating certain messages. For example, individuals with high self-esteem may state an opinion confidently even without sufficient evidence. You might be quicker to question their veracity than that of speakers whose low self-esteem would prevent them from supporting unproven viewpoints.

MATURITY. Of the many personality variables, the one that most strongly affects communication is level of *maturity.* It is difficult to pinpoint the stage at which a person matures psychologically, but we usually judge a person as mature when he or she is able to function independently in a social setting. One measure of such maturity is the individual's ability to satisfy psychological needs for things such as independence, approval, affection, and so forth. What this means in a communication setting is the absence of intrapersonal conflicts that might intrude on objective transmission and interpretation of messages.

Defense Mechanisms

We all suffer from varying degrees of anxiety. For most of us, anxiety stems from intrapersonal conflicts—conflicts between inner psychological needs and external realities. If severe enough, anxiety can distort your perception of yourself and your environment and thus act as a barrier to communication with others.

The self must find various ways to resolve the anxiety produced by such intrapersonal conflict. These methods, known as *defense mechanisms,* help us accept things that might otherwise cause emotional pain. Defense mechanisms, when used in moderation, aid our personal adjustment to the environment. If used to excess, however, they can become a crutch that distorts reality.

We introduce ourselves
To Planets and to Flowers
But with ourselves
Have etiquettes
Embarrassments
And awes.

EMILY DICKINSON

RATIONALIZATION. Defense mechanisms take many forms. Perhaps the best known is *rationalization,* an attempt to justify our failures or inadequacies. Most of us rationalize from time to time. For example, when Ellen was not hired for a job she wanted very badly, she rationalized her failure by claiming that the man who would have been her boss was threatened by her abilities. Tom rationalized his rejection by a law school by telling everyone that he really didn't want to go anyway.

PROJECTION.   Sometimes we ignore certain traits, motives, or behaviors in ourselves and attribute them to others. This defense mechanism is known as *projection.* Eleanor, who has a weight problem and is constantly dieting, goes to lunch with her friend Jan, a perfect size 8. When the women finish eating, Eleanor remarks, "I can tell you're still hungry." Actually, Jan is quite full. It is Eleanor who is still hungry.

INSULATION.   One way to resolve conflicts caused by contradictions is to isolate contradictory feelings and information. This defense mechanism is known as *insulation.* For example, a member of a radical group who protests police brutality by bombing a precinct headquarters has clearly insulated contradictory behaviors. This person is able to oppose violence on the one hand and participate in violence of a "different" sort on the other.

REACTION FORMATION.   Sometimes people deal with "undesirable" urges or behaviors with a defense mechanism known as *reaction formation.* This process involves denial of what you or society consider unacceptable feelings or behaviors, coupled with extreme advocacy of the opposite position. For example, someone who is easily aroused by pictures of nudes may deny this tendency by becoming an outspoken opponent of pornography.

IDENTIFICATION.   We have discussed the importance of identification in developing self-concept. The *identification* process can also be used as a defense mechanism against insecurity or inadequacy. Thus, adolescents, who often feel uncertain about themselves, may seek security by identifying themselves with stars of the entertainment or sports worlds. Such identification accounts for much of the popularity of personalities such as Elvis Presley, Madonna, Michael Jordan, and Sting.

REPRESSION.   Some people deal with unpleasant or unacceptable feelings, desires, or experiences by repressing them. *Repression* is a defense mechanism that keeps certain thoughts and feelings beneath the conscious level. Thus, children brought up in overly strict homes, where outbursts are severely punished, often learn to repress anger.

SUMMARY

The most basic level of communication is intrapersonal, involving the sending and receiving of messages within one individual. This is the level on which you communicate with yourself.

Intrapersonal communication is a

function of the physical self, the emotional self, the intellectual self, habits, and private versus public situations. In addition, the need for a unified conceptual system and the picture that you have of yourself—your self-concept—also strongly influence these self-communications. Your past experiences, reference groups, and accustomed roles combine in ever-changing relationships to form this self-concept. At the same time, internal and external stimuli affect the cognitive, emotional, and physiological processing of intrapersonal communication.

An individual's intrapersonal communication must be considered in any analysis of interpersonal communication situations. For example, personality variables such as manipulation, locus of control, dogmatism, tolerance for ambiguity, self-esteem, and maturity—and personal orientations, values, attitudes, and beliefs—all intrude on the objective sending and interpreting of interpersonal messages. Communication is further hampered by the many defense mechanisms that people use to minimize anxiety.

EXERCISES

Group Experiences

Who Are You?

DESCRIPTION: Understanding the many selves that exist inside you is not an easy task. In this activity you will repeatedly be asked the question, "Who are you?" At first the answers may come easily, but after several minutes you may be surprised at the increased difficulty you experience in answering the question. The purpose of this activity is to provide you with an opportunity to explore your perceptions of yourself.

PROCEDURE: Divide into dyads. For the first five minutes, Person A should ask Person B the question, "Who are you?" Person B should answer this question with very short and concise phrases, such as "I am a student." As soon as Person B supplies an answer, Person A should once again repeat the question, "Who are you?" After five minutes the roles should be reversed, and Person B should ask the question.

DISCUSSION: How did your answers illustrate (1) your perceptions of yourself and (2) others' perceptions of you? Do you have "multiple" concepts of yourself? What do your answers say about the degree to which your self-concept is negative or positive? Ask your partner who he or she perceives you to be, based on your answers to the question. How does the way you see yourself affect your communication with others?

Cocktail Party

DESCRIPTION: Feedback from other people often plays an important role in the way we feel about ourselves—it may cause us to reevaluate our perceptions of ourselves. This activity provides you with an opportunity to experience the extent to which positive and negative feedback affects your responses to others and your perceptions of yourself.

PROCEDURE: Each participant should receive a self-adhesive label to be worn on the forehead for this activity. Each label will have a short phrase written on it, such as:

Criticize Me   I'm Boring
I'm a Clown   Give Me Your Sexiest Look
Frown at Me   Smile at Me

When you are ready to begin the activity, all participants should have labels placed on their foreheads. *No one is permitted to tell you what your label says.* Participants should move around and talk to people as if they were at a cocktail party. The "cocktail party" should last from ten to 15 minutes, depending on the size of the group. As you talk with other people, you must respond to their labels (follow the directions on their labels) without actually telling them what their labels say. For example, if players are wearing labels saying, "I'm boring," you must act as if everything they say is dull. You can do this by yawning, walking away, closing your eyes, or using your voice to show disinterest.

DISCUSSION: Before you remove your label, try to guess what it says, based on the verbal and nonverbal feedback you have received. Next, classify your label—was it very negative, negative, neutral, positive, or very positive?
  Begin the discussion by asking all those people who were wearing negative or very negative labels to share their experiences. Did they have an emotional response to the feedback they received? For example, did they become withdrawn, introverted, or depressed during the cocktail party? Then ask those people who had positive labels if they were talkative, extroverted, smiling, and gregarious. How would consistent positive or negative feedback from significant others (parents, friends) affect your emotions and ultimately your perception of yourself?

Personal Experiences

1. We all seem to be affected, to varying degrees, by the type of feedback we receive from others. Observe the amount of positive, neutral, and negative feedback you receive during a two-hour period. How do the different types of feedback affect you? How would you react to a large amount of negative feedback?

2. Spend some time alone and consider people or groups with which you identify. Remember that identification is more than just imitation. When you identify with another person or a particular group, you see yourself as an extension of that person or group. What are the problems with identifying with another person or group? Why have you formed identifications with particular people or groups? What do your identifications reflect about your self-concept?

3. Keep a diary for a week. At the end of each day, record the feelings you experienced during the day. For example, you might write that you felt angry for most of the morning, but by the end of the day you felt very calm. At the end of the week, reread your log to determine if (a) you have experienced highly intense feelings that may properly be called emotions and (b) if those feelings were predominantly positive or negative. How does your inner world of feelings affect your communication with others?

Discussion Questions

1. To what extent can you achieve effective communication with another person without understanding his or her self-concept, attitudes, and beliefs?

2. What effect does a positive or negative self-concept have on your communication with others?

3. What characteristics distinguish achieved roles from ascribed ones?

4. How would you draw the Johari Window for (a) an intimate relationship, (b) a casual relationship, and (c) an initial interaction with another person? Remember that you can change the proportions of any square.

5. How do you use the various defense mechanisms in your daily activities?

Interpersonal Communication

KEY CONCEPTS AND TERMS

Interpersonal communication
Dyad
Functional communication theory
Linking function
Mentation function
Regulatory function
Relational communication theory
Control
One-up message
One-down message
Complementary relationship
Symmetrical relationship
Trust
Trusting
Trustworthiness
Intimacy
Coordinated management
   of meaning theory
Constitutive rule
Regulative rule

Self-disclosure
Feedback
Feedforward
Attraction
Initiating
Experimenting
Intensifying
Integrating
Bonding
Differentiating
Circumscribing
Stagnating
Avoiding
Terminating
Alternating monologue
Stimulus-response interaction
Interaction with feedback
Interaction with empathy
Conflict management

D anny had just finished her paper for the conference, a task that had taken more than 18 months to complete, including research time. As she looked over at her husband, Rich, she smiled. He was working on the other computer in their tiny, cluttered office and putting the finishing touches on his paper as well. Although the papers would be competing for slots on the same panel, Danny and Rich were confident that both papers would be accepted.

A month later, Danny came running into the house, yelling and waving an envelope in her hand. As she called Rich's name, she realized he was not home yet. So she sat on the couch for a moment and stared at the label. The letter was addressed to her. What would it say? She felt sure that both papers had been accepted. Quickly, Danny ripped off the end of the envelope and opened the letter with trembling hands. Her paper had landed! Rich's paper had not. He would be crushed, and their relationship would probably suffer.

Feeling delighted, yet ambivalent about the development, Danny didn't know quite what to do. Rich was not only her husband, but also her lover and best friend. Now Laurel, their mutual friend and chairperson of the interest group, had asked Danny to break the news to him. What would she do?

Fortunately, the scenario you have just read is fictitious. However, it is based on a composite of events that friends and colleagues of mine have experienced. (You guessed it. The names were changed to protect the innocent.) Although most of us probably will never be placed in this position during our lifetimes, we all have had moments when we have felt alone and isolated. At these times, we feel the need to reach out to others and to share our feelings and ideas. This sharing of experiences—both positive and negative—is known as **interpersonal communication.** It is the extension of ourselves to other people and their extensions toward us.

In the previous chapter we examined *intra*personal communication and analyzed the messages that are sent and received within an individual. However, the term "communication" is most often identified with information that is shared between or among individuals, or interpersonal communication.

AN INTERPERSONAL COMMUNICATION MODEL

Interpersonal communication can occur in any environment, be it formal (the lecture hall) or informal (the check-out line). Most interpersonal messages are informal, however, and stem from everyday, face-to-face encounters. Think of your own communication. From your first "Good morning" to your last "See you tomorrow," your interpersonal communication is usually spontaneous, unplanned, and loosely organized, probably even ungrammatical. With the exception of telephone conversations, most of this communication involves people close enough to see and touch each other. This makes sending and receiving messages much easier and eliminates the need for the kind of formal rules followed in debates, news conferences, or other public speaking situations.

DYADIC VERSUS SMALL GROUP COMMUNICATION

Most interpersonal communication involves a *dyad,* or two people in close contact. As a result, the potential for sending, receiving, and evaluating messages is divided between the two halves of the dyad (see Figure 6–1). That is, both participants alternate from one role to the other—sometimes originating messages, at other times responding to them. Both roles provide a means for exchanging information, but neither is complete in itself; if one participant only listened, and the other only spoke, communication would soon break down. Thus, communication in a dyad is very much a shared responsibility. Equally shared responsibility differentiates a dyad from a small group. (We will examine small group communication more completely in Chapter 7.) In small groups, the balance of communication shifts. Because each participant has a different role and status in the group, the potential for sending and receiving messages is not evenly divided. Furthermore, group members not only serve as sources or destinations of messages, but they also function as channels to relay the messages of others.

Purpose further differentiates interpersonal and group communication. Many groups are problem-centered; that is, members are working together for a defined purpose, usually decision making or problem solving. In contrast, interpersonal communication in dyads focuses on the *sharing of meaning.* Although interpersonal dyads may also solve problems or make decisions, their messages convey a wider range of feelings and emotions. The information they exchange is not just the dry, factual material common in a

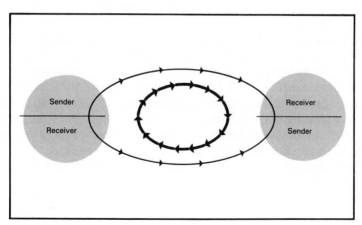

FIGURE 6–1
Dyadic Communication

sales meeting, for example. Rather, it consists of meanings derived from personal experiences and observations. These interpersonal messages have a significant psychological impact: The process of translating thoughts into verbal and nonverbal messages increases the communicator's awareness of his or her feelings and self-concept. In turn, the listener's responses confirm or alter these feelings. With effective interpersonal communication, this process becomes reciprocal; both participants strengthen themselves and each other through the sharing of meanings and emotions.

To help you more clearly understand the process of interpersonal communication, this chapter will focus on various interpersonal communication theories as well as on variables that affect interpersonal relationships. As Watson and Barker have noted, a variety of factors affect interpersonal relationships, including temporal, physical, social, cultural, emotional, and intellectual factors.[1] Additionally, we will examine the growth and decline of interpersonal relationships and discuss how we can more effectively manage interpersonal communication. By the time you have completed this chapter, we hope you will have taken the time to examine your own interpersonal behaviors. Such self-analysis is critical to the development and maintenance of healthy interpersonal relationships.

THEORIES OF INTERPERSONAL COMMUNICATION

Although the study of interpersonal communication may seem relatively straightforward when you first consider it, a perusal of the many different approaches to its study reveals the true complexity of the subject. For example, some communication theorists are interested in the functions of interpersonal communication, while others focus solely on dimensions of interpersonal relationships. Still other communication specialists are interested in how meanings are created and interpreted, while others address variables that affect interpersonal communication. In short, interpersonal communication may be viewed in a variety of ways, each of which can help us to better understand the overall communication process.

In order to introduce you to the study of interpersonal communication, the following sections will focus on three specific theories of interpersonal communication: functional communication theory, which addresses the functions of interpersonal communication; relational communication theory, which focuses on dimensions of interpersonal relationships; and the theory of the coordinated management of meaning. This final theory addresses meanings in interpersonal relationships and the rules through which we construct interpersonal communication.

---

[1] K. W. Watson and L. L. Barker, *Interpersonal and Relational Communication* (Scottsdale, Ariz.: Gorsuch Scarisbrick, 1990), 6.

Functions of Interpersonal Communication

According to the ***functional communication theory,*** we use interpersonal communication for a variety of reasons. For example, through interpersonal communication, we are better able to understand our world. Talking through a problem with a friend or business associate in order to better understand a situation is an illustration of this function. At other times, we communicate interpersonally in order to think and evaluate more effectively. For example, when Julie asks for input from her staff in order to help her make a more informed decision, she is illustrating another interpersonal function. We also communicate interpersonally in order to change behavior in some way, whether that behavior is our own or someone else's.

For communication specialists Frank Dance and Carl Larson, interpersonal communication serves precisely these three functions. More specifically, it (1) provides a ***linking function*** between a person and his or her environment; (2) allows us to conceptualize, remember, and plan, each a part of the ***mentation function;*** and (3) serves to regulate our own and others' behavior, the ***regulatory function.***[2]

To illustrate the importance of these three functions, first imagine a world in which communication would not allow you to relate to the outside world, but instead would only let you communicate with yourself—intrapersonally. (Incidentally, you probably would be unable to communicate even with yourself without interpersonal communication.) Then imagine a world in which you could not relate to other people. Not only would a world such as this be a very lonely place in which to live, but you also would probably be unable to survive for much longer than an hour. Through interpersonal communication, we are nurtured as infants—physically, emotionally, and intellectually. In addition, we develop cultural, social, and psychological ties with the world through interpersonal communication. In short, interpersonal interactions allow us to *function* more practically in life. The functional theory of interpersonal communication was developed for this reason.

Relational Communication Theory

Unlike the functional theory of interpersonal communication, which focuses solely on communication functions, ***relational communication theory*** addresses interpersonal communication by examining dimensions of interpersonal relationships.

According to communication theorists Edna Rogers-Millar and Frank Millar, three dimensions of interpersonal relationships are important: the control, trust, and intimacy dimensions of relationships. Created and

---

[2]F. E. X. Dance and C. E. Larson, *The Functions of Human Communication* (New York: Holt, Rinehart & Winston, 1976).

sustained primarily through interpersonal messages, these three dimensions reflect and define the nature of the relationship.[3]

The first dimension, or the **control** dimension of interpersonal relationships, focuses on the distribution of power in a relationship, particularly the power to direct the nature of the interaction. This dimension is usually reflected in the number of messages we use to exert or relinquish relational control. For example, a message such as the following exerts control: "I'm really tired this evening, Jan. Let's stay home and watch a movie!" In addition, "control" is reflected in our general tendency to accept or reject a source's statements of control. Look at the following conversation between Bob and Sandy:

> *Bob:* (slamming door) Honey, I'm home. . . . Is anybody here?
> *Sandy:* (coming through living room door) Hello, sweetheart. Yes, I'm home.
> *Bob:* Good, I was hoping to find you here. We only have a couple of minutes before we have to go!
> *Sandy:* Before we have to go where?
> *Bob:* Let's talk while we're getting ready. The boss has invited us out to dinner at 7:00, and it's already 6:30. I can't believe he expected us to go on such short notice.
> *Sandy:* That's O.K., honey. Dinner here can wait until tomorrow. I'll go and put it in the refrigerator before I change.

In the previous conversation, Bob tended to use messages that exerted control. Rather than asking Sandy how she felt about the change in plans, he took control and made the decision for them. Messages that exert control are called **one-up messages.** On the other hand, Sandy responded in a way that accepted Bob's control. She did so by using a greater number of messages that were **one-down** in nature, or which relinquished control to Bob. Relationships that are characterized by this pattern of interaction are called **complementary relationships.** In a complementary relationship, one person generally is more dominant than the other. If Sandy had argued with Bob and refused to accept his control, the relationship would have been characterized as more **symmetrical** at that point. In a symmetrical relationship, partners mirror each other's behavior more often.

The second dimension of interpersonal relationships is the **trust** dimension, which is defined uniquely when compared with other current definitions of trust. Trust is defined by Rogers-Millar and Millar as "the responsible acceptance of the control dimension." Although this definition

---

[3]F. E. Millar and L. E. Rogers, "A Relational Approach to Interpersonal Communication," in Gerald Miller, ed., *Explorations in Interpersonal Communication* (Beverly Hills, Calif.: Sage, 1976), 87–103.

may seem alien at first, trust indeed involves a belief that the other person will not exploit us. It is this aspect of trust on which Rogers-Millar and Millar base their definition of trust. **Trusting** involves an admission of dependency on the part of the persons involved. In turn, **trustworthiness** is defined as the acceptance of an obligation not to exploit control. Both trusting and trustworthiness go hand in hand to create our feelings of trust.

The third dimension of interpersonal relationships, for Rogers-Millar and Millar, is the **intimacy** dimension, or the degree to which two can uniquely meet one another's needs. For example, if Hal meets all of Jennifer's needs and Jennifer doesn't feel the need for additional relationships, for Jennifer the relationship would be defined as an intimate one. However, if Hal is unable to meet all of Jennifer's interpersonal needs, the relationship for Jennifer would be described as lower in overall intimacy.

Control, trust, and intimacy are three important dimensions of interpersonal communication. Each has the potential to affect the nature of our relationships. For example, researchers have found that the less often two people exert control simultaneously, the more satisfaction they will experience in the relationship. However, if one-up messages are always followed by one-down messages, the two people will be less likely to experience empathy for one another. These are only two of many findings that have been discovered as a function of the relational communication theory. As you can see, the theory has much to offer to communication students; it can allow us to make specific predictions about interpersonal outcomes.

The Coordinated Management of Meaning

Unlike the two theories of interpersonal communication we have already addressed, the **coordinated management of meaning theory,** CMM for short, is a meaning-centered theory of communication. In other words, its primary focus is on meanings in interpersonal communication, and on how we coordinate and manage meanings in everyday life.

Perhaps one of the most compelling arguments that CMM theorists make is that all communication is best viewed as the coordination of rules for interacting with others.[4] For example, if you and I were to meet for the first time, we both would bring to that initial meeting certain rules about interactions. To illustrate, my rules might include the following:

1. When meeting someone for the first time, I should smile and say, "hello."
2. When one meets another person, it is generally considered polite to shake his or her hand.
3. If I am interested in that person, I should maintain a fair amount of direct eye contact.

---

[4]W. B. Pearce and V. Cronen, *Communication, Action, and Meaning* (New York: Praeger, 1980).

In turn, you also might bring these rules to our initial interaction. Once we move through the behaviors that are guided by these rules, however, what should we say to each other next? Should I inquire about your health? Your background? Whether you have read the latest edition of *Communication?* What meanings should I assign to your words and should you assign to mine?

According to Pearce and Cronen, the two primary developers of CMM theory, two sets of rules help to answer these questions and allow us to coordinate the interaction. The first of these rules, or **constitutive rules**, define what a given act or behavior should "count as" and allow us to decide what each other's behavior "means." Using CMM notation, this type of rule could be written something like this:

initial meeting

smile ⟶ sign of
        friendliness

Or, "In the context of an initial meeting, a smile may be taken to count as a sign of friendliness." As you can see, the symbol ⎤ simply designates the situation or context, while the arrow ⟶ is used to designate what the given behavior (in this instance, a smile) should "count as."

Regulative rules, on the other hand, tell us how we should behave in a given situation. For example, the following regulative rule might apply during our initial interaction:

initial interaction

other person ⊃ I should smile
smiles   in return

Or, "In the context of an initial interaction, if the other person smiles, then I should smile in return." At this point, the only unfamiliar symbol in this rule is the symbol ⊃, which says, "If you do x, then I should respond with y."

Although these examples are exceptionally simple, very complex acts may be described in a similar fashion. In addition, CMM theory allows us to see how these rules actually mesh—in other words, how we actually coordinate meanings. To illustrate this coordinated management of meaning, Figure 6–2 describes a potential sequence that might occur during our (same) initial meeting.

As you can see, communication indeed may be defined as the coordination of individual rules and the meanings that we attribute to resulting behaviors. In short, for CMM theorists, effective communication is viewed as a function of two ingredients: (1) a mutually shared system of rules and (2) the coordinated management of meanings that results.

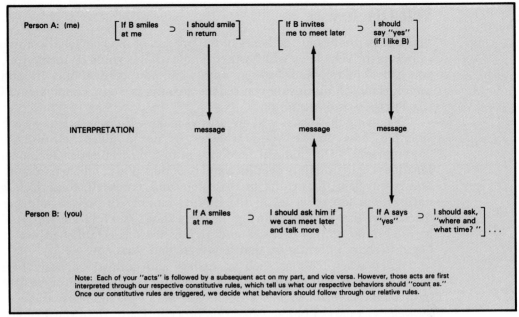

Note: Each of your "acts" is followed by a subsequent act on my part, and vice versa. However, those acts are first interpreted through our respective constitutive rules, which tell us what our respective behaviors should "count as." Once our constitutive rules are triggered, we decide what behaviors should follow through our relative rules.

Source: Adapted from W. B. Pearce and V. Cronen, *Communication, Action, and Meaning* (New York: Praeger, 1980), p. 174.

FIGURE 6–2

Coordinated Management of Meaning

VARIABLES AFFECTING INTERPERSONAL RELATIONSHIPS

In the previous section of this chapter, we identified three theories of interpersonal communication in order to show you how communication theorists currently conceptualize the interpersonal communication process. We hope that this discussion has helped to reveal the complexities associated with interpersonal communication. In order to help you further understand interpersonal communication, this section will focus on variables that affect interpersonal relationships, including self-disclosure, trust, feedback, non-verbal behavior, and interpersonal attraction. Our success or failure in addressing these variables in our own interpersonal communication determines how satisfying our interpersonal relationships will be.

The uttered part of a man's life, let us always repeat, bears to the unuttered, unconscious part a small unknown proportion. He himself never knows it, much less do others.

THOMAS CARLYLE

Self-Disclosure

Self-disclosure lies at the heart of the process of interpersonal communication. It is the vehicle by which others know what is going on inside you, what you are thinking and feeling, and what you care about. In addition, appropriate self-disclosure can reduce anxiety, increase comfort, and intensify interpersonal attraction.[5]

Knowing these facts will not always make self-disclosure any easier. For example, how do we know whether or not a given self-disclosure is "appropriate"? Our natural tendency is to hide feelings of incompetence, loneliness, guilt, anxiety over love and rejection, and conflicts based on anger and resentment. According to Hornstein and Truesdell, these feelings are natural and are reflected in the limited number of private and personal disclosures that we make during the early stages of a relationship. However, as the relationship progresses and greater trust is established, we usually begin to share information that is private and personal.[6]

Even when feelings such as anxiety and guilt are not involved in a relationship, self-disclosure may still be difficult because of well-learned habits that help us to avoid emotional pain. We all learn these evasive strategies as part of our socialization process. They are so rewarding that it becomes difficult to know when to put them away. Many people in our society are accustomed to hiding what they really want, think, or feel. For this reason, self-disclosure becomes a rare and valued gift. Confiding in others and receiving their confidences is, therefore, one of the most effective interpersonal communication tools we possess.

Because of the importance of self-disclosure to the development of interpersonal relationships, communication researchers have explored the nature of self-disclosure and its relationship to other important interpersonal concepts. Psychologist Steven Broder summarized research findings from a number of studies and found that people often reveal personal information in response to another person's disclosure, even when they do not like the other person very much. Such reciprocity plays an important role in social interaction. Additionally, Broder found that we disclose to people whom we like, but also that we like people more when they disclose to us. Thus, liking plays an important role in disclosure. Finally, Broder looked at the trust–disclosure relationship and found that research also documented this relationship. In short, we share intimate aspects of our lives with those whom we trust, despite the personal risk and feelings that accompany being "open." Generally, we do so because expressing ourselves gives us a sense of relief and improved psychological functioning. Despite the fear associated

---

[5]L. E. Lazowski and S. M. Andersen, "Self-Disclosure and Social Perception: The Impact of Private, Negative, and Extreme Communications," *Journal of Social Behavior and Personality,* 5, no. 2 (1990), 132.

[6]G. A. Hornstein and S. E. Truesdell, "Development of Intimate Conversation in Close Relationships," *Journal of Social and Clinical Psychology,* 7, no. 1 (1988), 49–64.

Self-disclosure is vital to healthy interpersonal communication.

with "getting something off our chests," we self-disclose in order to be closer to people about whom we care.[7]

As Broder's research demonstrates, self-disclosure is a vital component of interpersonal communication. However, the work of these scholars should perhaps be qualified in at least two ways. First, as Caltabiano and Smithson have noted, self-disclosure should increase in scope and intimacy as a relationship develops, in order for self-disclosure to be seen as appropriate. Second, during the acquaintanceship stage, positive disclosure of information (in contrast to negative disclosure) is seen as more appropriate, with positive disclosures viewed as more adjusted and emotionally stable than negative disclosures.[8] In short, during the initial stages of interpersonal relationships, it is best to avoid negative disclosure statements, particularly about oneself. Such disclosures reduce the chances that a relationship will be sought by the communication receiver.

---

[7]S. N. Broder, "Helping Students with Self-Disclosure," *School Counselor*, 34, no. 3 (1987), 182–187.

[8]M. L. Caltabiano and M. Smithson, "Variables Affecting the Perception of Self-Disclosure Appropriateness," *Journal of Social Psychology*, 120 (1983), 119–28.

Trust

Just as self-disclosure affects the nature of interpersonal relationships, so too does trust affect the quality of our interactions. We all have experienced the satisfaction that results from learning that we can trust a new acquaintance. Likewise, we know the importance of being trustworthy in return. According to Rogers-Millar and Millar, both of these trust dimensions must be in operation before interpersonal trust can develop in a relationship. As we stated earlier, *trust* may be best defined as an interaction between trusting and trustworthy behaviors. More specifically, it involves (1) an *admission* of dependency by all parties involved, and (2) the *acceptance* of an obligation not to exploit control.

As you know, however, trust does not just happen. Trusting another person develops over time. According to Gamble and Gamble, trust is established in four major ways:

1. The individuals who are involved must be willing to disclose themselves to the person of interest—trust precipitates trusting behaviors in others.
2. We must be willing to let the other person know he or she is accepted and supported—reducing threats to another's ego increases trust.
3. We must be willing to develop a cooperative rather than a competitive orientation; working to win in a relationship can destroy it.
4. Finally, we should trust people when trusting them is appropriate; taking inappropriate risks can be as destructive as not taking risks at all.[9]

In short, the "bottom line" regarding trust in relationships is threefold. First, trusting others generally encourages their trust in you. Second, you must be cooperative and supportive of the other person. Finally, trusting behavior may be appropriate or inappropriate, depending on the context or situation. Only you can decide when and how to trust another person. We hope that this discussion will help as you make these critical decisions.

The highest compact we can make with our fellow is—"Let there be truth between us two forevermore."

RALPH WALDO EMERSON

Feedback and Feedforward

Thus far, we have discussed how different theories of interpersonal communication can contribute to our knowledge of the communication process. Additionally, we have argued that self-disclosure and trust are important

---

[9]Adapted from T. K. Gamble and M. Gamble, *Contacts: Communicating Interpersonally* (New York: Random House, 1982), 226–28.

variables that influence the effectiveness of interpersonal communication. Another variable that influences interpersonal interactions is the extent to which we share feedback and feedforward with one another. We now turn to a brief discussion of these concepts.

Feedback, a term borrowed from computer technology, originally referred to a self-regulating mechanism that keeps machines running smoothly and efficiently. As we mentioned in Chapter 3, communication feedback keeps interpersonal relationships running smoothly. You provide this feedback by *paraphrasing* (thereby confirming or correcting your understanding of a message), by *asking questions* (thereby demonstrating your interest and your desire for more information), or by *responding with feeling statements* (thereby showing that you care about your partner). The following dialogue illustrates all three of these forms of feedback.

Andy: My trip to Paris last summer was the most interesting experience of my life.

Mark: You really enjoyed your stay in Paris. What did you like best?

Andy: Well, I lived in a dorm for foreign students, and I got to meet people from all over the world.

Mark: I can appreciate your pleasure in meeting people from different backgrounds. Two years ago my family hosted an exchange student from Zambia, and I really grew a lot from knowing him.

We often require feedback from others to shape our own behavior. This is especially true in social situations, in which we tend to monitor our own actions to conform to the behavior of the group. Social cues are the feedback that allows us to monitor our behavior. For example, at a party, high self-monitors are acutely aware of their behavior and model the actions of other guests. They talk quietly when others talk quietly, and they laugh at jokes that seem to amuse the other guests. In contrast, low self-monitors disregard this situational feedback and follow their own inclinations. They start dancing while other people are engaged in serious conversation or drink too much when others are drinking very little.

Concern about social feedback also helps speakers to plan communication strategies. For example, suppose that you are nervous about asking a co-worker for a date. From casual conversations during coffee breaks, you know that she likes sports, and you hope she will agree to meet you at next Saturday night's hockey game. On the other hand, you worry that she might consider Saturday night a "heavy" dating night, inappropriate for a first date. Your anticipation of feedback is known as **feedforward.** Feedforward in this situation permits you to set up two possible plans: the evening hockey game and an afternoon gymnastics exhibition. If she expresses hesitancy about going to the Saturday game, you can then switch to your contingency plan.

Nonverbal Behavior

Nonverbal behavior plays a strong, necessary role in interpersonal relationships. So much can be "said" by a smile, hug, or handclasp that words are often not needed.

As we mentioned in Chapter 4, eye behavior is especially important in interpersonal situations. For example, studies have shown that eye contact between close couples is much greater than that between casually dating couples. Besides showing interest and caring, eye contact also can express hostility or the desire for dominance. Indeed, competing athletes use staring as an aggressive gesture and an indication of their confidence level. In contrast, the avoided glance often signifies submission.

Touching is another important nonverbal factor in interpersonal relationships. Touching usually communicates intimacy: couples walk down the street with their arms around each other; a father caresses his baby; a child hugs her dog. Touching can also communicate status and power. Ask yourself who would be more likely to use a patronizing pat on the head or an aggressive poke in the chest: professor or student; policeman or detainee; physician or patient; boss or subordinate. Status differences related to sex are also revealed in touching behavior. Who is usually the first to hold the other's hand or to demonstrate physical affection in a male-female relationship? Women have come a long way, but it is still rare for them to make the first move by putting an arm around a date in a dark movie theater.

Interpersonal Attraction

Self-disclosure, trust, appropriate feedback, and nonverbal behavior all work together to increase your interpersonal effectiveness. Interestingly enough, this increased effectiveness somehow improves interpersonal attraction, the "good vibrations," "magnetism," or "invisible force" that somehow draws people together.

Attraction is a positive attitude, movement toward, or liking between two people. What causes this attraction is rarely "love at first sight." Rather, the cause can be found in the complex mix of variables within ourselves and within the other individual. Research indicates that many of the factors that determine attraction relate to interpersonal communication. For example, in their summary of the attraction literature, Neimeyer and Mitchell discuss several precursors to interpersonal attraction, including the need to feel close to someone, shared preferences for activities (such as athletics, cooking, or travel), physical attractiveness, and attitude similarity. Geographical (physical) proximity and closeness also affect our feelings of attraction and, hence, our interpersonal relationships.[10]

Consider the following example. Leah started taking yoga lessons at the YMCA. In the class she met a couple of people who shared many of her other

---

[10]R. A. Neimeyer and K. A. Mitchell, "Similarity and Attraction: A Longitudinal Study," *Journal of Social and Personal Relationships,* 5 (1988), 131.

Physical proximity positively affects interpersonal attraction.

interests, such as Eastern religion, natural foods, and meditation. The three students became close friends and continued to see each other after the lessons were over. Sharing a common territory, in this case the YMCA classroom, brought these students together. However, as Neimeyer and Mitchell have noted, similarity in attitudes and interests probably sustained the relationship following their initial interactions.

DEVELOPMENT OF DYADIC RELATIONSHIPS

Thus far, we have examined several skills that are important in interpersonal relationships. But where and how do relationships begin? What factors cause relational growth or disintegration? Recent popular literature suggests that individual personalities evolve over time through life experiences, acquired knowledge, and environmental factors. Interpersonal relationships also evolve in this way. Cultivating a lasting friendship can take months or even years. However, time is relevant. Two people also may experience love "at first sight." Ultimately, relationships progress through five different stages of development. These phases of relationship development will be discussed in the following section.

Phases of Relationship Development

Think for a moment about the types of relationships you are a part of in your family, school, job, and community. Each relationship has unique qualities that set it apart from others, even though the characteristics may be positive or negative. If we look back to the beginning of each of our relationships, we see that there are a variety of reasons for the involvement. Maybe at one time you needed special care (mother), information (teacher), service (postal carrier), or a lover (girlfriend or boyfriend). According to Mark Knapp, relationships follow characteristic patterns of development (coming together) and disintegration (coming apart). His five phases of relationship development are initiating, experimenting, intensifying, integrating, and bonding.[11]

INITIATING.   During the first stage of relationship development, we make conscious and unconscious judgments about others. Although we are cautious at this stage, we have usually sized up the other person within 15 seconds. David entered a singles' bar and scanned the room for prospective dancing partners. He stereotyped and classified available women according to personal preferences. After narrowing the field to two women, David determined his approach strategies. Finally, he began a conversation by asking, "Would you like a drink?" "Are you waiting for someone?" "You look like you need company," or "It was nice of you to save me this seat." Sometimes we *initiate* communication nonverbally. In the same situation, the girl at the bar could easily signal for David to leave by looking away, turning her back to him, or moving to another stool.

EXPERIMENTING.   After making initial contact, we begin *experimenting* with the unknown. This stage is known as the "do you know" period of interaction. Most relationships do not develop beyond this superficial point. We all can remember situations in which we used small talk to establish a friendly atmosphere. For example, after being introduced to her blind date, Renee attempts to find common interests by asking about Tom's major, family, favorite bars, job, and so on. Renee may not even be interested, but she asks questions to make the situation more comfortable. If initial interaction goes well, each person probes to determine whether pursuing the relationship is worthwhile.

---

[11]M. L. Knapp, *Interpersonal Communication and Human Relationships* (Boston: Allyn & Bacon, 1984).

INTENSIFYING. As relationships develop into friendships, participation and awareness are *intensified.* Gradually, steps are taken to strengthen the bond by asking for and reciprocating favors. Through self-disclosure and trust, the two personalities begin to blend. Statements such as "I've never told anyone this . . ." or "There is something you need to know: I was arrested when I was eighteen . . ." become more common. The verbal relationship usually changes, with the couple using nicknames, pet names, and slang. More time is spent sharing expectations, assumptions, and experiences. Nonverbal behaviors begin to communicate just as effectively as verbal ones. As a relationship intensifies, you notice mutual winks, nods, touches, and so on.

INTEGRATING. At the *integrating* point in relationship development, we agree to meet the expectations of the other person. Two people begin to share many commonalities, such as interests, attitudes, friends, and property. At this stage they do not completely lose their identity; however, there is a need to please the other person by giving in to his or her way of life. Not only do the individuals treat each other differently, but the two are now seen as a unit. In a dating relationship, Jim and Candy would tend to dress for each other. Jim is interested in racquetball, so Candy joins a beginning racquetball class. Candy collects antiques, and to help, Jim subscribes to the magazine *Treasures in Your Attic.* When friends have parties, Jim and Candy are invited together rather than individually.

BONDING. In the final stage of relationship development, serious commitments and sacrifices are made. In today's society, "commitment" involves marriage or a verbal commitment to live together. Sacrifices usually include a willingness to help with even the most difficult of personal problems and to give gifts or favors that require a substantial expenditure of time, money, and energy. The *bonding* of any relationship can become a powerful force in making the relationship better or worse. Marriage is the most accepted form of commitment and usually gains social and institutional support. However, the couple also usually has to agree to the rules and regulations of the contract. In many relationships, lasting commitment is seen as possible only in marriage. For this reason, many couples end up either splitting or getting married after years of dating. Trial bonding is also used at this stage. After living together secretly for two years, Bill and Amy decided to make their commitment legal by getting married.

Phases of Relationship Disintegration

As we all have experienced at one time or another, even our closest friends may go their separate ways over trivial matters, and many job changes are the result of negative interpersonal relationships rather than job dissatisfaction. Just as with relationship development, relationship disintegration may take years—or it can take a few seconds. After their children were married, David and Betty found that they had nothing left in common after 36 years

In interpersonal communication, participants strengthen themselves and each other through the sharing of meanings and emotions.

of marriage. Tom and Sam, identical twin brothers, never spoke to each other again after Tom saw Sam with his girlfriend, Lynne.

Thus far we have examined five patterns of relationship development. We will now look at patterns of disintegration. The five phases of relational disintegration are differentiating, circumscribing, stagnating, avoiding, and terminating.

DIFFERENTIATING.   Integration in a relationship signifies a union, and *differentiating* signifies a separation. Differences occur at every stage of relationship development, but with differentiating there is increased interpersonal distance. At this stage, differences become more and more apparent. The partners usually begin to want freedom and individuality. Both parties begin to play games that test the relationship and the other person's involvement. After Bob and Kathy had been dating for seven years, friends and relatives expected them to get married. During the last few years, however, the couple began experiencing different lifestyles, and they began to want different things out of life. At one time each knew what the other person wanted, but now they weren't so sure.

CIRCUMSCRIBING.   When relationships begin to disintegrate, there is less communication. Topics of conversation are controlled or **circumscribed** to reduce conflict and tension. On the surface everything appears to be all right, but underlying difficulties are evident. The presence of others increases interaction, and socially the relationship seems unaltered. Sally wondered, after having so much fun at her friend's party, why she and Chip sat in silence all the way home. At this stage of disintegration, there also tends to be less expression of commitment verbally and nonverbally. Affection is given only occasionally, and loving remarks are almost nonexistent.

STAGNATING.   During the *stagnating* stage, all efforts to communicate are abandoned. The interpersonal atmosphere is cold. Nonverbal messages are often the only feeling states expressed. As Jane got home from her dance recital, she was met with a cold stare from her husband. We wonder why individuals would continue a relationship that is so unrewarding. Many people stay in relationships because they want to punish the other person, they hope for reconciliation, or they want to avoid the pain of ending the relationship. Sandy was afraid she could not pay the rent on her own, so she continued to live with Angela, even though doing so was like having two roommates because Angela was living with Ron.

AVOIDING.   At this stage, one or both parties act as though the other person does not exist. Each person tries to find ways to *avoid* interaction. Meetings are often arranged so that there is someone else around, or excuses are made for not being able to be with the other person alone. Toward the end of this stage, one or both people seek a permanent state of separation. Linda called John on the phone because they had not communicated in two weeks. She said, "John, we need to talk this thing through. Can we get together this weekend? How about Monday? Do you have a test on Tuesday? Okay, then you tell me the next time that you are free, and I will change my plans."

TERMINATING. The *termination* of a relationship can be immediate or delayed. A friend may die of a heart attack, a marriage may dissolve because of an affair, or your company may transfer you to another city. Termination is dependent upon the type of relationship, perceived status of the relationship, effects of dissociation, and timing. As with relationship development, the final stage of relationship disintegration can occur suddenly with heated words over a poker game, or slowly and unobtrusively by failing to make plans to get together. Methods of termination are usually dependent upon future goals and expectations.

The stages of relationship development and disintegration can occur in the order in which we have just presented them, or they can start at any phase of development. In a crowded bar, a fight might end a relationship that was a minute old. If a person breaks into a movie theater ticket line, you quickly make a judgment and decide to avoid this person.

MANAGING INTERPERSONAL RELATIONSHIPS

To this point, we have emphasized the processes involved in interpersonal communication. In this section, we turn our attention to the people involved and how we may best "manage" interpersonal relationships.

Types of Relationships

Just as individuals are emotionally healthy and productive, or sick and ineffective, so too are interpersonal relationships. Manipulative involvements are a prime example. In such relationships, one or both members try to satisfy psychological needs by smothering the individuality or potential of the other. In manipulative relationships based on dependency, for example, one or both partners may be so "addicted" to the other that he or she drops all outside interests, activities, and friends. Just as the single-minded pursuit of a drug addict destroys his or her life, so can the dependency relationship destroy self-identity, self-respect, and all chances for growth and development. Many marriages suffer from these manipulative tendencies. Conversely, other marriages fail for the opposite reason: lack of involvement. When no effort is made to maintain a marriage, the relationship becomes boring and stale. Such marriages stifle personal growth and self-realization.

The ideal marriage, or any interpersonal relationship, is based on growth facilitation. The individuals involved are united but do not lose their identities. Through their shared communication, they achieve growth that they would not have reached on their own. In short, the whole exceeds the sum of its parts. The couple becomes not two separate individuals but a pair—more sensitive, loving, and stable than they had been before.

Levels of Social Interaction

Depending on the type of interpersonal relationship, different forms of communication or social interaction will take place.

ALTERNATING MONOLOGUE. The least productive and least fulfilling kind of communication, often seen in manipulative relationships, is the *alternating monologue.* Each individual knows that the other is speaking but does not listen openly to what is being said. Each person is so preoccupied with his or her own concerns that there is no sharing or understanding of ideas. The end of one statement merely signals the beginning of an unrelated reply:

Bob: You wouldn't believe what I had to do at work today.
Grace: Oh, yes. Tonight I have to go over to school and take that exam.
Bob: I almost quit, I was so angry at the boss.
Grace: I cannot believe how hard I've studied for this test.
Bob: Maybe I'll quit—get away from it all and have some fun.
Grace: Hey, now you're talking. Have some fun. That's what I'll do tonight after the exam.

STIMULUS–RESPONSE INTERACTION. *Stimulus-response interactions* are no better. In these interactions, the speaker proceeds in a set manner, independent of any responses the listener may make. The librarian who requests information to issue a card or the salesman who wants to know what size hiking boots you wear is participating in this type of interaction. They already know what questions to ask, and the responses do not change them.

INTERACTION WITH FEEDBACK. Alternating monologues and stimulus-response interaction are alike in their neglect of feedback. *Interactions with feedback* are more common and more productive. For example, a political canvasser bases his comments on the responses he gets from the voter.

Scenario 1:
Canvasser: Excuse me, are you going to vote for Raymond Charles?
Voter: That socialist? No way would he have my vote!
Canvasser: Perhaps you received some wrong information about our candidate. Let me tell you a little about him.

or

Empathy means sharing others' joy and pain.

Scenario 2:

Canvasser: Excuse me, are you going to vote for Raymond Charles?

Voter: I don't know. But I do know I don't want to be pestered.

Canvasser: Excuse me. I'll just leave this information with you, so you can read it at your leisure.

Even in these feedback situations, responses may be based as much on habit or learning as on interpersonal factors. Because the canvasser has had many similar experiences in the past, his answers may be automatic, requiring no feedforward or feedback.

INTERACTION WITH EMPATHY. The most productive form of communication is ***interaction with empathy.*** Empathy means deep understanding of other people, identifying with their thoughts, feeling their pain, sharing their joy. Such empathy is typical of strong, healthy relationships. Indeed, empathic communicators know each other so well that they can predict the responses to their messages. For example, Mario says to himself, "I know if I tell May that I'm not crazy about her new dress, she'll be hurt. So instead I'll say, 'May, that dress looks great on you, but I think the green one is even more becoming.'" This illustrates the special feedforward that empathy can produce.

Managing Interpersonal Conflict

People who care about each other will get angry, but their intimacy should ensure healthy, productive conflict and the use of words, not to hurt, but to find out what is bothering each person. Then, bottled-up tensions can be released.

There is a big difference between this type of arguing and the destructive variety. Whereas healthy conflict stresses the facts, destructive conflict aims for the ego, with statements such as "You're ridiculous," and "Me? You should see yourself." The goal of an argument should be **conflict management,** not character defamation. Better to say, "I hate what you said," than "I hate you because you said it."

Gamble and Gamble propose six principles for managing interpersonal conflicts effectively and efficiently.

1. *Recognize that conflicts can be settled rationally.* A conflict has a better chance of being resolved if you do not pretend it doesn't exist, withdraw from discussing it, surrender to the other person, try to create distractions, find fault or lay blame, or attempt to force the other person to take your view.
2. *Define the conflict.* Ask yourself: Why are we in conflict? What is the nature of the conflict? Which of us feels more strongly about the issue? Then try to figure out a way that all can "win."

Successful conflict management aims at facts—not egos.

3. *Check your perceptions.* Perceptual distortions of the other person's behavior, position, or motivations can take place. At this time, attempt to determine whether you understand one another.

4. *Suggest possible solutions.* The goal at this stage is to put your heads together and come up with a variety of solutions. However, neither you nor the other person(s) should evaluate or condemn the suggested solutions at this time.

5. *Assess the alternative solutions and choose the best one.* Determine which solutions will let one party "win" at the other's expense, which solutions would allow both parties to lose, and which solutions let both parties win. Then choose the one that allows both people to win.

6. *Try out the solution and evaluate it.* Determine to what extent the selected solution is working or not working. Then make appropriate alternations in the plan.[12]

As you can see, interpersonal conflict can be managed successfully. However, doing so means taking the time and expending the necessary energy to talk through the conflict. We hope that the steps that Gamble and Gamble have listed will help you to be a more effective communicator. In addition, we hope that this chapter has provided you with the necessary "ammunition" to more effectively communicate in your interpersonal relationships.

---

[12]T. K. Gamble and M. Gamble, *Contacts: Communicating Interpersonally* (New York: Random House, 1982), 322–28.

SUMMARY

Interpersonal communication is the sharing of feelings and ideas with other people. Most interpersonal messages are informal exchanges in dyads—that is, between two people in close contact. The potential for sending, receiving, and evaluating messages is shared between the members of the dyad. The purpose of their communication usually focuses on the sharing of meaning as well.

Three specific theories of interpersonal communication can help us better understand the complexities of interpersonal communication. Functional communication theory addresses the functions of interpersonal communication, while relational communication theory focuses on three specific dimensions of interpersonal relationships. These dimensions are control, trust, and intimacy. Finally, the coordinated management of meaning theory focuses on meanings in interpersonal communication, as well as on the concept of coordination.

Skills related to self-disclosure, trust, feedback and feedforward, nonverbal communication, and interpersonal attraction combine to determine how successfully meaning will be conveyed in such dyadic communications.

Another important topic in the study of interpersonal communication concerns the phases of relationship development. Of the ten stages, initiating, experimenting, intensifying, integrating, and bonding represent the growth in relationships. The five phases of relationship disintegration are differentiating, circumscribing, stagnating, avoiding, and terminating.

Managing interpersonal relationships involves a number of factors. For example, the people involved often bring personality and environmental factors into the interpersonal setting. The variables also influence the success or failure of the communication process. For example, individuals with manipulative needs often destroy opportunities for communication that might aid personal growth and development of friends and associates.

Similarly, certain types of messages also limit effective social interaction. For instance, both alternating monologues, in which the speakers seem not to hear each other, and stimulus-response interactions, in which the speakers' set messages are unaffected by their listeners' replies, hinder effective communication. In contrast, interactions characterized by feedback and empathy build strong, healthy relationships.

Finally, managing relationships necessarily involves the management of conflict. Six principles that can help with this often difficult aspect of relationship management are the following: (1) Recognize that conflicts can be settled rationally; (2) define the conflict; (3) check your perceptions; (4) suggest possible solutions; (5) assess alternative solutions and choose the best one; and (6) try out the solution and evaluate it.

EXERCISES

Group Experiences

Positive-Negative

DESCRIPTION: One aspect of interpersonal attraction is the extent to which another person shares your attitudes and beliefs. Simply stated, we are more attracted to people who share our attitudes than to those who do not. Consider some of the relationships you have had with others. Relationships that you remember as positive probably were ones in which your ideas were readily and willingly accepted or at least supported. When you have a falling out with another person, you may both have reevaluated each other and may consider the attitudes of the other person to be strange. Because nobody wants to be considered strange, you leave the situation. The purpose of this activity is to magnify the emotional feelings a person has when his or her ideas are positively and negatively reinforced.

PROCEDURE: Divide into groups of four to six persons. Choose one person as the subject. Select a controversial topic of discussion or a topic that requires preparation (such as planning a picnic). During your discussion, accept and support all ideas suggested by the subject on the topic. Listen carefully to everything he or she has to say. After five minutes, select another subject. Then for the next five minutes, reject all comments presented by the second subject. Avoid listening. Let the subject know that you consider his or her beliefs to be strange, wrong, and worthless. The final part of this activity is a report from the subjects about the emotional states they experienced during the activity. The subjects should indicate how much they liked other group members, along with their reasons for liking or disliking them.

DISCUSSION: Most people surround themselves with people who agree with and reinforce their ideas. Let's face it—people who like us can't be all bad! The two subjects most likely had very different feelings about the group. Creating the actual emotional condition that you would feel in a real-life situation was probably difficult, because in the back of everyone's head is a little voice saying, "It's just an activity." However, the next time you are in a group that evaluates you either positively or negatively, watch your emotional state. Do you tend to gravitate more toward people who like you?

Mr. and Ms. Wonderful

DESCRIPTION: Everyone has varying opinions as to what they regard as attractive. During different periods of time, being pleasantly plump was "in" and looking like Twiggy was definitely "out." In fact, history records periods of time when women were sent to "fattening schools" to prepare for marriage. Today everyone runs to a spa to lose those extra ten to 15 pounds. Even within a given period and culture, people simply have different ideas about beauty. This activity will provide you with the opportunity to identify what characteristics of attraction you want in your Mr. or Ms. Wonderful.

PROCEDURE: Now is your chance to become an author and to write a heartrending description of an attractive person at a cocktail party. The scene is set. You, the author, are watching this person from afar. Your attraction is immense, and you watch his or her every move. Write a paragraph describing those physical characteristics that are so magnetic to you. Be adventurous, and use the following lines as an example:

> I couldn't keep my eyes off his amber-colored hair as it fell feathered from his face. His deep brown eyes were penetrating, and I imagined that they were looking directly at me. I liked the way he moved—with assurance and yet lightness.

The preceding paragraph is just a beginning. Be creative and write about the physical characteristics you would find attractive in another person. Share your descriptions of Mr. or Ms. Wonderful with others in the class. Read them out loud with the same emotion you used in writing the paragraph.

DISCUSSION: You probably found some of the paragraphs funny—maybe even ridiculous; the question is, "Would you have been attracted to the same characteristics others wrote about?" Discuss the sayings, "Beauty is in the eye of the beholder," and "Love is blind." Are they true? Do you ever see couples that you think are physically mismatched? The final question to consider is this: "What do you really want in a Mr. or Ms. Wonderful?"

Personal Experiences

1. Make a list of three people whom you like and three people whom you dislike. Consider each person separately and determine how they respond to you. Are they enthusiastic about your ideas? Do they share similar attitudes and beliefs with you? After you have answered these questions, reflect on this one. Do you tend to like people who positively reinforce you, and dislike those who negatively reinforce you?

2. Using Knapp's ten phases of relational growth, chart the growth and decline of some relationship that you were a part of in the past. Then compare it with a chart of some relationship in which you are currently involved. How are the two relationships alike? How are they different? What factors affected the former relationship? How can you avoid those events in your current relationship? Does "knowing" the phases of growth and decline help in any way? If so, how?

3. Make a list of communication strategies that you can use to make your interpersonal communication more effective. Which suggestions do you find easy or difficult to practice? How can you be more aware of the communication strategies that you use each day? How can you learn to practice effective strategies more consistently? How can you learn to avoid detrimental communication strategies?

Discussion Questions

1. What role do quarrels or arguments play in an interpersonal relationship?

2. How can theories of interpersonal communication help you in your day-to-day activities?

3. Explain how phases of development and disintegration evolve in interpersonal relationships.
4. What methods can be used to manage interpersonal conflict?

Small Group Communication

KEY CONCEPTS AND TERMS

Group
Small group
Primary group
Discussion group
Private or closed discussion group
Open or public discussion
Panel
Symposium
Forum
Problem-solving group
Fact-finding group
Evaluation group
Policymaking group
Quality circle
Bypassing
Functional role
Task-oriented role

Maintenance role
Self-serving role
Leadership
Leader
Democratic leader
Authoritarian leader
Laissez-faire leader
Cohesion
Intergroup conflict
Intragroup conflict
Conformity
Circle network
Wheel network
Y network
Chain network
All-channel network

Four of the five members of the planning committee had met three times when they heard the exasperating news. Trent, who had been appointed by the vice-president to attend the sessions, had yet to show up for the meetings. Now, as he stood scowling at the front of the room where Sam, Donna, Jennifer, and Doug were meeting, he informed them that their work must take a major turn. As he gave the committee this directive, he tossed each of them a document that was at least an inch thick. If only they had received the information inside the report a month ago, their efforts would have been rewarded. Now they would have to begin the process all over again.

Problem-solving groups, such as the one described above, are common in American businesses and corporations. They may meet to discuss such issues as marketing strategies, team product/service development, or how to crack the international marketplace. However, as you have seen in the previous illustration, each member of the group must pull his or her own weight if the group is to function effectively. Additionally, the group must be able to depend on each member to play the roles they have agreed to play.

In the following pages you will learn a number of communication principles that will aid you during small group interactions. Following a brief overview, we will discuss some distinctions between small and large groups and the outcomes that will generally accrue from each. We also will address several types of small groups and their purposes and functions. Once we have made these distinctions, we will provide you with basic ammunition that will help you participate more effectively in group interactions. We also will provide you with the tools to become a more effective small group leader and to optimize your contributions to the problem-solving process. From there, we will examine several factors that affect group outcomes and performance, such as personality, cohesion, and conflict. We will conclude by instructing you in the art of analyzing group interaction.

SMALL GROUP COMMUNICATION: AN OVERVIEW

Think for a moment about all the different groups to which you belong, whether they be social, political, family, academic, religious, vocational, or special interest groups. It is virtually impossible to exist independently of all groups. Researchers have estimated that the average person is a member of five or six groups at any one time and that the total number of small groups may be around 4 billion or 5 billion.

The existence of groups is a basic part of the democratic process. In a society such as ours, the group process plays a significant role in proposing and reviewing the laws that govern our land. The government does much of its work through various committees and subcommittees, which study and propose legislation. In addition, civic groups meet regularly to comment on the actions of government and ensure that the voice of the people will be heard. These groups protect the rights of the individual citizen.

The democratic aspect of the group goes beyond politics, however. The family that jointly decides where to go for winter vacation, the union members who meet to discuss contract demands, the student-faculty committee that determines college requirements and the consumer group that organizes a protest against dangerous toys are all participating in the democratic process on some level.

There are many different types of groups to which you can belong, and many benefits to be gained from participation in and observation of group behavior. Participation in certain groups can lead to increased personal rewards, which include change and growth in personality, self-concept, and behavior. Well-known groups such as Weight Watchers, Alcoholics Anonymous, and Smoke Enders are self-help groups that enable people to overcome undesirable habits. As a result of interpersonal interactions, group members derive strength and support from others who are working toward the same goals. Different groups develop as different needs are expressed. Some groups such as group therapy can contribute to the emotional well-being of the participants. Others may serve social as well as psychological needs.

Participation in groups can also result in professional rewards. A person's ability is often measured by how effectively he or she functions in a small group. A student who participates in student government may be asked to head a campus committee; the parent who functions effectively in a parent-teacher group may be encouraged to run for the school board; or the president of a local chapter of a charity organization may move up to head a regional division.

On a practical level, the study of group processes can help you function more effectively in the different groups to which you belong. For example, if you are aware of the various factors that can be barriers to decision making, you may be able to help your club, committee, or organization overcome them.

I know of no safe depository of the ultimate powers of society but the people themselves.

THOMAS JEFFERSON

DEFINITIONS

The Group

Before discussing the group process, we must decide what we mean by the term *group*. A **group** is any number of people who have a common goal, interact with one another to accomplish their goal, recognize one another's existence, and see themselves as part of a group. To test our definition, let's consider an example: people in line outside a movie theater. Is this a group? Certainly these people have a common goal; they are all waiting to see a particular film. But these people need not interact with one another to accomplish this goal, although each may be very aware of the presence of the others in line. Now, if someone were to try to sneak in at the front of the line and the people made a unified effort to keep the crasher out, we could say that during that period of time the random collection of people became a group. Looking at our definition, the unified effort to block the line crasher would call for group interaction and awareness of others.

The Small Group

Our main concern in this chapter is the small group. A **small group** is three or more people interacting face to face, with or without an assigned leader, in such a way that each person influences, and is influenced by, every other person in the group.

The small group may vary in size, but researchers generally agree that the best size is somewhere between five and seven members.

Certain generalizations can be made about small and large groups. For instance, small groups tend to be more informal and less structured, while larger groups may have to adopt formal rules to keep order. A small group can function effectively without a designated leader, but a large group may need a leader to maintain order and make sure the group performs efficiently. Theoretically, an increase in size increases the group's resource pool, since more people mean more information, ideas, and opinions. However, the larger the group, the less chance there is for individual participation and the greater the tendency for dominant or aggressive individuals to monopolize the discussion. This type of behavior causes the shy or less verbal person to withdraw from the interaction and feel a sense of frustration. After the large group has functioned for some time, a number of cliques tend to develop, which often hinders the group effort. Therefore, as the group becomes larger, there is greater difficulty in accomplishing a particular task.

SOME SMALL GROUPS AND THEIR FUNCTIONS

The two major types of small groups are primary groups and discussion groups.

The Primary Group

The **primary group,** or *psyche group*, functions as a support system for its members. Neighbors who get together daily, friends with whom you go to the movies once or twice a month, and the coffee klatch at work are all groups that usually enjoy conversation rather than discussion. Conversation is much more loosely structured than discussion and covers a variety of topics without a particular objective in mind. It is neither unusual nor particularly harmful for one member of a primary group to occasionally dominate the conversation. In a discussion group, in which members have a common objective, however, maintaining a balance between speaking and listening activity is essential. Such "rules" are alien to the primary group, which is generally social and tends to be quite informal.

The Discussion Group

In addition to the formality of discussion groups, a **discussion group** is characterized by the following:

1. *Face-to-face interaction.* A discussion cannot take place if group members do not respond, react, and adapt to the communication of other participants. The interaction must be continuous and flow from within the group. If the people merely state preconceived ideas in isolation, apart from the interaction, fruitful discussion cannot take place.
2. *Leadership.* Generally, a discussion group is characterized by the presence of one or more leaders. Although many small group experts insist that a designated leader must be present for a group to function effectively, our definition acknowledges the presence of leadership potential, or those instances in which one or more people assume leadership duties.
3. *Shared characteristics.* Discussion groups are distinguished from a "small aggregate" of people by the presence of a common characteristic. This common characteristic may range from similar religious beliefs to similar ethnic background, race, geographic location, social class, economic level, lifestyle, educational level, etc. A common characteristic may be assigned, assumed, or self-identified; however, as a rule, it does exist.
4. *Common purpose.* Ultimately, a common purpose or goal is the binding force of a discussion group, whether that goal is specific or broad in scope. Groups that are formed with no concrete goal in mind generally disband or disintegrate. Goal-directed behavior holds groups together. The more relevant the goal is, the more motivation that group members will have to maintain the group and their identification with it.[1]

Discussion groups can be either private or public. **Private** or **closed discussion groups** are those in which no audience listens or participates in the discussion. An executive council or a cabinet meeting is an example of a private discussion. An **open** or **public discussion** takes place before an audience. Open discussions may take the form of a **panel,** in which a group of well-informed people exchanges ideas before an audience. A group of doctors,

---

[1] L. L. Barker, K. J. Wahlers, K. W. Watson, and R. J. Kibler, *Groups in Process: An Introduction to Small Group Communication,* 3d ed. (Englewood Cliffs, N.J.: Prentice Hall, 1987), 43–44.

psychologists, and sociologists speaking about the effects of cocaine before a college audience would represent a panel discussion. Similar to the panel is a *symposium,* which is made up of experts who present their views one at a time. Five physicians who are talking to an audience of colleagues about progress in the field of organ transplants constitute a symposium. If the audience mentioned in these two examples were to actively participate in the discussion, the group would then be called a *forum.*

THE PROBLEM-SOLVING GROUP.   One of the most important kinds of discussion groups, the *problem-solving group,* is usually private. The most basic of these groups is the *fact-finding group,* whose purpose is to gather information about a particular issue or problem. This task usually requires considerable research. The information collected by the group may then serve as the basis for future policy discussions. One example of a fact-finding group is a committee of university students who volunteered to study the circumstances that led to the closing of their library on weekends and evenings. The university cited lack of funds as the reason for reducing hours. The student group found out how much money was distributed throughout the school and where possible sources of relief money might be located. Government officials often appoint fact-finding committees to investigate particular incidents or problems. For example, after a number of schools report a sharp increase in vandalism, a commission might be established to investigate the situation.

A group whose task stems directly from the fact-finding group is the *evaluation group.* This type of group uses the information that has been made available through investigation to determine the scope of a particular problem and the priorities in finding a solution. The group will then make recommendations to those who carry out policy. An example of an evaluation group would be a team of efficiency experts who are asked to make suggestions on how a factory's production might be increased while its costs are minimized. After an evaluation group offers its recommendations, the *policymaking group* may make particular changes or take certain actions. Sound policymaking must be based on fact finding and evaluation.

We have described the various kinds of problem-solving groups as though they operate in a sequence but separately from one another. This is not always the case. Any task group can perform any or all of these functions. Generally, the group involved in policymaking goes through the fact-finding and evaluation stages to ensure a carefully considered decision.

One example of a task group that systematically performs any or all of these functions is a quality circle. *Quality circles* are groups of three to ten people who meet periodically to suggest ways of improving work life, increasing employee commitment, implementing suggested changes, and building attitudes geared toward problem prevention.[2] As such, their

---

[2]B. H. Steele, P. Rue, L. Clement, and K. Zamostny, "Quality Circles: A Corporate Strategy Applied in a Student Services Setting," *Journal of College Student Personnel*, 28, no. 2 (March 1987), 146.

emphasis is on identifying and analyzing problems in an organization and on creating innovative solutions to those problems. Quality circles are one of the most popular management practices to emerge from Japan. They first surfaced in the United States during the 1980s.

PARTICIPATING IN SMALL GROUPS

Responsibilities

If a small group is going to function successfully, certain attitudes, actions, and behaviors of its members are important. Your first responsibility as a group participant is to keep an open mind toward the issue or problem as well as toward the other members of the group. You should try to remain objective during the course of the discussion and evaluate information and ideas independently. This means being aware of personal biases to make sure that they do not interfere with a willingness to listen to the ideas of others.

Showing sensitivity to the moods of others and the emotional tone of the group is also important. Sometimes what people say and mean are two different things. If you are sensitive to this fact, you may be able to "read" them more effectively. A different tone of voice, change in posture or body position, and other nonverbal cues may reinforce or contradict what group members are verbally communicating.

Individual members have an obligation to make sure that everyone participates in the group process. For example, a newcomer to the group may feel somewhat intimidated by the other members, particularly if they all know one another and have worked together for a long time. As a sensitive group member, you should try to make a new person feel at ease and draw him or her into the discussion.

Participation in a group often requires preparation or homework. Sometimes the group may agree to think about a problem or complete research on a particular subject before the next meeting. Following through on such assignments is essential. If not, time will be wasted, and those who have done their work will be frustrated and annoyed. For example, when the social committee of an organization was planning its Christmas party, each member of the committee was supposed to investigate the prices of different restaurants or catering halls. When only three of the seven members came prepared, the group's work was set back at least a week. As part of a group, you have an obligation to other people as well as to yourself.

Communicating

SPEAKING.   Because the group process depends on interaction among members, you must communicate your ideas and opinions as accurately and concisely as you can. Here are some ways to increase the effectiveness of your communication as a group member.

Effective small group communication involves speaking and listening.

1. If you find yourself mumbling or rambling, you may be saying something that is unimportant. Avoid speaking unless you have something to contribute.

2. Address your comments to the group as a whole. Involving everyone is essential to group success.

3. Organize your remarks whenever possible. Although group interaction is spontaneous by nature, you can prepare the information you are presenting before you arrive.

4. Relate your ideas or opinions to what others have said. Make connections clear whenever possible.

5. State only one point at a time so that the group can digest what you have said. Doing so will keep the discussion on track and allow the group to respond to individual points.

6. Ensure that everyone understands your comments by speaking clearly and using language to which the group can relate.

LISTENING AND FEEDBACK.   As a group member, you must be both a speaker and a listener. Listening effectively is as important as speaking effectively. Jimmy Celano and Jeff Salzman, founders of CareerTrack, one of America's top business seminar companies, suggest the following guidelines for "listening aggressively" in dyads or groups.

1. *Consciously concentrate.* When you enter a situation in which you know you will have to listen, put yourself into a "tuned-in" mode. "Bear down, suppress other thoughts, and focus."

2. *Visibly respond to the speaker.* Act interested, maintain eye contact, and demonstrate your interest verbally or nonverbally. The speaker will be far more likely to tell you what you need to know.

3. *Don't talk while you are listening.* This is like talking with your mouth full: highly rude. There's a difference between listening and waiting for your turn to talk.

4. *Create informal situations.* Formal communication settings can paralyze shy or less confident individuals. In informal settings, people will generally open up and reveal their true personalities.

5. *Avoid filtering out the negative.* When the news is good, we are "all ears"; when it's bad, we often tune out entirely. Effective listeners try to tune in during either situation.

6. *Sum up.* When you are listening for the purpose of understanding, paraphrase what's been said once the speaker comes to a natural pause. This will help to crystallize ideas, aid memory, and allow the speaker to clarify miscommunications.

7. *Interrogate—politely.* Asking questions will allow the speaker to know that you are serious about the information that he or she is sharing. Doing so may also help a shy speaker to feel more important and confident.

8. *Take notes, but not too many.* Listening and writing simultaneously may be difficult but is essential in the business world. To avoid missing what's being said, be selective. Write down key words, phrases, and statistics.

9. *Refuse to listen when a speaker is talking over your head or is incoherent.* Calculate the value of listening versus the consequences of not listening, and act accordingly.

10. *Avoid killing the messenger.* Whenever you hear bad news, avoid flying off the handle at the person who is delivering it. People will be less likely to cover up problems, and you will be able to keep abreast of the information needed to do your job. Welcome and reward the delivery of bad news—it's just as valuable as good news.

11. *Get to yes or no when you need a quick answer without the details.* If a quick response is impossible, use a "speeder-upper" such as, "Is it mostly yes or mostly no?" "Give me a headline," or, "In 25 words or less, what is your opinion?"

12. *Listen to more than just the words.* Research indicates that 93 percent of a speaker's message is communicated nonverbally. When listening during a discussion or problem-solving session, consider the speaker's facial expressions, eye behavior, posture, and gestures for what's really being said.[3]

---

[3]Adapted from J. Celano and J. Salzman, "Listen Aggressively," in *CareerTracking: 26 Success Shortcuts to the Top* (New York: Simon & Schuster, 1988), 111–18.

Sometimes, even though people try to listen carefully, a certain amount of misunderstanding takes place. Sending feedback is one way to help reduce such misunderstanding, and, as Celano and Salzman suggest, questions can be a valuable form of feedback. Actually, the use of questions can improve communication throughout the group process. At the outset, it helps for members to ask questions relating to the goals and objectives of the group as a whole as well as to the purpose of any particular meeting. Once these goals are established, questions about procedures should be asked. Even when conclusions have been reached, carefully thought-out questions can often refine these decisions to a considerable degree.

BYPASSING.   A variety of questions can overcome barriers to communication in small groups. One such barrier is called *bypassing,* a situation in which people are actually talking past each other. In such a situation people argue or reach an impasse when, in fact, they are in agreement.

A major cause of bypassing is ambiguity or vagueness on the part of some group members. Questions relating to interpretation or calling for explanation can help bring out the intended meaning. On the other hand, sometimes a person will use stigma words or phrases, such as "indecent" or "foaming-at-the-mouth radical," that are emotionally loaded. The person who uses this type of vocabulary is trying to provoke the rest of the group and cause conflict. Without accusing or intimidating the member who uses such language, other members should be quick to ask for clarification.

Norms

Over a period of time, small groups develop a set of norms, rules, and expectations that are unique to that group, based on the interactions among its members. According to small groups researcher Daniel Feldman, these norms are developed and enforced for four major reasons.[4] First, such norms are established in order to facilitate the group's survival. More specifically, they help to protect the group from outside interference. Second, group norms are developed and enforced for four major reasons: (1) to facilitate the group's survival; (2) to make more predictable the behaviors expected of group members; (3) to help the group avoid embarrassing interpersonal problems; and (4) to express the central values of the group and clarify aspects of the group's identity that are distinctive.

Norms can help to facilitate survival and protect the group from outside interferences. For example, consider a group of "little sisters," who are tapped each fall semester by many fraternities across the country. "Little sisters" in every fraternity develop a set of norms that are unique to the group. These norms will vary from fraternity to fraternity. For example, at one fraternity, "little sisters" may be known for their practical jokes, while at another, they may be notorious for throwing great parties. Anyone who does not conform to these norms may be ostracized by the group. In this instance, cohesiveness is important to the group in order to maintain group tradition.

Norms also increase the chances that group members know what is expected of them. For example, when a group first convenes, confusion may exist regarding who will keep the minutes. Consequently, a norm may be established that alternates the task among individual group members from meeting to meeting.

Third, norms are likely to be developed if they help a group avoid embarrassing interpersonal problems. For instance, groups might enforce norms that prohibit the discussion of romantic topics during a meeting.

Finally, group norms are established if they express the central values of the group and clarify what is distinctive about them. Indeed, one need look no further than the Hell's Angels to understand this function of norms. Each year at Christmas, the Hell's Angels take gifts to children in hospitals across the country and, if possible, take them out and let them sit on their bikes. This norm serves to reflect one of the group's central values: the importance of sharing love and hope with America's sick and needy children. In this instance, the norm guides and justifies the group's activities as well as defines and legitimizes its power.

---

[4]D. C. Feldman, "The Development and Enforcement of Group Norms," *Academy of Management Review,* 9 (1984), 47–53.

Sometimes members are unaware that group norms even exist until there is some specific change in the group. For example, members of a weekly scheduling meeting never realized that they followed a particular seating arrangement until the group was short a chair at one session and the usual pattern was disrupted. Similarly, members of a parent-teacher group were thrown off when a new member addressed them by their first names, which was not their usual practice.

These two examples concern norms that are outside the group discussion process. Other norms actually govern the course of the discussion. For example, it was pointed out to members of an activities committee that during their weekly meetings Richard would always bring the discussion back on course if it seemed to stray, and Elsa would call for periodic summaries of what had been said. Although these behaviors were accepted norms, they were never realized by the group until they were pointed out.

Functional Roles

In the previous example, while neither Richard nor Elsa filled the official role of leader, each filled a leadership role. Role structure is one of the most important kinds of norm a group can develop. Sometimes a role is determined by a person's relative status or position. For example, a student representative on the college personnel and planning board might defer to the head of a department because of his or her position relative to the student's own. Yet, while position is influential, role structure develops from within the group, and any and all members of a group can fill a variety of different functional roles. **Functional roles** are those that keep the discussion on course and aid the group in accomplishing its objectives.

The functional roles that develop within a group can be divided into two major categories: **task-oriented roles** and **maintenance roles.**

TASK-ORIENTED ROLES.　These roles are directly related to the group's goal, whether that goal is to gather information, make recommendations, solve a problem, or complete a project. In our example concerning the activities committee, Richard kept the discussion on track, and Elsa asked for summaries. Both were filling task-oriented roles. These are only two of several task-oriented behaviors. A more complete list of such roles would include the following:

1. *Information or opinion giver:* In this role a group member provides content or well-considered opinions that will help the group move more smoothly toward the best decision. Richard, for example, knows of various fund-raising activities that have worked well on other campuses. As an information giver, he would be aware of the salience of this information and would share any ideas that might contribute to his group's needs and set criteria.
2. *Information or opinion seeker:* The group member who takes on this role is usually the person who perceives that the group needs additional

data. For example, John might ask, "Do we have information that reflects the amount of money that might be raised through each alternative?"

3. *Expediter:* The individual in this role helps the group stick to its agenda and often leads the group back on course when it goes off on a tangent. As the activities committee begins to digress to an irrelevant topic, Elsa might say, "But weren't we in the process of deciding what criteria need to be applied?"

4. *Idea person:* The idea person is an imaginative group member who thinks originally, comes up with several alternatives, and quite often contributes an idea that serves as a basis for the final decision. In order to promote the carnival as the best decision, Jim and Carla might begin a debate on the pros and cons of the carnival as the best alternative.

5. *Analyzer:* This role is played by the individual who is highly skilled in problem solving, who moves the group rapidly to the core of the problem, and who, at times, examines the reasoning behind each contribution to the discussion. The analyzer is recognized by statements such as, "O.K., so far we've managed to narrow our choices to a circus, a car wash, or an auction. But aren't we overlooking the potential of the raffle that Dave suggested?"[5]

MAINTENANCE ROLES. Task-oriented behavior is essential in getting work done, but a group can only be productive if there is interaction among its members. ***Maintenance roles*** are concerned with the feelings of individual members and the emotional behavior of the group. Maintenance roles include the following:

1. *Active listener:* This role is played by the person who recognizes the contributions of others and who responds with specific verbal or nonverbal reinforcement. A nod of the head, a smile, or a verbal, "Great idea," represent the responses of an active and participating listener.

2. *Game leader:* The game leader is the individual who recognizes when the process is becoming tedious, when fatigue is setting in, or when the discussion is getting out of hand and who has a timely and uncanny ability to create an appropriate joke, digression, or comment to improve the spirits of the group. As tension begins to mount over the decision to be made, Andy might suggest, "Why don't we just quietly break into teams, with each team representing a solution, and let the winners of a pillow fight make the decision?"

3. *Harmonizer:* The harmonizer is the group member who is both perceptive and empathetic and who is able to reduce or reconcile differences and misunderstandings. When Steve and Karen seem almost ready to come to blows over the choice of a fund-raising project,

---

[5]Adapted from R. F. Verderber, *Communicate,* 5th ed. (Belmont, Calif.: Wadsworth, 1987), 228–231.

A leader, designated or not, is anyone who helps a group achieve its goals.

Julia might suggest that the two discover areas of agreement, rather than disagreement, and begin from there.

4. *Gatekeeper:* Gatekeepers make sure that channels of communication are open and that everyone has a chance to enter the discussion. When Elaine notices that Alison is exceptionally quiet during a committee meeting, she might encourage Alison by asking her opinion.

5. *Compromiser:* During the course of a discussion in which two prominent positions emerge, it is often the compromiser who must act in order to make the decision. In cases such as this, when two decisions may work equally well, the compromiser may be spotted through statements such as: "How can we reconcile these differences so that we all can agree?" or "Rick, Andy, you both have good ideas, but if you look a little closer, you'll see some similarities between the two ideas."

6. *Public relations—the front person:* The front person is the person who possesses skills at interacting with outside groups and individuals and who is skilled in public speaking and interpersonal relations. Because the decision that any group makes will affect other people, such a person is vital to solution implementation. Once a fund-raising committee decides on the best way to raise funds, its public relations person's job begins.[6]

_____

[6]Ibid, 231–234.

SELF-SERVING ROLES. Maintenance roles are extremely important in maximizing group efficiency, but sometimes members adopt *self-serving roles* that are counterproductive. These roles have a negative effect on the group's emotional climate as well as its ability to reach goals. Self-serving roles include:

1. *Aggressor*—the person who works for his or her own ends by criticizing or blaming others when things get rough.
2. *Blocker*—the person who blocks ideas from group acceptance by going off on tangents or rejecting suggestions on a personal basis.
3. *Competer*—the person who competes with others to gain attention.
4. *Special pleader*—the individual who has his or her own pet ideas and who, regardless of the group, works to integrate those into whatever is done.
5. *Joker*—the member of the group whose behavior includes clowning, mimicking, and generally disrupting the group. While the game leader plays a positive role in the maintenance of the group, the joker is only out for attention.
6. *Withdrawer*—the person who refuses to contribute or to be a part of the group.
7. *Monopolizer*—the group member who feels the need to talk all the time.[7]

The different roles we have been discussing operate in almost all group situations. Awareness of task-oriented and maintenance roles can enable you to overcome self-serving behavior and accomplish the group goal in a positive manner.

THE DEVELOPMENT OF A SMALL GROUP

Although we have discussed the major roles that are a part of small group interactions, we do not want to suggest that effective small group communication takes place either easily or overnight. Every group has to spend both time and energy learning how to communicate and work together. As Giammatteo and Giammatteo have stated, "It takes time for members, each different, to learn how they can fit into the group and contribute best. Often things seem 'all mixed up,' and group members may quite naturally become disturbed and discouraged—even aggravated at each other."[8] To help people

---

[7]Ibid, 234.
[8]M. Giammatteo and D. Giammatteo, *Forces on Leadership* (Reston, Va.: National Association of Secondary School Principals, 1981), 28.

understand these natural "growing pains," these researchers have pinpointed the following descriptive stages in the development process of small group interaction:

1. *"Groping":* When the group is first finding out how to plan and work together, they may not all agree. They don't know and understand each other well enough to really trust the others, and they still have to determine each others' skills, knowledge, situation, and attitudes. They often feel uncomfortable and "lost."

2. *"Griping":* The members become discouraged when they can't seem to work together, when there isn't much progress, and when their attempts are frustrated. They say the wrong things, play negative roles, and block group action because they are uncomfortable. This stage requires more "self–other" understanding and remembering that, although everyone is different, we all want to do a good job and to be liked by others. Learning to understand why people are griping and finding ways to work things out are essential skills for survival during this stage.

3. *"Grasping":* Ideas and suggestions are beginning to fit. Members begin to agree and can start to see some direction to group activity. Everyone begins to feel more comfortable. Now they are getting somewhere.

4. *"Grouping":* Members are getting to know each other and can understand and enjoy how each person works and fits into the scheme. Group goals, task roles, and maintenance roles come into play, and a surge of enthusiasm spreads through the group.

5. *"Group Action":* Now the group is in full swing, with members playing constructive roles. Leadership is shared, and everyone is participating. While it was difficult at first, learning to work well together was worth the effort. They have shared in making plans and decisions, have learned together, and feel that this is a good group with which to work. They are busy making their group more democratic.[9]

Once a small group moves into the latter three stages, the members are ready to tackle more important tasks. At times they will return to some of the early stages, but each time the process will be less disturbing and more effective.

LEADERS AND LEADERSHIP

In the example we have been discussing, we commented that both Richard and Elsa were filling leadership roles when they kept the discussion on course and asked for periodic summaries. These task-oriented roles demon-

---

[9]Ibid., 29.

strated leadership on their part, although neither of them was designated as the leader of the group. In the study of group dynamics, **leadership** is any kind of behavior that helps the group toward its goals, and a **leader** is any person who influences the group in this way. Therefore, according to these definitions, Richard and Elsa not only exhibited leadership, but in doing so became leaders of their group.

Sometimes one or more members of a group become leaders by assuming leadership roles, even if someone else has been assigned or elected to that role. Actually, it is possible for a group to demonstrate effective leadership even when there is no official leader. While it is most desirable for a group to have a designated leader to get things started, it is also good for a group to have shared leadership. For example, it is difficult for the person who assumes several task-oriented roles to assume maintenance roles as well. Sometimes one or two people will see to it that the social and emotional atmosphere of the group remains conducive to the completion of the goal, while another person will assume responsibility for task-oriented behavior.

Think for a moment about the groups to which you belong and the leadership roles you play. Are you more comfortable when assuming task roles, or are you more at ease when exhibiting maintenance behaviors? If you have not recently had the chance to "test" your leadership abilities (or if you have and wonder how well you may have done), take a moment to complete the Leadership Assessment Questionnaire provided in Figure 7–1. This questionnaire will help you determine your "leadership quotient."

THEORETICAL APPROACHES

Operating under the assumption that leaders are born, not made, early investigators of leadership looked for traits or characteristics that distinguish leaders from nonleaders. As a result, many of the early studies focused on attributes of great leaders, such as George Washington and Winston Churchill. These studies revealed that some leaders score higher on measures of intelligence, scholarship, dependability, responsibility, social participation, and even socioeconomic status. However, researchers could not agree that all leaders have these traits, or even which traits are more important than others.

Dissatisfied with the trait approach to leadership, researchers turned their attention to behaviors that are associated with effective leaders. From this research, scholars learned that leadership ability is partially related to increased amount of information, flexibility in opinions and approaches to problems, active participation in problem solving, and low authoritarianism. Using this approach, investigators also learned that effective leaders seem to be less opinionated and more agreeable than nonleaders. However, this approach also had many critics. These critics argued that no leader is likely to use a single set of leadership behaviors and that, across leaders, no single behavioral style prevails.

FIGURE 7–1

Leadership Assessment Questionnaire

Leadership skills play a vital role in small group interaction and ultimately in your ability as an organizational or corporate manager. Primarily, leadership skills affect the way people perform and the results they achieve.

What kind of leader are you? The following questionnaire will help you to make an initial assessment.

1. Would you rather be
   (a) the spokesperson for a group?
   (b) the captain of a team?
   (c) the commander of an army?

2. Would you consult with subordinates before making important decisions that will affect their work?
   (a) Nearly always—I value their experience.
   (b) Sometimes—it depends on how much time I have.
   (c) Never—I believe a leader should lead.

3. Do you believe that people should be allowed to participate in setting objectives for a group or an organization?
   (a) Always—I feel it's vital to get their commitment.
   (b) Sometimes—usually for the less important goals.
   (c) Never—they would simply try to persuade me to accept lower standards.

4. What do you consider to be the main benefit of delegation?
   (a) Makes life easier for the leader.
   (b) Helps to develop individual abilities.
   (c) Allows the leader to concentrate on higher-level work.

5. How much authority would you delegate to subordinates? Would you prefer for them to
   (a) check with you first before making important decisions?
   (b) decide for themselves whether to consult you?
   (c) act first and tell you later?

6. A subordinate turns in an outstanding performance on an important assignment. Would you
   (a) congratulate him or her personally and right away?
   (b) say nothing in case he or she might ask for more money?
   (c) congratulate him or her if you happened to meet?

7. You have to announce a very important policy change to your group. Would you
   (a) issue a memo or general circular, enclosing a copy of the new policy?
   (b) brief one of your lieutenants and ask him or her to communicate with the rest of the group?
   (c) call a meeting and explain the changes personally?

8. A subordinate's general performance begins to deteriorate sharply. Would you
   (a) threaten him or her with tough action unless he or she improves quickly?
   (b) discuss the problem to discover the cause?
   (c) ask the personnel department to investigate?

9. A subordinate suggests a radical new idea—which you feel is unsound. Would you
   (a) point out its weaknesses and encourage him or her to try again?
   (b) tell him or her it's impractical, too costly, or not the right time?
   (c) promise to think about it and then file it?

10. One of your people is depressed after missing a promotion. Would you
   (a) tell him or her not to worry—everyone must expect an occasional setback?
   (b) suggest what action he or she might take to become a stronger candidate for the next promotion vacancy?
   (c) tell him or her the job wouldn't have suited him or her anyway?

Now that you have completed the questionnaire, let's determine your *current* standing in the leadership ranks. (Remember, many leadership qualities must be learned! If your score is low on the questionnaire this time, you simply have more work to do to increase your leadership skills.)

The Analysis

1. a–0	3. a–10	5. a–0	7. a–5	9. a–10
b–10	b–5	b–10	b–0	b–5
c–5	c–0	c–5	c–10	c–0
2. a–10	4. a–0	6. a–10	8. a–0	10. a–5
b–5	b–5	b–0	b–10	b–10
c–0	c–10	c–5	c–5	c–0

Leadership Ratings

80–100 You are an excellent leader who knows how to motivate people to give their best. Any group led by you will exhibit high levels of trust and commitment.

55–79 You have a positive attitude about managing people and major errors of judgment are rare. Occasionally, you could be more adventurous.

25–54 You are much too cautious and may tend to stifle your subordinates' development. Try to have more confidence in yourself—and in other people.

0–24 You need to work on your leadership skills.

Source: Adapted from T. Farnsworth, "Test your leadership skills," in J. E. Adair, "The Building Blocks of Good Leadership," *International Management,* 38 (1983), 47, 50, 55, 77.

The third and most recent approach to the study of leadership focuses on situations and contingencies. Contingency theorists argue that no single "best" leadership style exists. Instead, effective leaders use behaviors that are appropriate to the situation and type of subordinates, tasks, decisions, and organizations involved. According to contingency theory, anyone who learns to find the right "fit" between their actions and the social setting can contribute to a group's success.[10]

From contingency theory, we have learned a number of important things about leadership. For example, you do not have to be the designated leader to discover that your group is straying from its agenda. Any member of the group who proposes a return to the agenda contributes positively to the group process. Similarly, any member who points out that there is a "hidden agenda" controlling group discussion (such as a disruptive ego battle or the promotion of special interests) contributes to the group process. Other major leadership behaviors include keeping the discussion centered on issues, insisting on the critical evaluation of evidence, and refusing to yield to social pressure. The experienced group member uses an issue-centered approach to rescue discussions that have fallen victim to personality clashes.

Styles of Leadership

There are three basic styles of leadership: democratic, authoritarian, and laissez-faire (see Figure 7–2). **Democratic** leaders guide, rather than direct, a group. Receptive to group members' suggestions, these leaders leave most of the actual decision making to the group itself. While this style of leadership is very popular, less experienced groups may feel lost when left on their own to this extent. The effectiveness of democratic leadership depends on the amount of power the leader has, the nature of the task, and the interpersonal relationships that exist among the leader and group members. Generally, groups with a democratic leader are more creative and consistent than groups with other types of leadership; however, the former fall behind in efficiency when compared with groups that have an authoritarian leader.

Authoritarian leaders are more directive than democratic leaders. They are strongly goal-oriented and have firm opinions on how to achieve these goals. If their competency is respected by group members, the group works well and efficiently; if not, conflict is likely to arise within the group.

The third type, *laissez-faire* leaders, avoid directing the group at all. As potential sources of information and feedback on group interaction, they function as observers and recorders and are available for advice when the group wants it. This kind of leadership is especially appropriate for groups engaged in creative activity, where more direction would limit or stifle creativity.

Regardless of the style of leadership, positive evaluations of the group's performance depend on the degree to which each member contributes to the

---

[10]N. W. Biggart and G. G. Hamilton, "An Institutional Theory of Leadership," *The Journal of Applied Behavioral Science*, 23, no. 4 (1987), 431.

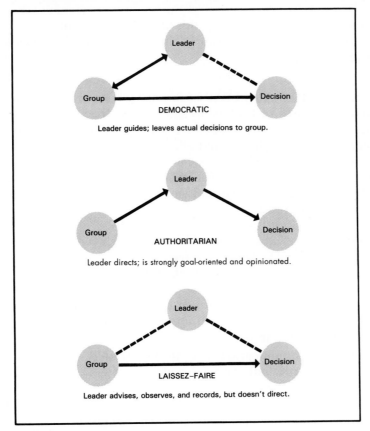

FIGURE 7-2
Three Basic Styles of Leadership

task and maintenance outcomes. In fact, as one study has shown, group members are evaluated more positively by the leader, whatever his or her style, when the latter attributes the group's performance to the group members' efforts.[11] To the extent that leaders believe that a performance is controlled by outside forces, such as the leader's direction, group members will be devalued by the leader.

EMERGENCE OF LEADERS. In groups that have no assigned leaders, functioning leaders often emerge through a process of elimination, not through a process of selection. Interviews with group members reveal that during the first phase of the elimination process, members who are uninformed, quiet, or dogmatic are removed from consideration. In the second, longer phase of elimination, overly authoritarian or verbally offensive individuals are knocked out of the running. In most cases in which

---

[11]D. Kipnis, S. Schmidt, K. Price, and C. Stitt, "Why Do I Like Thee: Is It Your Performance or My Orders?" *Journal of Applied Psychology*, 66 (1981), 328.

a consensus leader emerges (and this always happens in the most successful groups), a second person—a runner-up, so to speak—becomes an auxiliary leader or lieutenant.

SKILLS OF EFFECTIVE LEADERS.   As we have stated, earlier periods of research in the area of leadership emphasized the special traits or characteristics that were a part of effective leadership. More recently, leadership has been viewed in light of what effective leaders *do* rather than who they are. As a function of this more recent trend, several authors have attempted to summarize and categorize leadership skills. One such skill description is that of Giammatteo and Giammatteo. They list and briefly describe five of these major skill areas:

1. Skills of personal behavior. The effective leader:
   Is sensitive to feelings of the group.
   Identifies self with the needs of the group.
   Learns to listen attentively.
   Refrains from criticizing or ridiculing members' suggestions.
   Helps each member feel important and needed.
   Should not argue.
2. Skills of communication. The effective leader:
   Makes sure that everyone understands not only what is needed but why.
   Makes communication with the group a routine part of the job.
3. Skills in equality. The effective leader recognizes that:
   Everyone is important.
   Leadership is to be shared and is not a monopoly.
   A leader grows when leadership functions are dispersed.

The degree to which I can create relationships which facilitate the growth of others as separate persons is a measure of the growth I have achieved in myself.

CARL ROGERS

---

4. Skills of organization. The effective leader helps the group:
   Develop long-range and short-range objectives.
   Break big problems into small ones.
   Share opportunities and responsibilities.
   Plan, act, follow up, and evaluate.
5. Skills of self-examination. The effective leader:
   Is aware of motivations and motives guiding actions.
   Is aware of members' levels of hostility and tolerance so that appropriate countermeasures are taken.
   Is aware of their fact-finding behavior.

Helps the group members be aware of their own forces, attitudes, and values.[12]

Now that we have discussed leadership approaches, styles, and skills, we will turn to another important area of study in small group communication: the process of group problem solving.

PROBLEM SOLVING THROUGH GROUP DISCUSSION

We have all experienced the frustration that arises when a group of people cannot solve a problem that an individual could solve relatively quickly (such as four people trying to decide which movie to see). Researchers have discovered that the relative effectiveness of group decision making depends on the nature of the problem itself.

Groups are more effective in situations in which the pooling of data is necessary, or in which increased knowledge and a variety of approaches are required. In policy decisions, group participation leads to wider acceptance and better understanding of the solution. However, the group decision-making process is prone to problems that arise from any process involving human interaction. For some group members, winning an argument may become more important than finding a solution. Other group members may try to dominate the discussion, while others may habitually give in to win group acceptance. The four friends who cannot decide which film to see may actually be arguing about social dominance and not about movies at all.

A decision-making group is a group of people who work together to solve a problem by collecting information about the problem, reviewing that information and making a decision based on their findings. While we may ordinarily think of decision making as an unexciting or private process, decision-making groups play a central and public role in American life. During crucial strike negotiations, the media feature dramatic, up-to-the-minute accounts of union-management talks. If you are sensitive to the fact that decision making is a *process*, you can improve your own participation in group discussions and also contribute to the effectiveness of the overall group effort.

Kinds of Topics or Problems

Some topics or problems are better than others for group discussion. Those that are most appropriate to group discussion fall into three categories: problems of fact, value, and policy. It is important to identify these three

---

[12]Giammatteo and Giammatteo, 3–4.

distinct types of topics; decision-making discussions often break down because the participants do not understand the nature of the problems with which they are dealing.

PROBLEMS OF FACT. Problems of fact require that the group investigate the truth or falsity of assertions about actual events or conditions. "Did last week's fatal DC-10 crash result from a defective cargo hatch?" "Do air pollutants from chemical-producing plants pose a health hazard to local residents?" "Is the nation going through a depression?" Panels of experts are sometimes assembled to decide crucial factual issues. Ideally, the beliefs, attitudes, and values of group members do not affect the decision-making process here; instead, members act like detectives, defining their terms ("defective," "health hazard," "depression") and making logical deductions based on evidence. One group goal in discussions concerning problems of fact is to arrive at a correct and accurate description of the facts.

Interestingly, in this type of decision-making discussion, the fact that everyone agrees is no guarantee that the decision will be the correct one. Everyone may agree and still be wrong. Whether or not a good decision is made by a group considering a problem of fact is determined by how well the members have analyzed and interpreted the information on which their decision is based. For this reason, group members should see the "facts" before them in more or less the same light. To avoid misunderstanding, members should ask questions relating to the interpretation of particular words or ideas.

For example, suppose a group was planning a party for a friend. The guest of honor's availability on certain dates would, of course, be one of the important facts to be considered. Also important would be clearing up the confusion created if one friend suggests that the group buy a "substantial" gift as opposed to each person giving something individually. Some friends might think in terms of high price, while others might think that "substantial" referred to the gift itself, meaning something sturdy and practical. Someone has to clear up the confusion and ask for an agreed-upon definition before the problem can be solved.

PROBLEMS OF VALUE. With problems of value, group members base their discussion on attitudes, morals, and values. "Is a citizen ever justified in refusing to fight in a war?" "Should abortion be legalized?" There are no correct or incorrect answers to these questions, but there are acceptable or unacceptable answers. The group's goal and responsibility is to discover its own bases for acceptability and unacceptability.

Discussions concerning value will obviously differ from discussions of fact; values are individually held, and they are not always formed (or defended) on the basis of logic. However, more than one type of problem may be considered by any particular group. In the example used to illustrate problems of fact, questions of value might easily surface and demand attention before consideration of the facts could occur. For instance, questions concerning an appropriate gift might reflect individual values.

When one friend suggests that the group buy the guest of honor a fancy cigarette lighter, another friend might question whether the group should contribute to a bad habit. This question would reflect a difference in values.

On the other hand, during discussions of value, definitions must be agreed on and facts must be determined. "Are 'undeclared wars' or 'policing actions' to be considered in the same category as other wars?" "At what point is a fetus considered a human being?" Problems often arise when groups fail to distinguish value from fact. It is also important to remember that conclusions reached in discussions concerning values may be agreed upon by the participants, but this in no way means that these conclusions have been proven.

PROBLEMS OF POLICY. Problems of policy are the most common type of topic for formal decision-making groups, and they are frequently used as topics for class exercises in decision making. Problems of policy are involved in determining courses of action: "How should we allocate our advertising budget this year?" "Should U.S.–Soviet trade agreements be affected by Soviet emigration policies?"

Discussions concerning policy inevitably involve discussions of fact and value. Before deciding on the allocation of their advertising budget, business executives have to identify their target audience and their media habits. "How much time do they spend watching TV, listening to the radio, and reading magazines?" In order to determine the basis for U.S.–Soviet trade arrangements, policymakers have to deal with a question of value such as, "Does one government have the right to interfere in the internal affairs of another government?" Because discussions concerning policies are liable to raise a number of questions, members of the group should recognize when and whether they are addressing the same question. For example, if one senator is concerned with the adequacy of current U.S. grain supplies, another is worried about wheat deals in the past, and a third is upset about violations of human rights in Third World countries, their committee's discussion on trade agreements may become disrupted or blocked entirely. If, however, the three concerned members are able to identify these issues separately and agree to discuss them one at a time, they can conduct an effective and productive discussion.

For a moment, reconsider the questions that might be raised for our group that was planning a party. A question of policy might arise concerning the nature of the party itself. Should the party be a surprise or announced? Should the group send out written invitations or telephone the guests? These questions concern possible actions for the group to consider.

Research for Discussion

Conducting research for facts and evidence is a crucial part of the decision-making process. Brilhart has divided preparatory research into four distinct stages: (1) reviewing your own information; (2) gathering additional information; (3) evaluating information; and (4) reorganizing information and gathering more, if necessary.[13] Each of these stages will be discussed in the following paragraphs.

REVIEW YOUR OWN INFORMATION. Whatever your topic for discussion, you will inevitably have some ideas and background information. Now is the time to jot down everything you know about the topic and its causes and effects. Move from a freewheeling kind of thinking to a more organized mode of thought in which you note main issues, subsidiary questions, and supporting details. Make note of information that you don't know now but that would be useful for later discussion.

GATHER ADDITIONAL INFORMATION. This is the active phase of your research: Go out and observe the problem yourself. If your group is trying to come up with ways of reducing the theft of library books, go prowl around the library, watching for security leaks. A second source of information is interviews. Talk to experts; ask the head librarian for an analysis of the theft problem. More information about your topic can come from reading. Check magazines, professional journals, and books for the latest data on your problem. Other informal sources of information are all around you. Ask friends for their ideas about your topic; check TV and radio shows that might give you some useful information; or go to a campus lecture that deals with your topic.

EVALUATE YOUR INFORMATION. Now is the time for you to play the critic, distinguishing facts from opinions. As we noted earlier, statements of fact can be determined to be either true or false on the basis of evidence. Opinions can be neither proved nor disproved; they are not necessarily based on evidence, and they introduce the dangerous element of uncertainty into your discussion. While opinions may become useful in deciding questions of value or policy, it is essential that they be identified correctly. The head librarian's suggestion for installing antitheft devices may be a useful or expert opinion, but recognize it for what it is—an opinion, not a fact.

After you have separated fact from opinion, evaluate them both. To evaluate facts based on survey and statistical data, Brilhart suggests the following questions:

1. Are results based on a random or other scientific sample?
2. How are the questions asked? By whom?
3. Are the data collection procedures clearly explained? Are they appropriate?
4. Is the method of computing averages or trends described and appropriate?
5. Are the data interpreted and evaluated appropriately?[14]

---

[13]J. K. Brilhart, *Effective Group Discussion*, 5th ed. (Dubuque, Iowa: Wm. C. Brown, 1986), 81–92.
[14]Ibid., 89–90.

Unless a member of your group is trained in research or statistical methods, ask a researcher or statistician to help you determine the answers to the last two questions.

To evaluate a source's opinions and their resulting implications, Brilhart advises asking the following questions:

1. Is the person (or other source) a recognized expert on the subject?
2. Does the source have a vested interest that might have influenced the opinion?
3. How well does the source support his or her opinion with documented evidence? Is the evidence well organized, with supporting statistics, tables, and clear reasoning?
4. How consistent is this opinion with others that are expressed by the source? If the statement is not consistent with other opinions and predictions from the same person, is there an acceptable explanation for the change?
5. What are the implications of the opinion?[15]

Finally, test your evidence for accuracy, recency, and completeness. Old or partial information is not useful and may be misleading.

REORGANIZE YOUR INFORMATION AND GATHER MORE, IF NECESSARY.   After you have weeded out useless or unreliable information, you can recognize the hard evidence and make a tentative outline of your analysis of the problem as well as suggested steps for its solution. Remember at the close of this stage, you are engaged in a cooperative effort. Do not regard your research material as weapons stockpiled for battle—view it instead as a collection of accurate and objective information that can be shared with the group to help provide the basis for informed problem solving.

THE PROBLEM-SOLVING PROCESS

Dewey's Reflective Thinking Process

When we are confronted with a problem, we often forget that decision making or problem solving is a process. Studies have shown that people tend to respond to problems in an ordered series of steps. In his classic book *How We Think*, John Dewey identified five distinct phases in goal-directed or reflective thinking:

1. Recognizing the difficulty.
2. Defining or specifying the difficulty.

---

[15]Ibid., 90–91.

3. Raising suggestions for possible solutions and rational exploration of the ideas.

4. Selecting the best solution from among many proposals.

5. Carrying out the solution.[16]

A Standard Agenda for Decision Making

While Dewey's discussion originated as a description of rational thought, his influence has been so great that later scholars adopted and expanded these steps to form a standard agenda for decision making.

STEP 1: DEFINING THE PROBLEM. If a group has been given a specific and clearly defined problem, this step becomes unnecessary. In many cases, however, a group finds itself in the middle of a difficult situation, and a clear definition of the problem becomes an important part of the decision-making process.

Consider the following example. At a certain university, eating arrangements have become a problem for a large number of students; many students live off-campus, others have kitchens in their dorms, and commuters need only a few meals on campus a week. The university meal plan ticket is expensive, the cafeteria food is unappealing, and local grocery stores and restaurants are very expensive. A group of students concerned with this situation meets to share complaints. The students are aware of the situation, and some have vague ideas as to possible solutions, but they need to define their problem more clearly. At this stage they have two goals. They want to frame their definition of the problem to increase its "solvability," and in a way that will promote discussion and effective interaction. Clearly, posing the question so that it can be answered by a simple "yes" or "no" does little to define the problem.

The most effective definitions are problem centered rather than solution centered. "How can we get local supermarkets to lower their prices?" is a solution-centered definition of our sample problem. Hidden in this question is the assumption that there is only one way to solve the problem; this kind of definition effectively short-circuits the entire decision-making process. An alternative definition of the problem might be, "How can we improve grocery buying and dining facilities?" This question centers on the problem and does not limit the range of possible solutions from the beginning.

STEP 2: LIMITING THE TOPIC. After the problem has been defined, limits to the discussion must be set up based on relevance to the group, the importance of specific issues involved in the larger problem, and the amount of time available for discussion. For example, our hypothetical group is interested in the high price of groceries, but only in a certain sense. The group is not going to discuss a nationwide boycott of certain supermarket

---

[16]J. Dewey, *How We Think* (Boston: Heath, 1933), 106–15.

Which step of the problem-solving process could this be?

chains; it is interested in the problem of prices only in the immediate area. Similarly, the group has to limit its topic on the basis of the priority of specific issues. Should they focus on the problem of grocery buying, campus dining facilities, local restaurants or all three? Obviously, the group's definition of the problem will also depend on the amount of time available. Do they have only a few hours, or will they meet over a period of weeks or months?

STEP 3: ANALYZING THE DATA.   At this stage the group goes through its evidence, distinguishing relevant from irrelevant material, finding important details, searching for causes of the problem, and working out the dynamics of the situation. Our group might evaluate the quality of dining hall food in relation to its price, compare local supermarket prices with supermarket prices in other nearby towns, compile statistics on the number of students who do and do not have meal plan tickets, and collect figures on local restaurant prices.

STEP 4: ESTABLISHING CRITERIA FOR POSSIBLE SOLUTIONS.   The group must determine in advance what they expect from their proposed solutions. For example, our group might decide that its solution should meet three criteria: It should provide (1) nutritious and (2) tasty food to students (3) at prices they can afford. During this stage group members must keep from judging which of the proposed criteria are acceptable until all suggestions have been heard. The group then selects criteria that are acceptable to the majority.

STEP 5: SUGGESTING POSSIBLE SOLUTIONS.   During the "brainstorming" stage the quantity rather than the quality of proposed solutions is important. Again, the group must not try to come to a decision until all possible solutions have been heard. All possible approaches to the problem should be brought up and discussed: negotiating with the university to change dining hall policies, talking to local supermarket and restaurant owners about student discounts. These ideas and many more may prove to be worthwhile. Open-mindedness is the rule. Even seemingly impossible proposals may yield solutions as they are worked, improved, and modified. An excited, "Hey, let's start our own grocery store!" may provide just the inspiration for the organization of a student cooperative supermarket.

STEP 6: CHECKING THE INDIVIDUAL SOLUTION AGAINST THE ESTABLISHED CRITERIA.   Does each solution satisfy the standards the group has established? Do some of the proposed solutions satisfy the criteria better than others? At this point the group will throw out those solutions that fail to meet the established standards, and will evaluate the remaining solutions in light of the needs of the problem. In this stage the group must keep its discussion focused on issues, not personalities. Any proposed solution must be judged on its own merits—not on the popularity or loudness of its sponsor.

STEP 7: CARRYING OUT THE SOLUTION.   The group must decide how its solution may be carried out within the limitations of its authority, facilities, and budget. If our student group has decided to organize an alternative supermarket, should they hire an outside contractor to run the store, or should they run it themselves as a student cooperative? Do they have sufficient personnel, business expertise, and financing to run it themselves? Which plan would result in the lowest food prices? The group must choose the most efficient and effective means of carrying out their solution.

STEP 8: EVALUATING THE EFFECT OF THE SOLUTION.   After the solution has been implemented, various questions must be asked. Has it accomplished its purpose? Does the new student cooperative market provide better food at more reasonable prices? Has it satisfied the need? Do enough students use it to justify its existence? Can improvements be made to increase the effectiveness of the solution? Should students work at the cooperative without wages in return for even lower food prices?

The standard agenda that we have described is only a guide. It is useful only insofar as all group members are aware of it and accept it as a useful and organized way to approach the problem-solving process. Despite the orderliness of the standard agenda, its use does not guarantee effortless solutions. Several other factors affect the operation and outcomes of problem-solving groups.

OTHER FACTORS AFFECTING GROUP PERFORMANCE

Personality

One of the most fascinating aspects of group behavior is the uniqueness of every group due to the nature of its membership. There are many variables that influence group interaction, but the primary one is the different personality of each member of the group.

Each person contributes his or her own experiences, values, attitudes, and personality to the makeup of the group. For example, some people are shy and tend to sit back in a group situation, while more aggressive individuals may use the group as an audience for their assertiveness. While some people try to avoid conflict in a group, other people like to provoke conflict and enjoy the combative interaction that often follows. Perhaps you have participated in a group that you felt could have functioned more efficiently if two members had been less argumentative or if someone had been more dominant.

Undoubtedly, you have heard the expression "personality conflict" used to describe the irreconcilable clash of personalities. Such a difference in personality can sometimes cause a group to lose sight of its goal and remain unproductive. Yet differences in personality can have a positive effect on group interaction. For example, one person who is particularly task-oriented may counterbalance the member who is concerned with the behavior of the group. Similarly, a humorous individual can offset someone who is extremely serious or tense. The group is a complex entity because of the combination of different personalities. The next time you participate in a group or observe one in action, remember that the group is equal to and greater than the sum of the individual personalities of its members.

Cohesion

Groups develop personalities all their own. For example, some groups always seem to work smoothly and achieve their goals easily, while others are marked by conflict. Highly publicized mountain climbs such as those up Mt.

Everest provide an example of this second type of group. In the past, instances have arisen during which the climbers, who depend on each other for their survival, have not communicated effectively. Additionally, the overall group has been divided into two subgroups with quite different goals: the climbers, whose goal was to reach the summit as quickly and safely as possible, and the film crews, whose goal was to capture exciting footage. As a result, teamwork between the two subgroups disintegrated and ultimately jeopardized lives.

A communication expert would diagnose this problem as a lack of group cohesion or solidarity. **Cohesion** is the degree to which group members identify themselves as a team, rather than as just a collection of individuals. Cohesion arises from and reinforces shared values, attitudes, and standards of behavior. Cohesion is a crucial factor in a group's success. Highly cohesive groups are more likely to be productive, their members are more likely to feel personally satisfied by the group process, and their interpersonal communication is more effective.

Cohesive groups inspire feelings of loyalty because group members have an emotional investment in the life of the team. They share the same goals and are willing to make personal sacrifices for the good of the group. One compelling example of group cohesiveness was the "bonding" reflected during the 1988 rescue of baby Jessica McClure from the well at her parents' Texas home. The awe-inspiring teamwork of rescue workers, family, and friends during the frightening ordeal succeeded not only in becoming an international media event, but also in bringing the country together over the safety of the little girl. In short, group cohesiveness made the rescue of baby Jessica a reality.

Interaction in highly cohesive groups has several special characteristics. First, because individuals feel secure in these groups, they can tolerate some degree of productive conflict. Specifically, they feel free to offer both rewarding and punishing feedback to other group members.

Second, cohesive groups offer their members greater returns, or rewards, for their personal investment in the group. In the business world, these rewards may take the form of money; for example, a team assembling autos may be paid for the number of cars they produce each week, instead of being paid by the hour. In an academic situation, a professor may give the same grade to all students working on a group project, regardless of their individual contributions to the project. In both cases, cohesion increases as a result of a shared group goal. Members of the car assembly team will probably work harder to get more pay, and the students will work harder to get a better grade.

Third, cohesive groups offer psychological rewards—feelings of belonging and the friendship and respect of other people. Cohesive groups also offer their members the reward of prestige, which comes either from the social status of the group or from some group accomplishment. In either case, group members share the reflected glory of the group. Finally, participation in a cohesive group allows each member to experience achievement rewards, the satisfaction that comes from productive work, and the fulfillment that comes from contributing to a valuable cause or goal.

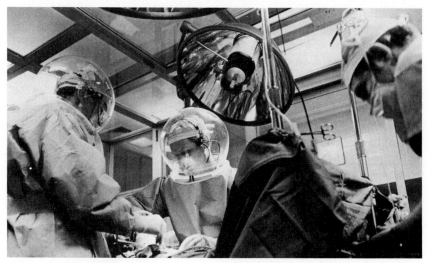

Cohesion is a major determinant of successful teamwork.

Conflict

The ideal group is highly cohesive, but groups, like most things in life, are rarely ideal, and conflict often emerges from group interaction. Conflict between groups—***intergroup conflict***—often benefits the groups involved by increasing goal-oriented activity and causing group members to value their work more highly. An extreme case is war, in which conflict strengthens in-group bonds by providing an outlet for tension and focusing a group's goals. Conflict usually occurs when there are two or more competing or incompatible responses to a single event. Thus, conflict may occur both within the group itself, when individuals experience differing needs or values, or between groups, when the groups have competing interests over the accomplishment of a cooperative goal.[17]

In the past it was believed that all ***intragroup conflict*** (conflict within a group) had the opposite effect—that it had a negative influence, reduced cohesion, decreased productivity, and caused group members to discredit their own achievements. Researchers now believe that some degree of intragroup conflict is useful and productive. It is possible that when conflict is appropriately channeled, it can contribute to more effective results. Of course, this kind of conflict is not a pitched battle but an issue-centered form of open discussion and confrontation that uses group problem-solving methods to achieve better solutions.

At times, intragroup conflict cannot be avoided. To cope, the group must be willing to work through its problems. The *first* step in this process is determining whether a conflict exists. To aid in the completion of this step,

---

[17]H. W. Cummings, L. Long, and M. Lewis, *Managing Communication in Organizations: An Introduction,* 2d ed. (Dubuque, Iowa: Gorsuch-Scarisbrick, 1987).

Schultz and Anderson suggest that group members should be willing to address four specific questions. First, do the parties involved believe or know that a conflict exists? A conflict is not a conflict unless all parties are aware of it. *Second*, are there incompatible goals? Conflict is almost always the result of one party's particular goals. For example, one group member may believe that the scope of a project is far too broad, while the leader of the group may feel that the project is manageable. *Third*, are scarce rewards involved? Conflict often results when rewards are perceived as limited or scarce. These include both tangible and intangible rewards, such as money or respect. *Finally*, what degree of interdependence and independence exists among the parties in conflict? Conflict seldom occurs if one of the parties is capable of functioning independently of all other group members. If the members could function independently, they probably would not be members of the group.[18]

Once the real source of conflict has been identified, the process of managing the conflict can begin. First, the group should determine the issues of the conflict. An examination of every conceivable issue from all sides should be considered. (In our earlier example of group conflict, the scope of a particular group project was the issue. At this stage, the group would listen to the speakers representing both sides.) Once the issues are identified, the group can translate the issues into goals and can rank them according to practicality and desirability. For example, Jeannie might suggest that the project be completed in two stages rather than one, given that the scope of the project is broad. Finally, the group should determine the direction and strategy that would best achieve the goal(s). At this point, the problem-solving process can be resumed.[19]

Conformity

Another important variable that influences groups is pressure to conform within the group. In and of itself, **conformity** is not a negative force. Sometimes, however, when consensus inhibits dissent, the pressure to conform, or "groupthink," can cause serious errors in decision making.[20] As previously discussed, many of the norms to which a group conforms are productive for the group and enable it to function more effectively.

While pressure to conform is sometimes so subtle that a group member may be totally unaware of it, at other times the pressure can be quite open. Group members may be pressured to conform, even when conformity means going against their better judgment. This sort of overt pressure can result in dissonance, which can erupt in open conflict or defiance.

---

[18]B. Schultz and J. Anderson, "Training in the Management of Conflict: A Communication Theory Perspective," *Small Group Behavior*, 15 (1984), 333–48.

[19]Ibid., 339–42.

[20]I. L. Janis, *Victims of Groupthink: A Psychological Study of Foreign Policy Decisions and Fiascos*, 2d ed. (Boston: Houghton Mifflin, 1982).

For example, an individual may verbally yield to group pressure but then exhibit contradictory behavior. Examine the following situation. Gil's bike club was going to sponsor a charity drive for an undetermined organization. Gil was anxious to support the local animal shelter, but the group made its final decision to support the nearby children's hospital. Gil reluctantly agreed, and the group believed that it had won him over to its side. Yet Gil was nowhere to be found when it came to active participation in the collection drive. In this case Gil told the group what it wanted to hear, but he refused to conform in his actions.

The consequence that may result when group members are pressured to conform will vary depending upon the situation, the force of the pressure, and the people involved. Consider another example. After three weeks of testimony, a jury was asked to determine the guilt or innocence of the accused. From the very outset, most of the jurors were convinced that the defendant was guilty. After three days of discussion, all but one of the jurors voted to convict the accused. The "holdout" was subjected to group pressure, both overt and subtle. Everyone was tired and anxious to go home. On the next day the twelfth juror gave in to the group pressure, and the accused was found guilty. In this instance group pressure—whether for good or ill (depending upon the actual guilt or innocence of the accused)—greatly affected a group's decision.

Some group members are more susceptible to group pressure than others. The following personality characteristics identify those who are most vulnerable to group pressure:

1. *Level of self-confidence.* The better one's self-concept, the more resistant one will be to group pressure.
2. *Regard for authority.* A closed-minded person, defined as one who relies on the accuracy and correctness of authority, will be more apt to conform to group pressure.
3. *Intelligence.* The greater one's intelligence, the less likely one is to conform.
4. *Need for social approval.* The greater one's need for approval, the more apt one is to conform.

Other variables that influence conformity concern the situation in which the group finds itself. Situational variables include:

1. *The size of the group.* Conformity usually increases as the size of the group increases, but only until there are four members; thereafter, conformity decreases as the group increases.
2. *Group structure.* Group structures that permit a great deal of interaction between members produce more conformity than those that limit interaction.
3. *Difficulty of the task.* Conformity usually increases as the task becomes more difficult.

4. *Degree of crisis or emergency.* The old adage that there is safety in numbers may account for the increase in conformity during a crisis situation. For example, a group of shipwrecked survivors floating on a raft in the middle of the ocean would probably exhibit a high degree of conformity since deviation from the norm could mean disaster.

Whatever the mechanisms affecting a particular group—personality, cohesion, conformity—every group member is responsible for making the most of the positive potential of these forces. By becoming a member of a group, you and others have elected to pursue certain objectives as a team. When goals are kept firmly in view, individual differences can often be recognized as the stumbling blocks they are and can be temporarily shelved while the solution is sought in an open-minded way.

Communication Networks

Another variable that influences the process of small group communication is the network of communication channels used in the group. The five most common communication networks are the circle, the wheel, the chain, the Y, and the all-channel networks. Distinguished by the concepts of *distance* among members and *centrality* of information flow, communication networks vary as a function of the transmission and reception of information from member to member. Figure 7–3 illustrates the most common communication networks in a five-member group.

In the **circle communication network,** members pass information from side to side. No one person has greater access to group members than any other person. Unlike the wheel, which has a leader at the center, the circle lets each group member be viewed as the leader at different times. Equal access to information means higher group morale and satisfaction. The circle network is especially effective for solving complex problems.

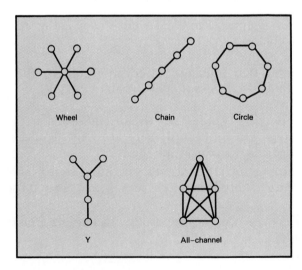

FIGURE 7–3
Common Communication Network Structures

Perhaps the most unique characteristic of the **wheel network** is its highly centralized flow of communication. The person at the center of the network controls the communication flow. Because all information is primarily sent and received from a central source, the wheel is especially suited for solving simple problems. Speed and efficiency are the hallmarks of the wheel. However, this network tends to produce less group satisfaction and poorer morale than the circle network.

Much as the wheel is viewed as a highly centralized communication structure, so are the **Y** and the **chain** characterized as more centralized. In both the Y and the chain, the person in the center is viewed as the leader, due to the flow of information that he or she sends and receives. Perhaps the most interesting aspect of the Y is its ability to identify coalitions. Thus, the Y structure is more characteristic of groups that have developed over time. As with the wheel, these communication networks are more adaptable to solving simple problems. Again, speed and accuracy are the name of the game.

The final communication network that is illustrated is the **all-channel structure**—generally considered to describe a leaderless group discussion. An example of an all-channel communication network might be the first meeting of a group of concerned citizens who wish to raise money for the needy in their community. No leader may emerge during the initial meeting of such a group. Over time, however, another communication network will emerge (for example, a circle or a wheel). In short, the all-channel network may be considered to be "no network at all." It is most often used to describe an initial group discussion.

Although this discussion of communication networks may seem a bit alien at first, you need only look to the small groups of which you are a member to discern their existence. The important thing to remember, however, is that satisfactory groups take time to develop. At first, group members may "jockey" for varying positions in the network, thus changing its form. Once the group is established, however, the particular pattern of communication should become of little consequence. The group's time can then be used to complete a project or to solve a problem.[21]

ANALYZING SMALL GROUP INTERACTION

The explanations and guidelines presented in this chapter can help you participate more fully and effectively in small groups. One way to apply these principles is to observe group interaction. You should now be able to

---

[21]For a more complete discussion of communication networks, see B. A. Fisher, *Small Group Decision Making: Communication and the Group Process*, 2d ed. (New York: McGraw-Hill, 1980); and J. Luft, *Group Processes: Introduction to Group Dynamics*, 3d ed. (Palo Alto, Calif.: Mayfield, 1984). Portions of this discussion were adapted from these sources.

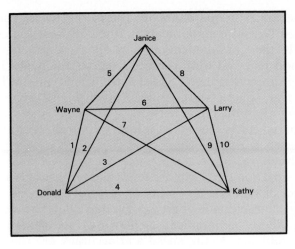

FIGURE 7–4
Channels of Communication
in a Five-Member Group

recognize characteristics of effective and ineffective small groups by examining group goals, member participation, types of listening and feedback, group roles, and styles of leadership.

Groups are often evaluated based on the outcomes and products the members produce. Group membership can be beneficial to some and detrimental to others. Alcoholics Anonymous is beneficial to a person who attends and never drinks again. The Humane Society may be seen as unsuccessful when animals have to be put to sleep because they are not adopted.

Groups are also evaluated based on what actually takes place during a group interaction or meeting. During the 1970s, Bales and Lashbrook developed quantitative (number and amount of member participation) and qualitative (evaluation of a member response in terms of benefit to the group) methods to analyze group interaction. Their guidelines are still used today to evaluate group effectiveness.[22]

For example, Figure 7–4 shows a five-member group with ten possible channels of communication (or an all-channel network). Using Lashbrook's method of group analysis, the lines among the group members represent group members' ability to respond (verbally and nonverbally) back and forth. Donald can initiate a conversation with Kathy just as easily as he can with Larry, Janice, or Wayne. By examining the number of times a person speaks, you can evaluate factors such as leadership style, member participation, roles, and so on. The small slashes on the lines in Figure 7–5 indicate the number of times each person spoke to another member during a specified period.

---

[22]Guidelines for group evaluation can be obtained from the following sources: E. M. Bodaken, W. B. Lashbrook, and M. Champagne, "Proana 5: A Computerized Technique for the Analysis of Small Group Interaction," *Western Speech*, 25 (1971), 112–15; R. F. Bales, *Personality and Interpersonal Behavior* (New York: Holt, Rinehart & Winston, 1970); R. F. Bales and S. P. Cohen, *SYMLOG: A System for the Multiple Level Observation of Groups* (New York: The Free Press, 1979).

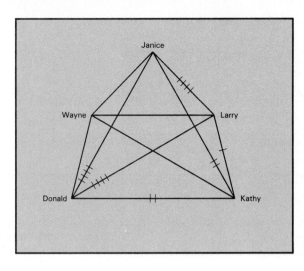

FIGURE 7–5
Number of Times a Group Member Spoke

If this were a family trying to decide where to go for a vacation, who do you think would have the most say? Probably the parents. In Figure 7–5, you'll notice that more communication is directed to Donald than to anyone else. We could assume that he is the father and that Janice is the mother. What would you guess about Kathy, Larry, and Wayne? Maybe Larry is the oldest child, because he interacts more than Kathy and Wayne, or maybe he is more assertive than they are. We might guess that Wayne is a small child or baby since no communication is directed to or from him.

If this were a business meeting, we might assume that Donald was the designated leader or chairman of the board. We could also guess that his leadership style is authoritarian. We would probably be concerned that Wayne did not participate, but he may have another function (for example, recorder, trainee). Much can be assumed from these simple diagrams. However, it is often important to determine the quality as well as the amount of interaction.

Decisions about the quality of communication are based on a number of factors. It is important to know whether the group's purpose serves a social or task function. For example, if the group meets socially to celebrate a member's birthday, then no one would expect organized, purposeful conversation. On the other hand, if a group meets with a specific goal, then the functions of group members are important. A group of surgeons deciding which patient will receive an eye donation would need to get to the point immediately without sharing the tales of their latest golf game or fishing expedition.

When observing a group that is task-oriented, we need to be aware of member functions. Does a member tell a joke just to get attention or to release tension? We also need to observe types of listening behavior and feedback. Do members listen to what is being said, or do they go off on a new tangent each time they speak? When a group is involved in brainstorming, are members accepting of others, or do they (verbally and nonverbally)

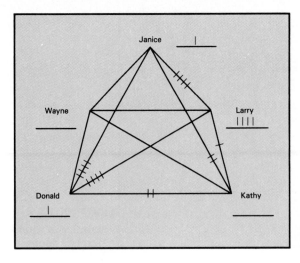

FIGURE 7-6
Diagram to Determine Productive Group Members

chastise others for "far-out" suggestions? Diagrams can be used to determine which members are most productive or meet group goals.

Figure 7–6 includes a space for interactions that are not beneficial to the group. For example, if Larry started talking about a song that he wrote when the group was assigning duties for a dance marathon to fight muscular dystrophy, he would not be adding to the group purpose and would be involved in nonpatterned interaction. A slash would be drawn beside his name and not on the line between members because he didn't add useful information or respond to a comment from another member.

SUMMARY

It is almost impossible to exist independently of all groups. Understanding the group process can help you get more out of your participation in groups. As a participant in a group, you have certain responsibilities. These include keeping an open mind to all ideas; showing sensitivity to other members; communicating ideas, opinions, and information as accurately and honestly as possible; using appropriate questions when necessary; and doing all the homework or preparation required.

It is also helpful to be able to analyze the role structures, norms, and outcomes that function in your group. Attention to the norms that develop will enable you to determine which of these are beneficial to the group and which are counterproductive. To further increase productivity, you and the other group members should assume various task-oriented roles, including information or opinion giving, information or opinion seeking, expediting, contributing ideas, and analyzing. These kinds of actions keep the discussion on course and aid the group in accomplishing its objectives.

You should also be concerned with the emotional behavior of the group. Concern for the social and emotional climate of the group is shown when members assume maintenance roles, which include active listening, game leading, harmonizing, gatekeeping, compromising, and "fronting" for the group. Indifference to the group and its goals often results in self-serving roles, which can obstruct the group's progress. Although each member in the group has his or her individual role to play, effective group interaction does not take place automatically. The group must go through several stages of development, including groping, griping, grasping, grouping, and group action.

Although some people seem to be good leaders by nature, specific leadership skills can be learned. Good leaders tend to have skills in the areas of personal behavior, communicating, equality, organization, and self-examination.

The three basic styles of leadership are democratic, authoritarian, and laissez-faire.

When approaching a problem, it is usually best to follow an orderly sequence to arrive at the best possible solution. Problems of fact, value, and policy can all be discussed by groups, but it is extremely important for the group to understand the agenda, which is based on John Dewey's pattern of reflective thinking. These steps are defining the problem, limiting the topic, analyzing the problem, establishing criteria or standards, suggesting possible solutions, checking individual solutions against all the criteria, carrying out the solution, and evaluating the effect of the solution on the problem.

Cohesion can be the key to effective group discussion and action. Groups that are not cohesive often fail to solve problems effectively. Loyalty and allegiance are fostered in cohesive groups. Conflict can destroy cohesion in a group, but at times it may also contribute to more effective results. It is the responsibility of all group members, not just the leader, to deal with conflict in an objective and reasonable manner. Conformity, when it is not forced, is very desirable, since consensus is one of the objectives of the group process.

Finally, the type of communication network in place in a given small group can affect overall performance. Highly centralized networks are more accurate when solving relatively simple problems. More complex problems are best addressed by less centralized communication networks.

EXERCISES

Group Experiences

Group Roles and Behavior

DESCRIPTION: Task-oriented and maintenance roles in groups are related to the roles people play in life. This activity is designed to explore the relationship between behaviors and roles. If you receive a "behavior" that seems contradictory to a role, try it anyway. They may work together better than you think!

PROCEDURE: Divide into groups of six. Write each of the following behaviors and roles on separate index cards:

Task Behaviors
Expediter
Analyzer
Opinion seeker

Maintenance Behaviors
Harmonizer
Gatekeeper
Public relations—the front person

Roles
Mr. Garcia: Runs a small grocery store.
Mrs. Garcia: Wife of Mr. Garcia and mother of seven children.
Father Hollen: Priest and dedicated missionary of his faith.
Dr. Redding: Scientist, winner of several international awards.
Ms. Valentine: Sales manager of Honeywell, Inc.
Elaine Warner: M.D., general practitioner.

Each group member should arbitrarily select a role card and a behavior card. Take five minutes and look up your behavior in the chapter to make that sure you understand what it involves. Do not show anyone the cards you selected.

All six members should meet as a group and play their assigned parts. The problem you face as a group is to decide which two people can leave the island where you are stranded. Only two people may leave, and there is no guarantee that they will be able to send help or reach their destination. For the people who stay on the island, there is plenty of fresh water, but food is scarce. Decide in 15 minutes.

DISCUSSION: Read aloud your role and describe the behavior you were asked to portray. Did you have trouble combining the role and behavior? Did you recognize the roles and behaviors that others were playing? Can you draw any conclusions regarding the relationship between roles and behaviors in groups?

The Power Trip

DESCRIPTION: The distinction between leaders and leadership has been discussed in this chapter. Leadership behavior (any behavior that helps a group clarify and achieve group goals) can be observed on both the verbal and nonverbal levels. This activity explores the relationship between power and leadership. During the activity, pay particular attention to the nonverbal behaviors that communicate influence, power, and dominance.

PROCEDURE: Divide into groups of six to eight members. Each group member should be given an equal amount of money. Although many variations are possible one method is to distribute ten pennies, one nickel, one dime, and one quarter to each participant.

Stage 1. For the first five minutes of the exercise, group members should be instructed to give some, all, or none of their money away to other members. However, during this time period they may not physically take money from another member. (A distinction is made between "taking" money and "receiving" money.) This means that they may not take money from any player, but they can accept money that is given to them.

Stage 2. The second stage of this exercise is the "taking" period. During the next five minutes, group members are instructed that they may "take" money from any group member, but they may no longer give money away. (This part of the exercise may become very lively, because group members may forcibly try to take money from a resistant member. This is an anticipated part of the exercise.)

Stage 3. At the end of the second five minutes, group members are told to stop and count the money they have. The group member who has accumulated the largest amount of money then becomes the group leader. All the members of the group must give the group leader their money so that the leader then has all the money for the group.

Stage 4. The leaders from each small group now come together to form their own "power" group. Their group members can stand around them and give them advice during the rest of the activity, but their group leader may not respond verbally to the comments.

Stage 5. Stages 1 and 2 (five minutes of giving, five minutes of taking) are repeated for the group leaders.

Stage 6. Each group leader should count the final amount of money collected. Each leader can decide whether to keep the money or to distribute it in some manner to the fellow group members. The decision of each group leader should be verbalized and carried out.

DISCUSSION: Is the person with the most power likely to be the leader? How are we persuaded to entrust other people with leadership authority? Is the use of money realistic and meaningful as a source of power? Is "power" a characteristic of a leader?

To Lead or Not to Lead

DESCRIPTION: The three types of leadership styles—democratic, authoritarian, and laissez-faire—are explored in this activity. The democratic leader guides rather than directs the group; the authoritarian leader is more directive than the democratic counterpart; the laissez-faire leader does not direct the group at all. In the following activity you will have an opportunity to experience the effects of all three types of leadership.

PROCEDURE: Divide into groups of six to eight members. The group should identify one person to play the democratic leader, one person to play the laissez-faire leader, and one person to play the authoritarian leader. The leadership should rotate every five minutes so that all three leaders have an opportunity to direct (or not direct) the group. Each group should select a task, such as planning a hike, a dance, a clean-up project for the city, or a recycling project.

DISCUSSION: After 15 minutes, each group should evaluate (1) its task orientation and (2) its social dimension (cohesion) during each type of leadership. Which type of leadership provided a balance between the task orientation and the social dimension? Did any particular type of leadership promote either the task orientation or the social dimension? Which type of leadership do you prefer? Why? Under which conditions would each of the three types of leadership be effective?

Questions As Feedback

DESCRIPTION: Questions can be a valuable source of feedback when they are used appropriately. Questions involve a matter of choice in terms of timing and the nature of the question itself. Sometimes a lack of questions can leave many issues unresolved in the minds of group members. This activity should help to make you aware of the appropriate use of questions of fact, value, and policy.

PROCEDURE: Divide into groups of five to seven members. There are two parts to this activity. The first part is to be done individually. Complete the "situations" given below by providing an example of a question of fact, value, and policy. After each group member has completed the situations, engage in a discussion to compare responses. The following situation and responses are offered as a sample.

Sample Situation

A group member's parent has recently passed away. Sandy suggests that a large arrangement of flowers be sent to the funeral home. Richard suggests that the money would be better used if it were sent to the American Cancer Society. Carol, who is somewhat concerned about the decision, suggests that the decision be postponed until all members are present.

Question of fact: What is meant by "large" in reference to an arrangement of flowers?

Question of value: Why the American Cancer Society? Why not another organization that has a broader appeal?

Question of policy: Should all members be asked to contribute a given amount of money, even if they do not support the final decision?

Situation 1

Michael was named as chairman of his department's picnic committee. Fulfilling his role as an authoritarian leader, Michael decided that the picnic should be held at a nice park that had good athletic facilities. In addition, he stated that it would cost $50, leaving $20 in the fund for the next six months. He pointed out to the committee members that the decision was entirely in the hands of the committee and was not subject to a vote by the student body. What questions of fact, value, and policy should be asked to clarify the issues?

Situation 2

Richard is sitting around with a group of old college friends, trying to plan a five-year reunion. The group is having difficulty locating the addresses of approximately 20 of the 200 classmates. Don suggests that they place an advertisement in the newspaper to attract these people. Carol and Sandy respond that this would be a waste of money and that the reunion should be planned with the 180 people for whom addresses are available. What questions of fact, value, and policy should be asked to clarify the issues?

DISCUSSION: Compare your responses with those of the other members of your group. Do you feel that in some cases a specific type of question is more appropriate? For example, is a question of fact more appropriate than a question of policy in a given situation? What are the repercussions for the group when questions are not asked? Do questions of fact, value, and policy help the group communication process in terms of clarifying its goal?

How Do You See the World?

DESCRIPTION: Decision-making discussions often break down because the participants fail to understand the nature of the questions being raised. A breakdown may also occur simply because each member is viewing the problem from a different perspective. A specific example would be one member arguing an issue from the basis of factual information, another from a value position, and another from the basis of policy. Although these three perspectives can be integrated in the discussion process, they may often hinder effective discussion when members refuse to acknowledge the existence of another perspective for viewing the problem or issue. This activity will demonstrate how a breakdown of communication can occur and will suggest alternative methods for avoiding and resolving breakdowns of a similar nature.

PROCEDURE: Divide into groups of five. Each participant should be given one of the roles described below. The audience should be informed as to the context of the situation but, if possible, should not be informed of the individual roles. The context of the situation is as follows. The student government has decided to take some type of action relating to off-campus housing. A subcommittee has been given the mandate (1) to determine if unfair and discriminatory practices by landlords against students exist and

(2) to suggest a plan of action to bring problems to the attention of the community. The following roles should be assigned to the participants:

Person A: You are a laissez-faire leader for the discussion group. You see your role as primarily one of observing and repeating what is happening and recording notes for the group.

Person B: You are concerned with facts only. Before you commit yourself to resolving this problem, you will need to know if there is a problem. Examples of questions you might ask include, "What are the landlord-tenant regulations?" and "What is meant by 'unfair' or 'discriminatory' practices?" Do not argue issues unless they involve sound facts that you can relate to. Always bring the discussion back to the facts that either are known in this case or need to be determined.

Person C: You are concerned with attitudes, morals, and values. "Are students justified in not paying rent when they feel that they have been treated unfairly?" "Does society have the right to treat students differently from other people who rent apartments?" Consider all issues from the humanistic point of view by raising questions of justice and injustice. Do not allow yourself to be pulled off these grounds during the discussion.

Person D: You are concerned with policy issues. "How much time and energy should be devoted to this problem relative to other pressing issues in student government?" "What authority do we have as a subcommittee to recommend or carry out particular solutions?" "Are there events in landlord-student discrimination that have already set a precedent?" In order to both ask and answer the type of questions you raise, you will need information based on facts and values. Probe the other discussion members to determine which issues are important to them. Find out how you can use their information to answer your questions.

Person E: For the first five minutes of this discussion, ask questions for clarification to determine whether you understand the other points of view. After that point, urge committee members to discuss separately each kind of issue that arises. Try to direct the decision-making process so that all issues are fairly but distinctly considered.

DISCUSSION: Did Persons B, C, and D continue to discuss separate issues of fact, value, and policy? If they did, you probably had an opportunity to see how the decision-making process breaks down. If each participant is discussing the same problem, but from a different perspective, it is unlikely that an acceptable resolution of the problem will be reached. Was Person E effective in convincing committee members to resolve issues of fact, value, and policy separately? If so, did this help the decision-making process? How can a discussion leader avoid the problems that result from trying to simultaneously argue issues of fact, value, and policy?

Group Discussion Contest

DESCRIPTION: This activity will provide you with an opportunity to either observe or participate in a group that uses a standard agenda for solving problems in a logical and objective manner. In this activity the group will be given a time limit to move through all the stages of discussion. In natural group discussion settings, it is unlikely that you would see a group move through all stages during one meeting, since most groups progress through the stages over longer periods of time. This activity can be considered a "speeded-up" version of a group engaged in a problem-solving task.

PROCEDURE: Divide into groups of five to seven members. Half of the groups should be observers, the other half participants. The following instructions are written for (1) the problem-solving groups and (2) the observation groups.

INSTRUCTIONS FOR PROBLEM-SOLVING GROUPS.   You have 40 minutes in which to discuss a problem from Step 1 through Step 8. The eight stages include:

Step 1: Defining the problem
Step 2: Limiting the topic
Step 3: Analyzing the problem
Step 4: Establishing criteria or standards for possible solutions
Step 5: Suggesting possible solutions
Step 6: Checking the individual solutions against all established criteria
Step 7: Carrying out the solution
Step 8: Evaluating the effect of the solution upon the problem.

Prior to the discussion, each member should have a thorough understanding of these steps. In addition, a problem area, such as downtown parking, low-income housing, quality of education, or medical services, should be selected by your group. Your 40 minutes officially begin *after* you have selected the problem area. Your primary task is to systematically evaluate the problem, using the steps above.

INSTRUCTIONS FOR OBSERVATION GROUPS.   The purpose of your group is to observe how effectively and efficiently the problem-solving group goes through the eight stages of problem resolution. In addition, you should observe leader emergence, group cohesion, and conflict resolution among group members. Focus your observation on the following questions, in addition to other questions that you feel are important:

1. Did the group discussion cover all eight stages of problem solving?
2. Was any stage either dismissed or given too much time? Why?

3. During which stage in the problem-solving task did you observe (a) leader emergence, (b) group conflict, and (c) group consensus?

4. What criteria would you use in determining whether the group was effective in its problem-solving task?

DISCUSSION: At the conclusion of the 40 minutes, each problem-solving group and its observation group should meet together for a 15-minute debriefing period. The observation group should have approximately five minutes to report its findings. The problem-solving group should then have an equal amount of time to respond to the observations. Finally, both groups should reach a consensus regarding (1) the effectiveness of the group discussion, (2) the identifiable leaders in the group, and (3) the efficiency with which the group proceeded through the eight stages of problem solving.

Personal Experiences

1. Attend a group meeting. Keep your participation to a minimum as you observe the task-oriented and maintenance behaviors used by other group members. Pay particular attention to whether members maintain the same role or change roles. Do any patterns emerge? For example, is one group member consistently a blocker when dealing with another member?

2. Choose a task-oriented or maintenance role that you can play in the next meeting you attend. Carefully study the behavior you select so that you can consistently display your chosen role. Following the meeting, ask other group members to respond to your behavior in the group. Then explain your experiment to the other group members so that they can understand what you did and why.

3. Select a group to observe for 30 minutes. While you are observing, apply the criteria you think are important for an effective group discussion. Then answer the question, "To what extent was the group effective during its discussion or problem-solving task?" After you have answered this question, reevaluate your criteria and make any revisions you feel would be appropriate.

4. Select a day during which you can observe your personal decision making. As you watch yourself making decisions, ask yourself the following questions. Which problems could be better resolved by a group than by an individual? What types of decisions do I usually seek advice on? When do I feel the need to share my decision making with another person?

5. Watch a television program that involves a lot of decision making (for instance, a detective program). To what extent were the decisions affected by (a) an authoritarian leader, (b) group pressure, or (c) a democratic or laissez-faire leader?

Group Discussion

1. How do you distinguish conversation from discussion in your everyday life?
2. How does bypassing affect the group process?
3. What distinguishes someone who exhibits leadership behavior from a leader?
4. In your opinion, to what extent is group pressure to conform in decision making instrumental, as contrasted to group pressure to carefully evaluate the evidence and options? Consider various types of decision-making groups, such as a jury, a senate subcommittee, and social groups.
5. Why is it important to understand the distinction between questions of fact, value, and policy in reference to group discussions?
6. Under what conditions would the three types of leadership (democratic, laissez-faire, and authoritarian) be most effective? Consider various types of groups, such as a shipwrecked crew, a dance committee, and a jury.
7. Think for a moment of the groups of which you are a member, and identify the communication networks that characterize them. Are those networks the most appropriate ones, given the nature of the task? If not, which network might be most effective?
8. Why is it important to analyze small group interaction? Consider differences between quantitative and qualitative analysis.

Organizational Communication

KEY CONCEPTS AND TERMS

Organization
Flexibility
Creativity
Increased availability
   of information
Term rewards and recognition
Variable compensation
Participative management
Task messages
Regulation and policy messages
Human messages
Innovative messages
Formal communication structure
Informal communication structure
Channel
Immediacy
Intermediary
Series transmission
Leveling

Sharpening
Assimilation
Network
Downward communication
Upward communication
Lateral or horizontal
   communication
Informal network
Professional
Networking
Interview
Employment interview
Appraisal interview
Exit interview
Directive interview
Nondirective interview
Business conference
Formal presentation

*K*ale hurried down the corridor, past the door to the auditorium. As she overheard the chief executive officer (CEO), she smiled. His voice was unmistakable—booming and intense—and now legendary at Madison Securities. Unable to resist the temptation, she opened the door, ever so slightly, and saw the CEO giving his annual report to the company's stockholders. Like clockwork, he was making his usual glowing remarks about the company's employees. Kale smiled and whispered the words "most valuable resource" in unison with him as he got to that part of the speech. He often used those words to describe his staff and always seemed to mean them.

That is why Kale and others were surprised when the CEO called a meeting of his staff one month later on a Monday morning. His meetings always were held on Friday afternoon after his usual round of golf. As Kale listened intently to the CEO's unusually quiet voice, she knew that something was amiss. Then it hit—those bitter words that no one expected. The company was cutting the staff by 20 percent. As Kale looked around the room at the faces of her colleagues, she could gauge nothing less than shock. Why had last month's message to the stockholders told such a different story?

Executives and managers all across the nation are often guilty of sending mixed messages. Mixed messages are those in which separate messages go to different audiences, one audience hears two different messages, or one's words contradict one's actions.[1] Although the use of mixed messages is not limited to serious situations such as that described above, they breed mistrust and reduce motivation in all communication contexts.

In short, effective communication is the key to success in any organization or workplace. In fact, research indicates that people with more highly developed communication abilities tend to be found at higher levels in the organizational hierarchy and tend to be promoted more often than people with less developed communication abilities.[2] Any job you take, whether as an attorney, construction worker, manager, salesperson, minister, psychiatrist, teacher, or patrol officer, requires the ability to communicate. This chapter is designed to help you understand communication in organizations and to provide you with guidelines for securing and maintaining a professional position most suitable to your needs.

WHAT IS AN ORGANIZATION?

In Chapter 7 you learned that a group consists of three or more persons with a common goal and the potential for interaction between members. You also learned that each of us is a member of at least five groups. You may be

---

[1]V. McClelland, "Mixed Signals Breed Mistrust," *Personnel Journal*, 66, no. 3 (1987), 26.

[2]B. D. Sypher and T. E. Zorn, Jr., "Communication-Related Abilities and Upward Mobility: A Longitudinal Investigation," *Human Communication Research*, 12, no. 3 (1986), 420–31.

wondering if these groups are also organizations. Not necessarily. **Organizations** are collected groups of people that are constructed to achieve specific goals that could not be met by individuals acting alone. Prior to and during the 1980s, organizations generally were characterized by division of labor, power centers (control by top management), substitutability of personnel, interdependence among organizational members or units, and coordination among those units. By the year 2000, many organizations across America will have a different look; they will be "flatter, leaner and more aggressive" than companies that characterized the '80s.[3] Specifically, organizations of the '90s and beyond will have six primary characteristics: flexibility, creativity, increased availability of information, team rewards and recognition, variable compensation, and participative management.

CHARACTERISTICS OF ORGANIZATIONS IN THE 1990S AND BEYOND

To be successful, organizations of the '90s and beyond must be characterized by **flexibility,** or the ability to perform a variety of different tasks effectively and efficiently. In the '90s, broader knowledge and experience concerning company operations and customer needs will be valued over depth of knowledge in a narrowly defined field. Such flexibility will also be valued more than endurance and loyalty.[4]

Indeed, one need look no further than the story of Scandinavian Airlines (SAS) to see the importance of this characteristic for organizational viability. During the 1980s, CEO Jan Carlzon turned the company's "top-down" style of management upside down and brought the crippled airline back into "the black" within a matter of months. Today, the day-to-day "management" of the company is in the hands of every member of the company. For example, in his book *Moments of Truth,* Carlzon recounts a story about how he received his first computer. Several members of his staff had decided that he needed to know when and why planes were delayed if he was going to run a successful airline. One day, while he was sitting at his desk, a young woman opened his door and rolled a computer and stand into his office. When he asked what she was doing, she told him. To this day, Carlzon can watch his terminal and determine if the company's planes are leaving on time. If a plane is delayed, he personally picks up a special phone that allows him to talk directly with his pilots and determine the problem. As a result, SAS is known as one of the most prompt and efficient airline carriers in the world. Carlzon's story embodies the essence of flexibility in the workplace.

A second characteristic of many organizations in the '90s is **creativity.** Creativity is defined here not only as originality of thought and use of

---

[3]J. H. Boyett and H. P. Conn, *Workplace 2000* (New York: Dutton, 1991), 2.
[4]Ibid., 4.

Interdependence is essential to effective organizational communication.

imagination, but also as a shared vision around which members of an organization can rally and direct their energies.[5] Creativity in the form of vision comes from two primary sources: (1) an ability to synthesize a great diversity of information in order to conceptualize new products or services and (2) the willingness to take risks to make the vision happen. After Steven Jobs stepped down from Apple Computer, he spent weeks reading science books in search of new ideas. While reading in the area of microbiology, he became intrigued with DNA and how it self-replicates. He placed a phone call to Nobel Prize–winning scientist Paul Berg, and arranged a lunch to talk about recombinant DNA. Jobs was curious about whether the Nobel laureate had ever attempted to speed up his experiments through computer simulations. Indeed, Berg *had* attempted to computer-simulate DNA recombinations; however, the primitive nature of the software and the expense involved in simulating such a complex phenomenon had prevented him from getting very far. With newfound excitement, Jobs decided to start a new computer company with this product in mind. His readings in microbiology and the

---

[5]J. Krantz, "Lessons from the Field: An Essay on the Crisis of Leadership in Contemporary Organizations," *The Journal of Applied Behavioral Science* 26, no. 1 (1990), 50.

meeting with Berg opened the door for the introduction of his next computer company.[6]

Increased availability of information and its effective use constitute the third characteristic of present and future organizations. This characteristic emerged with the age of computers and has redefined the concepts of efficiency and effectiveness in the workplace. Because of the prevalence of computers, organizations will continue to focus on the importance of computer literacy (and at least a rudimentary understanding of statistics) for its organizational members. People in the American work force who want to succeed will be required to have skills in the areas of data analysis and interpretation. They also will be asked to make recommendations based on their statistical and reasoning skills. Information sharing will be of great importance in sustaining such performances. As a result, an increased emphasis will be placed on performance reviews which, in turn, will direct and guide all organizational activities.[7]

The fourth characteristic of many present and future organizations is the use of *team rewards and recognition.* Because cooperation and teamwork have become central in many organizations, individuals who are able to operate effectively in teams are (and will be) the most valued organizational associates. Team leaders are those people who can assist the team in developing ideas, being innovative, overcoming challenges, and reaching consensus. Since peer pressure serves a vital function in team operations, the ability to communicate and develop relationships effectively are essential.[8] In the '90s, team rather than individual efforts will be emphasized and rewarded.

As an example of growing emphasis on the teamwork, consider how Hanes Knitwear decided to institute the team concept in their Sparta, North Carolina, plant.[9] During the 1970s, the Sparta plant was like many other American manufacturing plants: a good, "family" place to work with good pay and benefits, job security, and high individual incentives. However, in the 1980s, new plant management was brought in, and drastic changes resulted. With new performance standards, work methods, and attempts at increased productivity came employee dissatisfaction, decreased confidence, job insecurity, and low morale.

In 1985, an Atlanta-based consulting firm was hired to find out what was going on. After interviewing almost a third of the employees, the firm determined that the plant had experienced "change overload," and that part of the problem was a lack of employee understanding regarding the need for change, little two-way communication between management and employees, lack of communication and leadership skills on the part of management and supervisors, and too little team problem solving. The consulting firm recommended several risky and "revolutionary" ideas for alleviating the

---

[6]Boyett and Conn, 151–52.
[7]Ibid., 4–5.
[8]Ibid., 6.
[9]Ibid., 201–27.

problems. One of the primary recommendations was that changes be made in the area of teamwork. Specifically, the consultants recommended that more people be allowed to work in teams. (The team concept had been introduced by the new plant management, but its implementation had been a failure.) Additionally, the consultants recommended that certain teams be given training and follow-up coaching in problem-solving skills and be allowed to conduct in-depth problem solving. In short, the consulting firm was recommending true participative management.

Neither Hanes nor Sparta was willing to accept this idea at first. However, over time they did accept the new team concept and, between the spring of 1985 and fall of 1986, totally reversed a critical situation. Part of this reversal came from the plant's willingness to implement the team concept, with all of its nuances, and to reward team members accordingly.

Variable compensation is also predicted to be a characteristic of organizations in the future. By variable compensation, we mean that compensation for work will continue to take the form of base pay, but with less frequent or no annual increases. Instead of receiving raises, American workers will earn additional income through bonuses or incentive pay. The idea is based on a "pay-for-knowledge" system in which members will increase their base pay by learning and maintaining skills associated with multiple jobs in the organization. This type of reward flexibility will work well for highly motivated and skilled workers. Conversely, those workers who are less motivated or skilled will have fewer opportunities to increase their financial status in a major way.[10]

Finally, organizations in the 1990s are moving away from traditional management practices and toward an emphasis on *participative management.* The value of employee-operated companies was demonstrated by Jan Carlzon in our earlier example. As employees become more and more self-directed, they will need less and less supervision. Some futurists believe that supervisors will become a dying species by the year 2000. Supervisors will be replaced by team facilitators, who help teams manage communication and team relationships.[11]

COMMUNICATION DIMENSIONS IN ORGANIZATIONS

Think for a minute about the different organizations and businesses you've come in contact with in the last week. Now try to remember all the different channels of communication you used to get your message across to others. You may have called the power company to have electricity turned on, written a letter to a personnel director to ask about a summer job, told a

---

[10]Ibid., 6.
[11]Ibid., 7.

salesperson nonverbally that you are just looking and don't want any help, or ordered a hamburger and french fries over the intercom at a fast-food restaurant drive-thru.

You can probably think of a variety of other situations, but now focus your attention on the internal workings of an organization. How do companies communicate with their employees and customers? Organizations have structured ways of operating efficiently. At a supermarket, for example, a sign over the door reads "Customer Satisfaction Guaranteed." A customer gets home with a carton of milk and finds that it is sour. The customer returns the opened carton to a cashier, who refunds the money and tells a supervisor, who, in turn, tells the dairy manager, who tells the assistant store manager, who notifies the general store manager about the spoiled product. Organizations have different ways of communicating to ensure that everything functions smoothly. To help you better understand communication in organizations, the next section will examine (1) the types of messages sent in organizations, (2) formal and informal communication structures, and (3) communication networks.

Types of Messages Sent in Organizations

Communication in organizations takes a variety of forms. According to Goldhaber, these messages may be classified into one of four types: (1) task, (2) regulation/policy, (3) human, and (4) innovative.[12]

TASK MESSAGES. Messages that focus on the products, services, and activities of an organization are called *task messages.* Examples include messages about improving productivity, increased sales, quality of goods or services, and how to break into new markets. Task messages are necessary in order for members of an organization to complete activities associated with their jobs. Thus, messages associated with training, orientation sessions, and goal setting also qualify as task messages.

REGULATION/POLICY MESSAGES. *Regulation and policy messages* play a key role in organizational survival. These messages take the form of policy statements, organizational procedures, agendas, schedules, orders, and control measures that ensure that the organization will function properly. Regulation and policy messages also are associated with many formal and informal rules of the organization. For example, in many organizations, nepotism (the hiring of relatives) is discouraged as a rule.

HUMAN MESSAGES. Messages that focus on the relational element of the organization are termed *human messages.* These messages are associated with and directed by the attitudes, values, preferences, likes, and dislikes of organizational members. For example, at Georgia Power, every Friday is

[12]G. M. Goldhaber, *Organizational Communication*, 5th ed. (Dubuque, Iowa: Wm. C. Brown, 1990), 144–47.

designated "Jeans Day" for all employees. This informal "rule of conduct" takes into account the human element in the workplace. Praise for accomplishments, performance reviews, conflict management, rumors, counseling sessions, and social activities (such as coffee breaks and Christmas parties) are instances of human messages being communicated among organizational members.

INNOVATIVE MESSAGES. Messages that help an organization adapt to the changing environment are called ***innovative messages.*** Included in this category are messages associated with projects, new products or services, planning sessions, focus groups, and brainstorming sessions. For example, many companies have annual retreats for their employees in order to plan for the company's future. This retreat, its agenda, and the messages associated with it will take the form of innovative messages.

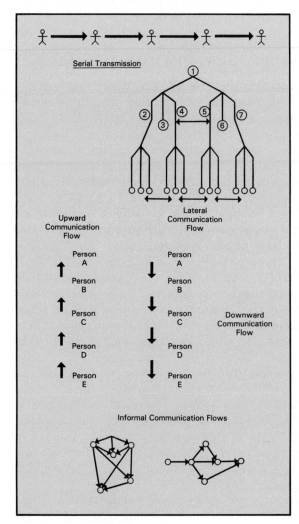

FIGURE 8–1

Networks Showing the Various Flows of Communication

Formal and Informal Communication

Messages that are sent through organizations may be classified as formal or informal. As we mentioned earlier, an organization's **formal communication structure** functions through rules, regulations, and procedures, and is characterized by more "formalized" channels of communication (see Figure 8–1).

At most universities, for example, students must petition for grade changes. Students first go to their instructor, the instructor then goes to the department chair, the department chair sends a memorandum to the dean of academic affairs, the dean sends notification to the records department, and the records typist finally notifies students about appropriate grade changes. Failure to properly follow the steps results in confusion, no grade change, and, ultimately, no action through the normal channels. Other organizations work similarly, with office workers reporting to supervisors, supervisors reporting to managers, and so on.

On the other hand, the **informal communication structure** of an organization is created wherever and whenever people meet and interact. It emerges on its own from interpersonal relationships within the organization. Social groups such as the water cooler crowd, the coffee lounge gang, or the lunch-hour jogging crew do not appear on any organizational chart; however, they serve at least eight vital organizational functions:

An informal communication structure.

1. They provide employees with a sense of belonging, security, and recognition.
2. They provide a way for employees to discuss their concerns in an open, friendly manner, thereby reducing stress and pressure.
3. They maintain a sense of personal integrity, self-respect, and free choice.
4. They facilitate formal communication.
5. They provide an informal network of interpersonal and group communication.
6. They provide an opportunity for social interactions.
7. They can be a source of practical information for managerial decision making.
8. They can produce future organizational leaders from within the ranks.[13]

In short, formal and informal communication structures work like the blades of a pair of scissors. Without both, an organization could not function effectively. The following section will explain how channels are used specifically to disseminate information in both formal and informal communication structures.

Communication Channels in Organizations

Organizations are linked through a series of communication **channels.** AT&T, MCI, and Sprint would have consumers believe that the telephone is the most effective channel of communication, when, in actuality, those organizations also use face-to-face interaction, letters, memoranda, and computerized messages to get information to others. Communication channels are often taken for granted, and we usually use the channel that is most economical and convenient. Currently, in order to save time, many people use the telephone to check facts like product prices, locations of businesses, and whether or not an establishment stays open on weekends; in the past, many people hopped into their cars and actually drove to the business in question.

Thoughtful consumers and organizations are becoming more aware of how channels affect the reception of messages. The channels we use to transmit messages send cues to receivers about how sources view the receiver and the message.

How the message is sent affects its degree of **immediacy,** or the degree of liking or disliking for a person or task. For example, rather than having to face a boss to quit, an employee might write a letter of resignation. The employee uses a less immediate channel of communication to avoid a personal confrontation. Channels of communication can be ranked in degree from the most to the least immediate.[14]

---

[13]Adapted from P. E. Han, "The Informal Organization You've Got to Live With," *Supervisory Management,* 28 (1983), 27–28.

[14]A. Mehrabian, *Silent Messages,* 2d ed. (Belmont, Calif.: Wadsworth, 1981).

1. Face-to-face
2. Picture phone
3. Telephone
4. Interactive computer
5. Telegram
6. Letter
7. Direct intermediary
8. Leaked rumor through an intermediary

As mentioned in Chapter 1, the most immediate channel of communication is face-to-face interaction. With face-to-face communication, participants are concerned with verbal as well as nonverbal behaviors, and receive direct feedback, which allows decisions to be made more quickly than with other channels. A customer who returns a camera in person is notified immediately that the camera will be repaired or replaced or that the money will be refunded. The use of picture phones also allows for verbal and nonverbal exchanges, but differences lie in the mechanical nature of the communication and in the power each person has to disrupt the communication process. The president of the textile company may use a picture phone to tell the personnel department that a hundred people must be laid off. Instead of listening to and watching the negative reactions, the president may then quickly sign off.

The next most immediate media include telephones and interactive computers. With the telephone, listeners attend to verbal and vocal cues, but there are no visual messages. Conversely, using interactive computers, communicators send and receive visual/verbal messages, but do not have the benefit of vocal cues. With telegrams and letters, we are even one more step removed. Nonverbal messages and direct feedback are eliminated with these two message forms. Because telegrams arrive more quickly than letters, however, they are considered more immediate. The immediacy of a letter is determined by whether or not it is handwritten, typed by the source, or typed by an intermediary. Job applicants feel more encouraged when a recruiter sends a hand-signed letter of acknowledgment rather than a signature-stamped form letter.

An **intermediary** is a messenger between the source and the receiver. When a direct intermediary is asked to deliver a message, immediacy is decreased because most of the original message is altered by the messenger. The least immediate communication channel is a leaked rumor through an intermediary. The message can be intentional or unintentional. An executive accountant, for example, may tell local freight lines in passing that the Internal Revenue Service will inspect the books of shipping companies in the near future, in hope that the companies will be prepared. Other information is leaked inadvertently, as when employees overhear news about promotions, new policies, and personnel shortages, and tell other employees before official notification is given.

Most communication in organizations occurs in a series. **Series transmissions** take place through a number of individuals who first act as receivers and then as senders of messages to others in the organization. Difficulties arise when intermediaries transmit messages inaccurately. How many times have you had to explain what you actually said when your message was taken out of context by someone else? For example, telling a friend that you don't want to go to a party could be misinterpreted to mean that you do not like the people giving the party. In fact, you might be tired, have an exam, or have other plans. Similar serial transmission problems often occur in organizations.

Research has shown that messages are distorted in one of three ways: leveling, sharpening, or assimilation. **Leveling** minimizes or omits information that may be important. For example, employees may say that they take only 15-minute breaks, when they actually take 20- to 30-minute breaks. **Sharpening** magnifies some details of the message. A secretary who overhears that there could be layoffs if production doesn't pick up might tell other secretaries that they are going to be laid off. The third and most important method of distorting messages is **assimilation.** When people assimilate, they transform messages to fit personal attitudes and expectations. Managers often ask assistant managers to give suggestions to new employees about selling techniques. The new employees could take the message as reinforcement or condemnation depending on their perceptions of the manager's and the assistant manager's motives. A desire for consistency in our attitudes and beliefs makes awareness of assimilation particularly important. Consistency of attitudes will be discussed more completely in Chapter 10.

NETWORKS

Channel selection and organizational network usage affect communication effectiveness. **Networks** are the interconnected channels or lines of communication used in organizations to pass information from one person to another. The flow of communication operates in downward, upward, lateral, and informal networks (Figure 8–1).

Downward communication directs information messages to subordinates. Messages include job instructions, individual evaluation (feedback), organizational procedures, training, and company-directed propaganda. Downward communication is solicited by employees who want feedback about their job performance, similar to the ways students seek results from tests, papers, and projects. Problems occur when information doesn't filter down to appropriate organizational levels. In addition, messages are often distorted and disrupted before they reach lower levels of the organization. For example, information may become distorted when the word "leaks out" that a company is planning layoffs, or when the chairman of the board is abruptly asked to resign by the board of directors.

Because downward communication is also seen as potentially threatening to employees, open communication between supervisors and subordinates becomes essential to organizational effectiveness. For example, when a supervisor calls and asks you to come to her office, you usually feel anxious because you are unsure of what issues are involved (job evaluation, promotion, and so on). Top management officials should also be selective in choosing the types of messages sent to subordinates. A personnel director who calls departmental meetings every Monday morning for the same pep talk will eventually be tuned out. Employees get bored with redundant information and tend to listen more carefully when meetings are scheduled only when necessary.

Upward communication is another network used in organizations. Managers need to encourage subordinates to send upward communication freely because it is an important indication of how effective downward communication has been. Since managers and superiors control the rewards of their employees through promotion, salary increase, or tenure, upward communication is offered cautiously by subordinates. Just as students refrain from criticism about courses and instructors until their grades have been posted, employees hesitate to criticize because they are afraid that what they say may influence their upward mobility. Through upward communication, however, subordinates can keep their supervisors informed of trends, incidents, changes and feelings. Additionally, by sending communication upward, they can inform supervisors of actual and potential problem areas—as well as opportunities for cost savings and increased output. The most useful way to improve upward communication, however, is by developing trust in the organization. With interpersonal trust at all hierarchical levels, employees feel free to comment both positively and negatively without fear of reprisal, and this freedom builds cohesiveness.

Lateral or *horizontal communication* takes place between peers at the same hierarchical levels. Its primary functions are task coordination, problem solving, information sharing, and conflict management.[15] Lateral communication often acts as a substitute for upward and downward communication when organizational members are frustrated or angry. Other factors that limit the frequency and effectiveness of lateral communication are rivalries, employee specialization, and lack of motivation. In instances such as these, lateral communication actually can become destructive. For example, employees may complain among themselves about an assembly line inspector who fails to check safety equipment. Over time they may even begin to sabotage his efforts. In short, as the quality of lateral communication increases, a number of positive outcomes occur. Problems can be solved, tasks can be coordinated, and overall conflict can be managed or avoided.

As we stated earlier in the chapter, *informal networks* also exist in organizations. Generally, they operate in the form of elaborate "grapevines." The grapevine was once thought to be characterized by disorganized, poorly defined lines of communication. However, research has shown that grapevines are faster and more accurate than formal lines of communication. During periods of excitement and insecurity, the grapevine becomes excep-

---

[15]Goldhaber, 160.

A classroom situation can use both upward and downward communication channels.

tionally active. For example, the installation of word processors in a secretarial pool may be perceived as a threat to overall job security. At times such as these, the grapevine will buzz with activity, and should be fed by managers with accurate information to keep the situation from getting out of hand. Should the situation become explosive, the results could be poor employee relations, decreased production, and employee layoffs.

The boundaries of all human organizations are defined and limited by the reach and efficiency of their communication networks.

OTTO LERBINGER

PROFESSIONALISM AND THE ORGANIZATION

The first part of this chapter examined organizational communication and the networks that exist in the organizational setting. We now turn to a consideration of professionalism in organizations. This section will examine "office politics" and the concept of networking. In addition, we will address the importance of personal appearance. Upon completion of this section, we hope you will have a clearer understanding of professionalism in the organizational setting.

Professionalism

What is a professional? A professional may be the punter for the Dallas Cowboys, the president of Exxon Corporation, an FBI agent, a CBS newscaster, an editor in a publishing company, a criminal lawyer, or a physical therapist. All **professionals,** no matter what their line of work, have one common characteristic: commitment to their jobs. Although new employees see themselves as professionals, maintaining a professional attitude can be difficult. Organizational success requires an understanding of how office politics and networking affect communication and professionalism in organizations. Each of these topics will now be addressed.

OFFICE POLITICS. We have all heard statements like: "She got the job because her father is a golfing buddy of the president," "He didn't deserve a promotion, but the top brass were snowed," or "There's no need to work hard, it's all political anyway." Like it or not, office politics does exist, and many bright, highly capable people fail at jobs because of their inability to cope with the situation. Professionals succeed by adapting to office politics and by establishing a power base that will allow themselves and others to function effectively. Such a power base may be developed by emphasizing and expanding your level of expertise and by creating liaisons with individuals who have access to pertinent information. Additionally, professionals can develop positive feelings and perceptions of relevant others, such as staff members and superiors. A third means of establishing a power base involves maximizing credibility with significant others. This not-so-difficult feat may be accomplished by joining outside professional groups from which one may receive recognition and support.[16]

However, once a power base is established, the professional must develop a set of strategies for implementing ideas and change—often the heart of success in any organization. Virginia Schein, a noted consultant in the area of organizational development, suggests using the following ten "power" strategies for overcoming office politics and implementing change:

1. *Present a nonthreatening image to others.* Learn the repertoire of acceptable arguments and highlight those aspects of your proposal that are most pertinent to your organization.
2. *Defuse opposition by bringing out conflict.* Inviting criticism and open discussion can enhance the process of organizational change. Doing so also allows you to keep up with your opposition and monitor resistance.
3. *Align with a powerful other, if possible.* Gaining management approval is another way of acquiring power and getting ideas off the ground.
4. *Develop liaisons* that maximize information flow and interactions with significant others.

---

[16]Adapted from V. E. Schein, "Organizational Realities: The Politics of Change," *Training and Development Journal,* 39 (February 1985), 37–41.

5. *Trade off short-term goals for long-term changes.* By solving a small problem for someone else, you will enhance your stature and set the stage for your ideas. In this way, "credit" can be cashed in later on projects in which you are interested.

6. *Strike while the iron is hot.* Follow up successful implementation of an idea with a request for approval to expedite a somewhat less popular program in which you believe.

7. *Conduct the necessary background research* in order to implement an idea successfully. Information is power. Additionally, it enhances credibility and esteem.

8. *Use a "neutral cover."* Associate your idea with an already approved and related noncontroversial companywide program. Then, build on the similarities that exist between that program and your more controversial idea.

9. *Inch along.* Begin with small changes and then "inch along" to more expansive aims. Avoid taking an "all-or-nothing" stance.

10. *Know when to withdraw.* If you find yourself competing with someone whom you know is incapable of succeeding, an unusual strategy is to withdraw openly and abruptly from the competition. If your hypothesis is correct about the competition, "higher-ups" may later come to you to implement change. (*Note:* This option may not be possible in many situations; however, it can be effective, given the appropriate circumstances.)[17]

NETWORKING.   Another vital dimension of professionalism is reflected in the concept of networking. **Networking** is the process of developing and using contacts for information, advice, and support. Male members of organizations have used informal networks for years to promote themselves professionally. These networks have taken the form of social clubs, civic organizations, and athletic groups. Recently women have begun to take the concept of networking one step further. As DeWine and Casbolt have noted, women have begun to deliberately formalize the activity by establishing "freestanding networks," or networks that link women with other women in an attempt to expand organizational contacts. The major objectives of such networking are (1) to provide women with opportunities to make organizational contacts, (2) to provide successful role models for women, (3) to generate solutions to problems, and (4) to effectively disseminate information.[18]

Whether you are male or female, just getting started or well underway in a professional career, networking with other professionals is important. Networking has become an important key to promotion and professional growth in organizations. As such, it is a vital concept to the professional.

---

[17]Ibid., 37–41.

[18]S. DeWine and D. Casbolt, "Networking: External Communication Systems for Female Organizational Members," *The Journal of Business Communication*, 20 (1983), 57–58.

PERSONAL APPEARANCE. Personal appearance has already been discussed in Chapter 4, but its importance cannot be overestimated. First impressions made by professionals serve a public relations function for organizations because appearance sends signals to others about attitudes, feelings, and personality. For many years IBM salespeople were required to wear dark suits or dresses, which stereotyped them as conservatives. Most companies no longer have stringent dress requirements for their employees, but clothing remains an important aspect of an organization's image. Thus, appropriate appearance is necessary for upward mobility within an organization. Observing people in higher management positions will indicate what attire is considered appropriate. When deciding what to wear to your first job interview, find out the dress of others who work in the position for which you are applying. Regardless of your size or sex, clothing should be coordinated in terms of color, line, texture, and style.

COMMUNICATION SITUATIONS

As a professional, you must be aware of various communication situations that exist in organizations. From what you have read thus far, you may think that succeeding in an organization involves little more than getting along with others and understanding office politics. While interpersonal relationships are important, the most important form of communication for upward mobility is the formal, structured communication in an organization. The three most common structured communication situations are the interview, the business conference, and the formal presentation.

The Interview

If you have answered survey questions for a public opinion firm, tried to get information from a local politician about foreign policy, answered questions when applying for a job, or talked about job preferences with a career planning counselor, you have participated in an interview. *Interviews* are the most common form of planned communication and are often defined as "a process of dyadic communication with a predetermined and serious purpose designed to interchange behavior and involving the asking and answering of questions." [19] Although interviews take place for a variety of purposes and in a variety of situations, we are most concerned with interviews in organizations.

TYPES OF INTERVIEWS. There are several different types of interviews, each requiring its own skills and offering its own benefits. During an *employment interview,* the employer tries to gain as much pertinent

---

[19]C. J. Stewart and W. B. Cash, *Interviewing: Principles and Practices*, 3d ed. (Dubuque, Iowa: Wm. C. Brown, 1983), 5.

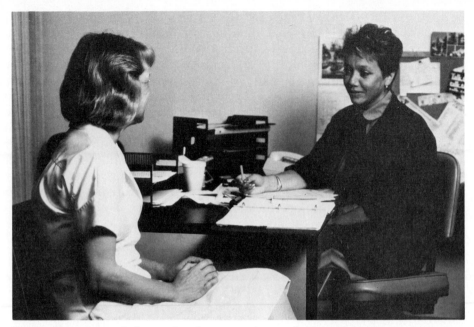

Gaining pertinent information is one major goal of employment interviews.

information about the applicant as possible. This kind of interview is usually broad in scope and deals with all areas of the interviewee's background and personality. The interviewer wants to find out about the applicant's work history, work habits, ability to relate to others, health, and other areas not covered extensively in the résumé or application form. Interviewees, however, do not become merely answer-producing machines. They have their own interests in mind and ask about things such as the working situation, benefits, salary, and opportunities. Thus, information is given and sought by both participants.[20]

In most companies employees are given **appraisal interviews** on a regular basis. In such an interview the worker's past performance and future potential are discussed. The discussion may cover a variety of topics, such as salary, job improvement, outside schooling, or physical health. The objective is clear—to let employees know how they are doing, how they need to improve job performance, and where they are headed. If conducted properly, appraisal interviews also let employees know that their employer cares about their work and their well-being.

When employees plan to leave their jobs, they are often given an **exit interview,** which is designed to find out how they feel about the company, the working environment, and other job conditions. The company can use this information to assess itself and make changes where necessary.

---

[20]For a more complete discussion concerning preparation for job interviews, see Appendix A.

APPROACHES TO INTERVIEWING. Be it an employment, appraisal, or exit interview, the participants can adopt one of two possible communication strategies: directive or nondirective. As an interviewer in a **directive interview,** you must have not only a general plan of what you wish to accomplish but also a step-by-step outline to follow. Although this type of interview has the advantage of being thorough, it may be so abrupt and impersonal that the interviewee is uncomfortable. As the following dialogue between the manager of a men's store and a job applicant illustrates, when you are a directive interviewer, you use frank, matter-of-fact questions, which give you complete control over the discussion. In this case, the store manager is seeking to fill an open sales position.

Interviewer: By looking at your résumé, I can see you already have experience in the retail business. What exactly did your job entail at the department store?

Interviewee: At first I was at the register, but later I waited on the customers and wrote out sales slips.

Interviewer: What did you enjoy most about the job?

Interviewee: I like people and especially helping them out. So, I really enjoyed giving them some help with their purchases and answering any questions they had.

Interviewer: Is there any particular reason for your leaving the job?

Interviewee: Since the store was so large, it was sort of impersonal. I want to work in a smaller place where I can deal more with the customers. The department store is often self-service.

Interviewer: Do you have any plans beyond salesperson?

Interviewee: Yes, I hope to advance to store manager some day.

In a **nondirective interview,** you give interviewees a great deal of leeway in their responses. This kind of interview is not entirely unstructured, however. If an interviewee strays from the subject, he or she is redirected back to the topic. The conversation may run freely, but the major points are developed by the interviewer. The disadvantage of this approach is that you may not obtain all the needed information. The advantage is that an informal atmosphere relaxes the interviewee and encourages him or her to speak freely. Here is an example of a nondirective exit interview:

Interviewer: John, I'm sorry to see you leave, but I hear you have a good job offer.

Interviewee: Yes, B&G Steel Company is looking for a foreman.

Interviewer: So, tell me all about it.

Interviewee: Well, I'll be managing about fifty people and getting a lot more money. This will help the problems with the family.

Interviewer: Problems?

Interviewee:	Yeah, you know how it is with two teenage kids . . . braces, sports, and school supplies. I liked this job and I really don't want to leave, but I didn't see any chance of promotion. And I couldn't wait any longer. Oh, and the new place is located pretty close to home, so I don't have such a long drive. The car is getting pretty run down, and just last week I thought it was a goner—couldn't start it up for hours!
Interviewer:	You said you liked your job here. Why?
Interviewee:	Well, the fellows in the shop are friendly, and the shop foreman is a good guy.

This sample shows both the strengths and weaknesses of the nondirective interview. Although the interviewee certainly feels relaxed, the interviewer has learned a lot about his personal problems but relatively little about working conditions at the shop. The ability to communicate effectively can obviously pay off in an interview situation.

The Business Conference

After you join the work force of an organization, the business conference will be your most frequent formal communication interaction. The **business conference,** or small group discussion, usually involves five to ten people who interact about organizational concerns. Meetings are usually designed to

A business conference.

Video teleconferencing is widely used as a method of formal communication for nationwide and multinational corporations.

disseminate information or to develop solutions to current organizational problems. A union spokesperson may explain to a small group of unionized automotive-employee leaders the latest features of their negotiated contract, while management personnel get together to discuss methods of dealing with union demands. The business conference is essential to every organization, and the principles presented in Chapter 7 concerning small group communication should provide information to help you participate more effectively both as a group member and as a group leader.

The Formal Presentation

The most structured form of organizational communication is the **formal presentation.** The responsibility is placed on one person to create interest and to motivate the audience to listen. The speaker sends a message orally with the aid of visual and audiovisual materials. A young architect showing a proposal for a new community sports arena to more established architects in the firm will carefully plan a verbal presentation explaining benefits, square footage, energy conservation features, space usage, costs, and so on, including visual aids to ensure clarity and receptivity of the message.

As an employee, you may be asked to explain new organizational policies, teach other employees about the proper use of technical equipment through demonstration, attempt to persuade employees to accept new ideas, and try to motivate employees to greater productivity. Individuals in organizations are unique, and you must understand them before preparing a message to meet their needs. Chapter 9 explains methods of audience analysis that should make your job easier. For a formal presentation you will also be concerned about your delivery, types of communication purposes, organization of messages, and how to secure the information to be included in your presentation. Careful consideration of the principles in Chapters 10, 11, and 12 should improve your formal presentation ability.

Visual aids can be an informal part of a formal presentation.

SUMMARY

Organizations are groups of individuals constructed and reconstructed to strive for specific goals that could not be met by individuals alone. Many organizations of the '90s are characterized by flexibility, creativity, increased availability of information, team rewards and recognition, variable compensation, and participative management. These qualities will become more pervasive as we near the year 2000.

Organizations also are characterized by four types of messages: task, regulation/policy, human, and innovative messages. These messages are affected by the structure of communication used in the organization. Formal structures function through organizational rules and regulations, while informal structures function through interpersonal relationships among employees. The importance of a message within the organizational structure determines the immediacy of the channel used, with important messages being delivered through oral channels, either alone or in combination with written channels.

Networks are the channels or lines used to transmit messages from one person to another. Communication networks operate in downward, upward, lateral, or informal modes. Because of the serial nature of communication in organizations, information is often distorted by leveling, sharpening, or assimilation.

After you have familiarized yourself with an organization's communication patterns and structures, it is important for you to understand professionalism and its role in the organization. Professionalism increases job satisfaction and productivity. Understanding the effects of office politics, networking, and personal appearance should improve communication in organizations.

Knowledge of office politics should help remind you to select group affiliations carefully. Professionals succeed by establishing a power base and developing a set of strategies for implementing ideas and change.

Networking is also a valuable tool for professionals' growth in organizations.

Networking involves the development and use of contacts for information, advice, and moral support. Likewise, maintaining a "professional" personal appearance contributes to others' perceptions of you as a professional.

Office politics is usually part of the informal communication structures, but for upward mobility, the formal, structured situations are most important. The most common formal communication situations are interviews, business conferences, and formal presentations. Knowing what to expect and which guidelines to follow should help you perform effectively.

EXERCISES

Group Experiences

Organizational Networks

DESCRIPTION: Organizations use a variety of networks to communicate with employees. Supervisors use downward communications to give instructions. Subordinates send upward communications to complain about working conditions. Peers communicate laterally to establish interpersonal bonds, and at times everyone communicates at once in haphazard informal networks. Networks are essential for interdepartmental coordination, but networks are often used inappropriately. This exercise is designed to provide experience in dealing with communication networks within organizations.

PROCEDURE: Divide into groups of five to seven persons. Within the groups, come up with a topic that could be used in the four communication networks. For example, each network is used in training programs in which new employees are instructed on the proper use of copying equipment, regulations, and so on. After the groups decide on topics, get group members to line up in rows (like a train). Exchange topics between the groups. With downward communication, the first person in the row should pass detailed instructions through channels until they reach their proper destination: person seven. (No feedback should be given, and all communication must move downward.) Next, divide the row into groups of two to three persons and discuss the message laterally; but again, remember that no interactions should take place with others in the chain. After a few minutes, form the rows again and send upward communication about the initial interaction. Finally, let members discuss the topic with whomever they wish.

DISCUSSION: Which communication network was the most satisfactory? You probably found that each situation contained unique problems. What problems were encountered with the networks? When would the use of one network be most effective? How could organizations improve their internal communication? What organizational network would you like to work in when you graduate?

Conference Compatibility

DESCRIPTION: One of the most important formal communication situations within an organization is the conference. Interaction patterns during conferences are affected by the purpose of the meeting, the methods of control during the meeting, and the group membership. This exercise shows how people participating in conferences affect conference outcomes.

PROCEDURE: Divide the class into male and female groups of five to seven people. Select a controversial topic that encourages active discussion (such as sexual freedom, abortion, or homosexuality). Each group should discuss the topic for five to ten minutes. Finally, change groups so that there is only one member of the opposite sex per group; again discuss the selected topic. After the second group discussion, have each member choose the group in which he or she felt most comfortable.

DISCUSSION: Share individual group selections with the rest of the class. What differences were there between the first and second group interactions? Why were there differences? How was the atmosphere affected by different-sex participants? How did your responses change with different group members? What does this exercise tell you about organizational conference effectiveness?

Personal Experiences

1. Find a local organization to observe for one day. Try to analyze the formal and informal communication structures. Determine the purposes and power structure of the organization. How would you fit into this organization? What kinds of office politics would you have to avoid? After you've decided whether or not you would feel comfortable in this organization, make a list of personal criteria that organizations must meet to satisfy your needs.

2. Set up an interview with someone in middle management in an organization. During the interview, ask that individual to discuss the concept of professionalism from his or her point of view. What is a

professional? What behaviors does he or she elicit? What examples does this person give of nonprofessional behavior? Then, examine your behavior in light of the talk you've had. How do you see your own behavior? How could you improve?

Discussion Questions

1. How can organizations improve their formal and informal communication structures?
2. What communication channels exist in organizations, and what role does immediacy play in their effectiveness?
3. How are messages distorted within an organization's structure? Formally? Informally?
4. Why is it important to understand office politics?

Ethics, Intentions, and the Speaker-Audience Relationship

KEY CONCEPTS AND TERMS

Public speaking
Public communication
Ends-justify-means approach
Social utility approach
Situation ethics approach
Credibility-centered approach
Speech to inform
Speech to persuade
Speech to entertain
Audience analysis
Demography
Belief

Value
Instrumental values
Terminal values
Casual audience
Passive or partially oriented
   audience
Selected audience
Concerted audience
Organized audience
Polarization
Social facilitation
Circular response

*J*amie had worked on her presentation for weeks. Her head virtually reeled as she put down her pen and wearily glanced out the window that overlooked the bay. As she watched the distant sailboats bobbing lazily on the water, she imagined herself dressed in her new red suit—making a splash with her boss and the other advertising executives who would be present. How could she lose? Her ideas were fresh; the facts and figures impressive. "At last," she said out loud, as she reached for her favorite chocolates, "everything has fallen into place."

The next day Jamie rose, showered quickly, and threw on her clothes. As she turned, she caught a glimpse of herself in the full-length mirror. "Ummm . . . ," she purred, "now go out there and knock their socks off." With a bagel in one hand and her briefcase in the other, she dashed out the door and headed down the steps toward the car. Between bites, she practiced first her opening lines, then the statistics that would provide the foundation for her entire presentation.

Upon arriving at the office, Jamie quickly disposed of her purse and headed down the long, austere corridor that led to the conference room. The expensive Titian artwork that lined the walls reminded her of the illustration she would use about halfway through her "act." As she entered the room, everyone turned to greet her. Jamie smiled and made a point to address each person who was present by name.

At last, after the joking and laughter subsided, Jamie began her well-researched presentation. Knowing that teasing and off-color jokes characterized the beginning of all such presentations with this group, she launched into a slightly "blue" story designed to make the transition. As she finished with the punch line and a devilish grin, she felt her smile melting and a silence descend on the room. Attempting to recover from the icy stares, she moved awkwardly but swiftly to the first major argument of the presentation.

As Jamie moved from point to point—attempting to captivate the others at every turn—the only feedback she received was a coolness that virtually permeated the air. Feeling slightly nauseated as she made her closing remarks, Jamie realized the fatal error she had made. Her research had been brilliant—her ideas beyond compare. But she had lost her audience at the outset by trying to be "just one of the boys."

As you can see from the above illustration, public speaking involves more than simply preparing a message. This form of communication also involves an ability to analyze your audience as well as to adjust a given message to its overall purpose. To aid you in learning how to succeed at these two tasks, this chapter focuses on a variety of topics ranging from the general purposes of a message to audience analysis. Additionally, you will discover some of the ethical responsibilities that you have as a speaker and the moral dilemmas that you may encounter along the way. Upon concluding this chapter, we hope that you will be well on your way toward success in public speaking settings. At the very least, we hope that you can avoid situations such as the one Jamie got herself into.

PUBLIC COMMUNICATION: AN OVERVIEW

Communication theory is relatively new, but the study of public speaking dates back to ancient Greece, when Aristotle and his contemporaries defined and practiced the principles of rhetoric. While these principles still provide the foundation of public speaking theory, modern styles of public speaking and public speaking situations are much less formal than they were in Aristotle's time. Even with less emphasis on formality, however, public speaking situations can intimidate people who are usually very talkative and outgoing. Although public speaking includes many of the same communication skills as other speaking situations, some people who are comfortable while talking in small groups feel anxious and experience communication apprehension in public speaking settings.

Perhaps these difficulties arise because *public speaking* differs from other forms of communication in two ways. First, a public speaking situation includes two distinct and separate roles: speaker and audience. Second, in this speaker-audience relationship, the speaker carries more responsibility for the communication interaction than does the audience. In other communication situations, speakers and listeners exchange roles and share this responsibility.

A public speaking situation need not be overly formal and imposing; it doesn't necessarily require a stage to separate the speaker from the audience. All of us participate in public speaking when we contribute to a class discussion, when we make a suggestion at a staff meeting, or when we tell a story at a party.

Public communication, like other forms of communication, serves several purposes. When a karate instructor gives a demonstration on self-defense, she uses public communication to instruct. When Ralph Nader speaks on the need for better consumer protection laws, he uses public communication to advocate his point of view. The mayor who delivers an annual Fourth of July speech to the townspeople uses the "soapbox" to stir feelings of patriotism. Public communication can also be used to praise and to blame, to accuse and to defend. When a local political candidate speaks to a community group, he may use public communication to blame the current officeholder for everything that's wrong with the community, while a Native American principal chief uses the same form of communication to praise community leaders for helping his or her tribe move toward greater self-determination and economic development. The prosecuting attorney who addresses a jury uses public communication to accuse the defendant of a crime. To accomplish the opposite end, Supreme Court Justice Clarence Thomas used his testimony during the 1991 Senate confirmation hearings as a means of defending himself against sexual harassment charges.

Since public speaking is such a useful tool for accomplishing a wide range of purposes, it is important to clear up some popular myths about speech making. The first is that the ability to make speeches is natural and

Clarence Thomas successfully used public communication to defend himself against charges of sexual harassment.

cannot be learned. While some people do have a talent for it, effective public speaking can be learned through training and practice. Students who take speech courses generally improve their speech-making ability and increase their self-confidence.

Effective public speaking depends on content and delivery. Contrary to popular opinion, good intentions are not enough when it comes to making a speech—they do not guarantee an effective presentation. Although someone may have something valuable to communicate, the message will be lost if the delivery is poor. Another misconception, however, is that it is not what you say that is important, but how you say it. The most eloquent delivery cannot save a meaningless message. Both content and delivery are important in achieving effective communication.

Finally, effective public speaking requires that the speaker be responsible for the message he or she presents. Although people who "speak their minds" are often praised for their stamina and courage, the effective speaker knows that, by virtue of gaining the opportunity to speak, she or he also acquires the chance to influence others. Reckless, irresponsible, or unethical speakers can cause great harm both to the members of the audience and to subsequent decisions they might make.

We turn now to one of the most important statements concerning public speaking: An effective speaker is one who begins with a sense of responsibility. Once we have considered the nature and implications of this statement, we may return to a discussion of the overall purposes of public speaking—to inform, to persuade, and to entertain.

ETHICAL RESPONSIBILITY AND THE PUBLIC SPEAKER

It would be naive to believe that all speakers possess the morality and good intentions included in Aristotle's concept of *ethos*. One need only study the persuasive tactics of someone like Hitler to be reminded that public communication can be used for evil as well as good. While ethical problems in communication are most often thought of only in a persuasive context, they apply to informative speaking as well. The student of communication must consider the ethics involved in all public communication.

Think for a moment about the nature of American politics today. Party candidates clash both between and within their ranks, and independent candidates clash with proponents of both. Although such "openness" is not inherently negative, speakers of one group often hurl insults at members of the opposing groups, and the recipients of these insults often respond in a similar manner. Because of the amount of time spent in such activities, the issues themselves are overlooked in many instances, and disenchanted voters who are genuinely concerned can do nothing but attempt, with little knowledge or trust, to choose the best candidate for a job.

American politics, however, is not the only arena in which ethics are problematic. In everyday life, ethics, morals, and responsibilities are called into question, leaving many to believe that ethical principles should be left to the individual. However, at least four different approaches regarding the bases of ethical behavior exist in this country today. These include the *ends-justify-means* approach, the *social utility* and the *situation ethics* approaches, and the *credibility-centered* approach to ethics and responsibility.[1] Before discussing each of these positions, however, we need a definition of ethics. For us, *ethics* will be defined as questions concerning the concepts of right versus wrong and good versus evil; in addition, ethics focuses on the nature of moral obligation.

Likewise, before we continue our discussion of ethical approaches, we must understand the nature of rhetorical (persuasive) principles themselves, or the means by which arguments are developed, understood, and critiqued. Principles of persuasion (or rhetorical principles)—like all principles addressing human behavior—are *amoral* in and of themselves. More specifically, they can be used for purposes that are evil or good. When applied to our discussion of the bases of ethical responsibilities, the same principle of amorality again applies. Each of these approaches can be used for right or for wrong. Armed with this understanding, we turn to the four approaches to ethics. As you will see, each approach has its merits and its potential pitfalls.

---

[1]B. E. Bradley, *Fundamentals of Speech Communication: The Credibility of Ideas*, 5th ed. (Dubuque, Iowa: Wm. C. Brown, 1988), 48–53.

Ends-Justify-Means Approach

When speakers believe the **ends justify the means** in attaining their goals, they adopt the position that any available means of persuasion may be used as long as the end result is honorable, just, or desirable. As a result of such a belief, however, speakers who take this position may distort the truth, conceal motives, twist reasoning, or make emotional appeals in order to prevent their listeners from making their own rational decisions.[2] The major flaw in this approach to ethics is that the speaker often believes that he or she has either the right or the ability to make such decisions. The 1990 invasion of Kuwait and the accompanying slaughter of innocent women, children, and animals by Iraqi soldiers is one instance in which the ends do not justify the heinous means. Likewise, the intentions and motivations underlying alleged FBI infiltration and disruption of groups such as the American Indian Movement are questionable at best.[3] In short, if we condone the use of such an approach to ethics, we must also be able to ensure that the end is in fact a good and justifiable end. Thus, it is imperative that the speaker who takes this approach be certain that the aims are justifiable and that the choice of rhetorical strategies is not based solely on the desire to achieve the aims or goals.

Social Utility Approach

When taking a **social utility approach** to ethics, the speaker determines which programs to advocate, based on his or her perceptions of the needs of a particular group. More specifically, he or she addresses two major questions in developing a program or message: (1) What program (or message) would most benefit the target group? and (2) What are the possible effects on other groups involved? If, for example, the president of a college decides that campus beautification is the most important priority, what is the best possible option to achieve that goal? This question would be the first that she would consider. Second, she would need to determine how that decision could affect the needs of other campus groups—for example, groups that advocate the need for faculty raises and stipend increases for graduate teaching assistants.

Situation Ethics Approach

The approach taken by a proponent of **situation ethics** is that consideration must be given to the nature of each individual situation before determining the "best" or "most loving" things to do. As a function of such goals, four factors are usually taken into account: (1) the desired end, (2) the means that

---

[2]Ibid., 48–49.

[3]P. Matthiessen, *In the Spirit of Crazy Horse* (New York: Viking, 1991), 106.

Ethical concerns play a major role in our everyday lives.

are to be used to achieve that end, (3) the motive behind the act, and (4) the consequences of the action.[4]

For example, the hospital administrator who argues that instances of euthanasia should be decided on a case-by-case basis would be advocating a situational approach to ethics. Although on first sight such an approach seems reasonable and rational, it can often lead to diverse decisions about particularly complex problems. If the life of a comatose patient is at stake, should one take into account the wishes and religious beliefs of the family? For some people the answer would be clear-cut; for others, it might not be so clear. In addition, the use of this approach requires both sophistication and objectivity on the part of its user or proponent—a sophistication and objectivity that the speaker may not possess.

Credibility-Centered Approach

The final approach on which we will focus is the **credibility-centered approach.** In using this approach, the speaker comes to the public commu-

[4]Bradley, 50.

nication setting with the objective of demonstrating, through particular methods, his or her competence and trustworthiness. As a result, the speaker:

1. Constructs a rational basis for argument based on a thorough review of all available information;
2. Presents evidence accurately;
3. Uses sound reasoning;
4. Retains objectivity with regard to groups or organizations with which he or she is affiliated;
5. Gives credit to all sources of information;
6. Stands firm on convictions;
7. Acknowledges when information is incomplete;
8. Avoids oversimplification;
9. Avoids the arousal of emotions on irrelevant bases.[5]

Perhaps this approach to public speaking contains the most effective overall treatment of ethics. However, it is up to the individual speaker to determine his or her own approach to achieving specific goals and objectives—*after* addressing the ethical considerations.

In American politics, it has become a norm for politicians to break promises to the public—promises that at one time got them elected into office. We are all familiar with the Iran-Contra hearings, during which high-ranking officials were found to have violated the public trust. We also have been bombarded with countless advertisements making misleading or exaggerated claims for products and services. We have seen newspapers, television, and radio select which news to report according to their editorial bias. Each of these examples represents an affront to our integrity and our sense of fairness and decency. Yet most of these affronts occur within the limits of the law. It is difficult to propose legislation that would protect our integrity but not infringe upon our basic rights. For example, how can a law govern campaign promises without infringing upon freedom of speech? How can a law determine on what page a particular news story should be printed? Aside from being impossible in a practical sense, the very idea suggests a violation of freedom of the press.

As students of communication, we must remember that ethics are separate from law and are based on our moral, and not our legal, system. It is up to every speaker to examine his or her own ethics and those of the speech before it is presented (see Figure 9–1).

---

[5]Ibid., 52–53.

FIGURE 9–1
Ten Questions for Examining Your Ethics as a Public Speaker

1. In determining your position regarding a topic, have you adequately examined all related facts? weighted them accordingly? separated facts from present loyalties?

2. Have you carefully looked at the issues and facts to determine how an "opponent" might view them? taken your "opponent's" point of view into account as you've constructed your message?

3. Have you closely examined the history and context of all facts to ensure that none has been taken out of context?

4. To whom do you give your loyalties? self? family? race? sex? boss? company? society? Have these loyalties affected your message in any way? If yes, how?

5. What is your intention in presenting the message? What are the probable consequences of making this presentation? Could limitations of knowledge on your part lead to harm rather than to good?

6. Whom could your message injure or adversely affect? Could you conduct a discussion with the potentially affected parties prior to the presentation?

7. Are you sure that your position will be valid in the long term as well as the short term?

8. Could you present this message to your boss, spouse, children, society, or creator without any qualms?

9. What is the potential of your message if it is understood? misunderstood?

10. Under what conditions would you allow exceptions to your point of view?

Source: Adapted from L. L. Nash, "Ethics Without the Sermon," in W. M. Hoffman and J. M. Moore, *Business Ethics: Readings and Cases in Corporate Morality,* 2d ed. (New York: McGraw-Hill, 1990), pp. 79–90. Reprinted by permission of the publisher.

PURPOSES OF COMMUNICATING IN THE PUBLIC SETTING

General Purposes

In order to be successful in a public speaking setting, you must have a clear purpose in mind: As the speaker, you must know whether you intend to inform, persuade, or entertain your listeners. Although these three goals often overlap and will be more fully discussed in the following chapter, we now take a brief look at each.

INFORMATION EXCHANGE. The exchange of information is basic to public communication, and all of us have participated in this type of communication situation. The *speech to inform* can take place in a variety of locations: on a football field, in a classroom, or in a convention hall. Similarly, the speech to inform can use a number of formats: instructions, reports, lectures, and demonstration talks are but a few examples. The coach explaining the strategy and tactics of a particular play informs the team through instructions. The surgeon informs colleagues about a new kidney transplant technique by delivering a report on the subject. Airline attendants inform passengers how to prepare for an emergency by demonstrating lifesaving equipment. All of these examples represent public speaking situations in which the speaker's main purpose is to inform.

Since the informative speaker's goal is to successfully transmit information, he or she must present the information in a way that holds the attention of the audience. Perhaps you can remember teachers who could put you to sleep even though they were talking about a topic that interested you. Or perhaps you have had the opposite experience, in which a professor brought to life a subject you had previously considered fatally boring.

The success of an informative speech depends on how well the material is understood. Even if the audience is motivated to listen and the speaker is dynamic, the final evaluation of success must be based on what was learned by the audience. A brilliant speech on newly discovered subatomic particles can be a failure if the audience cannot understand it.

Therefore, you must organize your speech to aid audience learning and aim for clarity and accuracy in your presentation.

PERSUASION. The purpose of persuasion is to influence an audience's behavior or way of thinking. The art of persuasion has been a subject of interest throughout history; it is a powerful tool that can be used for both good and evil. In defining persuasion as a means of bringing about behavior change, Aristotle said that a speaker could accomplish his or her end by using *logos* (logic and reasoning), *pathos* (an appeal to the emotions), and *ethos* (proof of the speaker's morality and credibility). We will define **persuasion** as a deliberate attempt to reinforce or change the attitudes, beliefs, or behavior of another person or group of people through communication.

ENTERTAINMENT. We can define the **speech to entertain** as one that is intended to bring the audience pleasure. Such a speech is usually humorous, or at least characterized by some degree of humor. A humorous speech may be gently amusing or boisterously funny. The effect depends upon the speaker's personality, delivery, and brand of humor. A speaker can use exaggeration, sarcasm, witticisms, or burlesque humor when presenting a speech to entertain.

Listeners expend much less effort during a speech to entertain than during an informative or persuasive speech. The very nature of the entertainment speech creates speaker-audience rapport. Usually, such a speech is considerably more informal than other forms of public speaking.

THE SPEAKER AND THE AUDIENCE: AUDIENCE ANALYSIS

Once you have determined your general purpose, it's time to take a look at the audience to whom you are planning to speak. Janet Elsea, president of a successful Washington, D.C., communication consulting firm, divides audiences into four major types: those that "love you," those that "think they are impartial," those that "couldn't care less," and those that "love you not." Because communication focuses on the mutual exchange of meanings, it is important to develop strategies and adjust content appropriately to each.[6]

Audiences that "love you" are those that are friendly and predisposed to you, your topic, or your viewpoint. With these groups, Elsea advises that you use an "open and warm" delivery, including increased eye contact, smiles, gestures, and body movement. She also recommends that you vary your overall speech rate and loudness—and use examples, illustrations, humor, anecdotes, and personal testimony as supporting material.[7]

Most of us like to believe that we are calm, rational, and objective when, in fact, research indicates the opposite—that is, we generally approach controversial topics with our minds made up. Because audiences *think* they are objective, however, their perceptions should be honored. Thus, when attempting to speak to an audience on a controversial topic, use a delivery style that is dispassionate, even, and controlled. Additionally, focus on facts and figures, expert testimony, and comparisons and contrasts as primary forms of evidence. Avoid humor, personal stories, and flashy visual aids, and organize your materials in the most precise and least controversial fashion possible. Finally, allow time for a question-and-answer session.[8]

The third type of audience to which we, at times, must speak is that which basically "couldn't care less." (If you think for a moment, you probably can identify at least one instance when you—yes, you—were a member of such an audience.) As a speaker in a situation such as this, your ally is a dynamic speaking style. According to Elsea, dynamic speakers are those who vary their speech rate, loudness levels, movement, gestures, facial expressions, and eye behavior. Additionally, they limit themselves to brief and interesting remarks. Supporting materials that will attract such audiences include the use of humor, cartoons, and anecdotes; interesting visual aids; metaphors; quotations; and startling statistics. Conversely, you will lose an apathetic audience if you stand behind the lectern without moving, pass out reading materials, or use boring overheads. Finally, "fewer than three major points" should be the rule.[9]

Audiences that "love you not" represent the fourth type of audience that

---

[6]J. G. Elsea, "Strategies for Effective Presentations," *Personnel Journal*, 64, 9 (1985), 31–32.
[7]Ibid., 31–32.
[8]Ibid., 31–32.
[9]Ibid.

Elsea identifies. Such audiences look for chances to ridicule you and to spin the situation out of control. To handle this type of audience, remain calm, and speak slowly and evenly. Force yourself to use gestures purposefully and to avoid random movements. Select supporting materials that are data-based and derived from expert testimony. Avoid anecdotes and jokes, for they may anger or irritate your audience. If possible, avoid question-and-answer sessions, but, if they are a must, insist on a moderator, written questions, and a definite time frame. Elsea also suggests that you make a final statement after you have taken the last question.[10]

As you can see, communication in the public setting is much like that in other settings: It too involves both a listener and a speaker. A speaker's ideas, speaking style, and nonverbal behavior are only a part of successful delivery—the listener is equally important. How do you determine the type of audience to whom you will be speaking? The answer lies in the concept of **audience analysis,** or the act of acquainting yourself with your listeners before giving a speech.

For of the three elements in speech making—speaker, subject, and person addressed—it is the last one, the hearer, that determines the speech's end and object.

ARISTOTLE

Of course, it is impossible to know everything about the members of your audience, but you can aim for a realistic assessment of the overall situation. First, try to learn about those aspects of the audience that will have the greatest effect on its listening behavior. Then, if time and circumstances permit, acquaint yourself with other factors. Let's say that you are going to give a speech on current unemployment problems. It would be more important to learn about the socioeconomic occupational backgrounds of your audience than about its religious affiliations.

Keep in mind that your own attitudes and stereotypes can influence the way you relate to your listeners. You should overcome your biases so that they will not limit your ability to judge how others think and feel.

Remember, too, that people change with time, and so will your audiences. An analysis made several weeks before you speak may not alter drastically by the time you are heard, but some minor changes will naturally occur. Even if you have done a careful job of audience analysis before you walk to the podium, your listeners may change their attitudes *while* you are talking. Prior analysis is only the beginning of understanding and relating to your listeners. While speaking, you must continue your examination, looking for audience reaction to the ideas you are presenting. What clues are your listeners giving you? What are their facial expressions? Are their eyes on you?

---

[10]Ibid.

Are they squirming in their seats, laughing, whispering, applauding? A successful speaker knows how to pick up on such cues, accept them, and then adapt the speech accordingly.

Demographic Analysis

What are the ages of the members of the audience? What is their average salary? Is one sex more represented than the other? What kinds of jobs do the people hold? What is their level of education or religious background? These are some of the questions asked when analyzing the demographic characteristics of an audience. **Demography** is the statistical study of populations. In the demographic approach to audience analysis, specific factual information is recorded upon which probable audience reaction is based.

AGE. Consider the ages of your audience members when planning your speech. People of different ages like different clothes, listen to different music, and have many different attitudes and beliefs. It is hardly surprising, then, that young, middle-aged, and older people react differently as audience members.

Winston Price, a writer of popular songs for all age groups, was often called on to talk about his career and about music in general. His speeches usually resulted in a strong, positive reaction from the audience. One of the reasons for his success was his ability to alter the approach and content of his speech depending on the average age of his audience. When speaking to teenagers, he dealt primarily with "top ten" hits and popular rock groups, but these were quickly put aside when he spoke to senior citizens, to whom he talked about entertainers such as Frank Sinatra, Lawrence Welk, and Guy Lombardo. If Price spoke to an audience composed of all ages, he approached the subject in more general terms, giving examples that appealed to all members instead of a select few.

EDUCATIONAL LEVEL. Before giving a speech, try to estimate your audience's educational level. This will help you to know what vocabulary, sentence structure, and abstract ideas will be appropriate. Also, it will let you know how many examples and definitions you will have to give in order to be understood. If you speak below your listeners' educational level, they more than likely will be not only bored but also angry when they discover they are being patronized. Likewise, if the audience is not as educated as you are, keep the vocabulary and structure of your speech at the audience's level. Too many speakers throw in technical, difficult terms to show how much they know. Your purpose as a speaker is to communicate, not to boost your ego.

Remember, there is not necessarily a correlation between the amount of education your audience members have and their degree of understanding and knowledge of a specific subject. Besides knowing your audience's educational level, you should, if possible, determine the amount of informa-

What are some of the demographic characteristics of this audience?

tion it already has on the subject you will discuss. Before giving your speech, try to find out whether or not your listeners have done any reading on the subject, observed it, or perhaps even participated in it. You might want to talk about hang gliding because you went once or twice, but there could be members of the audience who are real pros and could speak more knowledgeably about the sport. Through analysis of your audience's knowledge, you will be able to take advantage of what your listeners already know and give them the additional information they need.

SOCIOECONOMIC STATUS. Many of your listeners' values and attitudes are based on their economic background, so this aspect should also be taken into consideration when planning your speech. If, for example, you are asked to discuss the school budget for the coming year, a subject that influences tax level, you should be aware of the economic status of your listeners and the weight of their current tax burden.

Audience members are also influenced by their social background and experiences and by the attitudes and values they have developed. No one can totally escape his or her past. Social background, in fact, is often considered to have the strongest effect on listeners, being more important than religion, age, or sex.

OCCUPATION. People's occupations often give clues to their educational level as well as to their information on and interest in certain subjects. Although both car mechanics and accountants may be interested in future modes of transportation, the former group would probably be more interested in a new engine part.

Different occupational groups may be concerned about different aspects of a topic. For example, postal clerks might want to know how a postal law will affect their present salaries, while publishers may be interested in how the law will influence their mailing costs. Similarly, newspaper editors may be interested in learning the facts about a new superhighway, urban planners about the ways it will change the city's environment, and construction workers about the possibility of new job openings.

SEX. In the past, men and women were often thought to be interested in entirely different things. With the advent of the women's movement and the entrance of women into every field of endeavor, this "obvious" generalization about men and women is no longer appropriate. Some women are not only interested in automobiles, but they also race them. Some men are not only appreciative of needlework, but they produce it, too. Therefore, it is harder to differentiate audience interests on the basis of sex than it was in the past.

Awareness concerning political affiliations is critical to speaking effectively in public.

Nonetheless, the sensitive speaker may still be able to discern meaningful, if sometimes subtle, differences between audiences composed of men or women. For example, as a result of early socialization, males have been taught to listen more for facts, while females have been reinforced for effectively decoding relational cues. Likewise, scholars have recently suggested that women have a tendency to integrate emotion into the rational analyses of problems, rather than separating emotional behavior from verbal analysis.[11] The implication of these differences is that as a speaker, you may need to take these variables into account. However, you must keep in mind that generalizations are just that—and that there are countless exceptions.

GROUP MEMBERSHIP.   If you are asked to speak to a specific group or organization, such as the Young Republicans or the American Medical Association, you are one step ahead of the analysis game. The groups people belong to give you many clues to their other demographic characteristics. Most clubs or associations have certain guidelines they wish all members to follow—religious groups follow certain moral codes, political associations advocate certain partisan positions, and so on.

Referring to your audience's association in your speech can sometimes create a closer speaker-listener bond. Let's say you are trying to persuade a group of women faculty members at the local community college to support with financial assistance and volunteer service a newly established women's health center. You might draw a parallel between their fierce battle against the college administration for more equitable salaries for male and female faculty members and your own group's attempt to provide good, low-cost health services despite the opposition of the community's medical hierarchy, composed mostly of men. If you are able to identify the group memberships of audience members, you may gain insight into their attitudes and determine in advance what their reactions will be to your speech.

CULTURAL BACKGROUND.   America has been called a veritable "melting pot" of cultures: African-American, Caucasian, Native American, Hispanic, Asian, Middle Eastern—the list goes on. In labeling the United States in this way, however, we often overlook the diversity that gives individuals their unique cultural and personal identities. As speakers, buying into this metaphor means missing out on vital information—information regarding attitudes, beliefs, values, habits, needs, and often definitions of appropriate communication behavior.

For example, an emphasis on family, community, and harmony with nature still permeates the lives of most traditional Native Americans in this country. Likewise, for citizens of Asian descent, family and company loyalty often supersede individual or personal rights. Thus, to approach members of a tribal council with a proposal to buy and develop sacred lands at "fair market price" would produce responses ranging from disdain to open

---

[11]Y. Christen, *Sex Differences: Modern Biology and the Unisex Fallacy* (New Brunswick, N.J.: Transaction Publishers, 1991), 68–69.

hostility. Recommending to a group of Japanese businessmen that they fire or force into early retirement their older employees would quickly destroy your credibility with the former as an international management consultant.

To gain insights into any audience that is potentially culturally diverse, learn as much as you can (in advance) about that audience's attitudes, values, beliefs, and perceptions of appropriate communication behavior. A good place to begin is the travel, personal improvement, and business sections at your local bookstore. Another is talking with representatives of that culture prior to making your presentation.

Psychological Variables

BELIEFS AND VALUES. According to psychologist Milton Rokeach, **beliefs** are probability statements about the existence of things, or statements about the relationships between an object and another quality or thing. For example, we may "believe in God" or believe that God is omnipotent—the former being a belief in something and the latter being a belief in a quality-object relationship. **Values,** on the other hand, are specific types of beliefs that are central to our lives and act as life guides. According to Rokeach, values may take one of two forms: those that are guidelines for living and on which we base our daily behavior (*instrumental values*), and the ultimate aim or aims toward which we work (*terminal values*). An example of terminal values might be the desire to have a comfortable life. Being ambitious or cheerful is an example of an instrumental value.[12]

Many of our beliefs and values are acquired early in childhood and, although somewhat altered by new experiences, remain the basis of many of our thoughts and actions. As a speaker, you must therefore pay close attention to these elements when analyzing your audiences. As we mentioned earlier, you can appeal to an audience's values in order to persuade them to accept your point of view; but in order to achieve this end, you must be sensitive both to your own value structure and to that of the members of your audience. You must seek out the common ground that will give clues to their value structure. Let's suppose that you are going to talk to the Veterans of Foreign Wars about capital punishment, but you do not know their basic convictions. Before delivering your speech, you could read recent newspaper and magazine articles about the VFW's reaction to present-day political issues. From these you would be able to infer some of their basic beliefs and adapt the approach of your speech accordingly. Remember, however, that group associations do not always present the whole picture. The views of Democrats and Republicans, for example, often overlap on specific issues; not all Democrats feel one way and all Republicans another.

---

[12]Discussion adapted from S. W. Littlejohn, *Theories of Human Communication*, 3d ed. (Belmont, Calif.: Wadsworth, 1989), 90–91.

An audience's attitudes about a speaker often determine his or her success or failure.

Audience Attitudes

TOWARD THE SPEAKER. No matter how well you know your subject and how capable you are of speaking about it, you will not be effective if the audience dislikes you or strongly disagrees with your ideas. An audience's attitudes about the speaker often determine his or her success or failure in communicating the desired message.

What criteria influence an audience's decisions about a speaker? Studies show that audiences base their attitudes on a variety of things. Some are meaningful, such as the person's experience, and others petty, such as whether or not the speaker is a member of the "in-group" and whether he or she is liked or disliked. For example, researchers have found a "black sheep" effect to exist when it comes to in-group speaker evaluations. Specifically, audiences more positively evaluate likable in-group speakers than likable out-group speakers. However, if an in-group speaker is not well-liked, he or she will be evaluated more negatively than an unlikable out-group speaker.[13] In most cases, however, a speaker's success depends on the listeners' confidence or faith in him or her and what they feel is the speaker's worth or

---

[13]J. M. Marques and V. Y. Yzerbyt, "The Black Sheep Effect: Judgmental Extremity Towards Ingroup Members in Inter- and Intra-Group Situations," *European Journal of Social Psychology*, 18 (1988), 287–92.

competence. As was pointed out earlier, this is usually referred to as speaker *credibility*, or ethos.

As difficult as it may be to "see ourselves as others see us," it is extremely important for you as a speaker to try to estimate what the audience will think of you. Whether this information is uncovered through informal conversation or through direct questioning of prospective audience members, you should seek out both the positive and the negative expectations of the audience. With this information you can make a deliberate effort to structure the message in such a way as to reinforce the positive expectations and diminish the negative ones.

TOWARD THE SUBJECT.   As stated earlier, if your audience's attitude toward the subject of your speech is favorable, your task is easier. All you have to do is give the subject a fresh approach and reinforce your ideas. But what do you do if your audience is neutral? People who have no opinions on a particular topic will probably listen to both sides of the issue and keep their minds open to all information and attempts at persuasion. At the same time, though, they may be critical of everything they hear. Neutrality toward a subject does not mean indifference to it. Neutral listeners are concerned about the subject but have not yet made any final decisions about it. As politicians have discovered, these open-minded audience members may be very important to the outcome of a persuasive speech: They can still be moved to either side of an issue. This movement is possible, however, only if the speaker presents sound evidence to support his or her ideas, relates to the audience by sharing experiences, and answers all questions from the floor.

If you feel that your audience is indifferent to your topic, make your speech as interesting as possible. You can do this by finding an appealing, exciting way to cover the topic, by using attention-getting devices, and by playing upon other interests the members of your audience may have that are related to your subject area. The yacht club members might not be concerned with world politics, but they could be interested in the political implications of maritime law. Mathematics might be exciting to elementary school students when related to their everyday adventures or to magic tricks.

If you know that your audience is negatively disposed toward your subject, remember Elsea's advice to be calm and controlled. Additionally, for audiences that are extremely hostile, try these five steps:

1. If possible, pinpoint the specific cause(s) of your audience's hostility.
2. Determine the point(s) on which you and the audience agree and demonstrate similarity with your listeners regarding these issues.
3. As you move to the points on which you disagree, maintain a heightened sense of neutrality and respect for the audience's position.
4. Discuss thoroughly the value (advantages and disadvantages) of your position on each point of disagreement.
5. Organize and deliver the message in such a way that each point leads to the conclusions you want the audience to draw.

Take, for example, Career Day at George Washington High, an inner-city school. Rose, a dance instructor, had been asked to talk about the career of a professional dancer to an assembly of high school juniors. Long before she approached the podium, she knew she was going to face an uninterested, if not antagonistic, audience. But Rose was prepared.

> You know, many football players, such as Herschel Walker, learn ballet in order to limber up and play better. Those who have tried ballet have found that it has made them more agile and has enabled them to run faster and kick farther. But football players aren't the only athletes who learn ballet; it is practiced by many gymnasts, track stars, and swimmers, as well.

By approaching her speech in this way, Rose was able to accomplish several purposes: She lessened the opposition to her topic, gave the students someone with whom to identify, and dispelled some of the negative stereotypes connected with her subject area.

Other ways to combat audience indifference or opposition include adjusting your message, such as by omitting key discrepant statements, making the message less specific, taking a less extreme position, or using weaker language; and spending more time on issues and problems rather than on solutions. The most important thing to remember when confronting a negative audience, again, is to remain as calm as possible. If you hope to persuade your listeners, be careful not to show anger or impatience with their differing viewpoints. It is quite possible for you and your audience to disagree without losing respect for one another's opinions. If you present yourself and your speech in a fair and reasonable way, you may not only be able to get people to listen to your different ideas, but you may gain some converts as well.

TOWARD YOUR PURPOSE.   Every speech you make should have a definite purpose. Without the focus a well-defined purpose provides, your speech may be nothing but a collection of statements with no overall meaning. You will recall that the purpose of any speech is to inform, persuade, or entertain.

Speeches can, of course, have aspects of all three purposes, but there should be only one specific, unifying goal. If you give a speech in support of the liberalization of marijuana laws, you may inform your audience of the history of the drug's use, and perhaps relate some interesting anecdotes, but these are only means to help you accomplish your primary goal of persuasion.

The purpose of your speech will often directly depend on the audience's attitude toward the topic. Let's say that your listeners are already in favor of decriminalizing marijuana. Your purpose then is not to persuade but rather to reinforce their beliefs and inform them of the appropriate actions they can take in support of their beliefs. If your listeners are rigidly opposed to your topic, however, it might be best not to try to persuade them but simply to inform them of the facts and hope that, as a result, your audience will have obtained a more well-rounded impression of the topic. If your audience is neutral or only partially opposed, persuasion would probably be the best approach, while the interest and attention of a totally indifferent audience can often be focused on a particular issue by an entertaining delivery.

A good speaker will try to base the purpose of his or her speech on the desires and expectations of the audience. Listeners are more apt to pay attention to a speech they are prepared for and consider appropriate to their beliefs and the situation. The chances of a speech's success are greater if both the speaker and the listeners have the same purpose in mind.

Nothing angers an audience more than believing that a speaker's purpose is one thing and finding out that it is something entirely different.

> The presentation of a well-known Black poet was eagerly awaited by an audience composed mostly of admirers of her work and would-be writers. Their disappointment was tinged with anger when instead of discussing her poetry, she delivered a powerful attack on Caucasian middle-class attitudes toward black Americans.

> Charles Marsden, a fashion designer, was asked by a women's club to speak on the history of clothing. The members felt resentful when the lecture turned out to be a sales pitch for Marsden's latest line of women's fashions.

The irritation of the audience members in both cases did the speakers much harm. Had the poet and the designer given the expected information in a pleasing manner, they would have related well to their listeners and greatly furthered their personal causes.

If, prior to your speech, you can discover your audience's purpose and demands, you will know how to adapt your speech to increase the likelihood of a successful outcome.

METHODS OF INVESTIGATING YOUR AUDIENCE

When preparing a speech for one of your college classes, you already know the age, sex, relative economic status, and race of the class members. You can also make accurate guesses about their opinions on issues such as reinstitution of the draft, job opportunities, and higher education. Difficulties occur when you are asked to speak to groups of people that you know relatively little about (in terms of their demographic characteristics, values, beliefs, and attitudes).

Invitation Committee

The most obvious place to begin seeking information is from the people who invited you to speak. Immediately, questions will come to mind, such as: How many people will attend? Are there any specific time limitations or expectations? What does the audience know about the subject? Will they be required to attend? What are their ages? At first, being startled by the invitation, you may not ask all the necessary questions. If this is the case, don't hesitate to ask for additional information about your prospective audience.

Mass Media Sources

Other valuable audience information comes from reading community newspapers and magazines, listening to local radio stations, and watching local television programs. It may even be a good idea to subscribe to various publications for a few weeks before you speak, to get an idea of important issues in the geographical area. Through the mass media you'll find the concerns that are uppermost in the listeners' minds, such as police or teachers' strikes, sports playoffs, or human interest issues such as the activities of the local humane society. Even if your topic is not one of general community interest, being informed about local concerns can aid you in preparing examples and illustrations relevant to your audience.

Public Opinion Polls and Surveys

Over the years we have seen the importance of polls in predicting election results. Politicians are extremely concerned about how their platforms are accepted and how popular they are in particular areas. The information received from polls and surveys helps the candidates determine the best method of presenting their arguments and themselves. Beginning speakers can also gain insight from similar information without going to the expense of conducting actual surveys. References such as the *Gallup Opinion Index*, *Public Opinion Polls*, and *Public Opinion Quarterly* provide useful data on a variety of topics for different geographical regions of the country.

Personal Interviews

If you live nearby your prospective audience, much can be learned about them by talking with local people. Interviews with local leaders and citizens can give you a clearer picture about who is being affected on issues such as waste water facilities, local parks and recreation departments, and health facilities. Even if you don't live nearby, after arriving in a particular area, you can talk to people with whom you come in contact (for example, taxi drivers or hotel managers) to find out the latest issues of concern and even language styles that might be appropriate for your particular speech.

OTHER AUDIENCE CONSIDERATIONS

Audience Types

In 1935, H. L. Hollingworth developed a classification system that described audiences on the basis of their organization and orientation toward the situation in which the speech is given.[14] This now classic approach to

---

[14]H. L. Hollingworth, *The Psychology of the Audience* (New York: American Book, 1935), 19–32.

audiences is still highly pertinent today. As you will see, speaking before each of these audience types entails unique problems and responsibilities.

CASUAL AUDIENCES. Frequently, in large cities, people walking down the street will stop and listen to a soapbox orator preaching religion or some other cause, or watch an entertainer such as a magician or musician. Hollingworth calls such pedestrian audiences *casual.* These so-called audiences show very little, if any, homogeneity and, in fact, are barely audiences at all. They are just small groups of people who have gathered for a short time at the same place.

Soapbox orators or street entertainers who address casual audiences must first get the attention of the pedestrians passing by. This means that they have to spend a lot of time on their speech preparation and delivery. Each street orator attempts to develop his or her own unique speaking style—a specific way to hook the attention of the pedestrians. But, more important, these speakers have to *keep* the casual audience there. This means getting the listeners involved. The orator will perhaps fire questions into the crowd, and the entertainer may ask listeners to participate, emotionally or physically.

PASSIVE AUDIENCES. The second type of audience is *passive,* or *partially oriented,* and is usually composed of captive listeners. The people who make up this kind of audience have no choice but to listen to the speaker. A

A casual audience.

church congregation listening to a sermon or club members listening to the after-luncheon speaker are examples of passive audiences.

Speakers who confront passive audiences must gain the attention of the listeners and arouse their interest in the subject matter. In order to accomplish this, they can appeal to one or more of the interests that almost all audiences have in common. All people share basic primary interests or needs. Financial security, for instance, is one of the most basic needs of all persons. Almost everyone wants to hear about ways of earning or saving money. If you are trying to get the attention of your audience members, use some examples that are close to home and, especially, close to their wallets.

A comedian can only last till he either takes himself serious or his audience takes him serious.

WILL ROGERS

There are other common interests that, although not vital to personal welfare, appeal to audiences. Sports and hobbies are examples of such *secondary interests*. Suppose you are making a speech about an area of land you think should be converted into a state park. You might draw upon the secondary interests of your audience to advance your argument. If you have ascertained beforehand that audience members are outdoors enthusiasts, you could talk about the hiking trails, camping sites, and observation points that could be made available by such a state park. Or, if they are animal lovers, you might list the types of animals that would be protected in the park. Which secondary interests you draw on will depend on your specific audience and the results of your analysis.

Momentary interests are things that concern us for only a short time and are then replaced by other issues. A new television show or news event may be on everyone's lips for a couple of days. A speaker's reference to such a topic can be used to arouse the attention of the audience. An awareness of the momentary interests of an audience can be a great asset to the speaker.

SELECTED AUDIENCES. Audiences who have collected for a specific purpose are referred to as **selected** audiences. These listeners normally attend a speech because they have some previous interest in the subject. Examples of such selected audiences are environmentalists who come to hear a lecture on the ozone layer, students of the occult attending a talk on witchcraft, and members of the Farmers of America learning about a new irrigation technique.

While "interest catchers" are helpful with passive audiences, what are your responsibilities toward selected audiences that have met for a specific purpose? First, you need not try to attract attention; you already have it. Instead, you should strive to make a strong impression on your listeners so that they remember what you have said after your speech is over. A group of parents who wish to impress upon their fellow PTA members the seriousness of conditions existing in the school might invite an engineer first to inspect the buildings and then to come to the next meeting to discuss the leaking roof, unsafe staircases, and broken windows.

CONCERTED AUDIENCES. In many manufacturing companies across America, "business teams" made up of five to 15 persons have begun to meet regularly to discuss problems and issues regarding the quality of their products. These teams make up a *concerted* audience, one that has an active purpose and mutual interests, but no set separation of labor or strict organization of authority. Furthermore, the concerted audience has a high degree of orientation toward the speaker and his or her purpose. An Alcoholics Anonymous meeting is another example of this kind of audience.

Concerted audiences are already impressed and are ready to be led to action. The speaker must therefore enforce the audience's convictions— persuading members and directing their action. Audiences may have very strong attitudes, but having such attitudes and acting on them are two different things. For example, many women who attend National Organization for Women (NOW) meetings have definite pro–women's rights views. This does not always mean that they are taking action, however. A vibrant speaker may be needed to motivate these women to take legal action in cases of discrimination, for example.

ORGANIZED AUDIENCES. Finally, there is the *organized* audience, in which listeners are totally directed toward the speaker and all labor and authority lines are strictly designated. A Minnesota Vikings coach lecturing his football team on the upcoming game against the Green Bay Packers is speaking to an organized audience.

Organized audiences are ready for action, but they often have no direction. The speaker's responsibility in this case is to give the listeners specific instructions on the action plans. The Vikings coach will discuss specific football moves before the big game with the Packers. The labor leader will advise the union members about where and when they should picket.

Effects of the Environment

Is your speech being given in a large room or in a small one? Are the chairs comfortable? How are they arranged? What kind of lighting is there, and how good are the acoustics? All of these questions deal with the physical setting of your speech, which will greatly influence your audience's behavior.

Take the room itself, for instance. People will act differently if they are sitting in a large auditorium, a small classroom, or a house. Compare an audience listening to a formal lecture in a classroom with one that listens to the same speech in a coffee shop or outside under a tree.

The noises or other distractions around you must also be taken into consideration. Is the room quiet, or must you compete with the sounds of traffic outside and distractions such as loud air conditioning inside? You should learn how to adapt to such situations. You can project your voice over the noises, pause to let an intrusion pass, or incorporate the competing stimuli into the speech.

While in office, President Ronald Reagan often used noise from his helicopter to his advantage when dealing with members of the press. Rather than shout over the noise or approach the press corps close enough to hear them, he would simply cup his hand over his ear, shrug, and mouth the words, "I can't hear you." In this way, Reagan made use of the competing stimuli and avoided answering questions that he may have been unprepared to address at the time.

The atmosphere in a large auditorium with hundreds of unrelated people is, of course, very formal. Listeners usually sit in straight chairs, and all face the speaker. Compare this with a small, informal gathering in someone's home, where the listeners and the speaker have a much more intimate relationship. The listeners are more prone to ask questions and offer comments. In turn, the speaker can feel more at ease and less formal, and can more easily relate to the listeners. Additionally, he or she can use nonverbal communication more effectively to show sincerity and concern for those who are present.

The size of the audience is a physical condition that affects both your audience's behavior and your reactions to it. You will probably be more

The size of an audience affects its behavior and reactions.

formal with large audiences than with small ones. You will also have to use more pronounced gestures and a louder voice when addressing a large audience so that members in the back rows get the full impact of the message. In a smaller group, your facial expressions and small body movements will communicate much more effectively.

The Speaker-Audience Interaction

What distinguishes an audience from a random collection of people? Three things happen when groups of people progress from a mere gathering to audience status.

POLARIZATION. The first thing that happens is *polarization,* which provides the structure for an unorganized group of people. It is at this point that audience members recognize their role as listeners and accept someone else as a speaker. Two distinct roles, then, come into existence. While the polarized audience is separate from the speaker, it is also connected to him or her by the communication that occurs. Various aspects of the public speaking situation contribute to polarization, such as seating arrangements in which the chairs face the speaker, or the stage or platform from which the speaker delivers the speech.

Polarization is both normal and necessary in public speaking situations. However, polarization can become too extreme when either speaker or audience becomes alienated from the other. Shortly after his inauguration, President George Bush accepted invitations to attend meetings at two elite, "males only" professional clubs in Washington, D.C. By doing so he drew fire from the American press and damaged his credibility with feminists all across the country. Additionally, he created the potential for polarization in future meetings with this latter, highly influential audience.

SOCIAL FACILITATION. The fact that people behave differently as a function of the presence or absence of other people is called *social facilitation.* This phenomenon emerges in a number of situations. For example, when we drive with a passenger in the car, we generally drive more slowly, require larger gaps between cars when we pull out into an intersection, and stop more often at stop signs than when we drive alone.[15] Likewise, when we watch a situation comedy on television by ourselves, we may not laugh aloud, even if we think the program is funny. With friends, however, we may be prompted to laugh long and loud. Social facilitation may not occur immediately. For example, a formal audience attending a theater performance may take some time to "warm up." Few people want to be the first to applaud, cheer, clap hands to the music, or stand for an ovation. Audience members look to one another for reinforcement.

---

[15]J. S. Baxter, A. S. R. Manstead, S. G. Stradling, K. A. Campbell, J. T. Reason, and D. Parker, "Social Facilitation and Driver Behavior," *British Journal of Psychology,* 81 (1990), 351–60.

Imagine that you are watching the performance of a Russian dance troupe. At the beginning of the performance, the members of the audience may be very quiet. A few people tap their feet or drum their fingers in time to the music, but most are relatively unresponsive. But as the rhythm of the music and the exuberant movements on stage affect more and more of the members of the audience, a drastic change can occur. Before you know it, you, like everyone else, may find yourself stamping your feet, clapping your hands, and cheering. Even listeners who are usually very quiet and reserved can be influenced by the excitement of an audience.

CIRCULAR RESPONSE. When the kind of communication that happens between listeners occurs between the audience and the speaker, the phenomenon is called *circular response.* The speaker says something and the audience responds with nods, applause, or frowns. From these responses the speaker knows how best to slant what he or she says next to hold the attention of the listeners. If the response is favorable, the speaker may exert more effort, which in turn leads to more audience responses, and so on. This mutual feedback heightens the participation of both speaker and listeners and strengthens the bonds between them.

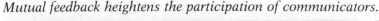

Mutual feedback heightens the participation of communicators.

Audience Analysis Checklist

Audience analysis is an art, not a science. Just think of all the variations and combinations that can occur in an audience's demographic and attitudinal characteristics. It is plain to see how difficult, if not impossible, it is to set down specific step-by-step rules to cover all the variables of any particular audience. However, Table 9–1 provides a checklist of some of the basics of audience analysis that can help you construct an effective speech.

TABLE 9–1
Audience Analysis

SUBJECT AND PURPOSE	
Subject:	Your general subject area.
Purpose:	To entertain, persuade, or inform.
Specific purpose:	What you want your audience to learn; what action or response you want.
Expected purpose:	What your audience thinks the purpose is.

GENERAL CHARACTERISTICS	
Personality:	Open/closed-minded, active/passive, tired/alert, calm/angry, other, mixed.
Knowledge of subject:	None—little, moderate, professional
Knowledge of speaker:	None—little, same background, family member, friend.

DEMOGRAPHICS	
Age:	Up to 12, 13–21, 22–40, 41–65, over 65, mixed.
Education;	Elementary, high school, college, graduate school, mixed.
Environment:	Rural, town, small/large city, urban, industrialized, suburbs, other, mixed.
Economic:	Poor, lower-middle, upper-middle, wealthy, mixed.
Occupation:	Unemployed, student, homemaker, mixed, trade, professional, other, mixed.
Sex:	Male, female, mixed.
Group membership:	Sports clubs, lodges, occupational clubs, interest clubs, other, mixed.
Cultural background:	Homogeneous, heterogeneous.
Classification:	Casual, passive, selected, concerted, organized.

ATTITUDES, BELIEFS, VALUES	
Political:	Republican/Democrat, liberal/conservative, independent, other, mixed.
Religious:	Catholic, Protestant, Jewish, other, mixed.
Attitude toward speaker:	Favorable, opposed, neutral, indifferent.
Attitude toward subject:	Favorable, opposed, neutral, indifferent.
Attitude toward purpose:	Favorable, opposed, neutral, indifferent.

ENVIRONMENTAL FACTORS	
Physical setting:	Formal/informal, large/small room, indoors/outdoors, other.
Competing stimuli:	Quiet, moderate, noisy.
Size:	Small, moderate-sized, large.
Density:	Scattered, moderate, compact.
Proximity:	Audience close to speaker/far from speaker, seated in front row/back row/sides.

Source: Adapted from G. Wiseman and L. Barker, *A Workbook for Speech/Interpersonal Communication* (San Francisco: Chandler, 1967).

1. Before choosing my speech purpose and topic, do I know the demographic characteristics of my audience, including age, education, occupation, personality, and so forth?

2. Have I a fairly clear notion of how much and what kind of knowledge my audience has about my topic? Will the range of knowledge among audience members be broad or narrow?

3. Have I discovered those basic religious, political, social, and moral beliefs, values, and attitudes that could affect this audience's understanding of my speech topic? Are there likely to be beliefs, values, or attitudes that may interfere with the audience's acceptance of my point of view, arguments, evidence, or examples? Have I taken these into account in planning my speech material?

4. Have I made an objective attempt to learn my audience's attitudes toward my intended purpose, my speech topic, and myself?

5. Do I know what type of audience I will be facing? If I know, have I chosen the level and emphasis of speech materials appropriate for a casual, passive, selected, concerted, or organized audience?

6. Did I consider environmental factors that could affect the comprehension or acceptance of my ideas? Can I describe and analyze the physical setting and note its good and bad points? Are there any potential competing stimuli for which I can plan adjustments?

7. What is the occasion for which I am to speak? Is this a regular monthly meeting of Athletes in Action or an annual honors banquet? Is it the Fourth of July, or Valentine's Day?

The answers to these questions will provide you with the information you need to increase the chances of a successful presentation.

SUMMARY

Public speaking differs from other forms of communication in two essential ways: (1) Public speaking situations require two distinct roles, those of speaker and of audience, and (2) in the speaker-audience relationship, the speaker carries more responsibility for the communication interaction than does the audience.

Perhaps the most important consideration to be made before speech preparation is ethical responsibility. There appear to be four approaches to ethics: (1) ends-justify-means approach, (2) social utility approach, (3) situation ethics approach, and (4) credibility-centered approach. After dealing with ethical considerations, the speaker should select both general and specific purposes. The selection should be based on the speaker's own knowledge and interests as well as on a thorough audience analysis.

One system of audience analysis is the demographic approach. This involves the gathering of particular and factual information to predict audience reaction. A speech may be planned according to factors such as the age, educational level, and socioeconomic status of the audience. Other useful considerations are the occupations, gender, group affiliations, and cultural background of audience members. It is important to avoid stereotyping the audience, however. Demography is best used in a factual, impartial, and nonprejudiced manner.

Other variables that the effective communicator should consider are the beliefs, values, and attitudes of the audience. Familiarity with the political or religious character of the audience may provide many clues about listeners' basic beliefs and common values or convictions.

Effective communication is not likely to take place if listeners are alienated by the speaker, the subject, or the speaker's purpose. A good speaker must present the speech in a way that will emphasize the positive attitudes of the audience while minimizing its negative reactions. A message that is geared to the desires and expectations of the audience will be received more readily than one that is not.

Speaking situations vary according to audience type. There are casual, passive, selected, concerted, and organized audiences, and the responsibility of the speaker is different in each case.

The person who speaks to the casual or passive audience must first attract and then hold the attention of the listeners. The select audience is a group that has met for a specific purpose, and the goal of the speaker should be to strongly impress the intended message upon them. The concerted audience is already impressed but has not yet been directed to action. In this case the speaker may try to reinforce established attitudes and motivate the listeners to take action. The final kind of audience is the organized audience. In this situation the listeners have already been persuaded of the necessity for action and are willing to carry out the specific directions of the speaker.

An intelligent public speaker must be aware of the effects of environment upon communication. Audiences react differently in large, small, formal, and informal speaking situations. Therefore, conflicting noises and distractions should be taken into account and prepared for, in order to make the smoothest possible presentation.

Those who wish to understand how a group of individuals becomes an audience and how audience reaction works should study the speaker-audience relationship. Polarization, the division of roles, establishes the speaker as separate from the listeners and establishes the connection between the two. Social facilitation involves the internal reaction of an audience. Audience members reinforce the reactions of one another. Circular response involves the speaker in the sharing of excitement.

Audience analysis is an art, and like all arts must be practiced and developed by each speaker. Students of audience analysis who keep in mind the characteristics and values of the listeners, the type of audience they are addressing, and the environment in which they are making the speech are on their way to becoming effective communicators.

EXERCISES

Group Experiences

Ghostwriting

DESCRIPTION: Many audience variables need to be considered when preparing a speech or presentation for a group. Analyzing the audience is a key element in public presentations. This activity will give you the opportunity to "advise" a speaker on the elements that should be considered for a given audience and topic.

PROCEDURE: Divide into groups of four to six members. Write each of the following topics and targets on a separate piece of paper.

Topics
1. The use of marijuana should be decriminalized.
2. Women should serve their husbands.
3. All families should be limited to two children.
4. Wearing seat belts should be required for all passengers in cars and buses.
5. Wearing helmets should be required for all motorcyclists.

Audiences
1. Veterans groups, 50 males, ages 25–50.
2. College students, 30 males and females, ages 18–30.
3. Feminist group, 40 females, ages 18–60.
4. Hell's Angels, 30 males, ages 20–35.
5. Daughters of the American Revolution, 25 females, ages 30–80.

Each group should select one topic and one target audience and should prepare a list of recommendations for things the speaker should consider. In preparing this list, the following factors should be considered:

Demographic characteristics
Educational level
Socioeconomic status
Personality
Sex
Group membership

Cultural background
Psychological characteristics
Audience beliefs and values
Audience attitude toward the
  subject and purpose of the
  speech

Although you have not been given all of the information just listed, you will have to make inferences about these variables.

Examples of recommendations include:

1. Avoid the use of idiomatic expressions. This is a professional audience that will expect the use of professional language.
2. You will need to loosen the group up so that they will feel comfortable with one another, since they do not know one another.

Each group should identify its topic and target audience. Then the list of recommendations should be read. Finally, the other groups should evaluate each list.

DISCUSSION: Did the group make logical inferences about the given audience? Did the recommendations reflect the appropriate concerns for the given audience? Were any important recommendations omitted? Do you think that the consideration of audience variables is important in writing an effective speech?

Audience Types

DESCRIPTION: Hollingworth developed a classification system that described audiences on the basis of their organization and orientation toward the speech situation. His audience types include casual, passive, selected, concerted, and organized audiences. This activity will give you a chance to use the Hollingworth classification system.

PROCEDURE: Each person should make up an example of two audience types. The examples should be collected and read aloud to the class. As each example is read, you should classify it as casual, passive, selected, concerted, or organized. After everyone has classified each example, the correct answers should be determined by class discussion. Check your score to see how many correct classifications you made.

DISCUSSION: Beyond the classification of audiences, of what value is the Hollingworth system? How could you use it in preparing a speech for a particular group?

Warm Up

DESCRIPTION: One of the most difficult tasks for a speaker to perform is to try to "warm up" a formal audience. Few people want to be the first to yell, clap hands to music, or even stand for an ovation. This activity will give you an opportunity to develop various warm-up techniques for different audiences.

PROCEDURE: This activity can be done either by groups or by individuals. The procedure is the same for both formats. Two descriptions of specific audiences are provided below. You are to write down all possible alternatives for warming up the given group. Your suggestions should be specific. Some examples include the following:

1. Tell a joke related specifically to the audience.
2. Bring several members of the audience in front of the group to participate in a demonstration.
3. Socialize with the group before your speech in an effort to relax them.

Setting 1

You have been asked to speak on malpractice insurance before a group of physicians. You are an attorney and have been active in lawsuits against physicians. Some members of the group resent the fact that you have been asked to speak to them. These members see you as the enemy.

Setting 2

You work for the Total Woman franchise. Your message to all women is that they should consider their husbands to be first and foremost in their lives. You have been asked to address a group of husbands who are experiencing some marital difficulties.

DISCUSSION: Have you given careful consideration to the techniques you have selected? Do any of your techniques involve nonverbal behavior, such as smiling or standing close to your audience? What are some indications that an audience is warming up to you as a speaker?

Personal Experiences

1. Observe a speaker in action, but spend most of your time watching for audience response. What cues did you observe that indicated attentiveness, boredom, interest, or anger? Could you tell when (or if) the speaker won or lost the audience?
2. Have you ever considered how much information you have about people based on age alone? Consider each of the following time periods during which people were born: What do you know about people who were born during 1931–1940; 1941–1950; 1951–1960; 1961–1970; 1971–1980; 1981–1990? Who were or are their idols? What was or is the political climate they experienced?
3. Can you remember a speech that was well received by the audience? To what extent did the speaker's adapting to the audience make the speech a success?

Discussion Questions

1. How does group membership provide you with clues for presenting an effective speech?

2. What questions should you ask about an audience's cultural background before constructing a speech?

3. What environmental effects should be considered in preparing a speech for a selected audience?

4. How can you assess audience attitudes toward (a) the speaker, (b) the subject, and (c) the purpose of the speech?

5. How might an awareness of the concept of social facilitation affect your preparation of a speech for a formal audience?

10

Communication Goals

Information Exchange, Persuasion, Entertainment

KEY CONCEPTS AND TERMS

Intrinsic motivation
Extrinsic motivation
Repetition
Visual aid
Platform
Speech to convince
Speech to stimulate
Speech to move audience to action
Logos
Deductive reasoning
Inductive reasoning
Reasoning
Pathos
Reward appeal
Fear-arousing appeal
Ethos
Qualification/expertness
Safety/trustworthiness
Compliance/dynamism

Normative/identification
Experiential-schematic function of
    attitudes
Defensive function of attitudes
Self-expressive function of altitudes
One-sided presentation
Two-sided presentation
Forewarning
Humor
Primacy effect
Recency effect
Speech to welcome
Award presentation
Acceptance speech
After-dinner speech
Farewell speech
Eulogy
Impromptu speech

When the Xerox Corporation first explored the distribution of its copy equipment nationwide, it began with the knowledge that the company was short of salespeople with professional sales skills. To meet the company's growing needs, Xerox created a training program that is still recognized as a leader today. Developed by a team of psychologists and the most experienced and successful members of its sales force, the training program was built on the premise that sales calls would be more effective if they included an "initial benefit statement." This statement would act not only to introduce the company's equipment by delineating its positive attributes, but it would also catch the customers' attention and give them a reason to buy.[1]

Since its development, this technique has played a major role in sales training programs across the nation. Because of their persuasiveness, benefit statements are employed successfully in a variety of business presentations. From their subtle use in television commercials, which suggest that we will be more happy, successful, or sexy if we use a particular product, to their more direct use by salespeople, activists, and politicians, this technique gives a targeted audience a strong incentive to listen and pay attention.

In this chapter we will focus on a number of techniques for presenting a persuasive message. However, our discussion will not be limited solely to *persuasion* as a goal, but will also focus on two other purposes of public speaking: *information exchange* and *entertainment*. As you saw in the previous chapter, you must not only know who your audience is, but you must also have a specific purpose in mind in order to be a successful speaker. Armed with this knowledge and a clear understanding of the three primary purposes of public speaking, you can begin to construct messages that win the enthusiasm and support of any audience.

INFORMATION EXCHANGE

Ways to Increase Learning

In order to facilitate audience learning, a major goal of informative speaking, you must organize your speech for clarity and accuracy. However, there are several additional ways in which a speaker can increase audience learning while presenting a speech to inform. Careful attention to these areas not only improves the chances that an audience will remember what is said but also can contribute to the ease with which the speaker is able to deliver the message.

---

[1]J. MacLachlan, "Making a Message Memorable and Persuasive," *Journal of Advertising Research*, 23, no. 6 (1983–84), 51–59.

MOTIVATION. The most significant factor in increasing learning is motivation. Before you can learn you must listen, and before you listen you must be motivated to do so. The motivation may come from within (*intrinsic motivation*) or from an outside source (*extrinsic motivation*). For example, when Maria attended a seminar on crime prevention, she went because she wanted to learn how to protect herself. On the other hand, her roommate Stephanie went because her sociology professor promised to give extra credit to students who wrote reports on the seminar. Maria's motivation to listen and learn was intrinsic; Stephanie's motivation was extrinsic. Although learning theorists disagree as to which form of motivation creates a greater increase in learning, we do know that an individual needs some type of motivation to listen to and then to learn the information being conveyed by a speaker.

If a speaker gives an audience a reason or reasons for learning the information, ideas, or skills presented, the audience gives more effort to the learning process. For example, when a representative comes to speak from the American Cancer Society and encourages the women in the audience to have a Pap smear and a breast examination and then teaches them how to conduct breast self-examinations, she would probably tell them that doing so will increase the chances of early detection of cancer.

ORGANIZATION. It is also the speaker's responsibility to organize his or her ideas so that the information presented to the audience is logical and easy to follow. There has been considerable research done on how the organization of a speaker's message can affect listener comprehension, speaker credibility, and listener frustration. In general, the findings of these studies support the claim that the organization of a message influences the audience in its interpretation and evaluation of a message. In studies designed to test the effects of message structure and style on listener evaluations, results indicate that messages that are more organized, logical, predictable, and factual are perceived as more comprehensible and persuasive than messages without these particular attributes.[2] You would probably reach a similar conclusion based on personal experience. Undoubtedly, you find it much easier to understand a speaker who presents ideas clearly and logically than one who is disorganized. Most of us have trouble grasping the main idea of speakers who jump ahead of themselves or who backtrack to fill in information they left out.

EFFECTIVE DEVELOPMENT OF IDEAS. Speakers who are presenting new information must develop their ideas effectively to sustain listener attention and motivation and thereby increase learning. There are specific techniques speakers can use to do this. One technique is to mix new and

---

[2]V. Hazleton, W. R. Cupach, and J. Liska, "Message Style: An Investigation of the Perceived Characteristics of Persuasive Messages," *Journal of Social Behavior and Personality*, 1, no. 4 (1986), 565–74.

familiar ideas. Although the purpose of the speech may be to present new and useful information, it is important to connect this information with something that the audience already knows. It is always easier for listeners to understand something they have experienced or can relate to. A person discussing the detrimental effects of television violence on small children would include examples of shows the audience has seen to make the information more meaningful.

Another technique a speaker can use to sustain listener attention combines the elements of conflict and suspense. If a speaker can emphasize opposition or competition through an appropriate image, the audience is more likely to note and remember that particular point. For example, an ecologist might refer to the "race" among the industrial nations to exhaust the earth's resources.

A strong image can serve as a focal point for a speech and give the listeners a major concept upon which they can hang other important bits of information. One key phrase can later trigger a listener's recall of important, related information. A historian describing the circumstances that led to the American Civil War could use the image of a fork in the road, one path leading to an urban, industrialized North, the other to a rural, agrarian South.

In recent years educators have talked about the need for relevance. You have no doubt sat through many speeches wondering what the information being conveyed had to do with you and your life. A speaker who can take ideas and associate them with the audience's present concerns will increase listener attention and interest. For example, an anthropologist could add interest to a discussion of primitive tribal rites by comparing them to some of the customs and rituals of various modern cultures and societies.

Effective visual aids help make ideas more clear, vivid, and concrete.

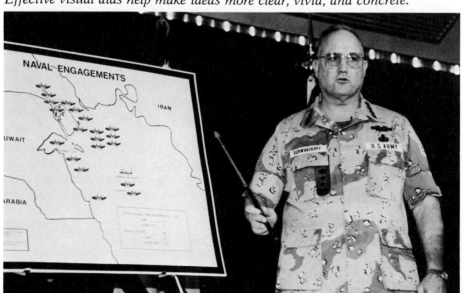

Another way in which a speaker can develop ideas effectively and increase learning is through the use of concrete, specific images that convey a sense of realism and vividness. A student delivering a speech on the World Trade Center in New York emphasized the enormity of the structure by pointing out that the building had close to 40,000 doorknobs. Although this bit of trivia is not in itself important, it made a more vivid and lasting impression than would have been made if the speaker had just informed the audience of the building's dimensions.

REPETITION. In every informative speech, regardless of subject, some information is more important than the rest, and it is the speaker's responsibility to convey this to the audience. An effective speaker will increase audience learning by emphasizing the most important information through *repetition.* A speaker can mention a point, underline its importance, mention it again in the middle of the speech, and repeat it at the conclusion. A recording engineer giving a talk to a class of would-be studio technicians might want to emphasize the need for organization during a recording session. He may mention it in the introduction simply as a "crucial factor." In the body of the speech, the engineer might quote the current hourly cost of studio time, pointing to the need for an organized use of every single minute. Finally, in the conclusion, organization might once again be stressed as a necessary element of good production.

VISUAL AIDS. In addition to using verbal pictures created through imagery, the speaker may improve a presentation by using a variety of diagrams, graphs, and photographs. In turn, these learning tools may be presented by using a variety of media, including flipcharts, overhead projectors, handouts, charts, drawings, opaque projectors, slide projectors, and films or videotapes.

There are several advantages to using *visual aids* such as those listed above. Visual aids:

1. Reinforce the presentation;
2. Simplify complex problems;
3. Help maintain group interest and attention;
4. Clarify important concepts for note-taking purposes; and
5. Aid in maximizing your credibility and professionalism.

Visual aids, then, can be of great value to you when you are presenting. To be most useful, however, they should be clear, legible, essential, accurate, and neat. You also must learn to handle visual aids effectively. To optimize effectiveness, make sure to:

Do:
1. Explain the visual aids' significance and relate them to your presentation.
2. Give the audience enough time to view and understand the visual aids.

3. Check all mechanical equipment before the presentation.
4. Use the hand closest to the visual aid to point.
5. Make sure that visual aids are large enough for all to see.
6. Keep visual aids simple.
7. Cover visual aids before and after using them.
8. Practice with visual aids beforehand.
9. Be creative with colors and designs.
10. Come prepared to deal with potential hazards before your presentation begins.

Don't:
1. Turn your back on the audience when referring to a visual aid.
2. Overuse visual aids during a presentation.
3. Place materials or aids in the hands of listeners during the speech.
4. Talk to your visual aids.
5. Apologize for the quality of your visual aids.[3]

A park official may decide to use color slides of various national forests in his presentation. As he talks of the size of the forests, he may show aerial shots to emphasize the number of square miles covered with trees. While describing the wildlife protected in the national parks, he may show slides of various animals and birds. When he wants to make clear the necessity of preventing forest fires, he may follow a series of beautiful images with one of the blackened and smoking ruin of a forest. By means of contrast, and by leaving this last image on the screen for a number of minutes, he will surely give his audience a clear idea of the damage and waste caused by a careless camper.

Audience Participation

While most of our discussion of the informative speech has focused on the presentation of information by the speaker, we should mention those situations in which the audience participates in the exchange of information. One popular format in which this occurs is the *platform.*

A platform format might be used at a public hearing on drainage problems, where citizens report on property damage from recent flooding, and officials relate their efforts to deal with the situation. Similarly, there may be an exchange situation on campus, where the college financial adviser gives an informative speech on how to earn money working part-time, after which a number of students relate the various ways they have found to earn money for tuition.

---

[3] K. W. Watson and L. L. Barker, *Presentation Skills Manual: A Guide to Effective Oral Presentations* (New Orleans, La: Spectra, Inc., 1991), 27–32.

The classroom also offers an opportunity for the presentation and exchange of information. Examples would be a home economics class in which students share their special recipes; a crafts class in which students do demonstrations of glassblowing, needlepoint, and pottery; and a philosophy class in which students explain their orientations to life. In each case, while the primary speaker may be the instructor, the audience also participates in the exchange of information.

PERSUASION

The degree to which an audience is actually persuaded will, of course, vary. A speaker who intends to persuade may (1) convince, (2) stimulate, or (3) move the audience to action. A person who attempts to **convince** intends to get the audience to think, believe, or feel a certain way. A person engaged in a debate, a minister preaching on the evils of materialism, and a business executive who thinks the company should merge with another firm may all use persuasion to convince their audience of a particular belief.

Another type of persuasion comes in the form of **stimulation.** Generally, a person who wants to stimulate an audience will attempt to reaffirm or strengthen preexisting beliefs or feelings. For example, the union leader who addresses members as they march on a picket line is trying to reinforce their belief in the importance of the strike while strengthening their feelings of solidarity.

The third level of persuasion is the speech that uses persuasion to **move members of an audience to action.** For example, if a product on the market skyrockets in cost or is believed to be hazardous to public health, different consumer groups may rally support from people around the country for an immediate boycott.

Although we make a distinction between the different degrees of persuasion, keep in mind that these purposes overlap. Obviously, before you can successfully move an audience to act, you must convince them. Because it is easier to get an audience to believe in something than to get them to act on it, the speaker who wants to activate an audience must use different techniques than the speaker who merely wants to convince.

Informative Versus Persuasive Communication

Perhaps the best way to understand persuasive communication is, first, to contrast it with informative communication. Persuasive communication differs from informative communication in three ways:

1. *Climate or environment.* When a speaker delivers an informative message, the relationship between the speaker and the audience is usually neutral. However, when a speaker delivers a persuasive

message, there is an emotional atmosphere that may be hostile or inspiring, depending upon the situation.

2. *Response sought.* More so than an informative speech, a persuasive speech will aim for a higher degree of audience involvement or action.

3. *Goals to be achieved.* The goal of an informative speech is to present an audience with new and useful information, which it is hoped they will understand and learn from. The goal of a persuasive speech is to change an attitude or belief, or to bring about some form of action. An informative speech that focuses on what furriers have done to date to stop the slaughter of animals on the endangered species list will be less controversial than a persuasive speech whose goal is to gain support for a boycott of the local furrier.

There are several approaches to persuasion that can help you more clearly understand the persuasive process. These include the Aristotelian approach as well as more contemporary approaches to the study of attitudes. Given the relevance of these approaches to our understanding of persuasion, we will begin by discussing each of them.

APPROACHES TO PERSUASION

The Aristotelian Approach

According to Aristotle, a speaker who wishes to create a persuasive message can choose among three persuasive modes, or appeals, in order to make his or her message effective. Aristotle labeled these appeals *logos*, *pathos*, and *ethos*.

> *Rhetoric may be defined as the faculty of observing in any given case the available means of persuasion.*
>
> ARISTOTLE

LOGOS: REASONING. *Logos* refers to a rational approach to persuasion. Based on logic and argumentation, logos is intended to appeal to an individual's sense of reason. For example, a physician trying to convince her colleagues of the value of an experimental surgical technique would do so most successfully if she uses a rational approach. Citing research studies and including statistics of successes and failures might persuade the listeners to adopt the technique. A member of a consulting firm trying to persuade a business person to adopt an efficiency plan must present hard facts and solid figures to show how the proposed plan will either increase productivity or eliminate waste.

Aside from facts and figures, logos includes the use of two basic types of reasoning: deductive and inductive. **Deductive reasoning** moves from the

The logos, pathos, and ethos of a public speaking situation are not only recognized but controlled by an effective speaker.

general to the specific. The best known form of deductive reasoning is the syllogism. The following is a classic example.

> All men are mortal.
> Socrates is a man.
> Therefore, Socrates is mortal.

A syllogism illustrates the deductive process very clearly; the final conclusion follows logically from the first generalization.

Inductive reasoning moves from the specific to the general. If your favorite disc jockey plays two enjoyable selections from a newly released compact disc, you may induce that the entire CD is good and decide to buy it. Sherlock Holmes was known for his ability to draw accurate conclusions about a crime on the basis of specific information or clues.

Of course, both deductive and inductive reasoning can be false. Consider an observer at an athletic event who notices that all of the track stars are wearing a particular brand of running shoes. He purchases a pair for his son and is disappointed when the boy fails to finish a marathon sponsored by the local youth organization. Just because a large number of great runners wear these shoes does not mean that everyone who wears them will be a great runner. The deductive process in this instance is fallacious and unreliable.

An example of false induction might be found in the case of a young woman who hires a small moving company to transport her furniture to her new home in another state. As she unpacks the shipping cases, she discovers that many things have been damaged, and she angrily resolves never to trust a small company again. In reality, many small companies are just as reliable as the larger ones, but she has falsely induced from her particular experience that all small company operations will be equally poor.

When you draw conclusions or make assertions, you must be able to support them by supplying the audience with the basis for your reasoning. In other words, you must convince the audience that your arguments are based on logical thinking.

Reasoning is that process of thinking by which an individual arrives at conclusions. A detective, a scientist, a labor mediator, and a public speaker all use the reasoning process as a tool of their respective trades. The ability to reason or think in a logical way is one of the distinguishing characteristics of the human mind. It is through reason that humans learn about their surroundings and generalize about their environment. Without this ability we could neither adapt nor function successfully in this world.

PATHOS: FEELING. A speaker may decide that *pathos,* an appeal to the emotions, will be more effective than logos, an appeal to reason. The effectiveness of emotional appeals depends on the audience's motivation to listen and respond, the credibility of the appeals, and the speaker's intent in creating the message.[4] Pathos is especially effective in situations in which emotions tend to override logic. Pathos includes reward appeals, fear-arousing appeals, and appeals to needs, desires, and values.

A *reward appeal* promises the listener some personal gain or profit if he or she believes or behaves in the manner suggested by the speaker. The intended reward may be either material or psychological. For example, a high school dropout who hears a speaker at a job placement center may be persuaded to attend night school to get his diploma if he is made to feel that it will better his chances for obtaining gainful employment. When the same individual attends his first class at the adult education center, he may be even more determined to finish if the instructor speaks about the increased self-confidence and sense of achievement he may expect as a result of his efforts.

The opposite of the reward appeal is the *fear-arousing appeal.* People tend to be more vulnerable to persuasion if they perceive a threat to themselves or their loved ones. An effective speaker can capitalize on a

---

[4]M. R. Robberson and R. W. Rogers, "Beyond Fear Appeals: Negative and Positive Persuasive Appeals to Health and Self-Esteem," *Journal of Applied Social Psychology,* 18, no. 3 (1988), 277–87.

Effective speakers capitalize on fear to enhance a persuasive message.

person's fear in order to enhance a persuasive message. Advertisements for home fire alarms and various safety products are examples of this approach.

Fear appeals are often used when the issue is public health. Televised public service announcements regarding AIDS, drinking and driving, and smoking are primary examples. However, fear appeals can be used in a number of other settings as well. Think for a moment about the following scenario, which resulted in harm to a university student. In a scenery workshop for the theater department of a university, the instructor presented the ground rules for participation in the class. Along with reminders to show up on time and to clean up before leaving, the students were advised to use the power saws only if supervised, to wear safety goggles and aprons when needed, to remove their jewelry, and to tie their hair back if it was long. The teacher did not really make clear the possibilities for serious harm to his audience, and the students were only too eager to start hammering and sawing. Some weeks later, one student lost his footing on a ladder and almost dislocated his arm when the leather thong bracelet he wore around his wrist caught on a protruding nail. In this case a greater fear appeal might have spared someone a badly wrenched shoulder and a puncture wound in the palm of his hand.

While certain fear appeals are justified, others become scare tactics. People are easily persuaded when they are made to feel threatened. Residents of a small middle-class neighborhood in New York City became vehemently opposed to the building of a low-income housing project when community leaders made them fearful that the project would mean an increase in crime and a deterioration of the neighborhood. Although the arguments used were purely emotional, they aroused enough fear and opposition to delay the building for some time.

In the previous example, the fear appeal was directed at a need for safety and security. Other psychological *needs* can be targets for the persuasive speaker as well. The need to be loved, the need to be respected, and the need for self-fulfillment can all be used as means of persuading an individual to change attitudes, beliefs, or behavior.

An effective speaker can also use human *desires* as a means of persuasion. When an attractive actress advertises an automobile, the appeal is intended to be sexual. Similarly, promises that a particular soap or cologne will make a man virile or a woman enticing are definitely based on an emotional appeal to desire. Other common targets for the effective persuader are the desire to be powerful, the desire to be unique, and the desire to remain youthful.

Yet another type of emotional appeal aims at our sense of *values*, perhaps best defined as preferred end states (such as freedom or equality) and preferred ways of doing things (such as being honest or ambitious).[5] Homer and Kahle have identified nine highly important values for most Americans. In no certain order, these include (1) self-fulfillment; (2) excitement; (3) a sense of accomplishment; (4) self-respect; (5) a sense of belonging; (6) being well-respected; (7) security; (8) fun and enjoyment; and (9) warm relationships.[6] Speakers who understand what their audiences value can create messages that produce increased understanding or overall influence. For example, when addressing an audience regarding the importance of being tested for the AIDS virus, a speaker who appeals to the audience's need for security (value 7) and who tells how the virus devastated an important relationship in her own life (value 9) will be more persuasive than a speaker who simply argues that the audience "owes it to society" to be tested.

As stated earlier, a good persuasive speaker will take care not to alienate his or her audience with a badly organized message. One of our primary concerns as listeners is how the organization of a message will affect us on an emotional level. Studies have shown that a well-organized message prevents listeners from feeling frustrated or angry and consequently increases the chance for an appeal to more sympathetic emotions. The importance of this factor is relative to individual listeners, since some people need greater structure than others to make sense of a message.

---

[5]A. Tesser and D. R. Shaffer, "Attitudes and Attitude Change," *Annual Review of Psychology*, 41 (1990), 479–523.

[6]P. M. Homer and L. R. Kahle, "A Structural Equation Test of the Value-Attitude-Behavior Hierarchy," *Journal of Personality and Social Psychology*, 54, no. 4 (1988), 638–46.

Credibility is a function of both expertise and trustworthiness.

ETHOS: SOURCE CREDIBILITY. *Ethos,* or source credibility, is the way in which a speaker is perceived by the audience. According to Aristotle, speakers will be held in high esteem if they are perceived as intelligent and moral and if they demonstrate good will toward the audience. Aristotle believed that these qualities alone were enough to create attitude change. Today we tend to analyze a speaker's ethos in terms of his or her expertise and trustworthiness. Source credibility contributes much to the persuasiveness of a message when the audience has no direct experience or knowledge of the topic.[7] However, whether the audience is informed or not, the speaker must be perceived as trustworthy and knowledgeable in order to carry any weight. If the author is perceived to be informed yet dishonest or devious, the speaker's persuasiveness will be undermined.

Sometimes a speaker's ethos will be established long before a particular speaking situation. For example, a Nobel Prize–winning physicist will probably be highly regarded by an audience because of prior accomplishments. His or her message would probably be more persuasive than that of a local high school science teacher, even if they presented identical messages.

When speakers lack ethos, however, it is harder for them to persuade. Let us look at the following situation: A college president, distrusted by the student body because he or she overreacted and called in the police to deal with a nonviolent protest, convened a conference of the student government to persuade students not to discuss the protest incident with the media. The

[7]W. Chenghuan and D. R. Shaffer, "Susceptibility to Persuasive Appeals as a Function of Source Credibility and Prior Experience with the Attitude Object," *Journal of Personality and Social Psychology*, 52, no. 4 (1987), 677–88.

president's ethos at this time was very low, and the students were particularly resistant to this persuasive attempt.

In many situations, however, a speaker is unknown to the audience and approaches the situation without a reputation of any kind. In this case the speaker must *establish* ethos, or credibility, so that the audience will perceive him or her as knowledgeable and trustworthy.

One factor that is influential in establishing ethos is organization. Aside from affecting comprehension, the organization of a speech affects speaker credibility. Studies in this area have shown that a speaker who is well organized in his or her presentation will be regarded as a more credible source than a speaker who is disorganized.

Interestingly, however, an audience's perception of source credibility can change in midstream, as demonstrated dramatically by national reaction in 1985 to Coca-Cola's announcement that they were changing the 99-year-old formula and offering consumers a modified formula called New Coke. Most of the advertising was geared toward convincing consumers that New Coke was different and even better than the original Coke. Bill Cosby was selected to star in the ads, based on his popularity and potential audience influence. Although the advertisements were aimed primarily at Pepsi drinkers in hopes that they would try New Coke and switch their brand loyalties, the ads also focused on loyal Coke drinkers who might be persuaded that the new product was as good as or even better than the old formula. However, the Coca-Cola Company was astounded by the results. Much to their delight, consumers who did not usually drink Coke were more favorable toward New Coke. However, to their horror, a "boomerang effect" resulted for loyal consumers. Consumers who regularly bought the original formula revolted in response to the change and were actually unfavorable toward the product with the New Coke label. The Coca-Cola Company reacted with lightning speed and launched a new campaign to market the old formula under the name Coke Classic. (Interestingly, the overall national reaction to Coke's campaign was recaptured in an experiment by Pierce in 1987. Loyal consumers were found to be positive toward the cola with the standard Coke label, but negative toward the product when it was called New Coke.[8])

The following is a partial list of factors related to source credibility.[9]

1. *Qualification/expertness:* This component of credibility operates when listeners are convinced that a source has enough training, ability, and experience to merit belief. For example, a nuclear physicist who presents a lecture on radioactivity would be rated higher on this dimension of credibility than would a high school student reading a report to a physics class.

---

[8]W. D. Pierce, "Which Coke Is It? Social Influence in the Marketplace," *Psychological Reports*, 60 (1987), 279–86.

[9]Adapted from R. N. Bostrom, "The Components of Credibility," in *Persuasion* (Englewood Cliffs, N.J.: Prentice-Hall, 1983), 71–74.

2. *Safety/trustworthiness:* This factor operates when a source is believed to be telling the truth and not presenting falsehoods to the listeners. For example, someone who makes money selling video- and audiotapes for real estate sales would be rated as less credible and persuasive on this dimension than would a realtor and friend of the family who is talking with you about real estate.

3. *Compliance/dynamism:* Sources who have either real or implicit power in a relationship often are more believable and persuasive than those who do not have power.

4. *Normative/identification:* Finally, credibility arises when a source is identified with a particular group that is important to the listener. To illustrate, Tommy is a chapter member of a local conservation club. When he discovers that James Kingry, president of the national organization, is to be a guest lecturer in one of his classes, Tommy will probably perceive that Dr. Kingry is a more credible source than his classmates will, even though Dr. Kingry is speaking on a topic unrelated to conservation or ecology.

Contemporary Approaches

Clearly, Aristotle made a significant theoretic contribution to our understanding of communication by focusing attention on strategies and attributes of the *source* that bring about persuasion. More recent advances, however, have focused on the nature of *receivers*, particularly their attitudes and the process of attitude change. Tesser and Shaffer (1990) have identified three major contemporary approaches to the study of attitude change. These include studies that address (1) the structure of attitudes, (2) attitudes as predictors of behavior, and (3) the functions that attitudes serve.[10] We now turn to a brief overview of each approach.

THE STRUCTURE OF ATTITUDES. A number of differing views currently exist regarding the structure of attitudes. However, recent advances in cognitive psychology suggest that our attitudes may best be viewed as associative networks much like (cognitive) maps, with our beliefs and feelings connected both within and between our attitudes. Thus, when we hear a message, a process of "spreading activation" takes place. In other words, the activation of one attitude (such as our attitude toward racism and bigotry on campus) will "prime" or make it easier for a source to tap other elements in the map (such as our beliefs and feelings about a campus crime that was racially motivated).

How does this information on attitudes help us to be more effective public speakers? Understanding that we all have cognitive maps—some more simple and some more complex—allows us to find better ways to reach and activate the attitudes of our audience. For example, a number of

---

[10]Tesser and Shaffer, 479.

variables affect our attitude structures, such as the amount of information we have on a given topic as well as how and to what extent we integrate that information. If you are speaking to an audience with expertise in your area or about some controversial issue, audience members are more likely to have knowledge both for and against your position on the subject. Thus, you will need to develop a speech that is two-sided in nature or that takes into account the sophistication of your audience's knowledge structures.

ATTITUDES AS PREDICTORS OF BEHAVIOR. Recent research by Ajzen and associates has shown that the best predictor of a given behavior is our intentions, and that our intentions are a function of (1) our attitude toward the behavior, (2) whether we believe significant others in our lives would condone and encourage the behavior, (3) the extent to which we believe we can control the outcome or results of that behavior, and (4) alternative behaviors that are available to us.[11] So powerful is this information that Ajzen and others have been able to use it to more accurately predict a variety of human behaviors, including dental hygiene, alcohol and drug use, self-examination for breast cancer, ability to quit smoking, consistency in following an exercise program, use of contraceptives, and voting behavior.

If Ajzen's theory, outlined above, has helped predict these behaviors, the theory has major implications for those of us who are interested in the nature of persuasion. For example, if you want to persuade your roommates to wash their breakfast dishes before they leave for class, Ajzen might argue that your best chance of convincing them will involve making an initial attitude assessment. This assessment should include your roommates' current attitudes toward washing dishes (positive, negative, or neutral), whether they will feel significantly rewarded by you (and each other) for washing the dishes, the extent to which they believe that washing dishes will result in desired rewards or avoided punishments, and other, alternative behaviors available to them (such as not washing dishes). Once you have made this assessment, you can begin the process of developing a message that will best fit your "profile" of their attitudes and intentions. For instance, you will need to take a more active approach if you know that they are negative toward washing dishes, feel unrewarded for doing them, believe that no significant rewards will ensue even if they change their behavior, and think that not washing dishes is the best alternative for them so far. Based on this assessment and some creative problem solving, you may be able to come up with a persuasive message. For example, you might try offering to do their dishes if they agree to make up your bed—something you loathe doing but they do well and consistently. In short, by understanding the attitudes and intentions that underlie behavior, you can better construct messages that get the results *you* intend.

---

[11]I. Ajzen, "Attitudes Structure and Behavior," in A. R. Pratkanis, S. J. Breckler, and A. G. Greenwald (Eds.), *Attitude Structure and Function* (Hillsdale, N.J.: Lawrence Erlbaum Associates), 241–74.

THE FUNCTIONS OF ATTITUDES. The third area of attitude research addressed by Tesser and Shaffer that has implications for public speakers is that of attitude functions. Work in this area has been conducted since the 1940s. However, a more recent study by Herek resulted in the classification of attitudes into three major functions: (1) experiential-schematic, (2) defensive, and (3) self-expressive.[12]

Generally, the ***experiential-schematic function of attitudes*** involves the general cognitive maps that we develop about a target object, issue, person, or group (such as "needles," socialized medicine, our doctor, or medical personnel as a whole). More importantly, attitudes of this type exist as a function of our experiences with the target in question and whether those experiences have been positive, negative, or neutral. To illustrate, think for a moment about your current attitude toward lesbians or gay men. According to functional theorists, your attitude will be positive if (1) someone you care about has chosen this lifestyle; (2) you have had a positive personal experience with a person who has chosen this lifestyle (for instance, you have become friends); (3) you feel that it is likely that you will interact in the future with people who are gay or lesbian; and/or (4) you have had positive personal experiences with people who have gay or lesbian family members or friends. Conversely, functional theorists argue that, if you have had negative past experiences in one or more of these domains, you will probably have a negative attitude toward someone who leads a gay or lesbian lifestyle.[13] In short, if an attitude is serving an experiential-schematic function, that attitude will be based on past experiences you have had with the object, issue, person, or group in question.

The second function of attitudes is the ***defensive function.*** We generally hold and express attitudes that are defensive in nature whenever we experience some form of personal anxiety or insecurity regarding the target in question. Additionally, defensive attitudes involve two major steps: the projection of unacceptable motives onto the target in question and expression of hostility as a result.[14] To illustrate, consider the following scenario. You have just been given two 50-yard-line tickets to the Super Bowl and are on your way to the game. The Los Angeles Raiders are playing the Washington Redskins. You are—and have been—a Redskins fan all of your life. You have even brought along a foam tomahawk (commandeered from a friend who is an Atlanta Braves fan) to help you cheer the team. You are pumped and excited as you park the car and walk with your best friend toward the gate. However, to reach the gate, you notice that you will have to walk through a group of Native American protesters to get to your seats. How will you behave? What attitudes will drive your behavior? Functional theorists would argue that, if you prefer to avoid thinking about the protesters and their concerns because doing so makes you feel anxious, or if

---

[12]G. M. Kerek, "Can Functions Be Measured? A New Perspective on the Functional Approach to Attitudes," *Social Psychology Quarterly*, 50, no. 4 (December 1987), 285–303.

[13]Ibid., 296.

[14]Ibid., 288–89.

you experience personal feelings of discomfort as you walk through their picket line, you will probably exhibit behavior that is based on a defensive attitude. For example, you may feel uneasy and a little guilty for having screamed a "war whoop" seconds before you noticed them. Or you may even grumble to yourself as you approach the protesters that they are "trying to ruin the game." As you reach the area in which they are located, you may feel the need to avoid eye contact, to look down as you pass by, or to ignore their words and concerns. If your attitude is highly defensive, you may find yourself name calling, getting into a fight, or engaging in some other equally undesirable behavior. From a public speaker's perspective (that of the Native American protesters, in this example), such a situation is especially difficult. The "speakers" are dealing with a potentially volatile issue—in this case, especially if you (1) live to be a Redskins fan, (2) like the mascot, and (3) love doing the tomahawk chop when your team is winning! Thus, the protesters must find ways of raising your awareness without calling out the defensive function of your attitudes—a task that is difficult at best.

The third function of attitudes is the *self-expressive function.* Self-expressive attitudes emerge every time we use our attitudes as a vehicle for expressing values that are important to us, such as having a comfortable life, a sense of accomplishment, a peaceful world, freedom, pleasure, inner harmony, or self-respect. Opinions that are based on self-expressive attitudes also involve (1) how we think people who are close to us would respond to a given target, and (2) how the target is viewed by people whose opinions we value most.[15] If we have a positive self-expressive attitude toward a target (for example, someone whom we know is carrying the HIV virus), we generally will take a "live and let live" approach regarding that person. In this instance, we will value his or her individual rights and need for personal expression—as we would with anyone who is diagnosed as HIV positive.

On the other hand, if we have a negative self-expressive attitude, we generally will resort to traditional or religious standards of what is right or wrong when perceiving the target. Think for a moment about news stories you have heard about communities banding together against a family that has a child with AIDS. In many instances, such behavior was "justifiable" to the townspeople—only as long as "everyone else" (significant others) held the same attitude. However, as soon as attitudes changed on the part of key people, or a celebrity (such as Elton John or Michael Jackson) became involved, the town generally changed its overall attitude and views. (Sadly enough, such attitudes change slowly—and often too late to make a difference in the lives of the "target.")

The question becomes, How can we use this information to become more effective public speakers? Research in the area of attitude change reveals that information that is directly related to the functions that an attitude serves will be more persuasive than that which addresses concerns other than those of the three aforementioned functions.[16] For example, one

---

[15]Ibid., 296.
[16]Tesser and Shaffer, 502–3.

study reviewed by Tesser and Shaffer revealed that messages (ads) that appeal to the "self-expressive" function of attitudes (to product image) have a positive impact on image-conscious people, for whom many attitudes serve a self-expressive function. Interestingly, the reverse would be true for people whose attitudes are driven by an experiential-schematic function. For the latter, messages that appeal to product quality over image would be more persuasive.

The ramifications of this and similar findings in attitude research are far-reaching for students of persuasion. Armed with an understanding of the structure and functions of attitudes, you are faced with a very real dilemma: determining what attitudes are driving your audience's behavior and finding ways to tap the "appropriate" attitude. That is your task and greatest challenge. However, by treating this new-found knowledge as a critical element of your audience analysis, you may begin to construct messages that are more appropriate to the audience and occasion. Given a clearer understanding of how attitudes affect behavior, we may begin a more systematic approach to understanding the structure of persuasive messages.

PERSUASIVE TECHNIQUES

We have thus far discussed the theories of persuasion. You may now be wondering about specific techniques that can be used in delivering persuasive messages. Indeed, using at least one of six techniques may help you construct an effective speech. These techniques include the uses of one-sided versus two-sided arguments, evidence, forewarnings, humor, primacy and recency effects, and effective conclusions. Each of these techniques will be discussed in the following pages.

ONE-SIDED VERSUS TWO-SIDED ARGUMENTS. When presenting a speech to persuade, a speaker must decide whether to present both sides of an issue or argument or only the side he or she is supporting. The effectiveness of either a *one-sided* or a *two-sided presentation* is determined by several factors.

In general, a two-sided argument is more effective when the audience is opposed to the speaker's point of view, when it is well educated, and when it will be exposed to opposing arguments in the future. On the other hand, the one-sided argument is more effective if the audience is predisposed to the speaker's position. For example, the woman who is in favor of abortion does not need to hear a counterargument in order to strengthen her belief. One-sided arguments also tend to be more effective if the audience is less well educated and if it will not be confronted with later attempts at persuasion.

The effective speaker in a two-sided approach can present both sides of an issue and pick apart the opposing argument in order to strengthen his or her own position. For example, a prosecuting attorney can repeat arguments put forth by the defendant and then proceed to show that these arguments are weak, inappropriate, or false.

USE OF EVIDENCE. While you might expect that the use of evidence could only enhance a persuasive message, studies in this area have come up with inconsistent and contradictory findings. While some researchers have concluded that the use of evidence is advantageous, others have shown it to be of little significance. In general, the persuasive communicator must assess the subject and audience before relying on evidence to make the speech effective.

For example, an efficiency expert who wants to persuade a group of office managers to use a new type of computer would be wise to include statistical data as evidence. The subject of efficiency is technical, and the audience is used to problem solving based on facts and figures. The listeners will be intent on hearing accurate information before allowing themselves to be persuaded.

If speakers have low credibility with their audience, the use of evidence may do little to enhance their position. The audience may "tune out" the facts and figures, thinking them to be as ill-founded and unreliable as the speakers themselves. On the other hand, speakers before audiences that perceive them as highly credible need not include evidence in their presentations. The audiences will accept their messages at face value.

When the speaker is perceived by the listener to have authority or economic power over others, the use of evidence will be superfluous. The promise of reward for those who agree and punishment for those who do not will be enough. Similarly, when listeners hold the speaker in a position of respect, they may allow themselves to be persuaded without hearing much hard evidence, in order to win the speaker's approval.

FOREWARNING. Does foreknowledge of a speaker's intent have any effect on the persuasion process? According to Hiromi Fukada, a Japanese expert in the area of persuasion, prior knowledge of a speaker's intent when he or she plans to present a fear-arousing message reduces the effect of that message by stimulating anticipatory counterarguments.[17] In other words, when an audience is *forewarned* of a speaker's intent to use fear-arousing appeals, audience members will generate arguments that are counter to that of the speaker during the actual presentation and will remain more resistant than audiences not forewarned throughout the message.

Of course, a speaker's intent is often well established long before he or she begins the presentation. For example, when a number of tenants refused to pay a rent increase, the landlord went before the tenants' organization. The landlord's intent was perfectly clear. The audience knew he was there to convince them that they should pay the rent increase and that the increase would mean better service. In a case like this, where the purpose is no secret, effective speakers will reveal their intent in the introduction and give a preview of what they are going to say. It thus appears that they are trying to be straight with the audience instead of trying to manipulate them.

---

[17]H. Fukada, "Psychological Processes Mediating Persuasion-Inhibiting Effect of Forewarning in Fear-Arousing Communication," *Psychological Reports*, 58 (1986), 87–90.

HUMOR. Another variable that the persuasive speaker should consider is the use of *humor.* Once again, studies have provided contradictory findings as to whether the use of humor enhances the persuasive attempt or detracts from it. However, if used properly, humor can loosen up a tense atmosphere, make people feel good, increase audience responsiveness, and reveal a more human side of you as a public speaker. Additionally, if used judiciously, humor can help emphasize certain key points and make ideas memorable. The reader is advised to remember that great care must be taken to minimize perceptions that you are speaking to entertain. Expert speakers have learned that humor is best used to keep the audience involved.

To help speakers use humor more effectively, Dorothy Leeds, author of *PowerSpeak*, offers the following suggestions.

1. When you tell a story or joke, have fun with it. Your face should wear a smile and your eyes should twinkle or reflect some form of mischievousness. If you don't have fun, your audience won't have fun, and your efforts at humor will be lost.

2. Stay with the essential elements of a story or joke; avoid giving too much detail. Deliver your story briskly. Then give your audience all the time it needs to respond. Timing is everything with humor.

3. Make direct eye contact with individual members of your audience when delivering a joke. Look left to right and around the room at different people as you deliver the punch line. Practicing humor before the event will help you appear spontaneous and comfortable with your story or joke.

4. Practice telling your joke or story in different ways. After a presentation, evaluate the effectiveness of your approach and make appropriate changes the next time you give a similar presentation.

5. After delivering a humorous story or joke, move directly to the point you are making. Doing so will help the climax of your presentation to be more effective.[18]

PRIMACY AND RECENCY. An important element in organizing your message so that it will have the greatest impact is to determine the placement of various arguments and key points. There are two effects that you should consider in this organization: primacy and recency. In some cases arguments presented first in the speech tend to have the greatest effect in creating attitude change. This is an example of *primacy* organization. Sometimes, though, strong arguments presented near the end of a speech seem to be more persuasive. When arguments are presented in this order, a *recency* effect occurs.

To say that one pattern of organization is always more effective than another is incorrect, since existing information is contradictory. It is known,

---

[18]Adapted from D. Leeds, *PowerSpeak: The Complete Guide to Persuasive Public Speaking and Presenting,* (New York: Prentice Hall Press, 1988), 117–18.

however, that certain factors may influence the effectiveness of placing an argument first or last. These variables include the nature of the message, audience position relative to that of the speaker, the interval between arguments, and so forth. The effect of primacy-recency on the organization of arguments within one message and on the order of two opposing messages has been studied. Although research has not provided any firm rules for the order of presentation of ideas, some general guidelines have emerged. It is important to remember, however, that these are not conclusive or final.

1. With one-sided persuasive messages, build to a climax by using weaker arguments at the beginning and stronger ones toward the end. Doing so produces a greater effect on the audience than an anticlimactic arrangement.

2. When presenting a two-sided, pro and con argument, present the first half in a climactic order and the second half in an anticlimactic form. In other words, build to your strongest supporting argument as you present the "pros" of your position, and move from the strongest to the weakest opposing evidence as you present the "con" side of your proposal.

3. Underscore weaker arguments with stronger ones when delivering a one-sided message. If a strong argument is followed by several weaker ones, you will lessen the total impact.

4. Present strong arguments in a set or close to one another to help your audience better remember the material.

5. In a two-sided message, give your arguments before you present those of the opposition.[19]

THE CONCLUSION. Conclusions serve three primary functions in a public presentation. They (1) provide the audience with a sense of closure, (2) allow you to repeat your main points for emphasis, and (3) encourage your audience to rethink how your message applies to their everyday lives.[20] As such, effective conclusions are those that directly relate to the introduction and the purpose of the speech, thereby bringing the speech and audience full circle. Additionally, they request agreement if you desire a particular response by the audience (such as drawing a similar conclusion to yours on the issue of human rights), or they appeal for action if your presentation is persuasive in nature (such as signing up for a free AIDS screening test being given at the health center over the next ten days.)

To help you construct more effective conclusions and to end your presentation with finesse and style, consider the following suggestions:

---

[19]A. J. Clark, "An Exploratory Study of Order Effect in Persuasive Communication," *Southern Speech Communication Journal*, 39 (1974), 322–32.

[20]J. K. Brilhart, J. S. Bourhis, B. R. Miley, and C. A. Berquist, *Practical Public Speaking* (New York: HarperCollins Publishers, 1992), 176.

1. Summarize the main points in your speech, just as you (may have) previewed them in the introduction. Doing so will help your audience better remember your central ideas.

2. Do not present any new information or ideas in your conclusion. Avoiding this pitfall will help your audience stay more focused on your primary points.

3. Finish with style; try concluding with a quotation, a startling statistic, humor, a rhetorical question, or a direct appeal. Challenge yourself. Stay away from the age-old phrase, "In conclusion. . . ."

4. When delivering a persuasive message, find ways to motivate your audience to action. Appealing for definite action will challenge audience members to assess the full impact of your message for them as individuals.

5. When appropriate, refer back to the opening of your speech. Returning to a story, joke, statistic, or any other effective introductory device will help the audience to better achieve psychological closure.

PERSUASIVE SITUATIONS

Persuasive communication is widespread. One of the most obvious settings in which persuasion occurs is in the courtroom. Here the court must decide whether there is enough evidence to warrant a trial, or a jury must decide upon the guilt or innocence of the accused. The prosecuting attorney may use a logical form of persuasion to convince the jury of the defendant's guilt: "The culprit was also described by several witnesses as a middle-aged man wearing unusually large sunglasses and a bright green athletic jacket. The defendant was arrested several blocks from the scene of the crime wearing such a jacket. The sunglasses were found in a trash can in a nearby parking lot. From the color of his jacket and the fact that the sunglasses were found near the scene, it naturally follows that he is the man responsible for the burglary."

A defending attorney may appeal to the emotions of the jury. "The defendant was wearing a green athletic jacket, but he was on his way to his son's Little League game at the local ball park. This is the kind of family man who is more likely to wear an American flag tie pin than a pair of gaudy sunglasses." By associating the defendant with the family, the favorite American sport, and patriotism, the defense counsel attempts to persuade the jury of his client's upright citizenship and innocence.

On a less dramatic but equally effective level, persuasion is also the basis of sales and advertising. A student selling magazines and a scout troop marketing cookies hope to gain access to your pocketbook as they sit outside your grocery store or travel door to door. A good salesperson can be so persuasive that many states have adopted legislation that enables a person to cancel an order or void a contract within several days of the initial sale. This type of law protects the consumer who may be "talked into something" by a persuasive salesperson.

Perhaps the most effective sales pitches are the ones that appear on television and radio or in newspapers and magazines. So powerful are these media that manufacturers invest millions of dollars annually in advertising costs. So persuasive are these media that a single 60-second commercial aired during the 1992 Super Bowl cost sponsors $1.7 million. While sponsors of such programming hope to entice the audience into buying their products—often, by introducing new multi-million-dollar ad campaigns—they also hope to expose the audience to new ideas and items. Many people go into the grocery store and buy a product that they have just heard about or seen advertised on television. Others are persuaded by their children to buy a new toy that has been bombarding the airwaves. Exposure and the power of suggestion account for much of the success of mass-media advertising.

Not all sales pitches come from manufacturers. In discussing persuasion, we must not overlook the charity drive. We tend to forget this form of selling, since the product we buy is either good will or a tax deduction. The most frequently used approach in a charity drive is the emotional appeal. While certain charity drives occur all year round, they seem to be most prevalent during holiday times, particularly around Christmas. The timing is not accidental; most people are more vulnerable and charitable at this time of year.

ENTERTAINMENT, CEREMONIAL, AND OTHER SPECIAL-OCCASION COMMUNICATION

In the beginning of this chapter we divided public communication according to purpose. We have already taken an in-depth look at speeches designed to inform and persuade. We are now ready to focus our attention on the third category, the speech to entertain and the special-occasion speech. While these two categories are often thought to be synonymous, it should be pointed out that special-occasion speeches include eulogies, farewells, and resignations, which are seldom meant to entertain. However, since many special-occasion speeches, such as introductions, acceptances, and after-dinner talks, are often intended to entertain, we will discuss them as separate but related in purpose.

Kinds of Special-Occasion Speeches

There are many different types of special-occasion and ceremonial speeches. Let us take a look at a few of the more familiar ones. A *welcoming speech* may be presented to an individual or an entire group about to join an organization or attending a particular meeting or seminar. The speaker who presents the welcoming speech should mention the group extending the welcome and should make some comment on the occasion. Perhaps you remember the dean of students presenting a welcoming speech at your freshman orientation. Similarly, when you graduate, a fellow student or member of the faculty will welcome the parents and friends of the graduates. A welcoming speech should be brief and to the point. It may be humorous in nature, depending on the situation or occasion.

Two additional special-occasion speeches are the **award presentation** and **acceptance speech.** You are probably familiar with these types of speeches from having seen televised presentations of the Oscar, Tony, and Emmy awards. It is likely that you have participated in some sort of award presentation as a presenter, recipient, or member of the audience. At some time in your life, you may have attended a high school awards assembly, a scouting club breakfast, or a church supper, where awards for superior performance were presented to deserving recipients. Whether an individual presents an award or receives one, he or she should emphasize the significance of the award. While the presentation speech focuses on the many ways in which the recipient qualifies for the award, the acceptance speech is a way of saying "thank you."

The **after-dinner speech** is often, but not always, a speech to entertain; certainly, it is intended to make the audience feel relaxed and comfortable. The content of the speech depends on the nature of the banquet. A more formal occasion will warrant a more serious presentation. The after-dinner

Acceptance speeches are a way to say "thank you."

speech at a hundred-dollar-a-plate political banquet will probably be more serious than the one presented at an annual fraternity ball. The after-dinner speech should be relatively brief, since other announcements, introductions, and speeches are usually on the agenda.

In a *farewell speech,* the speaker expresses regrets about leaving a particular group or organization and offers thanks to those who are left behind. A person who retires or is joining another company, the valedictorian of the high school graduating class, the employee who has joined the ranks of management, or the man or woman going off to join the military all share a common purpose in saying goodbye and thank you to the people they are leaving.

One particular type of farewell is the *eulogy,* a ceremonial speech marking someone's death. A eulogy may be presented at the funeral service or at a later date, as a memorial. Numerous memorial services are held on January 15 to mark the birthday of the Reverend Martin Luther King, Jr., renowned civil rights leader. The eulogy is a farewell speech that praises the virtues and accomplishments of the deceased. While a eulogy is often delivered by a member of the clergy, sometimes friends, family, or colleagues make the presentation in addition to or instead of the clergy.

Although there are numerous other special-occasion speeches, the last category we will discuss is the *impromptu speech.* "Impromptu" refers to the manner of presentation. An impromptu speech is one that is made on the spot, without any sort of preparation. Someone who wins an unexpected award will be expected to give an impromptu acceptance speech. Someone filling in at the last minute for a scheduled speaker may be asked to give an impromptu welcoming or after-dinner speech. The most important thing to remember when delivering an impromptu speech is to stick to the topic and try to present your speech in an organized and interesting manner.

Principles of Effectiveness

In any special-occasion speech or speech to entertain, there are several principles of effectiveness that you should consider. The first of these is to use humor appropriately. Remember that not all speeches or occasions should have a humorous approach. If the occasion does call for humor, you must decide if your speech should be really funny or just mildly amusing. Humor should be used as a means of accomplishing your purpose, not of offending or distracting your audience.

Another principle is to have a central theme. This is particularly important in special-occasion speeches. The speaker should know his or her purpose and relate the entire speech to that purpose.

Finally, the speaker should avoid belaboring points and should be clear, cogent, and brief. These qualities are particularly desirable in ceremonial or special-occasion speeches.

Chances are that at some time in your life you will be asked to deliver a special-occasion speech or a speech to entertain. It might be at a community affair, at a political banquet, or at a class reunion. If you keep these principles in mind, you will increase your chances of success.

SUMMARY

The major communication goals are information exchange, persuasion, and entertainment. In the first case, the speaker must aim for audience learning and comprehension. In the second, the speaker tries to modify the attitudes, beliefs, or behavior of the listener. A speaker whose purpose is entertainment must strive to amuse or please the audience.

When presenting an informative speech, the speaker must keep in mind the factors that affect audience learning. The speaker must try to motivate the audience to listen and learn. The message must be organized, and ideas must be effectively developed. The speaker may emphasize important information by repetition or by the use of visual aids. Information exchange may take the form of audience participation.

Comprehending approaches to persuasion across the ages can help us better understand the persuasive process. The Aristotelian approach takes a source-oriented perspective and provides us with three modes of persuasion: logos, pathos, and ethos. Much recent work in persuasion has been based on more of a receiver orientation, emphasizing the structure of attitudes, attitudes as predictors of behavior, and the functions of attitudes. Three specific attitude functions addressed in this chapter were the experiential-schematic, defensive, and self-expressive functions.

In addition to the tools this information provides in persuasive situations, a speaker may increase the persuasive effects of his or her presentation through the use of specific speaking techniques. An appropriate use of one- and two-sided arguments, sound and sufficient evidence, or forewarning of purpose may help to change the attitude of the listener. Explicit conclusions and the proper use of humor may also be persuasive. Consideration of the primacy-recency effect, the arrangement of ideas and arguments within the speech, may also improve the potential for successful persuasion.

The final kind of public communication is the speech to entertain, whether for ceremonies or for other special occasions. The entertaining speech is intended to bring pleasure and amusement to the listener. The special-occasion speech may be a way of saying thank you, farewell, or congratulations. It may be an occasion for awarding praise or it may be a eulogy. Appropriate use of humor; a clear, concise, and well-organized presentation; and a central idea are important elements of effectiveness in any of these communication situations.

EXERCISES

Group Experiences

Before and After

DESCRIPTION: Most individuals need some type of motivation to listen to, and then learn, the information that is conveyed by the speaker. Without even realizing it, most of us continually provide reasons for another person to listen to us in a dyadic conversation. If you are attracted to another person, this may provide extrinsic motivation for you to listen to what he or she has to say. On the other hand, if you have been with a person over time, attraction may no longer serve as an extrinsic motivator. In cases such as these, another form of motivation would have to be developed in order to maintain interest in the conversation. This activity will help you understand the connection between interest level and motivation.

PROCEDURE: This is a role-playing activity that is most effectively used as a demonstration technique in front of the class. There are two roles, one played by a female and the other played by a male. The team should be asked to play the following three scenes.

Before

This is your first date. You are sitting in a nightclub. You are both extremely attracted to one another and excited about being together. You hang on every word the other person says because you don't want to miss anything. Show your interest in the other person both verbally and nonverbally.

During

You have been dating for four months. You are at the nightclub again. Your relationship is gradually shifting to where you are more interested in the music than in each other. You listen to each other on an off-and-on basis.

After

You have been together for a long, long time. You are at the nightclub again. You have heard everything the other person has to say "a million times." Neither one of you listens to what the other person is saying. Carry on an entire conversation where you misinterpret or do not listen to what the other person is saying.

DISCUSSION: This activity demonstrates the existence of extrinsic motivation (attraction to the other person) in the "before" scene. The "during" scene demonstrates the minimal existence of extrinsic motivation, while the "after" scene demonstrates the complete absence of extrinsic motivation for listening to the other person. Logically, it can be assumed that extrinsic motivation can be replaced with intrinsic motivation, which then would increase the listening level. Can you think of a time during which you listened to another person with the absence of extrinsic or intrinsic motivation? Can you provide motivation for others to listen to you on both a physical and a psychological level? In your daily conversations, do you provide motivation for the other person(s) to listen?

The 60-Second Commercial

DESCRIPTION: Research suggests that many different variables should be considered when planning a speech for a particular audience. Some of the considerations include extrinsic and intrinsic motivation, organization, effective development of ideas, repetition, and visual presentation. This activity will provide you with the opportunity to use a variety of techniques in an attempt to persuade the audience to remember your product.

PROCEDURE: You are to design a 60-second commercial on a fictitious product or service. You will be paying a high price for 60 seconds of prime time, so the commercial should be designed with extreme care. Your purpose is to motivate your audience to remember the name of your product. Be creative in the design of your commercial.

DISCUSSION: The class period following the presentation of the commercials should be used to test which products were remembered. Take out paper and pencil and list all the products you remember. Next to each product you should identify why you remembered the product. After everyone has completed these lists, check to see which products were remembered the most. Why were some products remembered, while others were not? Consider the repetition, organization, and visual presentation of the message. Do you think it is difficult to develop a "persuasive" message?

How's Your Ethos?

DESCRIPTION: Ethos, or source credibility, refers to the way in which a speaker is perceived by the audience. Some of the findings related to source credibility include:

1. Receivers tend to accept conclusions advocated by sources perceived as competent and trustworthy.
2. A high-credibility source can produce more attitude change than a low-credibility source, even with highly ego-involved receivers.
3. When a receiver identifies with a source, it may enhance the source's chances of producing attitude change.
4. The receiver's attraction for a source increases as similarity of attitude between the two increases.
5. The status of the speaker can affect his or her persuasiveness.

The following activity provides you with an opportunity to see how these principles work.

PROCEDURE: Which of the above principles of source credibility does this example illustrate?

Sample Situation

In an Arizona state prison, a program was presented on adapting to society after living in prison. Two speakers addressed the group of inmates. The first speaker was Dr. Sharon Stone, a noted psychologist in the area of social adjustment. The second speaker was Ron Harnick, a former inmate who had spent five years in the state prison system. The inmates showed greater interest in listening to Ron Harnick, and, consequently, his speech had a much greater impact than Dr. Stone's.

Two principles can be identified in this example. Principle 3 suggests that when a receiver identifies with a source, it may enhance the source's chances of producing attitude change. In this case it can be observed that the inmates (receivers) identified with Harnick (source) because of the time the latter spent in prison. Principle 4 suggests that the receiver's attraction for a source increases as attitudinal similarity between the two increases. It may be assumed that the inmates perceived Harnick to have greater attitudinal similarity with them as compared with Dr. Stone.

Now that you have a sample description, divide into dyads and write an example that will serve to illustrate each principle. You may use one example to illustrate two principles. Each dyad should read one example to the rest of the class and ask the other students to explain the applicable principle of source credibility.

DISCUSSION: After writing and listening to various examples, can you identify other principles of source credibility? What are some of the ways in which you can be perceived as more credible? Which methods are most commonly employed by politicians to enhance their credibility?

Personal Experiences

1. Think for a moment about the last time you responded very positively or negatively to an event that occurred on your campus. That "event" might have been a protest, a heated debate, or a celebration surrounding a major victory by an athlete or team from your school. Now think of the attitudes that you had about the issues associated with that event and what attitudinal function may have been called out that contributed to your response. Was that attitude experiential-schematic, defensive, or self-expressive in nature? Did you feel your behavior being physically driven by that attitude? Have you ever found yourself embarrassed days after a behavioral response because you simply "lost control"? How does knowledge of the structure and functions of your attitudes help you diagnose your own behavior? How can you use this information to help you as you deal with other people in your everyday life? in public speaking settings?

2. Obtain a copy of a transcript of a speech, or attend a speaking situation in which the speaker is clearly attempting to persuade his or her audience. Was the speaker ethical? List your criteria for a code of ethics in public speaking.

3. A common misconception about public speaking is that the ability to make speeches is instinctive and cannot be learned. Interview one or two people in your community who are considered to be effective speakers. Find out how they began public speaking. Were they ever afraid to speak in front of groups? Did they ever deliver a "bomb"?

Discussion Questions

1. What are the criteria used to distinguish public communication from private communication?
2. What is an example of a persuasive speech to (a) convince, (b) stimulate, and (c) actuate?
3. Are the qualities of ethos, pathos, and logos inherent in every good speech? Why? Why not?
4. Under what circumstances would a one-sided argument be more effective than a two-sided argument?
5. What forms of motivation would be most effective to use when speaking to a group of college students?
6. In what ways do persuasive messages affect your day-to-day activities?
7. What techniques can a speaker employ to increase audience participation?
8. What are some creative ways you can think of to repeat the same information in different forms?

11

Developing and Organizing the Message

KEY CONCEPTS AND TERMS

Personal interview
Survey
Introduction
Thesis statement
Body
Conclusion
Transition
Topical pattern
Chronological pattern
Spatial pattern
Increasing levels of difficulty
pattern
Chain-of-events pattern
Inductive pattern

Deductive pattern
Cause-and-effect pattern
Problem-solution method
Progression
Real example
Hypothetical example
Extended example
Illustration
Anecdote
Description
Comparison-contrast
Operational definition
Statistics
Testimony

As Drew sat in his office pondering how he could best structure his presentation for the board, his eye caught a glimpse of an old photograph that had been with him for years. Framed in oak and sitting at eye level on the mantel, the photo seemed to come to life as his gaze traveled lazily toward the crackling fire. As his eyelids grew heavy, Drew found himself returning to an earlier time in his life—a time when he, Bobby Harper, and Randall Morris, the subject matter of that old photo, would camp out and tell ghost stories in the woods beside the creek. Hypnotized by the flames, Drew could almost hear the wind through the trees and the words that Bobby whispered. Bobby's voice had always trailed into a whisper when he got to the scariest parts.

As he heard the owl's hoot and the final words of Bobby's story, Drew actually experienced the "startle reflex" that he always associated with Bobby's dramatic conclusions. Jarred into reality, Drew sat upright with a start and looked suspiciously around the room. Then his eyes traveled back to the photo on the mantel, and he slowly began to smile. "*That's* how I'll approach this presentation," Drew said to himself. "I'll create a story that'll keep 'em hanging on every word." As he reached for the pad and pencil that had now been idle for over an hour, he scribbled notes that would transform his message into a colorful story. With two hours to spare and new-found inspiration, Drew knew he had this presentation in the bag.

All of us have probably experienced childhood memories such as Drew's—memories of sitting around a campfire telling ghost stories. Interestingly enough, it's no different when we're grown: Stories can bring to life the main point that we are making and capture the imagination of the audience. Like every good story, a public speech has an introduction and conclusion. Both also have climactic moments, color, and imagery.

In this chapter you will learn how to create more effective presentations by using many of the principles that successful storytellers use. However, public speakers, like storytellers, must be prepared. Speaking in public is a challenge that requires selecting a topic or approach that will enthrall, gathering information that will add not only substance but also color and form, and organizing the message with the rhythm and ebb and flow of a story. More than any other in the book, this chapter is a kind of handbook of do's and don't's. It is meant to give you practical advice. The suggestions on how to choose your topic and gather source materials will provide you with the foundation for creating more effective presentations. Likewise, we hope the information on organizing and supporting the body of your speech and on preparing an effective outline will help. (Appendix B illustrates how the process works by presenting and annotating an effective speech.) Given the importance of each of these elements to public speakers and storytellers alike, we now turn to a discussion of how to select and narrow presentation topics.

SELECTING THE TOPIC

Finding a suitable topic is sometimes half the battle. In some instances there is no choice. The topic may already have been decided for the speaker. For example, a union representative may be invited by the membership to discuss pension benefits at the monthly meeting, or a veterinarian who services a rural community may be asked by the local farmers to discuss precautions against cattle diseases.

You and the Topic

When you must choose your own topic, however, you should keep certain guidelines in mind. The first of these guidelines concerns you, the speaker—your knowledge, your interests, and your convictions. To help you realize the importance of these elements, consider the following illustration.

Penny was a "thirty-something" graduate student who had returned to school later in life. Over the course of the years, she had experienced several traumatic events, a number of which had fueled her interest in the study of communication. One day, as a graduate teaching assistant for the basic communication course, she made a decision to provide her students with an example of an informative speech. The speech she gave was one she had presented to several groups in the past on the topic of AIDS, and one that was based on her own personal experience. Penny introduced the topic of her speech by telling the following story.

> Once upon a time there were a boy and a girl who were the best of friends. They shared the same interests—skiing, cycling, the theater—and the same circle of friends. One day they looked into each other's eyes and saw that something was different. The friendship had turned to love. Soon after, they were married. Everyone came to the wedding and celebrated their union. The couple was perfect. Everyone had known that one day they would be together.
>
> For six months, their marriage was the epitome of bliss. The couple delighted in making each other happy. One morning the boy gently awakened the girl and said, "Sweetheart, I have something to tell you." The girl smiled and rolled over to face the boy she loved. His next words were, "Honey, I'm gay." The marriage was annulled immediately. It took years for the boy and girl to each put the pieces of their lives back together, but finally they did.

With a pause to cue her audience, Penny then switched from third to first person. "One day, five years later, the phone rang. I got up and said, 'Hello.' It was Wayne. He said, 'Hello, sweetheart. I've got something to tell you.'" At that moment in her speech, Penny's audience froze. Her next words were beyond their comprehension: "Wayne said, 'I've tested positive for the AIDS virus. I think you had better be checked.'"

As Penny moved from her story to the body of the speech, which focused on myths and information about the HIV virus as well as how to go about being tested, she later said she could have heard a pin drop until the very end of her presentation. To her surprise, she also was approached about her speech for several weeks by students whom she didn't know. Apparently, her students had been so affected by the presentation that they had gone home and told their friends. Penny's ultimate realization about the impact of her speech came almost three weeks later. A student who had heard about her came up and asked her where he could go to be tested. He was afraid of the results, but her story had given him the courage to face reality.

Penny's story is true. She was one of our graduate students. Of course, her name has been changed for this book. However, if you meet her one day, in the halls of a university in which she is teaching, she will probably tell you about the time that she found a way to teach her students three critical public speaking concepts. In this instance, she discovered a way to make them see the value of considering the following three elements:

1. Know your topic.
2. Be interested in your topic.
3. Believe in your topic.

Penny's speech provides a perfect example of how to follow these three guidelines. Penny knew her topic well. After experiencing the trauma of a broken marriage and having to take the AIDS test, she made a point of learning more about the HIV virus. Her life depended on this knowledge, and once she learned that she had tested negative, she decided to share her experience with others. It's always easier to discuss subjects about which you are familiar than ones about which you know very little. Although a good speaker researches any topic, previous knowledge of the subject can make the selection process easier.

Obviously, Penny's topic was also interesting to her. If your life is changed completely in one moment by as few as three words, you are going to be interested. However, you need not have experienced anything quite so dramatic as that which Penny experienced to be truly interested in your subject. For example, if you are an art history major, you probably will feel more comfortable discussing Leonardo da Vinci than talking about the advantages of solar energy. If you are genuinely interested in the subject on which you are to speak, your enthusiasm will be communicated to your audience when you deliver your speech. Interest in your topic also increases your motivation to investigate and research it thoroughly.

Finally, like Penny, you should consider your personal values and beliefs when selecting a topic. Make sure that your beliefs and the topic you choose are compatible. This is particularly important in persuasive speaking. For instance, you can hardly expect your audience to be convinced of the need for tougher environmental laws if you yourself are not firmly convinced. A firm belief in your topic will make the presentation more vital to you and to your audience.

NARROWING THE TOPIC

Once you have selected a topic, you must narrow it so that it is workable. Don't be like the high school student who decided to deliver his first speech ever on "the French Revolution." How narrow should your topic be? That depends upon your purpose. The thrust of a speech will vary according to whether it is intended to inform, persuade, or entertain. For example, in a well-coordinated effort, several elected city officials addressed their fellow citizens on the financial crisis in their city. The focus of each individual address was different. In a formal televised statement, the mayor, whose purpose was to inform the public of the crisis situation, focused on the current fiscal deficits and the long-range consequences of inaction. At a later press conference, a councilman outlined the kinds of legislation necessary to relieve the crisis situation. A third member of the city council was given the job of persuading the citizens who attended a town meeting to write letters or send telegrams to state and federal government officials encouraging them to pass legislation to relieve the financial crisis. Although each speech dealt with the finances of the city, the thrust of each address was determined by the speaker's purpose.

A good speaker should consider personal purposes and goals as well. These, too, will aid you in achieving desired results and in fully informing the audiences. One way that you might begin is to make a list of objectives, ideas, opinions, and conclusions that you have drawn (keeping in mind, of course, the audience and time limits involved!). Next, ask yourself the following five questions:

1. *Who* in the audience am I targeting for a change in attitude or behavior—for instance, those who are opposed to my view? those who are neutral? those who already feel as I do about the topic?
2. *What* actions do I want my audience to undertake as a result of my speech—for example, write Congress? contribute money? alter their personal behavior? change their attitude regarding my topic? be motivated to change?
3. *When* do I want the audience to take the actions that I am encouraging them to take—immediately? within the week? from this point on in their lives?
4. *Where* should the audience turn for more information if they need it? Can I provide them with enough information to bring about the desired action?
5. *How* should I structure my message in order to bring about the desired actions—include stories, examples, or statistics? build a one-sided or two-sided presentation? use a cause-effect or problem-solution organizational pattern?

Determining your central thought is a final consideration when defining and narrowing your topic. One of the most glaring speaking errors of beginners and poor speakers is lack of focus. As noted earlier, good speeches are much like other works of art—stories, musical compositions, paintings, plays, or literary works. They consist of separate elements that become unified into a whole by means of a central idea or thought.

GATHERING SOURCE MATERIALS

After selecting your topic and narrowing it, you can begin to collect the materials you need to build your speech.

Use of Sources

It is usually to your advantage to select from a wide variety of sources. The type and number of sources you use will depend on the specific purpose of your speech. When presenting an informative speech on a controversial issue, you should always secure information on at least two opposing views, especially when one source of information is biased. For example, if you were presenting a speech on "rising gasoline costs," you might find that the explanations of the shortage and the consequent increase in prices presented in an oil company publication would be quite different from the facts and arguments put forth in a consumer group pamphlet. In a situation like this, you should consult several sources in order to get the true picture. Of course, when presenting a persuasive speech, you may choose to include only those sources that support your particular point of view. Even then, it is important to be aware of the opposition.

Whether you conduct an interview, read a magazine article, or watch a videotape, it is essential to take notes. Your notes should include summaries of the information and direct quotations, particularly if you plan to use them in your speech. Ethical considerations and accuracy necessitate the use of a quotation in the context in which it was found. When direct quotations are not in order, summaries of information are sufficient.

You as Source

The most basic and obvious source at your disposal is yourself. Whether you realize it or not, you represent a storehouse of knowledge, experience, and observations. The fact that you remember paying 20 cents for a slice of pizza when you were in junior high school may be trivial. If you are going to give an informative speech on inflation and the cost of living, however, this information could suddenly assume significance. In general, personal anecdotes, examples, experiences, and observations make a speech more meaningful for the speaker and more colorful for the audience.

What type of planning is necessary when the interviewee is unknown to the interviewer?

Interviews

You will often find that the best source of materials for a particular subject is another person or group of people. In that case you may want to gather your material by conducting an interview.

PERSONAL INTERVIEW. A *personal interview* is conducted on a one-to-one basis with a person who has information or knowledge about the topic of your speech. For example, if you were to present a speech on penal reform, you might want to interview an attorney, an inmate, a judge, and other individuals connected with the penal system. If you were presenting an informative speech on a particular diet fad, you might find it valuable to interview a doctor, a nutritionist, someone who had success with the diet, and someone who did not. Although a personal interview may provide a sizable amount of material, information or opinions obtained by this method should not be considered definitive. The impact an interview will have on your audience depends on how that particular audience judges the credibility of your source.

Regardless of the subject, a good interview requires good technique. If you choose to conduct an interview, keep certain things in mind:

1. Remember your purpose and topic and avoid getting sidetracked.

2. As an interviewer, you should try to make the person you interview feel comfortable and willing to talk. Obviously, a cooperative interviewee will make your task much easier.

3. Be prepared for the interview and have definite questions in mind.

4. Since you are trying to find out specific information or opinions, phrase your questions in such a way that they will bring clear responses.

If the topic of your speech lends itself to a personal interview and an appropriate interviewee is available, you will find this method an invaluable source of material.

SURVEY. At times you may need to conduct a survey rather than a personal interview. A *survey* is a detailed gathering of information by questionnaire, observation, interview, and so forth. A survey enables you to gain a cross-section of information and opinions. Suppose you were giving an informative speech on the sexual mores of today's college students. You might wish to conduct a survey of as large a sample of your fellow students as possible in order to obtain some firsthand information. As in the case of the personal interview, the information and opinions obtained through a survey are not meant to be definitive. Although both sources are most useful when used informally, the validity of a survey can be judged in terms of the standardization of questions and the selection of participants.

A young historian went to the Ivory Coast to tape legends from an Akan tribal chief.

Printed Material

Printed material has long been relied on as the main source of information for speech content. Such material includes books, magazines, journals, pamphlets, newspapers, diaries, almanacs, encyclopedias, and so on. There are so many different types of printed material that it is essential to know how to locate these different sources and use them properly. Information about some subjects is found almost exclusively in printed material. For example, historical information that cannot be gained through a personal interview may be found in books or in a journal, and reports about current breakthroughs in science or medicine might be located in professional journals or magazines.

Today, thanks to microfiche and microfilm, printed material can be stored in a minimum amount of space. Libraries are the primary storage houses for printed material, but you may find it necessary or beneficial to search out other sources. If you were doing a speech on alcoholism, you could find printed information in the vertical file of the library, or you might visit a local branch of Alcoholics Anonymous and pick up pamphlets or newsletters regarding their programs and services. Many such special interest groups, consumer organizations, churches, trade unions, and so on, publish their own small newspapers or booklets about their activities.

Electronic Media

Modern technology has provided us with additional sources of material in the form of electronic media. Films, television, cassettes, records, computerized databases, and videotapes are all valuable sources of information that can aid you in the preparation of a speech. For example, the now famous Zapruder film of the Kennedy assassination has proven to be a vital source of evidence for those who urge further investigation of the shooting. Since the advent of videotape, many events have been captured on film and are available as source material for the speaker.

PARTS OF THE SPEECH

All speeches, regardless of their purpose or length, should be composed of three basic units: the introduction, the body, and the conclusion. Each of these parts serves at least one function that is essential to the effectiveness of the speech. Although each part of the speech should flow smoothly into the next, each unit should be identifiable upon analysis of the text.

Examine the following two brief speeches, which were prepared for a training seminar for magazine salespeople. Read each presentation carefully and decide which one is more effective.

Speech 1

There are many different magazines from which a person can choose. For the sports enthusiast, there are magazines like *Sports Illustrated* and *Field and Stream*. The homemaker might want to learn new recipes or tips on decorating from the *Ladies Home Journal* or *Redbook*. Those who enjoy literary magazines may turn to the *Saturday Review* or *The New Yorker*, while others may be interested in general news magazines like *Time* or *Newsweek*. These magazines vary in price and frequency of publication and are available through our subscription service.

Speech 2

Have you ever been stuck in a doctor's office or train station without anything to keep your mind off waiting? Or maybe you were stuck inside with a cold or waiting for a delivery? Perhaps if you had an interesting magazine to read, the waiting wouldn't seem so long.

There are many different and interesting magazines from which one can choose. For the sports enthusiast, there are magazines such as *Sports Illustrated* and *Field and Stream*. The homemaker might want to learn a new recipe or tips on decorating from a magazine like the *Ladies Home Journal* or *Redbook*. Those who enjoy literary magazines may be interested in reading a copy of the *Saturday Review* or *The New Yorker*, while others might be interested in a general news magazine like *Time* or *Newsweek*. These are just a few of the many magazines which can be readily purchased by subscription.

The number of magazines published is quite large. One can safely say that there is a magazine for every area of interest, whether it be crafts, sports, science, health, automobiles, food, fashion, gardening, or anything else. And what makes it even better is that they are all available through subscription.

Although these two speeches contain basically the same information, the second speech is obviously more effective. It has a carefully developed introduction, body, and conclusion.

The Introduction

The *introduction* of a speech must first catch and then focus audience attention as well as preview the body of the speech. Sometimes just getting started is one of the most crucial and difficult tasks in presenting a speech.

Often a speaker has to compete with a noisy or inattentive crowd. In such cases it is even more important to capture the audience's attention with an effective introduction.

In addition to the initial benefit statement mentioned at the beginning of Chapter 10, several other standard devices can serve as an effective introduction. These include the use of a startling statement ("By the year 2025, the earth will run out of food"), a rhetorical question ("Did you ever wonder what your life would be like had you been born in another era?"), statistics ("Only 1,400 out of 2,000 college freshmen will earn their degree"), a humorous statement ("If all the world's a stage, then a lot of us get bit parts"), or a famous quotation (from Abraham Lincoln: "You can fool all the people some of the time, and some of the people all the time, but you cannot

A speech in preparation: a portion of President John F. Kennedy's inaugural address.

fool all the people all of the time"). Of course, sometimes one statement produces two or more effects. For example, the statement "One out of every two marriages ends in divorce" uses statistics but may also be somewhat shocking to an audience.

THESIS STATEMENT. The introduction of a speech should also include a *thesis statement* that presents the specific purpose of the speech. The purpose can sometimes be worked into the opening device for getting attention. For example, a museum sponsor might begin a fund-raising speech with the following:

> You don't have to go to a peep show to see some of the most beautiful nudes imaginable. Some of the world's most famous nudes can be found right here in our museum. But, unless we can find a way to raise $20,000 for maintenance costs, these nudes are going to be left out in the cold!

The opening line of this introductory paragraph begins with an unexpected or startling statement. Chances are, at least a few ears will perk up with the words "peep show." The remainder of the paragraph suggests that the museum is in financial trouble and must raise money to continue its operations. The last sentence suggests the purpose of the speech and gives some insight into what the main text will be about.

Regardless of the technique you use in your opening, be sure that the introduction is appropriate, is in good taste, and says exactly what you want it to say. You should not use a joke or anecdote unless it is appropriate to the occasion and relevant to the subject. You should avoid telling a joke or humorous story unless you feel perfectly comfortable with it. Remember, not everyone is a comedian. You should also omit irrelevant "warm-up material" and clichéd beginnings such as, "A funny thing happened to me on the way. . . ." Your introduction should be relatively brief and direct.

The Body

The effective introduction previews the main text of the speech and leads directly into the body. The **body** is generally the largest part of the speech and is intended to present the main points, elaborate on them, and clarify when necessary. It is also a function of the body to develop clear transitions between different ideas.

In an informative speech, the body contains the bulk of the information you wish to present. In a persuasive speech, the body contains the arguments and evidence that support the speaker's position, as well as a refutation of any counterarguments. For example, if you were trying to persuade your audience to support the abolition of capital punishment, the body of the speech would probably include moral and legal arguments along with appropriate supporting material. You might also include statistics to disprove the standard counterarguments, which contend that capital punishment is a deterrent to crime, or those that attempt to justify capital punishment on the basis of "an eye for an eye."

Industry in art is a necessity—not a virtue—and any evidence of the same, in the production, is a blemish, not a quality; a proof, not of achievement, but of absolutely insufficient work, for work alone will efface the footsteps of work.

JAMES MCNEILL WHISTLER

The body of a persuasive speech should include a discussion of the nature, effects, and causes of the problem, issue, or controversy. A politician who is trying to change the juvenile justice system because it is too lenient might want to include statistics showing a high percentage of juvenile felonies, case histories of chronic juvenile offenders, and the opinions of sources who have experience in the legal system. The speaker should show why the particular problem is meaningful to the audience. The politician

Persuasive messages generally contain moral and legal arguments.

might try to convince the audience that it is no longer safe to go outside or that children and the elderly increasingly fall prey to juvenile criminals.

The body is the longest and most detailed part of your speech, so the arrangement of its ideas is very important. There are certain patterns of organization you can follow to help you structure the body of your speech effectively. These patterns of organization include a topical pattern, a chronological pattern, a spatial pattern, and various other patterns. Because the organization of the body is so important to effective speech making, we will discuss these structural arrangements in greater depth later in the chapter. Simply stated, however, the body of the speech should be presented in a way that is logical, coherent, and easy to follow.

The Conclusion

A speech isn't over until the speaker walks away from the podium. Therefore, the ***conclusion*** of the speech is as important as the introduction. Although the major portion of the speech is presented in the body, it is the conclusion that can leave a lasting impression.

In general, the conclusion of an informative speech should offer a restatement of the major ideas and a summary of the overall content. Concluding a speech on what to look for in buying a car, a speaker might restate specific guidelines such as economy, safety, and size as well as summarize the ways in which these guidelines can assist the buyer. Similarly, a demonstration talk on how to make a macramé wall hanging should end with a summary of the necessary materials and specific steps involved.

The conclusion of a speech gives you an opportunity to tie up loose ends and bring the speech to a unified finish. As it is impossible for the audience to listen to and remember everything that is said, the conclusion should emphasize the main points so that the audience knows what was most important.

The conclusion of a persuasive speech may be used to arouse the audience to action. Let's examine the conclusion to the speech presented by our museum sponsor:

> In conclusion, ladies and gentlemen and patrons of the arts, it is time to as-sure our magnificent paintings a place inside our museum. For many years you have enjoyed the beauty of these fine paintings. Now it is time to give something in return. Take out your wallet or your checkbook and give what you can to help raise the $20,000 we need to keep our museum doors open!

This concluding paragraph underscores the purpose of the speech and asks for some action on the part of the audience. A concluding call for action need not always be financial, of course. The president of a parents' group may end an address with a plea to parents to keep their children home from school as a protest against a cutback in school services. Or a union delegate might ask an audience to join a boycott of crops picked by nonunion workers. A political candidate might conclude a rally by asking for volunteers to distribute campaign literature. In each case the call for action would be strongest in the concluding paragraph.

Regardless of purpose, the concluding paragraph should round out the speech and bring it to a satisfying close. The final sentence should signal the end of the speech so that the audience will know that it is over. The speaker may want to close with an emphatic statement or use one of the devices mentioned in our discussion of the introduction. For example, if you want to leave the audience thinking, you might pose a rhetorical question. Or, depending upon the content of the speech, you might want to conclude with a famous quotation.

Sometimes you might want to coordinate the conclusion with the introduction by using the same type of device, or even the same statement.

*Using visual aids can help summarize key points at the conclusion of a
message.*

For instance, a community leader who opens with the quotation from
Abraham Lincoln that we mentioned earlier may close the speech in the
following way: "You cannot fool all the people all of the time; and all of us
here tonight know that *now* is the time to demand an end to the irresponsible
actions of the City Council." Using the same quotation or same set of
statistics not only reinforces a point but also lends your speech a sense of
closure and balance.

Transitions

We should not overlook the use of transitions as an important aspect of
speech organization. A **transition** is the bridge that allows one idea to flow
smoothly into the next.

The most important transitions are those between the introduction and
the body and between the body and the conclusion. However, they are also
necessary between the main ideas within the body. For example, in a speech
presented at a block association meeting, a neighborhood detective was
discussing an increase in local crimes. One major point was that in recent
years there seemed to have been a tremendous increase in auto thefts and

robberies. To lead into his next point, the detective added, "But, unfortunately, the problem has not remained in the streets. Latest precinct reports show that household break-ins and burglaries in the area are up 50 percent over last year." The shift from crime on the street to crime indoors was smoothly made by a simple transitional statement.

The complexity of a transitional bridge depends upon how similar the two ideas are that are being connected. Sometimes just a few words or a simple sentence will do. For example, certain phrases, such as "in addition to," "aside from," and "in conclusion," are often used as transitional bridges.

When ideas are not closely related, you may need a more substantial transition—in other words, something that draws a connection between the two ideas or parts. A woman speaking to a group of senior citizens may wish to convince them of the need for an urban renewal project and at the same time assure them of the preservation of their neighborhood. The two points may be related in this way:

> Perhaps you feel that all of these changes I have proposed will destroy the charm of our downtown area. However, along with the plans for change are many plans for the restoration of our historical sites and parks. The kind of rebuilding now proposed will be in keeping with the tastes and needs of our community.

The effective use of transitions is one way to distinguish between a good speech and a mediocre one.

ARRANGEMENT OF THE BODY OF THE SPEECH

Patterns for Informative Speeches

We have already mentioned several standard patterns of organization that can help you structure your speech and present your ideas with the greatest effectiveness. The pattern you choose will probably depend on your topic. Certain subjects are best suited to particular patterns of organization. We will now discuss some of the standard patterns most frequently used in the informative speech. It is important to remember that audiences retain more information when speeches are logical and well organized.

TOPICAL PATTERN. One of the most frequently used organizational patterns is the *topical pattern,* in which information is presented according to a specific category or classification. This type of organization is particularly useful when the subject of the speech can be divided into subparts that form a whole. For example, a speaker at a children's concert might introduce the audience to various parts of the orchestra by using a topical approach. He could discuss the strings, then the brass, then the woodwinds, and finally the percussion instruments. Each of the major divisions could then be broken down according to the general characteristics of each group and the specific instruments within each category.

CHRONOLOGICAL PATTERN.   A second standard pattern of organization is the *chronological pattern,* which follows a subject in time. The chronological pattern is particularly useful when presenting biographical or historical information or when tracing the development of an idea, institution, or movement. A speech on the development of satellite communication could be presented in a chronological pattern by tracing the events from the launch of Sputnik I on October 4, 1957, to the most recent advances in satellite technology. Or a speech on American fashion in the twentieth century could be divided into decades and could mention such eras as the "flapper" style of the 1920s, the miniskirt of the 1960s, the "yuppie" look of the 1980s, and the return of the '60s look in the early 1990s.

A chronological speech may span centuries or days, depending on the scope of the topic. Because it is impossible to do justice to a topic that covers an enormous period of time, even in a speech that is an hour in length, the speaker must focus on the most important information. You must also make sure that the audience is aware of the time lapse between events, especially when the events or information you are discussing have occurred at uneven intervals. For example, in presenting a biographical sketch, you might connect one event to the next with phrases such as "two years later" or "in a matter of weeks" in order to give the audience some perspective as regards the time that has passed. The use of transitional phrases is particularly important when presenting a speech according to chronology.

Remember, nobody wants to hear innumerable small details. Even in everyday conversation, an unnecessarily detailed account of an event or an experience can become very boring. Children are often guilty of this practice. For example, you may ask a child what a certain television program was about, and he will repeat an endless sequence of events. Obviously, each step is not an integral part of the story. However, the child has not learned how to decide what information is most important. A speaker must be able to determine the most important information, for he or she cannot include too many ideas, events, or details without causing the speech to become lengthy and tiresome.

SPATIAL PATTERN.   Not every subject is suited to every pattern of organization. Topics based on the location of one part in relation to others or on a geographical progression may best be presented in a *spatial* order. A speech that traces the westward expansion of America might be divided according to the extension of different geographic boundaries. (Note that the same speech might be presented using a chronological order.) A speech based on Christopher Columbus's discovery of the New World might follow his historical routes.

A spatial organization may be appropriate for certain subjects not related to geography at all. For example, an architect presenting a speech on the Pyramids might approach the topic from a spatial order, emphasizing the relationship between one part of the structure and another. A spatial organization enables the audience to visualize the individual parts as they relate to one another in terms of the whole.

PATTERN OF INCREASING DIFFICULTY.   Because one of the primary factors in evaluating the success of an informative speech is audience understanding, the speaker must strive to present the speech as clearly and logically as possible. When a topic is relatively complex, the speaker may choose to use a pattern of organization based on *increasing levels of difficulty.* This type of structure is particularly helpful when presenting an informative talk on a subject with which the audience is unfamiliar. When a plant manager explains the changes that will take place within a factory because of the pending use of robotics, the manager may want to present the information in varying degrees of difficulty. Because the comprehension of some ideas is based on understanding other ideas, a pattern of increasing difficulty helps to ease the progression. Audiences feel much more comfortable after they have mastered an idea or understood some particular bit of information. By carefully building one idea upon another, a speaker can present increasingly complex material to an audience whose confidence in its own interpretive and evaluative abilities also increases.

CHAIN-OF-EVENTS PATTERN.   As the name implies, this pattern of organization is based on the development of a series of steps, with each step depending on the previous one. For example, a local congresswoman addressing members of the Young Democratic Club in her district might use the chain-of-events method to explain the sequence of events that must occur as a bill goes from the committee stage to its actual enactment as law. Similarly, a weatherman predicting a 50-50 chance of a snowstorm might outline the series of weather events that must occur in succession in order for the storm to develop. The *chain-of-events* method is particularly useful when giving a demonstration speech that explains a certain procedure. For example, a salesperson demonstrating the use of a personal computer would show the customer how to operate the computer according to step-by-step directions.

Patterns for Persuasive Speeches

Various patterns of organization are particularly well suited to the persuasive speech. While these methods are not restricted to persuasive speeches, they are often used in them. Remember that the purpose of a persuasive speech is to create attitude change within the listener or to motivate the listener to action.

INDUCTIVE PATTERN.   The first pattern is the *inductive pattern.* This particular pattern of organization is based on the process of inductive reasoning, which we discussed in the previous chapter. In an inductive argument, you present the audience with several specific cases that serve as the basis for a generalization. The specific cases must, of course, support the generalization. Therefore, you must avoid examples that are inconsistent with or contradictory to the generalization you wish to make.

The number of specifics necessary to formulate a sound generalization will vary. Although there are mathematical calculations to determine statistical validity, you can usually rely on common sense and intuition to decide upon the minimum number of specific cases that a particular argument demands. For example, a senior citizen who condemns all teenagers as "dope fiends," based on the solitary example of a neighbor's son, lacks a sufficient number of specific examples. Therefore, the generalization is invalid. When the generalization involves a large population, a greater number of specific cases is necessary.

Certain generalizations are easier to support than others. For example, U.S. health officials who sought to end the swine flu inoculation program used an inductive argument. Citing several incidents of paralysis as a side effect of the injection, officials provided enough evidence to ban the program. The argument might have followed this pattern:

Specifics: I. Specific cases of paralysis following inoculation.
                  A. Cases of paralysis in Florida.
                  B. Cases of paralysis in Denver.
                  C. Cases of paralysis in New Jersey.
Generalization: II. The swine flu inoculation can cause paralysis.
Conclusion: III. Therefore, the inoculation program is potentially hazardous and should be discontinued.

Based on the occurrence of cases of paralysis following the shots, health officials decided that the inoculation could conceivably have caused paralysis and therefore concluded that the program should be discontinued. The generalization that the inoculation could cause paralysis was evolved through an inductive process based on the occurrence of scattered cases of this side effect. While some experts discounted this argument, emphasizing that the percentage of cases of paralysis was quite small relative to the number of persons receiving the shot, the program was discontinued.

DEDUCTIVE PATTERN. The inverse of the inductive pattern is the ***deductive pattern,*** in which a speaker applies a generalization to specific cases. The generalization, if accepted by the audience, serves as the basis for an effective argument.

In a deductive pattern of organization, the speaker must draw a conclusion about a specific case based on its applicability to a previously accepted generalization. In Chapter 10 we mentioned the syllogism, which is the most common example of deductive reasoning. An effective argument can be organized in the form of a syllogism. For example, a concerned member of the community may offer the following deductive argument at a public transportation hearing:

Generalization: We are all agreed that traffic lights reduce accidents.

Specific:	There seem to be a lot of accidents at the intersection of 40th and Vine.
Conclusion:	Therefore, a light at the intersection of 40th and Vine would reduce the number of accidents.

If the traffic officials agree with the citizen's general statement, they might be quite willing to accept the solution. If the general statement is not accepted by an audience, however, the deductive argument will have little effect. Generalizations based on value judgments are most difficult to validate. Therefore, a speaker must have some insight into the nature of the audience. Let us examine the following deductive argument:

Generalization:	All war is immoral.
Specific:	Vietnam was a war.
Conclusion:	Vietnam was immoral.

The effectiveness of this deductive argument depends on the audience's acceptance of the general statement. Undoubtedly, an audience of conscientious objectors would accept this argument. However, the same argument would probably be vehemently rejected if presented before an audience of Veterans of Foreign Wars. Therefore, in preparing a deductive argument, the speaker must be sure that the audience will agree with the general statement.

CAUSE-AND-EFFECT PATTERN.   Closely related to the inductive argument is the ***cause-and-effect pattern.*** In this type of presentation, the speaker establishes a relationship between two events. The speaker attempts to convince the audience that this relationship is one of cause and effect, or that a certain result is the product of a specific event. For example, at a monthly sales meeting, an assistant buyer suggests that the increase in hosiery sales results from a new line of pantyhose. This argument could be confirmed; according to the record of sales, the new line of pantyhose contributed to an increase of 25 percent of the total volume of hosiery sales. Therefore, the new line of pantyhose (cause) produced an increase in sales (effect). However, not all cause-and-effect arguments can be mathematically determined. For example, how could you substantiate a claim that natural catastrophes such as earthquakes and floods increase as a result of our tampering with the atmosphere? Although it might be argued that these disasters have been more prevalent following milestones in space exploration, it would be impossible to draw a causal relationship between the two events.

One effect is often the result of several causes. For example, when a heretofore losing team moved into a new stadium and started to win, the cheering fans were convinced that the new stadium brought the team luck. In a case like this, the exact cause of the team's success would be a combination of things, including perhaps the new stadium, an increase in attendance, errors on the part of the opposition, the return of an important player after an injury, and so forth.

PROBLEM–SOLUTION PATTERN.   Another useful pattern of organization for the persuasive speech is the ***problem-solution method.*** This approach is much the same as the pattern of organization used in group discussions (see Chapter 7). The problem-solving method, first described by John Dewey, includes the following basic steps:

1. What is the nature of the problem?
2. What are the causes?
3. What are the possible solutions?
4. Which is the best solution?
5. How can this solution be put into effect?

Remember our traffic light example? Let's examine this example according to the problem-solution pattern. The nature of the problem concerns the number of accidents at the intersection of 40th and Vine. Causes of the problem include the use of this route as an alternative to the parkway, with a subsequent increase in traffic, and the lack of any traffic signs or personnel. Possible solutions include a traffic light, a police officer to direct traffic, rerouting the traffic, and a four-way stop sign at the intersection. The best solution would be a traffic light, since a police officer would be too costly, a four-way stop sign might prove confusing, and rerouting the traffic would cause congestion on neighboring roads. The solution could best be put into effect by a decision by the Department of Motor Vehicles and the installation of the light by the same agency.

The problem-solution pattern is based on a logical, step-by-step analysis of a particular problem. Of course, the analysis of any problem requires considerable research and investigation.

PRINCIPLES OF OUTLINING

Regardless of the organization pattern you select, an outline helps you in the preparation as well as the delivery of your speech. The outline is a tool that allows the speaker to categorize information and separate main ideas from subordinate ones. For example, in a topical presentation the speaker would classify each aspect of the subject as a main division of the outline. In our previous example of an informative speech on the parts of the orchestra, the string, brass, woodwind, and percussion sections would each be represented as a major category of the outline. Each category would then be subdivided into specific instruments and general characteristics. Part of such an outline would look like this:

Parts of the Orchestra

I. The Strings
   A. Types of Stringed Instruments
      1. Violin
      2. Viola
      3. Cello
      4. Double bass
      5. Harp
   B. Characteristics of Stringed Instruments
      1. Sounds produced by plucking, bowing, or striking strings
      2. Many are fretted
II. The Brass

A chronological pattern of organization may be used in an outline that divides the topic by specific intervals such as decades, years, or weeks, depending on the scope of the topic. For example, a speech on American automobiles in the twentieth century might be divided into discussions of types of cars at the turn of the century, in the 1920s, in the 1930s, and so forth.

Although the outlines may vary in form, the basic principles remain the same. Some speakers prefer to use Roman numerals for each major part of the speech, using I for the introduction, II for the body, and III for the conclusion. Capital letters are then used for main ideas within the text of the speech. However, regardless of the form, you should remember that details presented in an outline get more specific with each subdivision. Look at the outline in Figure 11–1. Notice how the two major divisions (I and II) relate

Successful speakers practice their speeches before appearing in public.

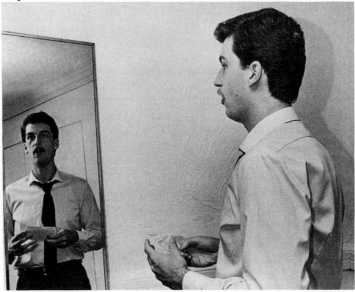

to the general topic of the outline (negative effects of air pollution). As you can see, the information gets more specific with each division, and each detail relates directly to the preceding category.

All forms of outlining share certain basic principles:

1. Keep your outline simple.
2. Account for all major parts of the speech.
3. Include at least two subpoints for each main point.
4. Use Roman numerals and indentation to structure your outline.
5. Organize main points and subpoints to underscore the relationships among them.
6. Arrange ideas in a logical progression.

Simplicity

An outline is used to assist, not confuse, the speaker. Therefore, as a speaker, you should keep your outline simple. Each line should represent a single thought or bit of information. Decide whether you want to use single words, phrases, or sentences, and then use them consistently throughout the outline. An outline is a valuable organizational tool if you don't let it become too cumbersome.

FIGURE 11–1
A Sample Outline

Title: Air Pollution: The Silent Killer

Thesis Statement: Air pollution has an adverse effect on world health and the environment; therefore, listeners should take an active role in reducing air pollution.

Introduction

   I. In the next 50 years, gas masks will not be reserved for war, but will be requisite for daily life.
      A. Current statistics regarding air pollution in major cities around the world
         1. London
         2. Paris
         3. Tokyo
         4. Moscow
         5. Montreal
      B. Current air pollution statistics in major U.S. cities
         1. New York
         2. Chicago
         3. Los Angeles
         4. Detroit
  II. What are the effects of air pollution, especially on world health and on the environment?

(Transition: First, let's address the growing relationship between air pollution and world health.)

Body

   I. How does air pollution affect health?
      A. Respiratory conditions associated with pollution
         1. Respiratory condition X
            a. Cases of X
            b. Deaths due to X
         2. Respiratory condition Y
            a. Cases of Y
            b. Deaths due to Y
      B. Allergies related to pollution
         1. Allergy Q
         2. Allergy Z

(Transition: Now that we've talked about the effects of air pollution on world health, let's turn to its impact on the environment.)

   II. How does air pollution affect the environment?
      A. Effects on agriculture
         1. Growth of vegetation
         2. Crop yield
      B. Effects on the atmosphere
         1. Increase in carbon dioxide level
         2. Destruction of ozone layer

(Transition: As you can see, air pollution is indeed a silent killer—of men, women, children, and the environment we live in.)

Conclusion

   I. Air pollution affects world health and increases destruction of the environment.
   II. Join with me in attempting to reduce the problem by carpooling more often and by encouraging Congress to take measures to reduce air pollution before it's too late.

Accountability

When outlining your speech, make sure to include all major parts, including the following:

1. title,
2. thesis statement,
3. introduction,
4. body,

5. conclusion, and

6. transition statements.

By accounting for all major parts of the speech in your actual outline, you will be better able to check your logic, ensure the inclusion of all major points, and better visualize your presentation as you both practice and ultimately deliver it. An example of a complete outline is provided in Figure 11–1.

Inclusion of Points

When you divide a main point in a presentation, use at least two subpoints to support that point. For example, under each Roman numeral you will need to include a "point B" if you have a "point A." Likewise, under point IA, you will need to have a "subpoint 2" if you include a "subpoint 1." The only exception to this rule might be if you are providing an example or illustration for a main point. In this event, the point you are illustrating would require no subdivision.

Use of Symbols and Indentation

Using symbols and indentation in an outline allows you to organize your points, logically arrange them, and show their intrinsic relationships. For example, if used correctly, numbers, letters, and indentation show which points are of equal status and which points are logically subordinate to others. In Figure 11–1, points I and II are of greatest importance, while points A and B are subpoints of each main point or arguments that are used to develop them.

To check yourself on the appropriateness of symbols or indentation, ask yourself, "Do subdivisions A, B, and C all relate to main point I? What about A, B, and C under point II?" If the answers to these questions are "yes" and you indeed have symbolized distinctions correctly, you can avoid sloppy outlines and sloppy thinking, both of which adversely affect the effectiveness of a speech.

Underscoring Relationships

Remember that all points within a subdivision must be related. For example, consider the following partial outline on bicentennial sights in the eastern United States.

Bicentennial Sights in the Eastern United States
I. Sights in Massachusetts
   A. Concord
   B. Plymouth Rock
   C. Boston Harbor
   D. Liberty Bell

If you know your American history, you will observe that entry D is out of place, since the Liberty Bell is in Pennsylvania. Incorrect placement of information is a relationship problem. Although the example just cited is quite obvious, the speaker may sometimes have a difficult time finding an appropriate spot for information. If the information is essential, it may be necessary to reorganize categories.

Logical Progression

It is important to arrange ideas in some sort of logical *progression.* For example, in a speech about local government, the speaker might identify the three main categories of the outline as local government in the city, in the county, and in the township. The speaker should then decide upon the order of these main categories, based on either ascending or descending order of complexity or size. The speaker should select a logical progression of ideas and remain consistent in the arrangement of major ideas and subordinate points.

SUPPORTING MATERIAL

One of the advantages of using an outline is that it enables you to see if you have adequate supporting material. Supporting material serves a variety of functions and is essential to all speeches, whether they are to inform, persuade, or entertain.

Clarification

One of the basic functions of supporting material is to clarify an idea, opinion, or argument. Remember that in an informative speech, your goal is for the audience to understand your message. In a persuasive speech, you want the audience to understand your position. If you want to entertain or impress an audience with a story of perilous travels in the desert, you may need to make clear the distances between watering places or the hostile nature of the surrounding peoples. Clarification is an important aspect of all speeches.

EXAMPLES. You can clarify an idea, opinion, or concept in many ways. One way is to use an example. The example may be real, hypothetical, or extended. Examples have been given throughout this text to help you better understand particular concepts. Some of the examples have been real, others hypothetical. A *real example* refers to an event or incident that actually happened. A *hypothetical example* is based on something that could possibly occur but that did not really happen. In the previous section on the organization of persuasive speeches, we offered two examples of inductive reasoning. The swine flu inoculation example was based on real events; the pantyhose example was hypothetical. Yet both examples helped to clarify a description of the inductive pattern that otherwise might have been meaningless to the reader.

An *extended example* is one that is carried out to considerable length in order to clarify or emphasize a very important idea. Often when athletes and rock stars speak to young audiences and advise them to "say *no* to drugs," they offer examples of their own personal experiences as users, and then extend the example to what might happen to audience members who do the same. Their extended examples are real. However, a speaker can extend a hypothetical example as well. For instance, a dietician might discuss the future health problems of a hypothetical family that is indifferent to the impact of nutrition in its members' daily lives.

ILLUSTRATIONS. Another means of clarification is the use of *illustrations.* While examples are verbal illustrations, the speaker may sometimes find a visual aid very helpful in clarifying information. A surgeon delivering an informative speech on a new technique for open-heart surgery would probably find a series of diagrams useful in her presentation. If you have ever attempted to assemble an "easily assembled" piece of furniture or equipment, you may appreciate the value of a visual aid in clarifying otherwise confusing directions.

ANECDOTES. Speakers sometimes use an *anecdote* to clarify a particular idea or point of information. An anecdote is a brief story that relates to an important idea in the speech. It is particularly useful as an introductory device when appropriate to the overall topic of the speech. For instance, a young woman who wishes to give a humorous talk about college life may start with an anecdote about finding her mother's old raccoon coat in a trunk in the basement.

An anecdote may be real or imaginary, personal or impersonal. Although an anecdote does not offer any hard evidence, it does help clarify and emphasize your point or position. For example, a fire official delivering a speech to elementary school children on the dangers of false alarms might relate the well-known fable "The Boy Who Cried Wolf" as a way to clarify the message.

DEFINITIONS. After analyzing your topic and audience, you might decide that a definition of terms is necessary to make sure that the audience understands your points. Since language is often ambiguous, it is important that you clarify any misunderstanding relating to definitions of words.

There are several different ways to define a word, idea, or concept. Some ideas can be defined by *description.* For example, in a speech on the kibbutzim of Israel, a speaker might want to describe this type of communal living in order to clarify audience understanding of the topic.

Sometimes a word, idea, or concept can best be defined by *comparison* or *contrast.* A definition by comparison suggests the similarity of something unknown to something with which the audience is already familiar. Someone discussing musical instruments of the Middle Ages might define a lute by comparing it with a guitar. Similarly, a speaker may define a term through contrast. In the same lecture, the speaker might define a clavichord as an early ancestor of the piano, pointing out the essential differences between the two.

Sometimes a speaker has to provide the audience with an *operational definition,* one that is used only for the duration of the speech. For example, the president of a large corporation, addressing stockholders on the success of the company in the previous fiscal year, has to clarify what he or she means by "success." It is possible that the president's definition does not coincide with that of the stockholders.

Support

Some material is used to support rather than to clarify. Particularly in persuasive speeches, speakers must carefully provide material that gives substance to their message and enhances their position. Using evidence in a speech supports your position. It also enhances the listeners' learning process.

The source of authority may be expert opinion, official pronouncements, religious symbols, the pomp and ceremony of institutional practice, the sayings or doings of the socially elect, or even the printed word or the tone of voice.

DANIEL KATZ AND RICHARD L. SCHANCK

EXAMPLES. When using examples as a form of support, you must be sure to use a sufficient number to confirm your ideas or opinions. A journalist reporting on corruption in a city agency should be able to come up with several examples of wrongdoing in order to demonstrate the problem. While one incident might make an important story, many examples would be needed to prove widespread corruption.

You also must give examples that are representative or typical of the position you support. If a psychiatrist advocates a certain kind of therapy for severe depression, he or she might support this position by citing several examples of cases in which this therapy was successful. If the cases described were not cases of severe depression, the examples would be inappropriate and unsupportive.

Examples used to support a position must also be representative of the total picture. When the owner of a nursing home sought to defend himself against media charges of poor conditions, he cited the case of one elderly gentleman who found the home so comfortable that he wrote the owner a thank-you note. On investigation it was found that this example was atypical and certainly not representative of what most of the patients felt. A speaker must be extremely careful when choosing examples.

Another way to support your presentation is with facts and figures. **Statistics** can be very valuable if used skillfully. A business executive suggesting a merger with another company could incorporate statistics into the speech to show how the merger would be profitable for the firm. A scientist promoting a particular drug would cite statistical results of different experiments.

It must be stressed that statistics should be used with care. In most situations the speaker should round off statistics to the nearest whole number. Remember, the audience is hearing the statistics for the first time, and the numbers must be easily interpreted. Statistics can be intimidating, so avoid overwhelming your audience with too many facts and figures. Fractions and decimals are often confusing and add little to listener understanding. Approximations such as "close to 30 percent" or "over a quarter of a million" give a general picture without burdening the listener with specific numbers. Nonetheless, the speaker must know when it is important to use exact figures. For example, a proponent of a particular bill narrowly defeated in Congress may quote the exact figures when discussing

Fumbling

Preparation and delivery of a speech go hand in hand. One supports the other. In a delightful passage from *Night and Day,* Virginia Woolf describes a speaker who could have benefited from closer attention to both. A disaster such as this emphasizes the need for careful planning.

His paper was carefully written out, but in spite of this precaution Mr. Rodney managed to turn over two sheets instead of one, to choose the wrong sentence where two were written together, and to discover his own handwriting suddenly illegible. When he found himself possessed of a coherent passage, he shook it at his audience almost aggressively, and then fumbled for another. After a distressing search a fresh discovery would be made, and produced in the same way, until, by means of repeated attacks, he had stirred his audience to a degree of animation quite remarkable in these gatherings. Whether they were stirred by his enthusiasm for poetry or by the contortions which a human being was going through for their benefit, it would be hard to say. At length Mr. Rodney sat down impulsively in the middle of a sentence, and, after a pause of bewilderment, the audience expressed its relief at being able to laugh aloud in a decided outburst of applause.

Source: Virginia Woolf, *Night and Day* (New York: Harcourt Brace Jovanovich, A Harvest Book, 1948), 53.

the issue at a press conference to show that there had been considerable support for the legislation.

If you use statistics, you must always make them meaningful for the listener. One way to do this is to present the statistics in the form of comparisons. In a speech on state aid to education, for example, a senator may tell her audience of college students that "for every dollar you spend on tuition, the state legislature spends five to educate you." In this case, the relationship between student expense and state expense is made clear by comparison.

The ethical speaker will keep in mind that statistics are often misleading and that certain statistics can be found to "prove" almost anything. The speaker and the audience should be aware that statistics do not always give an accurate representation. For example, an audience was greatly impressed when a golfer reported that he came in third in a recent tournament until they found out that there were only three participants. It is a matter of ethics to avoid such misleading information and half-truths.

Testimony

You should not overlook the value of *testimony* as supportive material. A person's testimony can often add validity to an informative or persuasive speech. Of course, the value of testimony depends on the credibility of the source. Basically, testimony can be derived either from a direct witness to an event or from an expert in a particular field. The appropriate use of testimony is determined by the nature of the subject. For example, in discussing the safety hazards in building construction, a speaker might give the testimony of several people who survived the collapse of a recently constructed hotel.

Expert testimony often proves helpful in both persuasive and informative speeches. A speaker supporting the idea of a conspiracy in the Kennedy assassination might cite the testimony of ballistic experts who claimed that more than one gun was fired.

By being careful to provide support and clarification for the ideas in your speech, you can increase the chances that your audience will understand your message and be persuaded by it. Concern for your audience and the integrity of your presentation are key issues in the preparation of a speech. When an audience feels your concern, it is likely to reward you with a positive reaction to your speech and increased credibility.

It should now be evident to you that a well-prepared speech combines many skills and carefully selected elements. Take a look at the sample speech presented in Appendix B. Analysis of any effective speech will reveal the basics with which it was built.

SUMMARY

Careful planning, organization, and preparation are essential when speaking in public. Athletes train for competitive events, musicians rehearse for concerts, and artists sketch before they paint. In the same way, you must prepare yourself to go before your audience. The success of your delivery will largely depend upon how well you have organized your message.

Begin by selecting a topic that interests you or one that you have some previous knowledge of or familiarity with. Make sure, if your speech is supposed to be persuasive, that your personal convictions are in agreement with your topic.

Good speeches are focused. Decide your purpose in speaking: Will you inform, persuade, or entertain your audience? Your subject should not be too general but should serve as the unifying or central idea of your speech.

As you gather information for your speech, keep your purpose in mind. An objective discussion of a controversial issue requires presentation of opposing views. If your purpose is to persuade, you may rely upon those sources that support your view. There are a wide variety of sources of information. Draw on your own experience, personal interviews, or surveys when appropriate. Take advantage of the wide range of printed materials, films, recordings, and videotapes available.

Consider the functions of the three basic parts of your speech. The introduction serves to catch and focus audience attention. Use the standard introductory devices, statistics, rhetorical questions, famous quotes, and so forth, when appropriate. You present your main purpose

and set the tone for your speech in your introduction. The body of your speech will contain the bulk of information and elaboration of your main ideas. These main ideas should be connected by smooth transitions. The conclusion should be used to leave a lasting impression on your audience and to reemphasize your main idea.

As you organize the body of the speech, decide upon a pattern of arrangement. Informative speeches may be topical, chronological, or spatial or follow the patterns of increasing complexity or chain of events. Persuasive speeches may follow inductive or deductive reasoning or develop according to patterns of cause and effect or problems and solutions.

Your outline is a map—be sure to provide yourself with a workable guide for your delivery. Remember the six main principles of every effective outline: simplicity, accountability, inclusion of all major points, proper use of symbols and indentation, underscoring relationships, and logical progression.

Supporting material is important to clarify and substantiate your ideas. Use real, hypothetical, or extended examples when appropriate. Employ illustrations or anecdotes to clarify your points. Define your terms when necessary by description or by comparison or contrast with terms familiar to the audience. You may reinforce your main ideas with the use of statistics or testimony.

The importance of good preparation cannot be overestimated. Using the methods of organization outlined in this chapter will help you in effective public speaking.

EXERCISES

Group Experiences

Come On Up and Introduce Yourself!

DESCRIPTION: As outlined in this chapter, the introduction to a speech serves several important functions. One of these functions is to catch and then focus audience attention. If you fail to catch your audience in your introductory comments, it is unlikely that you will get its attention later. This activity will provide you with the opportunity to write several different types of introductions to the same speech.

PROCEDURE: Select a topic for a speech. Then outline the main body of the speech. You will not have to deliver the speech itself, but you will have to deliver "introductions" to the speech. Therefore, it is important that you determine the theme and organizational structure of the speech so that you can preview the body of the speech in your introduction. Now—write three different introductions for the same speech. You may wish to review the various methods suggested in this chapter, such as the use of a startling statement, a rhetorical question, or a humorous statement. Each introduction should be no longer than 60 seconds. After hearing the introduction, your audience should (1) be motivated to listen to your speech, (2) be able to identify your central theme, and (3) have a general idea about what you will cover in the body of your speech.

Each member of the class should be asked to deliver his or her introductions to the rest of the class. The introductions should be done so that no one person will present two or three consecutive introductions. Each introduction should be evaluated by class members, based on the following three scales:

Scale 1. Did the speaker motivate you to listen to the speech? (1) not at all motivated; (2) slightly motivated; (3) motivated; (4) highly motivated.

Scale 2. With what degree of accuracy do you think you can identify the speaker's main theme? (1) not at all accurately; (2) slightly accurately; (3) accurately; (4) highly accurately.

Scale 3. With what degree of accuracy do you think you can describe what the speaker will cover in the body of the speech? (1) not at all accurately; (2) slightly accurately; (3) accurately; (4) highly accurately.

Poise and self-confidence are two important aspects of successful public communication.

Each speaker should carefully review all the evaluations of his or her introductions. You may wish to add the total number of points possible for each scale and then the number of points actually received on each scale.

Discussion: After reviewing your point totals for each introduction and each scale, can you identify problems with a particular introduction or scale? Do you need to spend more time in preparing introductions? How did your introductions compare with the others presented?

Concluding Remarks

Note: The procedure for this activity is the same as for the activity just described, except that *conclusions* are presented instead of *introductions*.

Patterns

Description: Persuasive speech patterns can easily be identified as inductive, deductive, cause-and-effect, or problem-solution. The purpose of any persuasive speech is to create attitude change in the listener; the various patterns are alternative methods for pursuing that goal. The purpose of this activity is to familiarize you with persuasive speech patterns.

PROCEDURE: Locate three speech transcripts. Analyze each speech to determine the speech pattern used. Keep in mind that a speech may have a combination of patterns. After identifying the patterns in each speech, write a short outline for each. For example, if you have identified a deductive pattern, you should point out the generalization, the specific statement, and the conclusion. Bring your analyses to class.

Divide into groups of four. Compare your analyses of the three speeches. If there are discrepancies among group members as to the patterns used in the speeches, determine the specific conflict. After 45 minutes each group should have reached an agreement on the patterns used in each speech and should report its results to the class.

DISCUSSION: Did you experience any difficulty in analyzing the speeches? Do you believe that organization in a speech is important for producing attitude change? Why? Why not?

Personal Experiences

1. Start your own collection of jokes, stories, or other types of interesting introductions for speeches. Collect these from books, magazines, television, or public speakers. Your collection can be used for introductions to speeches, stories, or papers.
2. Develop a list of statements made by yourself and others that demonstrate some form of illogical reasoning. Then consider the problems that are created when illogical reasoning is used. How often do you make invalid claims?
3. Identify all the "creative" ways in which you could collect source materials for a speech. Consider, for example, cartoons, fairy tales, and poems. Too often we look only in the standard places (reference books, interviews) for material. Consider the creative use of collections of information parallel to a multimedia presentation.

Discussion Questions

1. What are some of the principles of outlining you should use in writing a speech?
2. What are the intended purposes of the introduction, body, and conclusion of a speech?
3. Provide an example of each of the following types of supporting material: illustrations, anecdotes, definitions, and examples.

4. Can a speech effectively use a combination of the spatial, chronological, and topical patterns of organization?
5. What are the factors you should consider when preparing to speak in public? (List the factors in the order in which you believe they should be considered.)

12

Speech Delivery

KEY CONCEPTS AND TERMS

Communication apprehension
Rapport
Delivery
Gesture
Vocal delivery
Phonation
Voice
Larynx (voice box)
Resonance
Articulation

Pitch
Volume
Rate
Vocal quality
Style
Accuracy
Clarity
Appropriateness
Economy
Lively quality

357

As a newcomer running for public office, Jerry knew that the success of his campaign would depend on his ability to make himself known and to garner the trust of his constituency. As his platform was basically the same as that of his opponent, Jerry felt that the presentation of his speech would be of even greater importance than the content of his message. As a result of this knowledge, and on the advice of his campaign manager, Jerry decided to videotape rehearsals of his speech and to play them back to determine specific areas on which he needed to work. After analyzing the replays, Jerry noticed that he seldom looked at the audience and often nervously jingled the change in his pocket. Although he interjected bits of humor in the speech, Jerry kept a solemn expression throughout, except once or twice when he nervously laughed. His gestures seemed awkward and his voice somewhat shaky. Fortunately, through the use of video as a tool, he was able to identify his specific delivery problems and overcome them.

Throughout history, public speakers like Jerry have been keenly aware of the importance of dynamic delivery. Prophets, poets, philosophers, and storytellers have practiced through the ages to capture the minds and imaginations of their audiences. As a modern student of communication, you too must develop your own unique manner of presentation. Even the most powerful speech can be ruined by a poor delivery, whereas a mediocre speech can be improved if delivered in a dynamic way.

We have already discussed body movement, gestures, eye contact, facial expressions, and paralanguage. However, we will now look more closely at these and other related behaviors in the context of public communication. While this chapter may not help you win an election, you will improve as a public speaker if you practice the principles outlined herein.

The importance of delivery goes beyond maintaining audience interest. Delivery affects speaker credibility, message comprehension, and persuasiveness.

A speaker's credibility can be established or destroyed during the presentation of a speech. Ethos, the audience's perception of a speaker as trustworthy and sincere, is greatly influenced by delivery. These audience perceptions are changed by nonverbal cues such as the speaker's appearance, facial expression, posture, and gestures.

However, the truly critical audience should always be aware of the difference between perception and reality. While an honest speaker may quite unconsciously project an image of sincerity and trustworthiness, a skillful speaker with the most selfish motives can sometimes create that same impression. For example, the prominent political figure who denies an accusation of wrongdoing can add to his credibility by looking directly at the audience, thereby gaining support with nonverbal communication.

Delivery also enhances message comprehension and retention. It does so primarily by eliminating many of the elements that can distract the listener from the message. For example, if Amanda presents a message without exchanging direct eye contact with her audience, she will never know whether she is getting her message across. Such feedback is vital in determining the impact of a message. Likewise, if Chris plays with his pen or the piece of chalk he is holding, he may distract the audience from his message, thus reducing the chances for message comprehension.

In addition to increasing message comprehension and speaker credibility, a strong delivery can add to the persuasive impact of a message. Perhaps one of the best examples of a speaker who uses delivery effectively is evangelist Billy Graham. Known for his sweeping gestures and his emotion-filled facial expressions, Graham maximizes his delivery for persuasive appeal.

COMMUNICATION APPREHENSION

If you were asked what you fear most, how would you respond? A national polling agency conducted a survey to discover what people fear most. Some of the greatest fears included accidents, death, and heights, but over 40 percent of those polled listed speaking in public as their greatest fear. (Fear of death finished second at 19 percent!)[1] Maybe you agree with that 40 percent. But what characteristic of public speaking causes knees to shake, stomachs to turn, voices to tremble, and palms to sweat? (Similar reactions are also associated with other communication situations, such as interviews and blind dates.)

Stage fright, or speech tension (***communication apprehension***), has for years been defined as a fear of the situation. Today, however, most communication scholars believe that these physiological responses are caused by anxiety rather than fear.[2] Fear is a spontaneous response, whereas anxiety involves the anticipation of an event. Fear is usually provoked by an outside stimulus, while anxiety stems from insecurities within a person. Most people don't feel the fear of an automobile accident until after they barely miss a car that failed to stop at a red light. However, before giving a speech, going to a job interview, or meeting a fiancée's parents, many of us feel nervous because we are concerned with and unsure of the outcome. Some of us start to destroy our confidence before speaking assignments are due by telling ourselves, "I can't do this," "I know I'll forget something," "I bore people," or "Nobody is interested in what I have to say." We need to find ways to build our confidence instead of tearing it down.

Before signing up for speech classes, many of us secretly hope that we won't have to get up to speak. Sometimes we can avoid speaking in front of others, but what about the occasions when there is no way out of giving a speech? It is important to realize that what you are feeling is a normal response. It is natural to feel nervous before a presentation. In fact, if you

[1]A. Kornblum, "Stage Fright in the Executive Suite," *Nation's Business*, 72 (December 1984), 56.
[2]M.J. Beatty, G.L. Balfantz, and A.Y. Kuwabara, "Trait-Like Qualities of Selected Variables Assumed to Be Transient Causes of Performance State Anxiety," *Communication Education*, 38 (July 1989), 277–89.

don't feel some anxiety, it is likely that your performance will lack the energy needed to keep the speech interesting to an audience. Many coaches check players' palms and energy levels before important games. Because people perform better when there is some tension, coaches select as starting players those who are excited and up for the game. So, if you feel tension before speaking, it is likely that you will perform more effectively than if you feel no tension at all.

Now that we know that speech anxiety is a normal response, you may say, "But everyone can tell I'm nervous, and this bothers me." Well, even if you manifest nervousness, most audience members will not notice it. In fact, research reveals that speakers report higher levels of anxiety than is attributed to them by their audience, and that their level of anxiety is not accurately detected by their audience.[3] Audiences simply do not notice nervousness unless speakers call attention to themselves by saying, "I'm sorry my voice is quivering," "Excuse the paper, but my hands are shaking," or "If I forget something, it's because I'm scared." If you're still not convinced, ask speakers you feel are confident if they were nervous. You'll probably find that they were, even though you didn't notice it.

We sometimes build our anticipation to such a degree that we have too much energy before a speech. The following suggestions should help both to improve your confidence and to control speech tension.

Practice

Rehearsing a speech helps to build both speaker confidence and self-concept. If you are not prepared, you will have reason to feel tense. Consider the following example. Jennifer had just finished writing her speech for the banquet honoring her as incoming president of the Young Democrats Club. As she placed the finishing touches on the manuscript, her mind immediately turned to the history paper she had to finish. She knew her speech well enough—she had just written it, hadn't she? She should do fine this evening without rehearsal.

When she arrived at the banquet, she was startled by the number of people who were there. She had not anticipated an audience of 125 people, and she surely had not expected the university president to come. As the time approached for Jennifer to speak, her feelings of apprehension escalated. Her heart raced, her knees grew weak, and her hands sweated profusely. Jennifer now regretted not having rehearsed her speech.

At last, the time for her speech arrived. Jennifer stood and faced the audience. As she looked down at her manuscript, anxiety gripped her. She had not taken the time to transfer her manuscript to note cards, nor had she underlined the key points on the manuscript itself. All of a sudden, she felt

---

[3]R.R. Behnke, C.R. Sawyer, and P.E. King, "The Communication of Public Speaking Anxiety," *Communication Education*, 36 (1987), 139.

herself go blank. What would she do? As she glanced at the blur of black ink on the paper, she realized her only recourse was to read her speech word for word.

Jennifer made it through the speech, as we all do, but her performance was less than stellar. She had blown an opportunity to motivate and challenge club members to greater action. Likewise, she had failed to show the university president the true level of her commitment to the club. If only she had rehearsed her speech, Jennifer could have performed more effectively and reduced her communication anxiety substantially.

Rehearsal can come in a number of forms. You can physically deliver your speech to a wall, mirror, friend, or video camera. You can run the speech through your mind the way a seasoned athlete visualizes performance before a competition, or you can deliver your presentation orally. Practicing will help you learn how both you and audiences will respond, especially if you videotape your performance or present it to a friend or group of friends. An audience of friends can also give you suggestions for improvement.

Use Physical Activity

Physical involvement in your speech helps use excess energy. If your energy has no normal outlet, it will manifest itself in trembling hands, knees, and voice. Using gestures and body movements helps use energy, emphasize points, and maintain audience attention. Like speeches, gestures and movements should be practiced and experimented with before the final presentation. If you feel that you have too much energy before speaking, try taking a few deep breaths, using isometric exercises, or using systematic relaxation.

Do Not Memorize, and Organize Well

When students try to memorize, they put themselves at a disadvantage. Speakers begin to worry about forgetting something—and usually do. If a speaker does forget, there are usually uncomfortable silences and abbreviated presentations. With proper preparation time, using a note card with a brief outline should be all that is necessary for prompting. Clear organization enables speakers to speak extemporaneously. It is much easier to remember points when they follow in a logical progression, so try to put them in sequences that build your confidence.

Get Involved with Your Topic

Confidence increases when speakers are interested in and involved with their topics. Topics should be so important and interesting to the speaker that he or she wants to get ideas across. Motivation and involvement in the topic helps focus attention on what is being said, rather than on who is saying it. As a side benefit, communication apprehension also decreases.[4]

Develop a Proper Attitude

Proper attitudes go along with topic involvement. Speakers have a responsibility to be sincerely interested in what they have to say. Speakers must also remind themselves that their physical responses are normal reactions. The audience is an important factor to consider. Audiences usually want speakers to succeed, especially in classroom situations. The classroom audience is generally the most sympathetic audience speakers will ever encounter.

PRINCIPLES

Look Natural

In order to make a successful presentation, a speaker should practice certain principles of good delivery. The first principle is to look natural. If you are stiff or artificial, you will look uncomfortable and awkward. The audience may see this as a lack of confidence, which might greatly affect their perceptions of your credibility. At the other extreme, if you seem theatrical or overly dramatic, you may be perceived as false and insincere. The good speaker strives for a natural, easygoing style of presentation.

Match Delivery and Content

The delivery should be carefully coordinated with the content of the speech. Body movement and vocal expression should add to the presentation, not detract from it. Superficial gestures and inappropriate facial expressions can distract the audience's attention. To illustrate, while practicing her welcoming speech for the annual Opera Ball, Lisa attempted to coordinate a gesture with her opening sentence, "We welcome you with open arms." Rehearsing time and time again, Lisa tried to find the right moment to hold out her arms, palms up, facing the audience. Obviously uncomfortable with the gesture, Lisa was unsure about whether it should be used before, during, or after her spoken welcome. Although we might have laughed at Lisa's awkwardness, should we have been present in the room, we could have helped her by suggesting that she use natural gestures that would complement her verbal

---

[4]S. Booth-Butterfield, "Instructional Interventions for Reducing Situational Anxiety and Avoidance," *Communication Education*, 37 (July 1988), 214–23.

message—and avoid those gestures that would distract from what she was trying to say.

Although particular gestures are often associated with specific phrases, such as the one Lisa used above, it is best for us to use a variety of gestures and vocal expressions. A sudden change in volume, a pause in delivery, or a firm shake of the head can all be effective in punctuating a particular idea or argument. However, the speaker's various vocal expressions and body actions should support the verbal message and not contradict it.

Make It Appropriate

Another principle of good delivery concerns the choice of an appropriate style of presentation. The delivery of a speech must be considered in relation to the audience, the situation, and the speaker. Chapter 9 discusses audience analysis in terms of message selection and preparation. An awareness of audience characteristics is also important in terms of delivery. For example, the tone of voice used when speaking to an audience of children is quite different from the tone of voice used when speaking to adults. Regardless of the age of the audience, the speaker should never talk down to them. "Talking down" is more often projected by delivery than content. For instance, teachers' attitudes toward their students can sometimes be inferred from their tone of voice. Students often resent teachers who give simple instructions with overenthusiastic energy, as if to say, "Now children, today

Nonverbal messages play a significant role in public presentations.

we are going to. . . ." While you may speak differently to children than to adults, you must remember that no audience, regardless of age, wants to be patronized.

A good speaker also takes into account any special disabilities that members of the audience may have. For example, if some audience members have hearing problems, the speaker should adjust his or her volume accordingly.

It is very important to make sure that the delivery is appropriate to the situation. To do this, you must first consider the occasion of the speech. For example, if you are delivering a eulogy at a funeral or memorial service, you should present your speech in a solemn manner. To do this, you should keep your volume low and the pace relatively slow. On the other hand, if you are delivering an after-dinner speech, you should seem enthusiastic and in good spirits. Lightness of tone, variation in pace, and free use of gestures, plus a happy expression on your face, are appropriate here.

You should also consider the setting for the speech. Your delivery will be influenced by whether the setting is a small conference room, an auditorium, or a large outdoor amphitheater. During important political debates, the candidates and their advisers usually visit the location of the debate beforehand. This helps them use each setting more effectively in terms of acoustics and space.

Obviously, your volume must vary according to the size of the acoustics of the setting. Size, acoustics, and seating arrangement also influence the basic mood or tone of your delivery. A casual, understated, and highly informal presentation may not come across well in a very large auditorium. On the other hand, a strict sense of formality can alienate the audience in a small and intimate setting. The effective speaker will choose the degree of formality according to the setting. A quiet, casual talk would be effective in a classroom, where the audience is close enough to perceive subtle gestures and expressions, but the same kind of presentation would be inappropriate in a concert hall.

Talking and eloquence are not the same; to speak, and to speak well, are two things. A fool may talk, but a wise man speaks.

BEN JONSON

Delivery must be appropriate to the speaker's personal style or manner. The key here is to know your own personality and behave naturally— remembering that being a speaker does not mean being an actor. For example, former President Jimmy Carter was noted for his natural, easygoing style during his election campaign. He was unpretentious in his manner, and his characteristic smile helped him establish a warm relationship with his audiences. Throughout the campaign, political observers watched him gain self-confidence and increase the effectiveness of his personal, informal style.

Improving

Don't be afraid to be natural, to let yourself show through. Don't pontificate, or talk down to your audience. Talk up to them. Don't overexplain what you want to say, but, instead, assume that your listeners have the intelligence to understand your various points as you make them. And, if you suddenly realize that you have forgotten to make a certain point, don't be afraid to interrupt yourself and say, "Oh, by the way, I forgot to mention—." This merely shows your audience that you are fallible and human and makes your audience *like* you.

As you start to speak, look around your audience and pick out the friendly faces, and talk to them. In every group there are always a few that are all smiles and eagerness for what you have to say. They are your blessed allies, and you should make use of them as such. If the sheer physical fact of an audience unnerves you, play mental tricks on yourself. Imagine, for example, that these people are all your dear, close friends, and that you are talking to them in your own living room. Then, when you have familiarized yourself with your audience, be alert for the moment when the faces become less friendly, when the fannies begin to stir uncomfortably in the chairs, or when the audience appears to be looking at its collective wristwatch. That's the moment to start winding it up. There's nothing wrong with leaving a few of your listeners wishing you'd said a little more. They'll like you for that, too.

Learn to recognize—and avoid—any personal mannerisms, facial or vocal, that you may have —nervous throatclearing, for example, or vocalized ("Uh . . . uh . . . uh . . .") pauses between sentences. Buy an inexpensive tape recorder, talk into it, and then listen to and analyze yourself. Use a mirror and study yourself. Do you grin too much, or gesticulate with your hands too much? This is particularly important in front of a television camera, where hands flying up in front of the picture frame seriously distract the viewer from you and what you are trying to say or sell. President Kennedy discovered that he had a habit of standing in front of an audience with his hands thrust in his pockets, jangling the keys and coins therein. It was his mother, Rose, who first pointed this out to him, and got him to stand with his hands hanging loosely at the sides, or resting easily on the lectern. It's all right to move about casually as you talk, to scratch your chin occasionally, to shift position slightly, to cross your legs from time to time—anything that makes you seem at ease and natural.

Source: From Stephen Birmingham, "How to Speak in Public Without Butterflies," in *Communication Vibrations,* ed. Larry L. Barker (Englewood Cliffs, N.J.: Prentice Hall, 1974), 66. Copyright 1973 by Stephen Birmingham. Reprinted by permission of the author and his agent, Brandt and Brandt.

Regardless of the situation, you will project honesty and sincerity if you are true to yourself. Aim for a delivery style that is consistent with your own personality.

Establish Rapport

If a speaker fails to develop and maintain a positive relationship with the audience throughout the presentation, the purpose of the speech will be lost. *Rapport* is almost entirely the result of delivery. For example, eye contact with the audience increases credibility and makes the audience more trusting of the speaker. A warm, conversational manner can achieve the same effect.

Rapport is also important because a good speaker-audience relationship can overshadow weak spots in the message itself. Entertainers devote much energy and talent to projecting a feeling of identification with their audiences. Bruce Springsteen, an American rock 'n' roll hero, is especially sensitive to the speaker-(singer)-audience relationship. As Clarence Clemons, a longtime friend and saxophonist in Springsteen's E Street Band, told *Newsweek* reporters, "He cares for every person in the audience." Although aware of the price of fame and the cruel isolation that rock stars often must suffer, Springsteen is unwilling to isolate himself "from the people he writes for." Instead, he continues to mingle with the public whenever he can.[5]

Speak the speech, I pray you, as I pronounced it to you, trippingly on the tongue; but if you mouth it, as many of your players do, I had as lief the town-crier spoke my lines. Nor do not saw the air too much with your hand, thus; but use all gently: for in the very torrent, tempest, and—as I may say—whirlwind of passion, you must acquire and beget a temperance, that may give it smoothness.

WILLIAM SHAKESPEARE, HAMLET

PHYSICAL DELIVERY

The term *delivery* covers many different elements of a speaker's presentation, including physical delivery and vocal expression. The physical elements of delivery can be divided into various body movements, such as posture, gestures, facial expressions, and eye contact. Also included in the physical aspect of the presentation is the way a speaker uses accessories, such as note cards or a lectern.

Posture and Body Movements

As a speaker, you must be aware of your body as an important source of communication. In fact, the body is so expressive in communicating ideas and feelings that many of our verbal expressions are based on descriptions of body movements. For example, a person who maintains a positive attitude in times of adversity is said to keep a "stiff upper lip." Someone in great suspense or suffering extreme anxiety is said to be "sitting on the edge of his seat." These figures of speech accurately describe the body movements of people in these situations. Someone watching a movie based on a Stephen

---

[5]B. Barol, "He's on Fire," *Newsweek* (5 August 1985), 48–49.

King novel may very well be sitting on the edge of his or her seat. Similarly, an actress who does not get a part in a play may be keeping a stiff upper lip to stop it from trembling.

Our body movements and posture are closely related to our physical and emotional states. On the physical level, posture can reveal whether a person is tired, energetic or in pain. On an emotional level, posture can reveal whether a person is tense, relaxed, depressed or excited. Posture also tells us something about a person's self-image. People with a healthy measure of self-confidence move about easily, stand up straight, and hold up their heads. Those individuals who are shy, ill at ease or ashamed of themselves are more likely to slump, slouch, and keep their heads and eyes lowered.

A speaker's body movements and posture influence an audience's perceptions in many ways. Although no firm rules exist regarding the delivery of a speech, you may want to consider the following basic guidelines when presenting a speech. In order to appear poised and confident, try standing comfortably "at ease," with your weight equally distributed over both feet. Find ways to make your body relax; if you are too stiff, the audience may begin to feel uncomfortable. At the other extreme, avoid slumping, leaning on the lectern, or standing with your weight distributed on one hip or the other. If your posture is too relaxed, you may be perceived as too casual.

As a speaker, your movements, like your posture, should be natural, not forced. Although you should stand relatively still and avoid pacing, natural movements can add to your delivery. You can use body movements to energize yourself and your audience. A speaker who does not move from one space seems dull and restrained. Appropriate body movements help to free the speaker from nervousness and spark the audience's attention. Body movements can also convey meanings. A speaker who leans forward when revealing something new suggests to the audience that they are being made privy to this information. A step toward the audience suggests that the speaker is embracing them and breaking the imaginary barrier between speaker and listeners.

Gestures

In addition to moving your whole body, you can use a variety of gestures. *Gestures* can convey many different meanings, depending upon the context. For example, the well-known American "peace" sign—made with the first and second fingers placed in a V-shape, the second and third fingers curled and touching the thumb—is a vulgar gesture in some other countries. As discussed in the chapter dealing with nonverbal communication, gestures also can convey meanings in and of themselves (as emblems), while others are used as a part of the verbal message.

Traditional gestures are those movements of the hands and arms that have been associated with particular meanings. The boxer who has won a fight might clasp his hands above his head in a gesture of victory. Similarly, the modest speaker might push the palm of his hand toward the audience to still listeners' applause.

Gestures can convey a variety of meanings, depending on style and context.

Other gestures are emphatic in nature and tend to punctuate the verbal message. When presenting a forceful argument, the speaker might pound a fist on the lectern to support the idea. Or a speaker may wave an index finger to focus the audience's attention on a particular thought. These gestures can serve to underscore the speaker's message, but should be used sparingly so that they don't lose their effectiveness.

Gestures can be descriptive in nature and work to enhance the verbal message. For example, try to describe a spiral staircase while keeping your hands behind your back. The feat is nearly impossible. Descriptive gestures are particularly effective when you ask the audience to visualize what you are saying. A simple gesture to illustrate size, quantity, shape, or distance can lend support to the speaker's description.

All gestures—traditional, emphatic, and descriptive—must be used purposefully if they are to add to your delivery. Here are a few guidelines to keep in mind when you use gestures:

1. Avoid gestures that make you feel uncomfortable. Awkward or self-conscious movements detract from your delivery.
2. Be careful to coordinate your gestures with what you are saying; timing is important here.
3. Avoid gestures that call attention to themselves apart from the spoken message.
4. Use gestures only when they will add to your presentation; gestures lose their effectiveness when you use them to excess. Can you imagine a speaker who pounds the lectern at each and every turn in the message? The result would probably be more humorous than forceful.

Facial Expressions

In public speaking, as in other interpersonal exchanges, facial expressions are important to communication. A look of disappointment, a smile of delight, or a frown of disapproval can all be more powerful than a spoken message. In fact, research documents that facial pleasantness on the part of a speaker enhances his or her perceived competence.[6]

Facial expressions are important in establishing rapport with the audience, but the skillful speaker does not want to manipulate the audience by using them. An audience can usually sense when a smile is phony in much the same way a parent can often tell when a child is lying. Once again, as with all body movements, facial expressions should be natural extensions of the verbal message. If you are genuine about the content of your speech, then your facial expressions will be consistent with your words.

---

[6]J.K. Burgoon, T. Birk, and M. Pfau, "Nonverbal Behaviors, Persuasion, and Credibility," *Human Communication Research*, 17, no. 1 (Fall 1990), 140–69.

Eye Contact

Of all the parts of the face, the eyes are the most important in establishing the speaker-audience relationship. Good eye contact helps to establish rapport and speaker credibility. A speaker who looks at the audience appears more straightforward and honest than one who does not. In a study concerning speaker eye contact conducted by Atkins in 1988, speakers were judged to have "good" eye contact if they looked at the audience 90 percent to 100 percent of the time. "Minimal" eye contact was defined as looking at the audience 10 percent to 50 percent of the time. How was minimal eye contact perceived by the college students who took part in her study? Results indicated that speakers with "little" (0 percent to 10 percent) or "minimal" eye contact were judged negatively on 70 percent of the personality traits on which they evaluated speakers.[7]

Although eye contact is important in delivery, it is impossible to look at the entire audience at one time. The effective speaker scans the audience and looks directly at individual members seated in various locations. An empty stare or unfocused, wandering eyes do not add to your delivery. To increase the effectiveness of eye contact, try to make all the members of the audience feel as if you are talking to them individually.

The Lectern and Note Cards

When speaking to an audience, it is usually more comfortable to stand behind a lectern. The key word here is stand, not *hide*. Because body movement is an essential aspect of delivery, you must be clearly visible to the audience. A speaker can use this spatial relationship by moving away from the lectern to develop rapport with the audience or by remaining behind it to preserve formality.

A lectern provides a space for your notes or outline. Of course, the use of written materials depends on the type of delivery. An impromptu speech, which by definition is without preparation, would not involve the use of notes. However, an extemporaneous speech, which is carefully prepared but not memorized, might require notes or an outline, especially if the speech is long or complicated. Of course, when a speech is to be read, the complete text must be available to the speaker.

When you use note cards, be sure to prepare them carefully and to number them consecutively. If you are using an overhead projector, slides, or a flip chart, indicate their use with a color code. For example, you might try writing the letters OH #1, SL #2, or FC #3 in a different color of ink at the top left-hand corner of the card. That way, when you need to show an overhead, you will know when to turn the machine (back) on and use the visual aid. Limit the number of note cards you use to as few as possible, and avoid rustling them (or papers) if you are wearing a microphone.

---

[7]C.P. Atkins, "Perceptions of Speakers with Minimal Eye Contact: Implications for Strutters," *Journal of Fluency Disorders*, 13 (1988), 429–36.

The second major element of a speaker's presentation is the voice. ***Vocal delivery*** involves the mechanics of vocalization, vocal characteristics (including pitch, volume, rate, and quality), and pronunciation. Inexperienced speakers often pay little attention to their vocal delivery, incorrectly believing that the voice cannot be altered in any way. Even though one's physical makeup influences vocal quality, much can be done to improve vocal delivery.

The Mechanics of Vocalization

To understand how to improve vocal delivery, it is important first to be aware of the mechanics of vocalization.[8] Voice and speech depend on phonation. In simple terms, ***phonation*** is the process by which air is pushed through the vocal cords, which then vibrate to produce sound. The sounds or tones produced in this way are what we call ***voice***. Because air is responsible for the vibration of the vocal cords, the breathing mechanism plays a basic part in phonation.

When you exhale, air from the lungs travels up the bronchial tubes to the larynx. (See Figure 12–1.) The ***larynx***, commonly known as the ***voice box***, contains two thin membranes, or vocal cords, which vibrate as the air passes through them. The sound waves that result from this vibration are the basic voice sound. Functioning like a valve, the vocal cords are controlled by muscles that regulate the amount of air passing through. In order to produce speech sounds, the cords move close enough together to partially block the escaping air and alter the tone produced.

The process of phonation is not complete until the sound produced in the larynx is resonated throughout the vocal chamber of the mouth, nose, and throat. ***Resonance*** is responsible for both the amplification and the enrichment of the voice. Without these chambers or cavities to give the sounds support and resonance, vocal quality would be quite unpleasant.

To better understand this process, place your finger on the bone of your nose and feel the vibration as you hum. The sound is resonating in the nasal cavity. When you have a cold or a stuffy nose, your voice sounds different without this additional resonance.

Articulation is the process by which voice is altered into recognizable speech sounds. These speech sounds consist of vowels and consonants, the building blocks of our speech. The consonants and vowels are formed when sounds are modified by the articulators. These include the lips, teeth, tongue, jaw, gum ridge, and palate, in addition to the nose, throat, and oral cavities. Consonants are produced as the articulators interfere with the passage of sound. Each consonant is produced by a different articulator as it interferes in some way with the flow of sound. For example, the "p" sound is made by

---

[8]V.A. Anderson, *Training the Speaking Voice*, 3d ed. (New York: Oxford University Press, 1977).

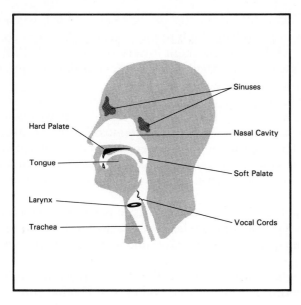

FIGURE 12-1
Elements of Vocal Delivery

joining the lips, which block the passage of air for a moment and are then quickly released. A "t" sound is produced when the tip of the tongue is placed along the gum ridge. The articulators in each case alter the sound produced by the vibrations of the vocal cords.

Vowels are produced by altering the size and shape of the nose, throat, and oral cavities. For example, contrast the shape of the mouth as you say "ah" and "oo." Unlike consonants, vowels do not require interference by the various articulators.

Poor articulation is usually the result of misuse of the articulators. For example, someone who has a lisp is not placing the tongue against the gum ridge to produce the "s" sound. Correction of this fault usually involves making a speaker aware of the error and having him or her practice the proper articulation of the sound.

Sometimes the problem is not one of carelessness or incorrect use. A person with a defective articulator will have problems producing proper speech sounds. For example, someone with an extreme overbite may have a lisp due to the improper meeting of the upper and lower teeth. With patience and practice, most people with such problems can improve their articulation to the point that their speech fault is negligible.

Vocal Characteristics

Now that you have a basic idea of how speech is produced, we can discuss the various characteristics of the voice. Vocal delivery involves four vocal characteristics: pitch, volume, rate, and quality.

PITCH. The *pitch* of the voice refers to how high or low the voice sounds. A person's natural pitch is determined in part by the length and width of the vocal cords. Women's vocal cords are characteristically thinner and longer than men's, so women have higher-pitched voices. Each voice can produce sounds ranging in pitch from high to low. Tensing the vocal cords produces a higher pitch, while relaxing them lowers the sound. Skillful singers and speakers are able to widen their pitch range and develop pitch control by practicing appropriate voice exercises.

When you have developed control of your pitch, you can use this skill to advantage. A variation in pitch adds color and vitality to a delivery and can also be used as a means of emphasis. The most boring speakers have little pitch variety. They speak in monotones, without emphasizing important points with their voices. As you may know, it is easy to be lulled to sleep by a monotonous voice, even when the topic of discussion is interesting.

VOLUME.   The second vocal characteristic is *volume*, which means intensity or loudness. Once again, as with pitch, each of us has a volume range that allows us to project various degrees of loudness, ranging from a whisper to a scream.

A person whose voice is perfectly audible in conversation may have difficulty projecting before a large audience. Therefore, in rehearsing the delivery of a speech, you must adjust your volume to the room in which you will be speaking. Obviously, the most brilliant oration is meaningless if you cannot be heard. You should also try to overcome any distracting noise that may interfere with the transmission of the message, such as sounds from electric fans or nearby traffic.

While the most important point is simply to be heard, you can also adjust volume to add to your overall presentation. Variation in volume makes you sound more dynamic, allows you to emphasize main ideas, and helps you underscore important arguments. If you build to a crescendo as you make major points, you will add impact to your message in the same way a musician does when playing a melody.

RATE.   *Rate* of speech is another important vocal characteristic. If you talk too quickly, the audience may not be able to keep pace. At the other extreme, if your speaking rate is too slow, the audience may lose interest. The main concern is audience comprehension. The nature and degree of difficulty of your message help determine a suitable rate of speech. A new or complicated message may call for a slower delivery than a subject with which the audience is familiar. An effective speaker will vary the rate of speech, pausing and slowing down to give emphasis to some material and speeding up at other points.

In addition to message comprehension, speech rate also affects an audience's perceptions of speaker competence and attractiveness. For example, a chemical engineer from New York travels to Georgia to give a lecture at a state university. Although he will arrive on campus with a certain amount of credibility because of his status, he will be evaluated less positively after the lecture if he speaks too slowly or too quickly. If his rate is too slow, he may be perceived as boring, monotonous, or (worse yet!) patronizing. Conversely, if he speaks too quickly, he not only will be less comprehensible, but also will be perceived as less approachable and, therefore, less attractive. A situation such as this one has the potential to arise any time that a speaker travels from one part of the country to another. In our experience, the overall speech rate of audience members who are reared in southern states such as Georgia, Alabama, and Mississippi is slightly slower than those reared in northeastern states. Thus, if you wish to have maximum impact on an audience, you also will need to take into account both your and their normal rates of speech.

QUALITY.   One of the most difficult characteristics to control is vocal quality. *Vocal quality* refers to the timbre of the voice, the characteristic that distinguishes one voice from another. A resonant quality is desirable, so that the voice sounds deep and mellow. Voices that are too thin, strident, nasal, or breathy sound unpleasant and should be improved. Each of these qualities is the result of poor phonation. Understanding the vocal process and doing voice exercises can improve vocal quality, but it takes time to change something that feels natural to you.

Factors Influencing Your Voice

In addition to voice exercises, other factors can influence the sound of your voice. The first of these is your physical makeup. This factor involves the various parts of the vocal mechanism described under phonation—namely, the lungs, vocal cords, larynx, and resonating chambers.

Psychological factors also influence a person's voice. When you are anxious or excited, the tension may localize in the vocal cords, creating a higher pitch than normal. If you are relaxed and at ease, your voice will sound much more pleasant.

A third factor that influences voice is environment. Members of the same family often seem to have similar voices. The similarity is partially genetic and partially environmental. You pick up inflections from the people around you, including family members, peers, and members of the same ethnic group.

In addition to the influence of your immediate circle of acquaintances, your voice is also affected by regional dialects. Different regions of a country have varying speech and voice patterns that make their use of voice and language unique. A person from the South may have a "drawl" that is quite distinct from the "twang" of a Midwesterner. However, regional differences usually affect pronunciation more than voice quality.

Improving Vocalization

The best way to improve your voice is through doing voice exercises. You must first be able to hear your own voice to decide which aspects need improvement. Try audiotaping your voice and playing it back on a tape recorder. Doing so will enable you to analyze your voice and practice a variety of exercises. You must decide, perhaps with the aid of a speech therapist or vocal coach, whether the problem concerns phonation, articulation, or pronunciation.

If the area in need of improvement is phonation, or the production of sound, then the problem may be one of force, duration, or quality. You might find that your voice often trails off at the end of a sentence, or that the volume is so low that you cannot be heard. In either case the problem is one of force.

Many people breathe incorrectly, and improper breathing can impair phonation. Some individuals lack force because they are not using their resonating chambers as efficiently as possible. Exercises to increase the use of these cavities add to a speaker's amplification.

Some people cannot speak for a long period of time without losing their voices. This can pose a serious problem for a person with many speaking engagements. Imagine the distress of politicians on the campaign trail who find their voices giving out after speaking for an extended period of time. Voice fatigue usually comes from improper use of the different parts of the vocal mechanism.

Basically, vocal sound should be supported by the partition of muscles and tendons between the chest and abdomen known as the *diaphragm*. This muscle is responsible for involuntary breathing and is one of the strongest muscles in the body. The muscles of the throat and the vocal cords are easily strained, while the diaphragm is virtually tireless. Through prescribed exercises you can learn to "support" your voice correctly and avoid hoarseness and voice loss. However, it takes time and practice to overcome bad habits that you have developed over the years. As mentioned previously, problems of articulation usually stem from careless speech habits. Unless a person must compensate for a physical defect such as a harelip, poor articulation can be improved by concentrated effort and practice. We can all be inspired by individuals who are born deaf and are never able to hear the sound of words. With a great deal of perseverance, many people who are hearing-impaired have learned to articulate well enough to be understood in conversation. Like these courageous individuals, you too can improve your articulation skills.

An understanding of how various sounds are made will help you improve articulation. Practice drills are good reinforcement for correcting problems of articulation, but you must make a conscious effort to carry over the correct production of speech sounds into everyday conversation as well as public speaking situations. Faulty articulation is particularly bad for the public speaker, since an audience is easily distracted by poor speech. Mumbling and speaking carelessly affect the audience's perception of you. A speaker whose pronunciation is clear and distinct makes a more favorable impression than does someone whose speech is sloppy.

Pronunciation

Pronunciation can be important to the improvement of both speech and voice. Standards of pronunciation are often determined by geographical area or imposed by occasion or education. Americans speak the same language, but pronunciation varies according to region. While geographic regions have changed in terms of speech patterns, one can still find a difference between

Northern, Midwestern, and Southern speech. In addition to the three major regions, there are numerous subdivisions. For example, New Yorkers do not sound like Bostonians, even though they are both considered Northern.

Certain speakers strive for what is called "standard American speech," the type of speech exemplified by Dan Rather and other national newscasters. Although still preferred in some circles, standard American pronunciation is not a prerequisite for success. Neither John F. Kennedy's New England dialect nor Jimmy Carter's Southern drawl kept either statesman from political success. The key is not regional dialect but careful articulation.

In addition to regional background, your pronunciation is influenced by the occasion and by your education. Certain situations such as job interviews or press conferences require careful pronunciation. Any person who speaks before a group should pay special attention to pronunciation. If a speaker makes an error, the audience's attention may be temporarily distracted. Poor pronunciation can create a bad impression.

Education affects pronunciation in the sense that exposure to language through reading, speaking, and listening results in increased vocabulary and knowledge of the way different words are pronounced. Education includes more than formal schooling. As you read, study, travel, and speak with educated people, your vocabulary and language skills, such as pronunciation improve.

There are several ways you, as a speaker, can improve pronunciation. If you are unsure of the way a word is pronounced, look it up in the dictionary. Be particularly careful to find out the proper pronunciation of the names of people and places mentioned in your speech. If you are quoting someone or acknowledging a particular person or organization, it is important to pronounce the name correctly.

Pronunciation, articulation, and phonation have always been concerns of the public speaker. Because we all rely on our voices for much of our communication, we should strive to improve our vocal delivery.

STYLE

We recognize that the Reverend Jesse Jackson has an effective style of oration, and we would all probably agree that Oliver North used a unique and powerful style of delivery at the Iran-contra hearings. But what is style?

In simple terms, *style* is the way an individual speaker gives ideas meaning through his or her particular brand of verbal expression and delivery. Style deals with both the wording and the delivery of the message. It includes the speaker's choice of words, the use of language, sentence structure, and the characteristics of delivery. Because style is made up of so many variables, each speaker's style is somewhat different. Some speakers have pet phrases that they include in their speeches, some are very plain-spoken, and others rely heavily on the use of metaphor or flowery language.

Style also applies to syntax, or sentence structure. A speaker may invert subject and verb to achieve a stylistic effect. For example, a disgusted sportscaster might say, "Never have I witnessed such a poor display of teamwork." Run-on or choppy sentences can also be used to achieve a stylistic effect. Although a good speaker should adhere to the rules of grammar, "poetic license" of sorts can be used to achieve a desired effect.

Our primary concern here is with the element of style that applies to a speaker's physical and vocal delivery. Of course, while every speaker develops a personal style, you should be able to adapt your style to fit the audience, occasion, topic, and purpose of your speech. Basically, your style may be formal or informal, with varying degrees in between.

Logically, a formal style is best suited for formal occasions. For example, we expect both a president's state of the union address and a college valedictory speech to be formal. A casual treatment of either of these speeches would demean their importance. The characteristics of a formal style include a serious and impersonal tone, correct use of grammar, sophisticated stylistic devices, and avoidance of slang. Physical and vocal aspects of a formal delivery style reflect dignity and seriousness.

A serious tone is projected by the manner in which you present yourself and your message. Although you need not be solemn, you should be dignified. There is no room for flippancy in a formal presentation. To emphasize the importance of the message, you should keep an impersonal tone by avoiding the use of personal pronouns.

More often than not, the speaking engagements in which we find ourselves tend to be more casual than formal and require a less formidable style. An informal style is characterized by a light and personal tone, use of fairly simple sentence structure and vocabulary, and a bending of grammatical rules, if necessary. An informal style allows the speaker to add warmth to the presentation with informal language and humor.

Very few speaking situations are either strictly formal or strictly informal. As most fall between the two extremes, you will have to adapt your style accordingly. For example, although we might think of an after-dinner speech as being informal, the appropriate presentation would depend on the nature of the occasion as well as the audience. You should evaluate each speaking situation individually to determine the right delivery.

Characteristics of Style

Although each speaker is different, there are certain desirable characteristics that help make any speaker's style effective. The first of these is **accuracy**, which requires a precise use of words. You may know what you want to say but have trouble getting the idea across to the audience. If an audience walks away not knowing what was said or misinterpreting the message, then you have failed in your basic purpose. As a speaker, you must choose the words that most accurately convey your message. Avoid words that are too abstract or general, as well as words that are open to many different interpretations. Words such as *good, bad,* and *nice* are really ambiguous and add little to a presentation.

Closely related to accuracy is *clarity*. The main consideration here is audience comprehension. A complicated description of a medical procedure that is perfectly clear to a surgeon may be totally confusing to an audience of lay people. Therefore, you must adapt your language and style to fit the needs of the audience.

Appropriateness is another characteristic of style. As mentioned previously, a speaker's style should fit the occasion, the audience, and the type and purpose of the speech. Each presentation should reflect consideration of all of these factors.

Another characteristic of effective style is *economy*, or the greatest efficiency of language. If you use the right words in the most efficient way, your message will be more meaningful. There is no need to use many words when a few will do. If you are concise, you generally will achieve accuracy and clarity as well. However, conciseness should not undermine comprehension, which sometimes makes it necessary to repeat ideas.

The final characteristic is a *lively quality* in the selection of words. Although economy is a virtue in terms of style, sometimes a speaker will use a phrase or expression that leaves a lasting impression on the audience. A poetic statement, a memorable expression, an unusual figure of speech, or a melodic phrase will jump out at the audience and capture its attention. The speaker must not overuse this quality, however, or the impact will be weakened.

An impressive style is not, of course, achieved without careful preparation and practice. Style, like good public speaking skills in general, *can* be learned, but not without the interest and effort it takes to achieve any valuable goal. If you are determined and strive to understand and use the communication principles suggested in this book, you will be rewarded with the attainment of your goal: satisfying communication and success in sharing yourself and your experiences with others.

SUMMARY

The importance of delivery in public speaking cannot be overestimated. A speaker's delivery is the vehicle for the communication of the message. Good delivery is essential in capturing and maintaining audience attention and also affects speaker credibility, audience comprehension, and persuasive impact.

Communication apprehension can affect a speaker's delivery. First believed to be fear of the speaking situation itself, apprehensiveness is currently viewed as stemming from anxiety and speaker insecurity. To overcome apprehension the speaker can do five things: (1) practice, (2) use physical activity, (3) avoid memorization and organize well, (4) get involved with the topic, and (5) develop a proper attitude.

Principles of good delivery include a natural appearance, consistency of expression and content, rapport with the listeners, and a presentation that is appropriate to the audience, the situation, and the speaker. The physical aspects of delivery include body movements, posture, gestures, facial expressions, eye contact, and the use of the lectern and note cards. An awareness and natural use of these elements can greatly enhance the verbal message.

The effective public speaker understands the vocal aspects of public speaking. Good phonation, resonance, and articulation are essential to message audibility and comprehension. An awareness of pitch, volume, rate, and voice quality will enable the speaker to capture and hold the listener's ear. Vocal delivery is influenced by physical, psychological, and environmental factors. Serious students of public speaking can improve their powers of vocalization by practicing appropriate vocal exercises.

Pronunciation is another element of vocal delivery not to be overlooked. Good pronunciation is essential to message comprehension and speaker credibility.

The style of delivery may be as important as the content of the message. The speaker may choose between varying degrees of formality. Most speakers eventually develop a unique personal style. Choice of words, use of language, and syntax are all effective stylistic elements. The speaker should aim for a style that is accurate, clear, appropriate to the occasion and setting, economical, and striking. Although this may seem a difficult task, the results will be worth the effort.

EXERCISES

Group Experiences

Coaching on the Sidelines

DESCRIPTION: Politicians have long been aware of the importance of public speaking. Today ghostwriters, communication consultants, and many other specialists work together to help "present" the politician to the public. This activity will give you the opportunity to act as coach or consultant to a politician.

PROCEDURE: Divide into dyads. You and your partner have been hired to help Laura Martinez present herself to the public for the upcoming campaign. Laura is totally inexperienced in public speaking. She does not know what to do with her hands, how fast to talk, what to say, or how to say it. Needless to say, you have a big job ahead of you. Write a plan for getting Laura ready for the public. You might want to incorporate some practice speaking sessions, including the use of videotape and so forth, to prepare Laura. Share your plan with the other groups and compare the strategy plans.

DISCUSSION: Did you forget any important steps in your plan? Can you improve a person's speaking ability? Can you create "charisma" in a person? How can delivery affect the credibility of a person?

Timing

DESCRIPTION: A good delivery is absolutely essential for a successful presentation, as are voice, gestures, and body stance. They all play an important role in a public speaking situation. A good delivery should be carefully coordinated with the content of the speech. If the gestures and facial expressions do not come at the right time, they will distract from the speech itself. This activity gives you an opportunity to see the effects on an audience of the timing of facial expressions and gestures.

PROCEDURE: If you have a theatrical flair or a dramatic side to your personality, then this is the activity for you. Write a three-minute speech designed to sell a product of your choice. Practice the delivery of the speech several times until you have completely *uncoordinated* your gestures and facial expressions with your words. This will be difficult, because when your voice is excited, your face will have to look bored. If you state that there are three good reasons to buy your product, you may want to use a hand gesture *after* you finish saying this. In whatever way possible, by making the timing wrong, your "presentation" should look like a comedy routine. Try it out by presenting it before a class or a group of people.

DISCUSSION: What were the reactions to your poorly timed talk? Did the audience remember what you had to say or the way you said it? Did you feel self-conscious or overdramatic? Whatever effect you created, chances are good that the lack of timing did hurt the impact of your speech. Next time you give a speech, be natural, and you will see that the facial expressions, gestures, and content of the speech will complement one another.

Voice Lessons

DESCRIPTION: A speaker's vocal delivery involves four things: pitch, volume, rate, and quality. By studying and practicing each quality, you can improve your speaking voice. The following voice drill is designed to help you identify specific characteristics of your voice.

PROCEDURE: Divide into dyads. With the help of your partner, practice the following line: "A person whose voice is perfectly audible in conversation may have difficulty projecting before a large audience." Say the line six times for each characteristic, focusing first on pitch, then volume, then rate, then quality. For instance, with rate, the first time you should say the line very slowly, and gradually get faster, so that by the sixth time you are saying it very fast. Your partner should select which repetition (first to sixth) is the best rate for an audience, and then do the same for the other characteristics.

Pitch: Go from a very high pitch to a very low pitch.

Volume: Go from a very soft voice to a very loud voice.

Rate: Go from speaking very slowly to speaking very quickly.

Quality: Go from a very nasal quality to a deep and resonant quality.

DISCUSSION: Are you surprised by any of the selections made by your partner? Feedback is important, particularly about the voice, for we cannot hear ourselves the way others hear us. A common problem in speaking is rate. Speakers tend to think they are speaking at a slower rate than they actually are. Try to remember and practice what your partner selected as the best rate, volume, pitch, and vocal quality for you.

Personal Experiences

1. Listen to a live speaker or a televised speech. Listen carefully to the vocal characteristics of the speaker (pitch, volume, rate, and quality). Is the speaker using his or her voice for maximum effectiveness? What things, if any, would you change about the speaker's voice?
2. Observe the kind of gestures you use when talking to another person. Do you use a lot of gestures? Do you make gestures in close to your body, or are they expansive? Do you feel self-conscious when you use your hands? You use gestures as a natural part of your everyday conversations; there is no reason why your gestures cannot be just as natural in a speech. Watch them. Feel comfortable with the way your hands move. If you feel comfortable, so will others.
3. Imagine that you are going to give a speech before an audience of a hundred people. In addition, you will be talking about something that excites you. Since looking forward to giving a speech is very important, what could you do to "psych" yourself up?

Discussion Questions

1. How can communication apprehension be used to *enhance* your delivery of a message?
2. What are the basic factors to consider in the presentation of a speech? Is any one factor more important than the others?
3. What physical aspects of a presentation are important for a speaker to consider?

4. What things make you "unique" as a speaker? (Consider style, vocal quality, delivery, and so on.)
5. What methods can you use to improve your delivery?
6. What plan would you make for yourself in order to improve your public speaking skills?

13

Communication Through the Mass Media

KEY CONCEPTS AND TERMS

Global village
Equal time rule
Diffusion of information
Change agent
Advertising
Demassification

Gatekeeper
Fairness doctrine
Homophily
Opinion leader
Public relations

*T*he Cultural Preservation Foundation had been in existence for five years without gaining much widespread success, in Katherine's opinion. She had been with the project for three years and knew that something would have to be done soon, or the program would be dropped and the foundation disbanded. Katherine decided it was time to bring in reinforcements. She picked up her phone and dialed. On the other end of the line, Lee answered his private line.

Lee was a marketing genius, and Katherine knew the questions she wanted to ask. She had gone to school with him and knew that if anyone could plan a productive marketing strategy, Lee could. Lee listened patiently to her questions: "How could the foundation make better use of its funds that were earmarked for advertising and promotion? What forms of media would be the most effective with a limited budget? How soon would the foundation begin to see results from a media campaign after it was begun?" Lee responded with the words Katherine wanted to hear: "No problem! Here's what I think we can do."

A week later, Katherine looked over all of the suggestions Lee had made. She was amazed at the number of opportunities the foundation had available to reach its public through mass media. Writing articles under the foundation name, making public service announcements at no expense, and using other options available to nonprofit organizations were just a few of the ideas that the foundation had never used. Lee suggested using a combination of media such as newspapers, radio, and television. Armed with this information, Katherine began to organize a campaign that would ultimately bring the foundation back on track.

The use of mass communication media, such as those that Katherine and Lee discussed above, is the topic of this chapter. Specifically, we will focus on the characteristics, functions, and effects of these various media in an attempt to help you understand their purpose and viability as communication tools.

MASS COMMUNICATION: AN OVERVIEW

Although all forms of mass communication affect our lives, the most widely used and influential forms are newspapers, radio, TV, and film. The importance of these media can best be expressed in numbers. There are approximately 10,000 different newspapers published in the United States, not including shoppers' guides, entertainment listings, and tabloids. The role of the newspaper keeps changing. At first it was entirely informative in nature; then, before the days of electronic media, it developed an important entertainment function, which disappeared after the advent of radio and TV. Yet today, because of keen competition among papers and other forms of media, newspapers once again include many features in addition to the daily news. This broad coverage of information is evidenced by the success of *USA*

Today. The New York Times also offers a weekly section devoted to the home, one to weekend entertainment, and another to lifestyles.

The medium is the message.

MARSHALL MCLUHAN

Although many of us in America are children of the television age, statistics about radio broadcasting help us realize the importance of radio both as a news medium and as an entertainment medium. There are close to 8,500 radio stations in the United States alone. Such a demand for the use of the airwaves has made it necessary to regulate the air frequencies and to use AM/FM bands in the interests of fairness and efficiency.

Interestingly enough, there are considerably fewer TV stations, with approximately 835 commercial stations and 280 educational channels. More than 100 cable and premium channels of programming extend the numbers even higher. In the majority of cities in the nation, private citizens also can rent air time from cable companies and produce their own shows.

CHARACTERISTICS OF MASS COMMUNICATION

Both print and electronic media share certain unique characteristics. Mass communication overcomes the barriers of time and space. This time phenomenon can be illustrated by "The Civil War," a serialized drama on PBS that chronicled the war from its inception to the final battle. Millions of viewers tuned in to watch the eight-part series of readings, artifacts, music, and reenactments that portrayed the conflicts as "real" and personal. Suddenly, events that had occurred 150 years ago were "alive" and "taking place" in homes across America.

The ability of mass communication to encompass vast boundaries of space is expressed by Marshall McLuhan's term *global village*. Global village suggests that the world is smaller than before because of advances in mass communication (especially the telephone, TV, satellites, and fiber optics). People in one part of the world can witness an event as it is taking place in another. People all over the world now share one another's joys and sorrows. For example, our joy in watching as each of the American and other hostages were released from Lebanon is certainly a contrast to the horrors we experienced as we watched scenes from the Gulf War or the crushed student uprising in Tiananmen Square in China. Advances in mass communication have made the world smaller. Indeed, the distance between people and the space between countries no longer seem as great a barrier to communication. For instance, recall how the entire world watched in wonder as the Berlin Wall came down.

Delayed Feedback

By definition, mass communication suggests a widespread audience separated from a source by a great distance. Therefore, a receiver's feedback or response to a message is most often limited and delayed. For example, a person watching a charity telethon may be moved to respond immediately by calling in a pledge. Yet the sheer mechanics of the situation create a certain delay in feedback. There are varying degrees of delayed feedback, ranging from a few minutes, as in the above situation, to several weeks or even months. Consumers responding to a TV commercial for a particular brand of deodorant may not purchase the product until their current supply runs out, which may be days or even weeks later. Consumers may not even realize that they are responding to a mass communication message. The fact that the source is inaccessible and that a medium is needed to transmit the response are major reasons for the delay in feedback. For example, if listeners are outraged by a remark heard on TV or radio, the best they can do is call the station. Yet even this action takes a certain amount of time and cannot represent total listener reaction, particularly in terms of nonverbal feedback.

> *The new source of power is not money in the hands of a few but information in the hands of many.*
>
> JOHN NAISBITT, MEGATRENDS

A television set on display at the 1939 New York World's Fair signals the beginnings of a new medium of mass communication.

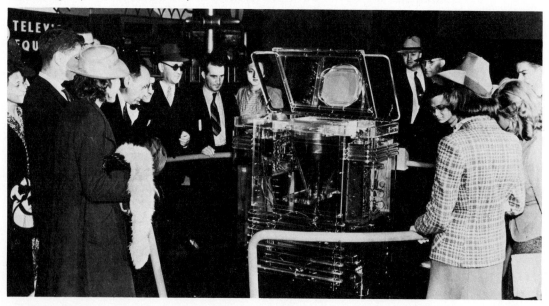

Gatekeeping

As one might expect, the enormous scope of mass communication requires some control in the selection and editing of the messages that are constantly transmitted to the mass audience. The term *gatekeeper*, originally used by Austrian psychologist Kurt Lewin to identify the people or organizations who control news items in the communications channel, has now come to mean any individual or organization that influences a mass communication message.[1] There are gatekeepers within the mass communication industry itself, within the government, and within big business. Each group sets certain standards and limitations that serve as guidelines for both content and delivery of a mass communication message.

INDUSTRY GATEKEEPING.   To understand the concept of gatekeeping, we need to examine the news media. Every major paper and news station is flooded with information fed to them by the major wire services, organizations that send news stories and features by direct telegraph to subscribing newspapers and TV and radio stations. Obviously, the news media cannot relay all of this information. Since neither time nor space allows for the printing or broadcasting of each and every news event, media personnel at various levels must determine which items they consider the most newsworthy. In effect, the information that is fed to the various news media goes through a filtering process. Stories that appear on the front page in a Midwest daily may be put on the back page of a New York newspaper, if they are printed at all. Yet you need not make comparisons across state lines to see that news selection and editing are very subjective. Examine two papers published in the same city and compare headline stories and the location of various news items. Sometimes a story that appears in the first few pages of one paper is entirely omitted in another. Writers, editors, publishers, and other media personnel determine length and placement of the news copy. While some stories must be included, they are often condensed or distorted. For example, an involved story about suspected corruption at the state or local level may be published as fact by news services in a different state or locality because they don't have the time or space to devote to a story that does not entirely influence their readers or viewers. This, then, is industry gatekeeping.

GOVERNMENT GATEKEEPING.   In addition to a filtering system that controls message selection, agencies such as the Federal Communications Commission (FCC) and the courts also influence media content. In their roles as gatekeepers, the FCC and the courts must protect the interests of the public. To ensure proper use of the public airwaves, the FCC issues a license before a station may broadcast. A license is granted for a period of three years, after which time the station's performance is evaluated. A review of the station must show that the station has abided by the rules and

---

[1]K. Lewin, "Frontiers in Group Dynamics," *Human Relations*, 1 (1947), 5–41.

regulations set forth by the FCC and that it has offered a public service. You may have noticed that sometimes when a TV or radio station's license is up for renewal, the station will invite letters from the audience to comment on how it has served the public interest. A station that has not been granted a license or that has had its license taken away may no longer broadcast.

Two important FCC controls are the equal time rule and the fairness doctrine. The **equal time rule** applies to candidates for political office. It says that a station must give all candidates the same amount of time under the same terms. Thus, if one candidate is interviewed by a station, other candidates must be given the same coverage. If a candidate buys air time to advertise his or her candidacy, other candidates must be given the same option, even if it means that the station has to preempt regular programming.

When the Kennedy-Nixon presidential debates were broadcast in 1960, Congress suspended the equal time rule so that stations would not be overwhelmed by requests to put many minor candidates on the air. Yet, in 1976 the FCC handled the Carter-Ford debates in a completely different way. Stations can bypass the equal time rule if coverage of a candidate is considered a newsworthy event. Therefore, the FCC concluded that the presidential debates sponsored by the League of Women Voters were a newsworthy event that should be reported, thereby getting around the equal time rule.

Unlike the equal time rule, which involves people, the fairness doctrine mainly involves issues. The **fairness doctrine** states that all stations must provide some time to discuss controversial issues and that each station must encourage opposing viewpoints. Therefore, if a station offers an editorial opposing school busing, it must ask for and air the views of a spokesperson in favor of the issue. Or, if in the course of a commentary a speaker denounces a particular person or organization, that individual or group must have the right to respond.

While all government attempts to control mass communication can be interpreted as infringements on constitutional rights, guidelines used to determine whether something is obscene or pornographic are particularly controversial. Although periodically revised, court rulings that define obscenity and pornography are characteristically vague. Decisions about obscenity are now left up to the individual community, which must decide if the material in question has any "redeeming social value," or—if taken as a whole—the material "appeals to prurient interest."

ECONOMIC GATEKEEPING. Advertisers are the primary financial support for mass media and thus control media industries to some extent. The broadcast media sell time, while the print media sell space. Because media buying is expensive, advertisers want some control over the content of anything they sponsor.

To illustrate the influence of a TV network sponsor, we can point out that during the McCarthy era in the early 1950s, a sponsor could dictate who could or could not work either on camera or behind the scenes of a program.

Some sponsors were known to blacklist anyone suspected of being sympathetic to the Communist Party.

The influence of advertisers goes beyond politics and has sometimes been known to dictate taste. Because the sponsor wants to capture a large audience to ensure the greatest exposure for the product, advertisers have been known to attempt to control content so that programming will appeal to the largest audience possible. For example, when the TV show *Quantum Leap* was preparing to air an episode involving prejudices against homosexuals, several of the show's regular sponsors threatened to pull their commercials. The show was aired, and the advertisers who ran their commercials received some of the largest audiences the show had ever had.

A sponsor's influence can sometimes work to the audience's advantage. For example, a sponsor might pressure the network to curb the amount of sex or violence in a program it sponsors.

MASS COMMUNICATION MEDIA

Now, more than at any time in history, we are a media society. No day goes by without our feeling the effects of mass communication. "That's not true," you may say. "I don't watch TV every day!" Maybe not, but did you listen to your radio or CD player on your way to school today? wear a Walkman the last time you jogged? read a book or magazine article in the last few days? rent a video or see what will be playing at the local movie theater this Friday night? We employ mass communication daily by using it to inform us of world events, to help escape into another realm, or to plan our weekends based on weather reports.

We have already examined the characteristics of mass communication. We will now look at four of the most important forms of mass communication: film, recording, radio, and television.

Film

From its beginning as a method of recording history, film has developed into a major form of recreation and entertainment. Film has been around longer than any other electronic medium, and it stays alive because it is the most creative and artistic of all media. The film experience shows us the universal emotions of love, hate, jealousy, fear, and delight. Each era has its own unique theme of the time. Trends have included the 1920s era of Charlie Chaplin silent films; the 1930s musicals with Fred Astaire and Ginger Rogers; the patriotic films featuring Humphrey Bogart in the 1940s; the 3-D and youth-oriented themes of the 1950s; the experience/involvement films such as *Psycho, The Sound of Music,* and the Beatles' movies of the 1960s; and the disaster films such as *The Poseidon Adventure, Jaws,* and *The Towering*

Inferno of the 1970s. The 1970s also gave us films of social comment such as *One Flew Over the Cuckoo's Nest, All the President's Men,* and *Coming Home;* the late 1970s and early 1980s often gave us movies focused on music, such as *Saturday Night Fever, The Buddy Holly Story, The Rose,* and *A Star is Born.* More recent films have also revealed an enchantment with and curiosity about space exploration and travel, particularly films such as *Star Wars, E. T., Close Encounters of the Third Kind, Cocoon* (parts I and II), and *My Stepmother Is an Alien.* The 1990s brought greater technical wizardry and special effects such as those in *Terminator II, Hook,* and *Beauty and the Beast.* Many recent movies have come in the form of remakes, such as *Father of the Bride* and *Cape Fear.* What's next? Although no one knows what next season will provide, we do know that there will be something for everyone, because film readily adapts to the events and needs of the times.

Recording

Is there a special song that reminds you of the first time you fell in love? Do you play a certain album when you're lonely and want to think? Can some music make you wiggle your toes or hop in the car? Music is everywhere in our society, from Muzak in doctors' offices to country and western or punk rock in the local nightclub. Just as we remember songs from different periods in our lives, we also remember different decades by the music that was popular at the time. The Big Band and swing era of the 1940s gave birth to the first recording hero, Frank Sinatra. The Comets arrived in 1955 with "Rock Around the Clock," and Elvis helped usher in rock 'n' roll in the late 1950s. The early 1960s were best known for the Beatles and later for songs of social discontent and alienation. The 1970s were a decade of no real trend, with gentler rock, hard rock, disco, punk rock, new wave music, and the rise of country and western music. During the 1980s, the trend was toward music that raises our social consciousness—for example, about famine (Michael Jackson and Quincy Jones, "We Are the World"), child abuse (Suzanne Vega, "Luca"), the plight of AIDS victims (Dionne Warwick, Elton John, and others, "Friends"), moral responsibility (U2, "The Joshua Tree"), and lifestyles (Tracy Chapman, "Fast Car"). The Band-Aid, Live-Aid, and Farm-Aid concerts represented a few of the efforts of musicians in that decade to step out and help their fellow humans.

In the 1990s, R.E.M., Kenny G., Mariah Carey, and Clint Black deal with emotions that run the gamut from love to angst. "Crossover" artists (ones that appeal to more than one listener segment) are at an all-time high. Rappers like Hammer are heard from coast to coast. 2 Live Crew challenges social barriers, while Madonna pushes the sexual barriers. Whitney Houston strengthens patriotic ties, and most current events in the world have a theme song.

The recording industry has music for all ages and tastes. When you visit a music store, the walls are filled on three sides to the ceiling with categories from A to Z. One visit can convince even the staunchest critic that the music industry is alive and well. Not everyone who tries to make it big succeeds.

But, in a garage band somewhere, the next Michael Jackson, Phil Collins, Barbra Streisand, or Stephen Sondheim is warming up to claim a place in the music world of tomorrow.

Radio

"This is Hits 96—all your favorite jazz." "Hot 95! The top 40 station of your choice." Driving with your windows down, you can hear radio stations galore as traffic goes by you. Ever sit at a traffic light and watch the person next to you sing along with the radio, commercials and all? Driving to class or to work, or driving out of town, many of us turn the radio dial, looking for a favorite station. It is usually fairly easy to find a station to meet our needs, since approximately 4,750 AM stations and 3,600 FM stations play all types of music. Although it has not always been so convenient, radio has been popular for over 50 years. During the 1930s and 1940s, radio was the television of today, with situation comedies, musicals, political addresses, and game shows. The late 1940s were a time of great change because of the development of television. Sponsors were quickly changing over to the visual medium. To save radio, a deejay format was introduced in 1951. With the deejay format, stations began to design programs for specific audiences; today we have everything from all-music to all-talk radio.

The success of radio is often attributed to its mobility. Portable transistors allow us to carry radios in our pockets and bring them anywhere, from beaches to offices. Radio is also the most reliable form of communication because it can use batteries instead of electricity. Further, radio is beneficial to advertising. Many small organizations that cannot afford the expense of TV commercials can still get inexpensive publicity through radio.

Television

You are a member of the television generation. Men, women, and children find it easier to identify with television personalities such as Bill Cosby, Roseanne Barr, Oprah Winfrey, or Tim Allen than with members of the president's cabinet or former schoolteachers. Television is the most powerful and influential mass medium. In 1941, only 5,000 to 10,000 homes in the United States had television; today, 98 percent of all homes in America have at least one TV.

Unlike film, recording, and radio, which now cater to specialized audiences, television designs programs to please every viewer. Cartoons, documentaries, soap operas, variety shows, game shows, adventure series, sports spectaculars, movies, news, educational programs, and family shows try to meet the needs of all viewers. Some people watch TV to satisfy social needs by receiving information from news shows, fireside chats, or *Meet the Press.* Others live vicariously through programs such as *International Outdoorsman* or *National Geographic: On Assignment.* People escape into other worlds and live fantasies by loving and hating men and women on soap operas such as *General Hospital* or *Days of Our Lives.* Still others reinforce their sense of values by watching shows such as *Home Front* and *Life Goes On*, in which good always triumphs over evil. The variety and flexibility of television make it America's most popular form of entertainment.

The average viewer of a given program reflects, to a large extent, the values of that program.

LARRY TRITTEN

FUNCTIONS OF MASS COMMUNICATION

In Chapter 10 we identified the purpose of public speaking: to inform, to entertain, and to persuade. Basically, these three purposes also describe the primary functions of mass media.

To Inform

Although there is considerable overlap among these three areas, one can say that the dissemination of information belongs primarily to the news media, both electronic and print. Yet the news media have come a long way from just "telling it like it is." Local news shows throughout the country have expanded their formats to include human-interest stories as well as news features. Co-anchors are now called "news teams." Friendly newscasters "share" the news with an audience rather than stating just the facts.[2] Viewers are now encouraged to participate in news gathering by using their home video cameras. The Rodney King incident in Los Angeles, in which police officers were filmed beating a suspected traffic violator, was one incident in which a home videotape became a part of the national news. A home video camera also captured footage of the inside of a tornado in the Midwest and made national news. Thus, ordinary people became a part of the news team. Even the actual coverage of the news has changed dramatically over the years. Instead of merely reporting events, reporters and broadcast journalists have become news analysts who discuss the implications of important news stories.

GOOD NEWS VERSUS BAD NEWS. Today, the broadcasting of news events is so immediate that the impact of a story "hot off the press" (or hot off the wires) can have a jolting effect. On certain days we may turn on the

---

[2]E. J. Whetmore, *Mediamerica*, 4th ed. (Belmont, Calif.: Wadsworth, 1991).

radio news report and hear nothing but bad news. A war, a famine, a plane crash, a murder can all be news events on any given day. The immediate reporting of these unfortunate events is bound to have an effect on listeners. Behavioral research in mass communication indicates that exposure to the media has automatic and direct effects. However, functional researchers believe that media effects occur over longer periods of time and are more complex than they were initially believed to be.[3]

Several studies also have been conducted to test the effects of good news versus bad news on people's feelings and perceptions about the media reporting the news. In one such study, subjects exposed to newspapers that were "heavy" on bad news rated the newspapers more negatively than newspapers reporting greater amounts of good news. Additionally, the newspaper's image as a "community watchdog" was rated higher for the "good news" issue than were those reporting higher numbers of fraud and malfeasance cases.[4]

Some individuals have a preference for receiving their news from newspapers, while others rely on TV or radio. Even within each medium, people usually select a particular newspaper or a particular channel for a report of the daily news. From *The New York Times*, Thomas Griffith explained two types of news found in a newspaper: " . . . The important and the interesting, and most readers . . . feel entitled to both. In fact, the simplest way to judge the coverage of any newspaper . . . is to measure which kind of news it accents the most. . . ."[5]

Newspapers and other print media suggest the significance of various stories by the space allotted to each story, its location in the paper, its layout, and the boldness of its headline. However, a story of great visual appeal or catastrophic dimension will probably have greater effect when seen on television.

PUBLIC BROADCASTING SERVICE. We cannot talk about the information media without mentioning educational television or the Public Broadcasting Service, a nonprofit organization that attempts to emphasize the educational and enlightening aspects of television. Unlike commercial networks, which sell air time to sponsors, educational stations buy programs from the PBS network with money obtained from donations, federal funds, and commercial grants. You might notice that at the beginning or end of a program on PBS, the source of funding for the program is announced: "This program was made possible by a grant from. . . ." This type of sponsorship, which eliminates the need for advertisers, represents one of the most striking differences between commercial and public broadcasting.

---

[3]H. Mendelsohn, "Socio-psychological Construction and the Mass Communication Effects Dialectic," *Communication Research*, 16, no. 6 (1989), 813–23.

[4]J. B. Haskins and M. M. Miller, "The Effects of Bad News and Good News on a Newspaper's Image," *Journalism Quarterly*, 61, no. 1 (1984), 3–13, 65.

[5]Whetmore, 38.

Unlike commercial networks, PBS has attempted to realize the educational values of television. Many of its programs are instructional in nature, the most widely known being *Sesame Street*, a program for preschool children.

PBS also provides a forum for many experimental and innovative programs that would be too risky for commercial sponsors. PBS does not aim its entire schedule of programs at a "mass audience"; instead, it offers programs that appeal to a limited audience, a practice that would be impossible for a commercial network. Unfortunately, the artistic principles and practices that make PBS unique also create difficulties. Aside from obvious financial difficulties, PBS stations are sometimes uncertain as to just what their educational function should be.

DIFFUSION OF INFORMATION. *Diffusion of information* refers to the way the public learns about news events, products, changes in policy, ideas, philosophies, and so forth. We might guess that most of our information comes from the mass media. However, studies have shown that although the mass media are particularly effective in informing the public of major news stories and events that have just occurred, they are much less effective when information has less news value or concerns something new about an event or idea that is already known. While many people learn about a famine or an earthquake through the media, information concerning a change in library hours or a change in traffic regulations must be diffused in a different manner. A study concerning unexpected news announcements revealed that fewer than 40 percent of their sample heard about the *Challenger* space shuttle disaster through the mass media. Additionally, they found that 59 percent heard about the disaster from other people.[6]

The diffusion of information from one individual to another is based on the principle of *homophily*, which is the degree to which two interacting individuals are similar in characteristics such as beliefs, values, education, social level, and so on. Diffusion of information occurs most often when a source and a receiver are alike. A student is more likely to acquire information from another student, a construction worker from another construction worker, and so on.

The diffusion of information can be analyzed in terms of change agents and opinion leaders. A *change agent* is someone who is responsible for making policy and creating change. By the nature of their position, change agents are usually not homophilous with the people to whom they must disseminate information. The change agent generally interacts with an *opinion leader*, who is more homophilous with the general public and disseminates information to them. Opinion leaders are usually respected by their peers and have considerable influence in forming and changing attitudes within their spheres of influence.

---

[6]R. W. Kubey and T. Peluso, "Emotional Response as a Cause of Interpersonal News Diffusion: The Case of the Space Shuttle Tragedy," *Journal of Broadcasting & Electronic Media*, 34, no. 1 (1990), 69–76.

Mass communication has certainly aided the diffusion of information. Opinion leaders rely on the mass media for reports of certain news events, which they in turn disseminate to the general public. For example, when the controversy regarding the building of a new nuclear power plant in Louisiana began, protest leaders relied heavily on the media for information. As new developments arose, protest leaders would report and analyze important events for their followers. Because of mass media as well as telephones and telegraphs, the process through which information is diffused has been greatly speeded up.

To Entertain

The most common function of mass communication is entertainment. Although radio, TV, and films function as information media, entertainment provides the primary source of their revenues.

Entertainment covers many different things. For example, entertainment sections in newspapers include comics, horoscopes, and advice columns, as well as crossword puzzles and other word games. In television, entertainment includes MTV, game shows, situation comedies, soap operas, movies, drama, variety shows, and sports events. Radio entertainment today consists primarily of music, although radio plays, talk shows, and comedy routines make a major contribution. When we talk about film, we are talking mainly about an entertainment medium, with the possible exception of documentaries. What do all these forms have in common? By nature, an entertainment medium is one that provides the consumer with some sort of escape or diversion from the realities and anxieties of daily living.

To Persuade

Another function of the mass media is persuasion, as presented by advertising for products, political candidates, service organizations, charities, businesses, and so forth. Both electronic and print media have great persuasive potential, but, depending on the nature of the message, a full-page ad in a major newspaper can sometimes have greater impact than a minute of air time. There are media specialists who analyze where and how messages should be placed to have the greatest influence. Recent research concerning persuasive appeals in political campaigns has shown that campaign strategies using "attack" commercials against other candidates were rated less favorably when followed by the opponent's "issue" commercials. This knowledge can aid political campaign managers in planning and programming their mass media campaigns more effectively.[7]

---

[7]B. L. Roddy and G. M. Garramore, "Appeals and Strategies of Negative Political Advertising," *Journal of Broadcasting & Electronic Media*, 32, no. 4 (1988), 415–27.

ADVERTISING

Each day our dreams, fears, desires, and concerns are analyzed by advertisers anxious to sell products. ***Advertising's*** chief purpose is to persuade people to buy, and to continue to buy, certain products. Radio and TV advertisements are geared to the particular audiences that will be tuned in. During a weekday afternoon, soap operas that attract millions of women are interrupted with commercials featuring products for laundry, cleansing, beauty, and feminine hygiene. Football games are sprinkled with commercials for beer, sturdy trucks, and men's underwear. Saturday morning TV is filled with advertisements for sugar-coated cereals and the latest action figures and toys of the future. Through demographic analysis, companies have learned about the types of people making up viewing audiences and what products they would be most interested in buying.

Many of you can easily recall certain advertising slogans or commercials. These advertising messages must do more than keep attention to be successful. No matter how interesting a radio or TV spot may be, if it fails to influence consumer buying habits, it fails. Advertising has been widely accepted in the print media, but many people view broadcast advertising as an invasion of privacy. They resent their lack of control over the type and length of commercials. For this reason, many TV viewers are turning to cable television or remote-control devices to turn off advertising. Commercials now invade local movie theaters and rental videotapes before you can see the feature presentation. Consumers can have a voice in methods of advertising. Because of consumer complaints about exaggerated claims, broadcast regulations now govern the content of advertisements.

One medium can be more successful than another for certain products. Radio is most effective in announcing items such as dry-cleaning specials, food discounts, and clothing sales, where the visual appeal is not as important as the information. TV is highly successful where both visual and verbal content is important. Seeing how a drop of super-strength glue suspends a 500-pound weight is more effective than just hearing about it.

Advertisers and politicians depend heavily on mass media. How else would sponsors promote new products, or candidates introduce themselves to the general public? Very often, however, consumers are unaware of the widespread influence of the mass media. A consumer may buy a product without realizing that the seed for that purchase was planted by a TV commercial or newspaper ad.

PUBLIC RELATIONS

While a fine line is drawn between advertising and public relations, advertising is generally concerned with selling a product, and public relations with selling an image. ***Public relations*** is a more subtle form of advertising, which is designed to influence attitudes and beliefs. McDonald's is interested in selling its food products, but it also tries to gain recognition by giving contributions to charity, sponsoring restaurant tours for children, and writing articles about employee satisfaction.

Corporations are not the only organizations interested in public relations. Nonprofit groups, governmental agencies, churches, and universities are all involved with publicity campaigns. These organizations use public relations agents and agencies to get specific information to the public via the news media. One of the goals of public relations is to utilize space free of charge. Television news coverage of a political candidate participating in a national walk-a-thon is probably more influential in projecting a favorable image than a 30-second, $50,000, prime-time TV spot would be.

Although many people resent the persuasive impact of advertising and public relations, we must also realize that this influence can sometimes be constructive. Self-help groups such as Alcoholics Anonymous and different social service agencies use the media to help make people aware of the groups' existence as well as to persuade those in need to seek out their help.

EFFECTS OF MASS MEDIA

Considerable controversy exists about whether mass media serve to reinforce or change preexisting ideas. This question has been studied in the context of both political campaigns and commercial advertising. In the 1940s and 1950s, studies by Bernard Perelson and Paul Lazarsfeld contradicted the long-held theory that people's voting habits were easily swayed by persuasive messages in the media. According to their studies, voting behavior is most influenced by family and acquaintances, and voters select those political messages that reinforce preexisting beliefs. Yet studies from the 1960s through the 1980s found that a voter may sometimes completely change his or her vote as a result of a political message. Thus far, the results of studies dealing with advertising are inconclusive. The question remains as to whether people are capable of withstanding ad campaigns or are manipulated by media sponsors.

Children and TV

There has been considerable investigation of the effects of TV on children. Not all findings are consistent. Some theories suggest that television provides vicarious reinforcement; that is, imaginary participation in an activity that is rewarding for the characters on the screen will reinforce this same type of behavior in a real-life situation. This does not imply a negative or positive value. Yet, when the activity is violent, or when youngsters cannot separate themselves from fantasy, this effect can be harmful. To support this

The Nature of the Medium

In accepting an honorary degree from the University of Notre Dame a few years ago, General David Sarnoff made this statement: "We are too prone to make technological instruments the scapegoats for the sins of those who wield them. The products of modern science are not in themselves good or bad, it is the way they are used that determines their values." This is the voice of the current somnambulism. Suppose we were to say, "Apple pie is in itself neither good nor bad; it is the way it is used that determines its value." Or, "The smallpox virus is in itself neither good nor bad; it is the way it is used that determines its value." Again, "Firearms are in themselves neither good nor bad; it is the way they are used that determines their value." That is, if the slugs reach the right people, firearms are good. If the TV tube fires the right ammunition at the right people, it is good. I am not being perverse. There is simply nothing in the Sarnoff statement that will bear scrutiny, for it ignores the nature of the medium, of any and all media, in the true Narcissus style of one hypnotized by the amputation and extension of his own being in a new technical form. General Sarnoff went on to explain his attitude to the technology of print, saying that it was true that print caused much trash to circulate, but it had also disseminated the Bible and the thoughts of seers and philosophers. It has never occurred to General Sarnoff that any technology could do anything but add itself on to what we already are.

Source: From Marshall McLuhan, *Understanding Media: The Extension of Man* (New York: McGraw-Hill, 1964). Reprinted by permission of the publisher.

claim, Sparks investigated developmental differences in children's reports of fear that is induced by mass-media programming. Results of his study revealed that younger children (ages five through seven) tend to report fright from programs that depict "impossible content" (that is, present grotesque, ugly figures or portray physical transformations of the main character), whereas older children (ages eight through eleven) report fright from programs that portray "possible events" or contain violent content.[8]

Another criticism of television is that it stifles a child's creativity. To prove this claim, a research team from the University of Southern California exposed 250 intellectually gifted elementary school students to three weeks of intensive television viewing. Based on pre-test and post-test evaluations, the study found that the children showed a "marked drop in all forms of creative abilities except verbal skills."[9] This study provided empirical data on an effect that many elementary school teachers have been observing for some time. A more recent study indicated a relationship between heavy television viewing and less advanced moral reasoning judgment in kindergarten students. How much effect early television viewing has on humans is

[8]G. G. Sparks, "Developmental Differences in Children's Reports of Fear Induced by the Mass Media," *Child Study Journal*, 16, no. 1 (1986), 55.

[9]"What TV Does to Kids," *Newsweek*, 21 February 1977, 63–70.

not yet known. Further studies that follow the development of children over time will tell us more about the ways in which viewing habits change our ability to view or participate in society.[10]

Because children watch television for a number of reasons, ranging from boredom to loneliness, they unknowingly become involved in a process of "observational learning"; that is, they learn certain things simply by watching the behavior of TV characters. The amount of observational learning that takes place depends upon several factors, which include the following:

1. The age of the child (two-year-olds are more prone than teens to imitate behavior, given that they are unable to see a relationship between behavior and motives).
2. A belief that behaving in the way presented on television will be rewarded.
3. The degree to which a child identifies with a television character.
4. The degree to which a child rehearses a given behavior by daydreaming about it or using it in make-believe play.[11]

Children learn many things through observation, including skills, values, norms, roles, and sex stereotypes. What a child learns can be either positive or negative, depending on behaviors he or she observes.

Another important effect of TV is that it often replaces parental influence and supplies role models for children and adolescents who have inadequate ones at home. The TV set can become a substitute parent, a baby-sitter, and a replacement for family interaction. This effect is not usually in the individual's best interest.

TV VIOLENCE. We cannot discuss TV and children without emphasizing the effects of TV violence. Once again, not all findings agree. However, an extensive body of literature demonstrates that exposure to television violence indeed contributes to increased levels of aggression among the young. In one such study, the researcher was interested in the effects of realistic TV violence versus fictional violence on aggression in children. To test the effects of violence, he presented to preadolescents a six-minute newscast that featured a fight scene as one story, and to a different group of children the identical fight scene as a part of a movie preview promotion. Both the fantasy and reality fight segments produced higher scores on a hypothetical situational aggression test than were obtained in the control group, which completed the test without having viewed either film segment. Alarmingly, Atkin also found that scores were higher on the aggression

---

[10]L. I. Rosenkoetter, A. C. Huston, and J. C. Wright, "Television and the Moral Judgment of the Young Child," *Journal of Applied Developmental Psychology,* 11 (1990), 123–37.
[11]D. Pearl, "Violence and Aggression," *Society,* 21 (1984), 17–22.

measure completed by children who viewed the news version than by children who viewed the fantasy segment of the fight scene.[12]

It is interesting to note how TV violence, in addition to producing aggressive behavior, affects our reactions to violence in real life. It is sometimes said that exposure to very violent scenes makes viewers more sensitive to the painful consequences of violent actions. Yet, there seems to be more support for the notion that TV violence "desensitizes" its audience to violence in real-life situations. According to this view, the audience becomes apathetic toward or accepting of violent acts in society.[13] However, recent research supports the theory that television viewing does not make us more violent. Researchers from this camp argue that each individual is born with a certain level of aggressiveness and that, as with alcoholism, only those susceptible to the effects of violence will show more aggressive behaviors.[14]

For example, one study examined how death was portrayed on television and the influence of these portrayals on a child's perceptions and ability to discuss death. The findings indicated that adolescents enjoyed watching violent deaths, but showed ambivalence about younger children viewing the same scenes. Many of the children were uncomfortable speaking to their parents about death, and often overestimated the amount of dying on television news and entertainment programs.[15]

The movie industry has also been faced with pressure concerning violence in films. The rating system imposed by the movie industry in the late 1960s was an attempt to deal with this matter, although both sex and violence determine the rating. While the rating system does not alter the content of a film, it does serve to keep children from seeing certain films and warns other viewers of what to expect. This same function is served by the disclaimers that precede certain TV programs.

TELEVISION COMMERCIALS. The effect of television advertising on children is another area of concern. Especially on Saturday mornings, children are bombarded by enticing cereal, candy, toy, and game commercials. In a 36-minute time period, at least six minutes are devoted to advertising. Like the advertising designed for adults, children's advertising encourages youngsters to persuade their parents to buy and use certain products. The commercials often offer rewards and prizes, such as iron-on decals and toys inside the box.

Parents display mixed emotions about children's television advertising. Faced with endless demands for certain products and specific brand names,

---

[12]C. Atkin, "Effects of Realistic TV Violence vs. Fictional Violence on Aggression," *Journalism Quarterly*, 60, no. 4 (1983), 615–21.

[13]B. G. Rule and T. J. Ferguson, "The Effects of Media Violence on Attitudes, Emotions, and Cognitions," *Journal of Social Issues*, 42, no. 3 (1986), 29–50.

[14]R. Lynn, S. Hampson, and E. Agahi, "Television Violence and Aggression: A Genotype-Environment, Correlation and Interaction Theory," *Social Behavior and Personality*, 17, no. 2 (1989), 143–64.

[15]H. Wass, J. L. Raup, and H. H. Sisler, "Adolescents and Death on Television: A Follow-Up Study," *Death Studies*, 13 (1989), 161–73.

they often feel at the mercy of televised commercials that have influenced their children. However, a study by Galst suggests that parents may have the resources to fight back—and to influence their children's preferences for snacks. In Galst's study, three- to six-year-old children were exposed over a four-week period to cartoons, with interjected commercials for food products with added sugar or commercials for food products with no added sugar. Additionally, pro-nutritional public service announcements (PSAs) were included in the segments, with or without additional adult comments to the children about the product portrayed. Following each televised segment, the children were allowed to select a snack from a snack table which included all advertised products to which the children had been exposed, as well as similar product types (such as additional candies and fruits). The form of intervention that was found to be most effective in reducing the selection of snacks with added sugar was exposure to commercials for food products without added sugar and pro-nutritional PSAs with accompanying positive evaluative comments by an adult.[16] Indeed, it seems that parents *can* fight back—but parental monitoring of television viewing is the key.

I am entirely persuaded that the American public is more reasonable, restrained and mature than most of the broadcast industry's planners believe. Their fear of controversy is not warranted by the evidence.

EDWARD R. MURROW

Political Campaigns

Although we have already touched on mass communication and politics, we should review some of the research designed to test the effects of mass media on political campaigns. Some people believe that mass communication is the key to political victory. Certain political observers even suggest that Michael Dukakis lost the 1988 presidential debates *and* the election because he was not as "telegenic" as his opponent (that is, he did not come over on television as well as George Bush did). Members of the press also were criticized for not focusing on the issues. Furthermore, while many people did not watch the political debates, they viewed the campaign advertisements as negative mudslinging. The 1988 presidential campaign was criticized for creating a new and lower standard for political advertising.[17]

Television, if used effectively, can aid a political campaign. However, candidates must be selective in choosing their strategies and media. In order

---

[16]J. P. Galst, "Television Food Commercials and Pro-nutritional Public Service Announcements as Determinants of Young Children's Snack Choices," *Child Development*, 51 (1980), 935–38.

[17]K. E. Andersen, "The Politics of Ethics and the Ethics of Politics," *American Behavioral Scientist*, 32, no. 4 (1989), 479–92.

Mass media reflect society's attitudes and shape our lives.

to use the television medium most effectively, candidates apparently have to purchase television spots to introduce themselves and their ideas. Although televised news coverage is free and spot commercials are expensive, the commercials have a much greater impact. Whether or not this exposure reinforces or changes viewers' voting habits is still unknown. In terms of exposure and information, however, the advertising spots have a much greater effect than television news coverage.

Of all forms of media, television is the most expensive and therefore must be used most efficiently. Advertising agencies may plan a media campaign for a political candidate in much the same way that they promote a new product. In fact, books such as *The Selling of the President*, by Joe McGinniss, have explored this similarity.

Sex Stereotyping

The mass media have usually reflected society's attitudes toward sex roles; so, until recently, little effort was made to contradict sex stereotypes. Women were portrayed as passive, while men were usually shown as aggressive and powerful. If you were to look at the TV programs of earlier decades, you might think that every woman in the country was a hard-working housewife who wanted only to stay home and care for husband and children.

Occasionally, a spitfire like Lucille Ball, Gale Storm, or Ann Sothern would show that women could have spunk, although their exploits always involved scheming and inevitably backfired. During the early days of TV, there were proportionately fewer women on TV than men, and seldom did you see them on a news program. In the print media, women's magazines catered to the housewife and mother, assuming that this was the only possible female audience.

While things have certainly not changed entirely, we have begun to see a shift. We now have TV situation comedies about single women (*Murphy Brown*) and widows (*Golden Girls*). We see these women as the family breadwinners, sometimes competing professionally with men. Women not only anchor night-time news programs (for instance, Barbara Walters, *20/20*); midday or "soft-news" programs anchored by women (Faith Daniels, *A Closer Look*) are on the rise. Recent trends in human-interest stories have opened doors to evening "news-info" specials hosted by women such as Jane Pauley, Maria Shriver, and Connie Chung.

The growing number of women in the work force has also brought about changes in movie themes. Consider the plot lines of *Working Girl, Baby Boom, Head Office*, and *Men Don't Leave*. Roles portraying lawyers, police officers, and corporate executives are no longer reserved for men. Magazines designed exclusively for the working woman are more readily available than ever before. A more balanced portrayal of modern society is evolving. The media are covering stories relevant to women as well as men.

Shaping of Events

The mass media are so important in our lives that they often have an effect on the shaping of the events they cover. Sometimes events are planned with an eye toward media coverage. The Super Bowl is a perfect example of a spectacular event that grew out of the media. On a smaller scale, basketball and football games that are broadcast live allow time out for a word from the sponsor.

There are numerous examples that show how media can shape events. A politician may delay a press conference until a broken TV camera is repaired, or a track star may be asked to repeat a final lap so that his or her action can be recorded on film. At one time, a group of people even speculated that the first landing on the moon was "faked" and that subsequent visits were nothing more than media manipulation.

The media sometimes overstep their bounds in shaping events. A major network was once accused of contributing money to invasionary forces in Haiti in return for the right to film the takeover. Although the event never came off, the thought that it might have succeeded is rather frightening.[18]

---

[18]D. R. Pember, *Mass Media in America*, 3d ed. (Chicago: Science Research Associates, 1983), 36.

Effects on Government

Related to media influence in shaping events is the effect of mass media on government. In a society where there is free speech and free press, the media serve as watchdogs over the government. For instance, the exposure of the Iran-contra connection ultimately resulted in congressional hearings that were broadcast live. This exposure later resulted in a trial for Oliver North, which also was broadcast live on television. Currently, the C-SPAN cable channel covers the daily proceedings of Congress 24 hours a day. In addition to the watchdog effect, the media also serve the government by disseminating information to the public.

APPEARING ON RADIO AND TELEVISION

Let's now turn our attention to behind the scenes and look at the organization of a broadcasting station. Because the broadcasting industry is dependent upon performers, we will conclude this section with some discussion about performing on radio and television.

About the Station

Jobs at a broadcasting station range from artistic to financial positions. While the organization of each individual station may vary, certain similarities do exist. Basically, the organization of all stations can be broken down into three major areas: management, sales, and production. Most stations run more smoothly and with fewer colorful people than those who work at WKRP.

Because broadcasting is a multimillion-dollar industry, the management area is of great importance. Management must assume the financial functions of accounting and bookkeeping as well as major responsibilities related to keeping the station in operation. Depending on the size of the station, distinctions may be made between general administrative functions and business management.

Because commercial broadcasting depends on selling air time to sponsors, the sales department of any station serves as its financial life-support system. Again, depending on size and volume of sales, some stations separate this department into two sections: one to deal with local sales and one to deal with national sales.

The production end of the broadcasting industry includes a variety of functions, some operational, others creative. One of the most important aspects of production is the programming department, which deals with the selection of programs and the scheduling of air time. Large stations tend to divide this department into major areas such as sports, arts, community affairs, and so on. Other production responsibilities include coordinating all operations and overseeing artistic considerations.

When you think of how complex the broadcasting industry has become, with many stations providing programming 24 hours a day, you can see the need for a highly specialized pattern or organization to ensure the smooth operation of the station.

Inside a Television Studio

A look inside a television studio reveals an array of cameras, monitors, and lights. The amount of equipment and sophistication of the video system is determined by the size and productivity of the station. Local stations have modest setups in comparison to the large studios of network-affiliated stations.

The first visit to a TV studio can be both fascinating and disillusioning. While the activity in the studio is very exciting, the discovery that so much of television is illusion may be disappointing. For example, you may find that the backdrop for a TV talk show, which looks so glamorous on the air, is really very ordinary. Or a set that is supposed to be the large and luxurious living room of your favorite soap opera character may turn out to be a

The camera operator coordinates the video and audio components of a production.

closet-sized piece of cardboard. Even the most basic television lighting and camera work can create many illusions, not to mention those created by the more sophisticated special-effects equipment.

A studio is divided into two areas: the main studio, where the camera work is done, and the control room, where the master console is located. The technicians who work this console are able to control the picture that viewers see at home. The individuals who monitor the video console can produce a composite picture by mixing images from two or more different cameras; they can dissolve from one shot to another; and, when the equipment is sophisticated enough, they can even create split-screen or superimposed images. For example, during a television debate the console may create a split-screen effect so that both opponents can be seen at the same time.

A study of the television studio is not complete without a look at the people who work on it. Unlike the character of Miles from *Murphy Brown*, the producer often is not seen in the studio as much as the director. The producer organizes a show, coordinates schedules, and supervises the overall production. Among his or her other responsibilities are the overseeing of financial matters, promotion, and the technical aspects of the production. It is the producer's job to see that a production runs smoothly.

While the producer is concerned with the production as a whole, the director is in charge of the creative aspects of the production. A good theater director is not necessarily a good television director, or vice versa. A good television director must make the most of the creative elements of television—for instance, the director must realize the sensitivity of the camera in picking up nuances and be sure that the camera captures the intended effect.

The producer and the director are powerless without the aid of other people whose jobs are also behind the scenes. The floor manager is an intermediary between the director and the actors. It is he or she who cues the actors and tells them where to stand, where to sit, where to cross the floor, and so on.

Camera operators are a necessity, as is the technical director. The latter is in charge of the control console, at which he or she coordinates the video and audio mechanisms.

The next time you watch your favorite television show, think about all the people and equipment that make it possible. Even the simplest news show requires sophisticated equipment and highly trained personnel.

Performing on Radio and Television

One of the most basic parts of the broadcasting industry is the "talent," the term used to describe the men and women who perform on radio and television. Usually thought of as having the glamorous jobs in the industry, the talent includes newscasters, sports announcers, actors, disc jockeys, and game show hosts, to name just a few.

Talent may also include amateurs who are invited to participate in local programs. In fact, you may one day be invited to discuss a school project or community event at a local broadcasting station. When you accept such an invitation, you should prepare for a communication environment that is different from any you have ever experienced. Understanding the conditions placed on professional performers will help you be a better communicator.

Regardless of their particular roles, performers must adapt to the medium in which they are working. For example, when working on radio or television, a performer must get used to working without feedback, since most often there is no audience present. Therefore, an individual must develop a sixth sense to determine the effect his or her material or delivery is having on the audience at home.

Other adjustments that a radio or television performer must make concern the limitations imposed by the audio and video equipment. On the air a radio performer must speak into the microphone; the TV performer must not only be near enough to the microphone but must also be in camera view. Therefore, natural movements and expressions must sometimes be consciously curtailed.

In addition, both radio and television performers must contend with numerous technical cues as well as technical distractions. Last-minute blocking changes, news footage, costume problems, or new lines can throw even the most veteran performer off his or her rhythm. In radio, machines used to play music or an advertisement might not work when they are supposed to. Of course, working on a tape that will be aired at a later time allows for retakes and editing, two luxuries that are not part of a live broadcast.

Film crew on location.

While there are certain similarities between performing on radio and television, there are also considerable differences. The radio performer's most important tool is his or her voice. Think about different radio personalities you have heard. What is it that you like or dislike about their voice quality or style? Many of the characteristics that we discussed in our chapter on delivery play an important part in radio performance. Rate, emphasis, vocal expression, pronunciation, and articulation are all areas that need much practice if you are interested in pursuing a career in broadcasting.

Performing on television adds many new dimensions to the list of "things to do" before going on the air. While a radio performer can hide behind a microphone, the television performer is under close scrutiny. Clothing, personal appearance, and body movements are extremely important. You may have noticed that when a station is breaking in a new sportscaster or newsperson, it takes a while before the person feels and looks comfortable before the camera. An unseasoned performer might very well feel self-conscious and uneasy when first appearing on television. Again, performers must learn to use the medium and make it work for them.

THE FUTURE OF MASS COMMUNICATION

Unlike other forms of communication, the development of mass communication has depended on advances in technology. The first major contribution to this development was the invention of the printing press, which led to the print media. For hundreds of years, print was the only form of mass communication. Radio, television, and film did not become realities until the twentieth century. Because the electronic media have such a powerful impact on our daily lives, it is almost impossible to imagine what our lives would be like without them.

Yet many advances in mass communication have occurred in just the last few decades. Words such as *DAT* (digital audio tape/technology), *CD* (compact disc), and *satellite* are now part of almost everyone's vocabulary, although they were developed only recently. The development of mass communication has certainly not stopped; we can expect that as our technology becomes even more sophisticated, there will continue to be additions to the realm of mass communication.

The Concept of Demassification

One way to view recent advances such as the introduction of satellite communication is through the concept of **demassification**. This term, coined by futurist Alvin Toffler, is closely tied to the notion that the wave of the future will be the use of channels of communication targeted at highly specialized interest groups rather than at the overall masses.

Indeed, we need only look around us to see that the age of demassification is already upon us. The present nature of the print media is only one example of the many changes that have been made in the process of transmitting information. No longer are the nation's major newspapers thriving as they did in earlier years. In the fast-paced world of high technology, particularly in the mass media, the oldest form of mass communication is losing readership every day to a virtual avalanche of highly specialized mini-circulation weeklies, biweeklies, and "shoppers" that serve specific communities and towns. Likewise, the deaths of major national magazines such as *Look* and the *Saturday Evening Post* (and their replacement by virtually thousands of mini-magazines targeted at small, special-interest markets!) seem to show that, indeed, demassified media are flexing their muscles. Pilots, homemakers, camera nuts, teenagers, tennis players, and men and women in general may purchase any number of periodicals targeted specifically at their interests. Likewise, the growing popularity of regional magazines such as New England's *Yankee*, Dallas's *D*, or *Western Farmer* seem to reflect the growing interests of an increasingly demassified audience.[19]

The print medium, however, is not the only medium that is courting the demassified audience. Television and radio are becoming more highly specialized. The late 1970s and early 1980s witnessed the emergence in radio of all-news radio stations aimed at the educated middle class; hard rock, soft rock, religious rock, and punk rock stations, each aimed at a different sector of the youth audience; classical music stations targeting upper-income adults; and foreign-language stations targeting the many ethnic groups that are part of our society.

The nature of television viewing has also changed in this direction during the 1980s and the 1990s. Think for a moment of the variety of options that we have: sports networks; all-news networks; cable systems; news, weather, and sports information services; and the emergence of systems such as Columbus, Ohio's QUBE—a two-way cable system that allows viewing audiences to send as well as receive information.[20]

Last, and perhaps one of the greatest contributors to the age of demassified media, is the current information explosion and technological advances in the computer world. Not only do computers facilitate the flow of information in the fast-paced interactions of corporations, but the computer has also made possible feats such as teleconferencing, the transmission of information through TELEX, "computer conferencing," and FAX. Computer conferencing allows two or more people to communicate through computer terminals in their offices or homes. An example of such a use of conferencing is the existence of the Electronic Information Exchange Service, which allows scientists, planners, and educators in several countries to conduct discussions about energy, economics, politics, or space satellites with one

[19]A. Toffler, *The New Wave* (New York: Bantam Books, 1981), 158–60.
[20]Ibid., 163.

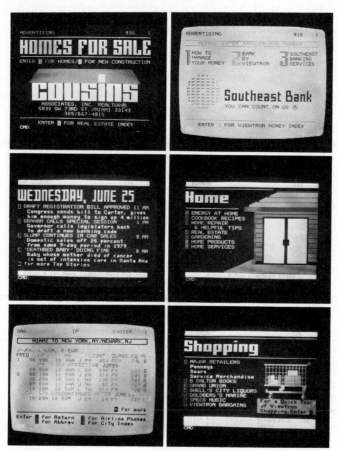

Computers make today's possibilities tomorrow's realities.

another through the use of teleprinters and video screens; they can use the system across varying time zones and at whatever time of the day or night they choose to work.[21]

As you can see, the shape of mass communication is rapidly changing. The possibilities are limitless, as the science fiction of today becomes the reality of tomorrow.

---

[21]Ibid., 252–53.

SUMMARY

Mass communication can be defined as the spreading of a message to an extended, mixed audience, using rapid means of reproduction and distribution, at a low unit cost to the consumer.

The most outstanding characteristic

of mass communication is its dependence on an intermediary channel to transmit a message from the initial source to a diverse audience. In addition, the sender-receiver relationship of the mass communication process suggests an element of delayed and limited feedback.

The scope of mass communication is enormous, overcoming the barriers of time and space. Because of this, regulation and direction are necessary. This control, known as gatekeeping, comes from the different media, the government, and various economic interests.

Mass communication media have continued influences on their audiences. Four forms of electronic media are film, recording, radio, and television. Each has been developed to meet the changing needs of our society.

Mass communication serves a number of functions. It can be used to inform, to persuade, and to entertain. The informative function of mass communication is primarily concerned with the news media. Newspapers and radio are still important forms of news media, and under some circumstances they are even more effective than TV in fulfilling this function.

The entertainment function of mass communication is quite diversified. Both comics in newspapers and a quiz show on TV entertain an audience. TV and film are primarily entertainment media.

The persuasive influence of the media is recognized in advertising for political candidates, service organizations, charities, and manufacturers. The relative persuasiveness of one medium over another depends upon the nature of the message as well as the individual medium.

While there has been considerable research on the effects of the mass media, many of the findings are inconclusive. Educators, psychologists, and sociologists are among those interested in the effects of mass media. Some of the areas they have explored include the effects of the media in terms of violence, politics, and government.

We also looked at the operations that go on behind the scenes at a broadcasting station, including station organization and management. We then commented on performing on radio and television. We can only guess where the advances of the future will lead us, as our discussion of demassification made this clear: Where we go from here is limited only by the boundaries of imagination.

EXERCISES

Group Experiences

Delayed Feedback

DESCRIPTION: Mass communication, by definition, suggests a widespread audience separated from a source by a considerable distance. As a result, a receiver's feedback or response to a message is usually limited and delayed. There are varying degrees of delayed feedback, ranging anywhere from a few minutes to several weeks or months. For example, a television commercial urging a customer to purchase a particular brand of detergent may have a delayed response of several weeks until the consumer runs out of his or her current brand of detergent. This activity will give you the opportunity to identify various degrees of delayed feedback.

PROCEDURE: Television and radio both operate on the premise that a receiver's feedback or response to a message is both limited and delayed. For this activity you are to identify two examples from radio or television of (1) immediate, (2) delayed, and (3) long-term feedback. For the purpose of this activity, we will define immediate feedback as a response that occurs within a 30-minute period; delayed feedback includes responses within up to two weeks; long-term feedback involves responses that require more than two weeks.

DISCUSSION: What are the effects of the varying degrees of delayed feedback on the receiver? Have you ever considered writing to a television show for a specific purpose and later decided that it would take too long to get an answer? Do you think that the nature of television and radio feedback reduces the number of written responses from viewers? How do television and radio stations attempt to accurately assess the feedback of receivers? Are you aware of the various degrees of delayed feedback with which you respond to mass media?

Industry Gatekeeping

DESCRIPTION: Every major newspaper and television station receives numerous stories fed to them by the wire services. However, neither time nor space allows for the printing or broadcasting of each and every news event. Media personnel at various levels determine which items they consider the most newsworthy. This activity will give you the opportunity to select the stories you and a team of experts consider to be the most newsworthy.

PROCEDURE: Divide into groups of four. You and your three group members will be industry gatekeepers. As a team, it is your responsibility to report the best news in the limited amount of air time available.

Each class member is responsible for bringing six news stories to class: two national stories, two state stories, and two local stories. From the pool of news items, each group should be given eight national, eight state, and eight local stories selected at random.

Each group is given 30 minutes to prepare a five-minute television newscast. During this preparation period group members should select the stories they feel are newsworthy. All group members should be involved in the broadcast. All newscasts should be evaluated by class members on a scale of poor, fair, average, good, or very good.

DISCUSSION: What variables contributed to a successful or unsuccessful newscast? What criteria did your group develop for the selection of news items? Do you consider the task of gatekeeping a difficult one? After listening to other newscasts, what criteria would you develop now for selecting items that are newsworthy?

The Big Debate

DESCRIPTION: One of the most compelling questions with regard to television is the effect of television on children and adolescents. Although there has been considerable research on the effects of television, findings are inconsistent. Some of the criticisms of television are that it stifles creativity, promotes violence, and has a negative effect on social morality. This activity will give you a chance to view both sides of the controversy.

PROCEDURE: All class members should research the effects of television on children and adolescents. Half the class should be instructed to find evidence to support the continuation of television programs, while the remaining half should find evidence of the negative effects of television. After the research has been collected, four class members should be selected to participate in a debate. One team (two members) will represent the position that television produces negative effects on children and adolescents (the negative position). The second team, also consisting of two members, will represent a major network (the affirmative position). The following format should be used for the debate:

> *Affirmative speaker 1:* 5 minutes
> *Negative speaker 1:* 5 minutes
> *Affirmative speaker 2:* 5 minutes
> *Negative speaker 2:* 5 minutes
> *Negative speaker 1:* 2 minutes
> *Affirmative speaker 1:* 2 minutes
> *Negative speaker 2:* 2 minutes
> *Affirmative speaker 2:* 2 minutes

Following the debate, the class members should reevaluate their positions on the topic.

DISCUSSION: What is your opinion on the effects of television on children and adolescents? Can you support your position with research findings? Can you identify any of the effects television has had on you? Can the effects of television be controlled or directed? How?

Personal Experiences

1. For a period of one week, watch a late-night movie every night. Try to watch a combination of romantic, humorous, violent, and horror shows.

Keep a TV dream diary in which you record in detail all the dreams that you have. It would be best to record your dreams first thing in the morning, before you do anything else. What relationship, if any, do your dreams have to the television shows that you viewed?

2. How are you influenced during presidential campaigns? List the various ways in which you receive information about the candidates. How many of those sources involve some form of mass communication, such as televised debates, radio, or newspapers? How has mass media changed national elections?

3. How does television reinforce or alter sex stereotypes? Select six different television serials and identify whether or not they reinforce sex stereotypes. Identify the methods by which programs characterize males and females according to sex stereotypes. Are there programs that attempt to change or even revise sex stereotypes?

Discussion Questions

1. How do mass media differ from other communication systems (intra-personal, interpersonal, and group communication)?

2. What are the positive and negative effects of television on its viewers?

3. What do you envision for the future of mass media? Describe the advances in technology that you feel will take place in the next 30 years. For instance, do you anticipate three-dimensional television in every home?

4. How does mass communication overcome the barriers of time and space?

5. Identify the television shows that are used primarily to (a) inform, (b) persuade, and (c) entertain. Are the most successful shows a combination of all three purposes?

Appendix A

Preparing for a Job Search

Anyone who has looked for a job knows that the interview is the most important step in the job-hunting process. If you do not perform well in a job interview, chances are you won't get the position, no matter how well qualified you are. Likewise, if you as the job interviewer do not know the correct skills, you may discourage qualified applicants or simply choose the wrong person for the job. Yet few executives and supervisors make an effort to learn specialized interviewing skills; they underestimate the importance of these interactions. Instead, they handle interviews with little advance planning, relying only on experience and improvisation. An understanding of the interviewer responsibilities should give you insights into how to prepare for your first interview.

RESPONSIBILITIES OF THE INTERVIEWER

Even though you may never be a personnel recruiter, there will be times when you will be responsible for conducting interviews. There are formal rules for interview situations. James Black, for example, offers a checklist of principles on sound interviewing practices.[1] Black first suggests that as an interviewer, you prepare yourself for the task of gathering a lot of information in a limited period of time. Because the interview is so short, you must decide in advance how much time you wish to devote to each area of discussion. Preparation also includes studying the data already received about the interviewee so that no time is wasted in asking unnecessary questions.

---

[1]J. Black, *How to Get Results from Interviewing* (New York: McGraw-Hill, 1970), 1.

Second, you must define your objectives and follow an organized plan to achieve them. A directionless interview is inefficient and will probably annoy the interviewee, giving him or her a poor impression of the company. Thus, the reason for the interview and the information to be obtained from it must be clear in the minds of both you and the person being interviewed.

Third, the environment of the interview must be considered. Positive communication often depends on comfortable surroundings. The room should be well lit and quiet. To ensure good eye contact and attentiveness, the two participants should always sit facing each other. The accommodations should be relaxed, pleasant, and above all, private. Taking telephone calls in the middle of an interview is rude and wastes valuable time.

Fourth, as the interview opens, it is up to you as the interviewer to break the ice—to make the other person feel at ease. Perhaps a question about an outside interest or about the person's family can serve this function. When interviewing, you should use words and phrases that the interviewee can understand. Trying to impress someone with your high-powered vocabulary will only block communication. Since you would like a productive interview, you must be able to develop a friendly relationship quickly, and, even more important, you must create a feeling of trust and confidence. The only way to do this is to be genuinely open and receptive rather than distant, authoritative, or condescending. These positive attitudes show the interviewee that you are sincerely interested in what he or she has to say.

Fifth, as the interviewer, you should decide the nature of the questions that will give you the necessary information. These questions should evoke more than a simple "yes" or "no," which would force you to do all of the talking. Also, the conversation must be free and open, and not become a cat-and-mouse game in which you try to trap the person with trick questions. In this situation you will lose the trust of the person you are interviewing, who will then reveal as little information as possible.

Sixth, you must listen attentively and intelligently. If your eyes wander or if you are constantly glancing at papers on the desk when you interview, the people you interview will feel uneasy. They will either speed up their answers or break off before they finish all that they have to say. On the other hand, if you show interest and attention, they will speak openly and freely and may even give more information than expected. Empathy is also important when listening. You should try to put yourself in the place of the person being interviewed and understand the real meaning behind the spoken words.

Seventh, interviewees should not be rushed into careless answers at the end because you must hurry them out. The interview should end gracefully and naturally. The interviewee will know it is coming to an end by the type of questions being asked and by the way you use your voice.

Eighth, at the end of the interview, interviewees must be told what to expect in the future: when they will find out whether they got the job, or what action will be taken to handle the matters that were discussed.

Finally, when the interviewee leaves, the interviewer's work must be completed. While the interview is fresh in your mind, you should make notes and evaluate the information you received. This evaluation should be as objective as possible. As the interviewer, you must put aside your own prejudices and must not distort the facts. Therefore, you must possess sound judgment, emotional stability, and the ability to make objective decisions.

Responsibilities of the Interviewee

Now that you are familiar with some of the tasks facing the interviewer, it's time to look at your responsibilities as an interviewee. You may think that all you'll need to do is to answer a few questions, but these questions will probably be the most difficult you've ever encountered, especially if you haven't prepared for the interview in advance. Job hunting is hard work, and sometimes even your preparation might seem difficult. The next few sections provide guidelines and principles to follow while preparing for your first interview.

SELF-EVALUATION. Do you know who you are? We all think we know ourselves pretty well, but during the next few minutes you may begin discovering parts of yourself that you never knew existed. The first step in preparing for your job search is to conduct a personal inventory. Most interviewees think they know the type of job they're looking for, where they'd like to work, the type of people they would enjoy working with, and so on, but campus recruiters find that students often fail to evaluate their personal and professional goals. Figures A–1 and A–2 give guidelines for you to follow when conducting personal and job inventories.

FIGURE A–1
Analyzing Your Personality Strengths

Listed are 50 characteristics that many employers consider positive and important. They are qualities that anyone could have, but not everyone does have. Rate yourself from "1" to "5" on each factor. Note that this list is not comprehensive; include other traits under number 51.*

	(Poor)		(Average)		(Excellent)
	1	2	3	4	5
1. Honest	( )	( )	( )	( )	( )
2. Dependable	( )	( )	( )	( )	( )
3. Motivated	( )	( )	( )	( )	( )
4. Assertive	( )	( )	( )	( )	( )
5. Outgoing	( )	( )	( )	( )	( )
6. Persistent	( )	( )	( )	( )	( )
7. Conscientious	( )	( )	( )	( )	( )
8. Ambitious	( )	( )	( )	( )	( )
9. Punctual	( )	( )	( )	( )	( )
10. Creative	( )	( )	( )	( )	( )

FIGURE A–1
(Continued)

	(Poor)		(Average)		(Excellent)
	1	2	3	4	5
11. Intelligent	( )	( )	( )	( )	( )
12. Mature	( )	( )	( )	( )	( )
13. Emotionally stable	( )	( )	( )	( )	( )
14. Enthusiastic	( )	( )	( )	( )	( )
15. Flexible	( )	( )	( )	( )	( )
16. Realistic	( )	( )	( )	( )	( )
17. Responsible	( )	( )	( )	( )	( )
18. Serious	( )	( )	( )	( )	( )
19. Pleasant	( )	( )	( )	( )	( )
20. Sincere	( )	( )	( )	( )	( )
21. Analytical	( )	( )	( )	( )	( )
22. Organized	( )	( )	( )	( )	( )
23. Appearance	( )	( )	(.)	( )	( )
24. Able to get along with co-workers	( )	( )	( )	( )	( )
25. Able to get along with supervisors	( )	( )	( )	( )	( )
26. Oral communication skills	( )	( )	( )	( )	( )
27. Written communication skills	( )	( )	( )	( )	( )
28. References	( )	( )	( )	( )	( )
29. School attendance	( )	( )	( )	( )	( )
30. Job attendance	( )	( )	( )	( )	( )
31. Willing to work long hours	( )	( )	( )	( )	( )
32. Willing to work evenings and weekends	( )	( )	( )	( )	( )
33. Willing to relocate	( )	( )	( )	( )	( )
34. Willing to travel	( )	( )	( )	( )	( )
35. Willing to commute a long distance	( )	( )	( )	( )	( )
36. Willing to start at the bottom and advance according to own merit	( )	( )	( )	( )	( )
37. Able to accept criticism	( )	( )	( )	( )	( )
38. Able to motivate others	( )	( )	( )	( )	( )
39. Able to follow through on something until it is done	( )	( )	( )	( )	( )
40. Able to make good use of time	( )	( )	( )	( )	( )
41. Goal- (or achievement-) oriented	( )	( )	( )	( )	( )
42. Show initiative	( )	( )	( )	( )	( )

(Continues)

FIGURE A–1
(Continued)

	(Poor) 1	2	(Average) 3	4	(Excellent) 5
43. Healthy	( )	( )	( )	( )	( )
44. Able to follow directions	( )	( )	( )	( )	( )
45. Detail-oriented	( )	( )	( )	( )	( )
46. Able to learn quickly	( )	( )	( )	( )	( )
47. Desire to work hard	( )	( )	( )	( )	( )
48. Moral standards	( )	( )	( )	( )	( )
49. Poised	( )	( )	( )	( )	( )
50. Growth potential	( )	( )	( )	( )	( )
51. Others	( )	( )	( )	( )	( )

*Beside any characteristic that you have rated as 4 or 5, describe an instance from your experience when you exhibited this quality. For example, "I showed dependability last summer when I . . . ."

Before you find a satisfactory position, you will need to evaluate your qualifications, preferences, knowledge, training, and experience. Don't just look at your strengths; also look at areas where you need improvement. A favorite question that recruiters ask applicants is, "Now that we have talked about some of your strong points, tell me some areas you feel weak in, and tell me what you are doing to overcome these weaknesses." That's a tough question, and unless you've prepared before the interview, you may have difficulty answering it effectively.

John, an English major, wants to work in a consulting firm developing written communication training programs for business and industry. After John makes a list of his skills and training, he realizes that he's never taken business courses. John can overcome this potential job-hunting weakness by taking appropriate business courses and/or by getting a part-time job in business.

The evaluation form in Figure A–3 is excerpted from *Jobs '77* by William N. Yeomans. It is designed to help you evaluate your job market-ability. By now you should have thought about who you are, what you have done, and what talents, skills, and interests you possess. With all this firmly in mind, complete this questionnaire. The scoring has not been scientifically tested, but it does view applicants in the same way organizations evaluate potential employees.

You may already know the type of positions for which you'd like to apply, but you may now know what's available to someone with your major, background, and skills. You may have chosen a major because the prospects for earnings looked good, the courses were easy, your parents suggested it, or it was something you'd always wanted to do. After getting your degree, and maybe after getting a job, you realize that you won't be challenged or happy

FIGURE A-2

Analyzing Factors of Importance to You in Jobs and Companies

Listed are factors that many people value in jobs and organizations. Rank the factors from "1" to "3" in terms of their importance to you. Put an asterisk beside the five most important factors.

1—Not Important   2—Average Importance   3—Very Important

	1	2	3
1. Challenge	( )	( )	( )
2. Responsibility	( )	( )	( )
3. Stability of company	( )	( )	( )
4. Security of job within company	( )	( )	( )
5. Size of company	( )	( )	( )
6. Training program	( )	( )	( )
7. Initial job duties	( )	( )	( )
8. Advancement opportunities	( )	( )	( )
9. Amount of contact with co-workers	( )	( )	( )
10. Amount of contact with the public	( )	( )	( )
11. Starting salary	( )	( )	( )
12. Financial rewards "down the road"	( )	( )	( )
13. Degree of independence	( )	( )	( )
14. Opportunity to show initiative	( )	( )	( )
15. Degree of employee involvement in decision making	( )	( )	( )
16. Opportunity to be creative	( )	( )	( )
17. Type of industry	( )	( )	( )
18. Company's reputation in the industry	( )	( )	( )
19. Prestige of job within the company	( )	( )	( )
20. Degree of results seen from job	( )	( )	( )
21. Variety of duties	( )	( )	( )
22. What the boss is like	( )	( )	( )
23. What the co-workers are like	( )	( )	( )

Source: From *Interviewing . . . A Job in Itself.* Copyright Lois Einhorn and The Career Center, Bloomington, Ind., 1977, 3–6.

working in this area for an extended period of time. Some people, for example, major in elementary education, get a job, and realize that children drive them crazy. Others get preprofessional degrees and then are not accepted into medical school, law school, or graduate school. What then? An inventory of your job preferences can help you look for positions to meet your needs. For additional help, go to your campus career planning office or to professional personnel agencies, study self-help manuals, or take a course on career planning. Laird Durham's book *100 Careers: How to Pick the One That's Best for You* is very useful. We hope that the exercises and examples in this section have given you greater insight into what your strengths,

FIGURE A–3
Job Marketability Evaluation Form

	Score
Scholastic Standing	
Phi Beta Kappa; top 10% of class	6
Top 25% of class	4
Top 50% of class	2
Lower 50% of class	0
Academic Rating of Your College	
Very high; Ivy League caliber	6
Good, well-respected academically	4
Not known for academic excellence	1
Barely accredited or not accredited	0
Work Experience	
Full-time work in your major field	6
Summer or part-time work in your major	4
Work in unrelated field	2
No work experience	0
College Expenses Earned Yourself	
75–100%	6
50–75%	4
25–50%	1
Under 25%	0
Campus Activities	
Major elected offices; many activities	4
Minor elected offices; some activities	2
No elected offices but some activities	1
No elected offices and no activities	0
Appearance	
All-American handsome or beautiful	4
Good-looking	3
Nice, but forgettable	1
Weird-looking	0
Personality	
Popularity plus. Well-liked; meet people easily	4
Pretty well-liked; meet people easily most of the time	3
Some friends; not too great at meeting people	1
Zero personality	0
Height (If Weight Is Proportionate)	
5'10" to 6'4" for men	3
5' to 6' for women	3
4'1" or under, 6' or over, or overweight, for women	0
Under 5'10", over 6'4", or overweight, for men	0

Bearing (Voice, Posture, Eye Contact)

Commanding, immediately impressive	3
Mostly impressive	2
Not too impressive	0
A laugh	0
Total Score	———

Results

35–42	Outstanding! You should be able to pick and choose a suitable position. However, people rarely score this high, so evaluate yourself again to be sure.
20–34	Excellent prospect. You should have several job possibilities without much trouble.
8–19	Average candidate. Job opportunities will depend on the economy and labor market. Need to try to develop some different areas to increase your chances.
0–7	Not so good. You will probably have difficulty in getting a desirable job. Need to think of ways to improve your score, or you may have evaluated yourself too severely.

---

weaknesses, training, preferences, and other qualifications are so that you'll know what you have to offer during a job search.

WRITTEN PREPARATION. You have now evaluated your assets and liabilities and know what you can expect from an organization. With your job objectives clearly in mind, you need to find a way to get an interview. The most widely used method of introducing yourself to an organization is through a letter of introduction and a *résumé*. Although cover letters and résumés are the most commonly used method of getting an interview, many have the opposite or no effect. Abbott P. Smith, a professional recruiting and placement specialist, gives 12 basic guidelines to help you ensure that your next résumé is not your obituary.[2]

1. Do some soul searching before you begin (conduct a personal and job inventory).
2. Write your objective (what do you want to do?).
3. Sell yourself (tell what you have done and what you can do).
4. Be brief and nonrepetitive (aim for a one-page résumé).

---

[2]A. P. Smith, "How to Make Sure Your Next Résumé Isn't an Obituary," *Training* (May 1977), 63–66.

5. Write it yourself (steer away from professional résumé-writing services).

6. List the jobs you have held (include job titles and dates).

7. Forget the references (applicants list references who will give positive comments).

8. List personal information first (name, address, phone number, etc.).

9. Don't elaborate on personal information (keep it brief).

10. Make it neat (this may be the time to invest in a professional typist or printing job).

11. Write a neat, short, personal cover letter (give reason for writing and what you know about the organization).

12. Put yourself into your résumé (find a way to stand out from the other candidates).

Résumé formats and what is included in résumés differ considerably. (Table A–1 lists résumé terms in order of importance.[3]) Figure A–4 provides

TABLE A–1
205 Personnel Managers' Ratings of Importance of Items in Résumé

RANK	IMPORTANT ITEMS	RANK	UNIMPORTANT ITEMS
1	Current address	26	Class standing
2	Past work experience	27	Sources for financing college studies
3	Major in college	28	References
4	Job objectives and goals	29	Percent of money earned for college
5	Date of availability for employment	30	Computer programming skills
6	Career objectives	31	Birthday and birthplace
7	Permanent address	32	Membership in honorary societies
8	Tenure on previous job	33	Membership in college social organizations
9	Colleges and universities attended	34	Offices held in social organizations
10	Specific physical limitations	35	Student body offices held
11	Job location requirements	36	Hobbies
12	Overall health status	37	Foreign language skills
13	Salary requirements	38	Marital status
14	Travel limitations	39	Complete college transcript
15	Minor in college	40	Height and weight
16	Grades in college major	41	Number of children
17	Military experience	42	Typing skills
18	Years in which degrees were awarded	43	Spouse's occupation
19	Overall grade point average	44	Spouse's educational level
20	Membership in professional organizations	45	Sex
21	Awards and scholarships received	46	Photograph
22	Grades in college minor	47	Complete high school transcript
23	Offices held in professional organizations	48	Personal data on parents
24	Statistical or mathematical skills	49	Race
25	Spouse's willingness to relocate	50	Religious preference

Source: Reprinted by permission of American Personnel and Guidance Association.

[3]H. S. Field and W. H. Holley, "Résumé Preparation: An Empirical Study of Personnel Managers' Perceptions," *The Vocational Guidance Quarterly* (March 1976), 234.

Clark Pager

Permanent Address	**Temporary Address**
134 Maytime Drive	2417 Broadway Street
Jericho, New York	New Orleans, Louisiana 70125
Telephone: (516) 822-8239	Telephone: (504) 861-0041

Job Objective

Full-time summer position working with law firm concerned with athletic arbitration.

Education

1988 to present B.A., 1992, Tulane University, New Orleans, Louisiana 70118
Adviser: Dr. Guy Peters
Major: Public Policy
Minor: Business
G.P.A.: 3.2 out of 4.0

1984–1988 Jericho High School, Jericho, New York 11753
Major: College Preparatory

Work Experience

summer 1988 to present Banquet waiter at the New Orleans Hotel to cover living expenses.

summer 1987 Courier and office clerk for Blau and Kramer Corporate Law Firm. Responsible for personal delivery of documents to the Security and Exchange Commission in Washington, D.C. Also responsible for updating law books.

summer 1986 Counselor and tennis instructor at Brant Lake Camp, Brant Lake, New York. Responsible for organizing, assisting, and instructing camp activities.

summer 1985 Courier and office clerk for Blau and Kramer Corporate Law Firm.

Extracurricular Activities

Responsible for organizing and running intramural sports for the College of Arts and Sciences.

Sports reporter for WTUL-FM, student-run radio station. Assemble and report the latest news concerning local, state, national, and world sports on a weekly basis.

special interests: Sports, theater arts, and travel.

References

Letters of recommendation and official transcripts will be furnished upon request.

an example of a résumé. You may be able to apply for several types of positions. If you do, you may need to write different résumés directing the content of each to a particular position. Applicants looking for a position in education usually use an academic vita, which has a different format. Some valuable source books to help with your preparation include *What Color Is Your Parachute?* by Richard Bolles (updated annually), and *How to Find a Job,* by Darold Larson. Just as the résumé is important, so too is your cover letter.

Field and Holley found that personnel managers consider five items important in a cover letter:[4]

1. The position the applicant is seeking.
2. The applicant's job objective.
3. The applicant's career objectives.
4. The applicant's reason for seeking employment.
5. The indication that the applicant knows something about the organization.

Because you are trying to get an interview with the personnel director, it is also advisable to request an interview in the cover letter and to refer to your enclosed résumé.

FINDING JOB POSSIBILITIES.   The interview is the most important step in the hiring process. Some of you may have a job waiting for you, but most of you must find a way to get an employment interview. Four major methods of securing a job interview include (1) answering want ads, (2) taking advantage of college placement centers, (3) visiting employment agencies, and (4) making cold calls.[5]

Want ads are the least popular form of organizational recruiting because they often expose employers to militants (EEOC), cost a lot of money, and release competitive information to other companies. Some companies use blind newspaper ads with only box numbers to give themselves greater flexibility. Because of the anonymous nature of a blind ad, the employer is not forced to answer inquiries, leak information to competitors, or conform to governmental equal employment opportunity guidelines. Although blind ads have advantages, they get fewer responses than labeled ads.

When reading want ads, you must learn to understand advertising tactics. Recruiters advertise for the maximum qualifications they can get,

---

[4]Ibid., 229–37.
[5]K. W. Stanat with P. Reardon, *Job Hunting Secrets and Tactics* (Milwaukee: Westwind Press, 1977).

with inflated requirements that are not absolute. Of course, some positions will require special expertise. A nurse shouldn't apply for a physician's position, and a brick mason shouldn't apply for an electrician's position. When answering an ad, you will be either offered the job, rejected, or offered a position not listed in the advertisement.

Newspaper ads usually ask you to send a résumé. If possible, you should avoid using the mail or telephone and try to answer the ad in person. We discussed immediacy earlier in this chapter and explained the importance of face-to-face communication when trying to get positive action. It's a lot easier for recruiters to throw a résumé in the trash if they've never met you personally.

The simplest way to get an interview is through your campus placement center. All you have to do is sign up; yet even with this easy procedure, many students fail to take advantage of placement center opportunities. Some think that their grade point average is too low, that only small companies recruit on college campuses, that companies look only for business majors, or that a lot of extracurricular activities are required. Students need to reevaluate the placement center interviewing option because it offers opportunities to students with a variety of backgrounds, experiences, and education.

It may help to familiarize yourself with how the placement center works. Placement offices usually have orientation meetings at the beginning of each quarter or semester, giving essential procedural information. The placement center provides forms and starts personal files for interested students (including alumni). Files include standard data sheets, résumés, letters of recommendation, and interviewing histories. Some centers also provide interview workshops, career counseling, career libraries, and employer information. Centers use open sign-up systems (first come, first served), staff sign-up systems (counselors place students), or card systems (batches of high- and low-priority cards are given for company preferences). No matter which system is used on your campus, you should go through your placement center to get valuable interviewing experience.

You may now be wondering what happens after you've signed up for an interview. Company recruiters are given placement center data sheets and a list of interviewee names with time slots. Your interview begins before you meet the recruiter, as he or she examines your placement file. Next, the recruiter enters the lobby or waiting area and calls your name. Introductions are made, handshakes are exchanged, and then you are led into a small room or partitioned area. The interview area usually consists of two chairs, with one placed behind a desk for the interviewer. Most campus interviews last from 15 to 20 minutes. At the end of the interview, recruiters usually tell you when you should be hearing from the company. Finally, after you leave, the recruiter quickly jots down impressions before moving on to the next interviewee. This can be a grueling process for both the recruiter and you; but again, you should get as much interviewing experience as possible.

A third method of getting an interview is through an employment agency. Employment agencies vary in size, style, cost, and purpose. Some agencies may have only one or two people placing applicants, while others have divisions for sales, management, engineering, professional, or technical positions. Agencies may treat you very professionally, with preinterview testing and counseling, or they may send you to an interview without preparation. Employment agencies stay in business through the fees they collect from either the employer or the interviewee or both. You may pay 10 percent to 20 percent of your first year's salary, or the company may pay all fees. As often as possible it is best to interview with fee-paid organizations. Some professional search agencies charge 20 percent and higher but guarantee job satisfaction, testing and training, and résumé-writing services. The purposes of employment agencies also differ. Agencies fill temporary vacancies, place technical or specialty personnel, find executives, or say they can place anyone.

Advantages of using employment agencies include their efficiency, saving time by having others do the searching for you, and confidentiality. One of the best methods of selecting an employment agency is to look at the classified section of your Sunday newspaper to see which agencies do the most advertising. Then scout several agencies and select two or three that seem most suited to your needs. Tell the agencies that you have registered with other agencies to let them know they have competition. As an interviewee, you must be prepared for critical analysis from agency counselors. They want to increase your job marketability and will sometimes get tough to help you perform more effectively during appointment interviews.

The final way to get an interview is by making cold calls. You can either send a résumé, or phone, or go in person. As mentioned earlier, it is best to go in person, yet this is probably the most difficult and ego-deflating situation of all. Having a job places you in a better bargaining position, but whether you have a job or not, you have to be persistent and make use of special cold-call tactics.

The best time to show up is about 10 A.M. or 3 P.M., because these are the least hectic times in organizations. When making plans, also try to go on Tuesday, Wednesday, or Thursday rather than Monday or Friday. The beginning of the week is busy and at the end of the week you'll find that the important people may be away. It is best to apply before November 15 and after January 1 because of holidays and fiscal years. If you want to make one friend before seeing a personnel director, it should be the company receptionist. Receptionists have the power to help or hurt your chances of getting an interview. However, even though you want to make friends with receptionists, don't give them your résumé. After you turn over your résumé, you lose bargaining power and may never get a chance to talk to the people who make hiring decisions. You'll learn tricks of the trade with experience. Just remember not to give up until you get the interviews you want.

RESEARCHING THE COMPANY. It is essential that you find out about the company before the actual interview. Just as you feel good when someone you meet knows something about you, recruiters are also flattered when you know something about what is important to them—their company. Know everything possible. The knowledge will increase your confidence and ease during the interview. However, remember too that timing is important. Don't interject some obscure company fact at inappropriate times.

The best place to begin is at your placement office. It usually has company literature, annual reports, brochures, and fliers. If not, write or phone the organization and ask someone there to send you the information. Next, try to talk with people who work in the organization. They'll give you greater insights than any written material could provide. Finally, local libraries usually have information in business periodicals, newspapers, stock market reports, and so on. The questions you will want to answer depend on the type of organization you are investigating. In applying for a teaching position, you'd want to know the number of schools in the district; for a manufacturing firm, you'd be interested in plant locations and competition; and for a bank, you'd probably like to know if it was nationally or state chartered and how many branches it had. Remember, the answers to the questions are intended to help you. Now that you have examined the responsibilities of interviewers and interviewees, you should be ready to think about your first interview. Your confidence should be high because you have evaluated yourself, completed a formal résumé, found the job openings, researched the company, and gotten an interview.

THE INTERVIEW

When you are being interviewed, your chief responsibility is to yourself. During an employment interview, you owe it to yourself to obtain as much information as you can, so that should you be offered the job, you can make an intelligent decision. Make sure you understand the requirements of the job (just what it is that you will be expected to do). If you don't understand something, ask questions until you do. State your qualifications in a positive way, and don't be afraid to mention potential weaknesses in your background (but try to balance them with strengths). The most important thing to do during any kind of interview is to communicate—listen, speak, question, respond, and understand.

The employment interview incorporates everything we've discussed about communication, and more. After your first interview you will be aware of additional areas that you'll need to prepare for the next time. One area that needs no further preparation is that of honesty. There is a misconception that you should say anything to get the job. However, this doesn't pay off. One young man decided to alter his grade point average on his résumé. Instead of putting down his cumulative average, he listed the average in his major course work, which was considerably higher. He interviewed with his placement center and was offered a job in a major duplicating corporation. After he accepted the position and had started training, the company sent for his college transcripts. The personnel director noticed the discrepancy between the grade point averages and called him in to ask him about it. After he told the director what he had done, he was fired for dishonesty.

Lying may not get you fired, but it could cause even more serious problems. New interviewees often fall into the trap of trying to please the interviewer with all their answers. If they are asked if they'd mind traveling, some say "no" even if they do; or they may say they enjoy working with people, when in actuality they would rather work by themselves or with machines. You may get a job, but your dishonesty will only hurt you. Too many people are miserable in positions they should never have accepted or applied for. When you see that you would be dissatisfied in a position you're applying for, acknowledge it to the recruiter. There may be another position that you'd be better suited for, or the recruiter can keep you in mind if something does become available.

We have already mentioned a few questions that are used during employment interviews. The following list of frequently asked questions should help prepare you further for your first interview. Questions are designed to serve as indicators of your personal background; human relations skills; work background; accident, safety, and health histories; education and training; and personal objectives.

1. What do you see yourself doing in five, 10, 15 years?
2. How have childhood experiences influenced you?
3. How would your closest friend describe you?
4. Why did you decide to go to your college or university?
5. If you could change anything about your education, what would it be?
6. Do you work well under pressure? (give some examples)
7. Would you rather be a leader or a follower?
8. What motivates you to give the most effort?
9. Are your grades a good indicator of your academic achievement? (explain)
10. Do you have plans for continued study? (explain)
11. How do you evaluate success?
12. Who is the person you admire most? (why?)
13. If you could have an ideal job, what would it be like?
14. Why should I hire you over other candidates?
15. Do you work better alone or with supervision? (explain)
16. Why are you interested in working for our company?
17. What have you learned from your mistakes?
18. What are you looking for in a job?
19. Are you a leader? (explain)
20. What qualities should an effective manager have?
21. How do you accept criticism? (explain)
22. Tell me about yourself.
23. What work experience helps qualify you for this position?
24. How do you spend your free time?
25. What qualities do you think I should be looking for in this position?

The ability to answer these and other questions should give you a good edge over unprepared candidates. Questions you will be asked are important, but you should also be giving some consideration to questions you should ask the interviewer. Toward the end of an employment interview, the interviewer usually asks if you have any questions. A few sample questions follow.

1. What type of training program do you have, and how long will it last?
2. What is the advancement potential in your organization?
3. Does your company help pay for employees to continue their education?
4. Will I have to relocate?
5. How are your employees evaluated?
6. What opportunities do you see for a person with my background?
7. What have been your most rewarding experiences with the company?
8. What is the employee turnover rate?
9. Does the company pay for moving expenses?
10. What weaknesses do you see that I should try to improve?

Job interviews do not consist solely of questions and answers. Several factors work together to make your interview a success or failure. The list of do's and don't's in Table A–2 should serve as a useful reminder before your interview. Making sure that you do all the do's will not necessarily land you a job, but doing one don't could cause you not to be hired.

In this section we have covered the three Ps of interviewing: preparation, presentation, and post-analysis. The preparation phase involves four steps: (1) self-inventory, (2) occupation inquiry, (3) preparation of letter of introduction and résumé, and (4) putting it all together. The interview presentation itself has four stages: introduction, background, matching, and

TABLE A–2
Some Do's and Don't's in Successful Interviewing

DO	DON'T
Act natural	Criticize yourself
Be prompt, neat, courteous	Be late
Prepare self and job analysis inventories	Present an extreme appearance
Ask relevant questions	Become impatient
Allow the employer to express himself or herself	Become emotional
	Oversell your case
Make yourself understood	Draw out the interview
Listen to the other person	Make elaborate promises
Present informative credentials	Come unprepared
Think of your potential service to the employer	Try to be funny
	Linger over what the company will do for you (such as benefits, salary, promotion)
Act positively	Unduly emphasize starting salary

Source: Reprinted from *Planning Your Future* by permission of the College Placement Council, the copyright holder. In R. A. Vogel and W. D. Brooks, *Business Communication* (Menlo Park, Calif.: Cummings, 1977), 42–43.

closing. The post-analysis calls for follow-up and reevaluation of your performance. The important thing to remember about this process is that no two interview situations will be exactly the same. The most you can do is understand the overall process; prepare for that process; and go in with a positive and professional attitude, thinking, "I have something to offer you."

AFTER THE INTERVIEW

Before breathing a sigh of relief, remember that your job search is not over yet. It is not complete until you've secured the position that you've applied for. After each interview, applicants can follow three simple steps to increase their chances of getting hired.

Immediately after leaving the interview, write down your recruiter's name, title, and address. Forgetting your interviewer's name could be detrimental to you later, when a secretary calls to set up a second interview and asks if you were interviewed by Mr. Barton, Ms. Kendall, or Mr. Barfield. The recruiter is now a personal contact with the organization, and all additional correspondence should be directed to him or her. You may be asked to send in letters of recommendation, transcripts, or job applications at later times, so be prepared.

After making sure that you remember your interviewer's name, find time to evaluate your interview participation by reconstructing the interview situation. Do you think that the outcome will be positive or negative? What impressions did you make? Why? After self-analysis you may remember biting your fingernails, interrupting the recruiter, looking at your watch, answering the wrong question, or using profanity. There is a tendency for us to focus on our mistakes rather than to look at the total process. Try to force yourself to remember areas of outstanding performance as well as areas that need improvement, so that your next interview will be more successful.

One last way to leave a favorable impression with a recruiter is to write a letter of appreciation. These letters usually thank the recruiter for his or her time and for the opportunity to meet, and express interest in the organization. You want the recruiter to remember you; even if a company doesn't have a position at the present time, it will be more likely to think of you in the future if you keep in touch. By following these three post-interview guidelines, you should increase your chances of success.

Appendix B

Sample Speech[*]

Introduction

getting
attention

I am here today in three capacities. The first is as a native Californian—this has been my home for most of my life, and I only regret that my job requires me to be away from the Golden State most of the time. I have been here, though, for most of the last month, enjoying the sun and the ocean, my friends and my family—including the newest addition, my four-year-old grandson.

establishing
ethos

I mention him—his name is Patrick Elton Dunne—because being here in California and seeing him has reminded me again of what a wonderful place this is to raise children, and also because my second capacity today is that of a parent—a person who has children, and now a grandchild as well, and who thinks often of the many large and small influences that shape our children into adults.

My third capacity today is that of a broadcaster, which I have been most of my adult life—a person who has some responsibility for one of those influences, the television set in the living room. It is only in the last few years that most of us, parents and broadcasters alike, have realized just how sizable a role television plays in the lives of our children. The realization has been a sobering one. We have spent a great deal of effort trying to discover just what it is that our children get from their television watching—and when we haven't liked the answers, trying to improve the situation. We have asked what the proper role of television ought to be in the growth of our children and where the responsibility for it lies. In the next few minutes, I would like to offer a few of my own conclusions on this subject.

stated
purpose

*Elton H. Rule (President, American Broadcasting Companies, Inc.), "Children's Television Viewing: The Parent's Role," in *Vital Speeches*, 43, 1(15 October 1976), 24–26. Speech was delivered before the Rotary Club of Los Angeles, Los Angeles, California, 3 September 1976.

Body

Let me begin by admitting one of my own personal prejudices. We have all heard a great deal about what's wrong with the younger generation: that they are alienated, apathetic, illiterate, promiscuous—and so forth. No doubt there are a good many children who do have those and other problems. But my own feeling is that, by and large, today's youngsters are turning out very well. At six and at 16, they are often surprisingly mature and interesting people—people who know more about their world, and themselves, than I would have expected.

If there's any truth to this impression, I also believe that the presence of television may have been one positive contributor. Television is, after all, a window on the world wider than any previous generation has ever known—one that offers an incredible exposure to people, places, and events that were once only topics in textbooks. And television is an effective communicator—from one recent study in Michigan State University, we know that there is a distinct correlation between how much television young children watch and how much they know about current events and discuss these events with their parents. More than that, television can aid personal, emotional development; in entertainment as well as informational programs, children can gain insights into how other people live, how they relate to each other, and especially how they deal with problems common to us all.

That's not to say television cannot cause problems for children. It can. This has been brought home to us very forcefully by parents of all descriptions since television began to assume a greater role in their home lives. Beginning about five years ago, our industry—and ABC in particular—embarked on an intense and still-continuing search for ways to improve its programs as they relate to younger viewers.

This effort has involved not only those in the industry, but a broad spectrum of educators and child psychiatrists, not to mention a great many parents and children. It has brought to the screen programs altogether new to the medium—from Saturday morning news programs for children to original weekday afternoon dramatic specials both for and about children. It has brought a new policy, called "family viewing," to evening television; it provides for early-evening programs which are suitable for viewing by the entire family. And it has completely changed the face of the weekend programs made specifically for children.

One major area of concern has been the portrayal of violence (or the threat of violence) in these programs. Early on, we at ABC pledged ourselves to eliminate gratuitous acts of violence from our programs, and as a result of similar actions throughout the industry, the overall amount of violence has been declining on television. To eliminate all acts of violence would be to deny reality, however, so we needed also to learn to ensure that what violence remained had constructive value. We knew relatively little about how to do this at the beginning, so we spent $1 million on two five-year research projects by three distinguished experts in the area.

That phase of their work is not completed, and from their findings we have been able to develop some workable guidelines for the producers of our

examples	programs and for our own editors. Let me cite some examples: The presentation of violence should exclude details which could be imitated by a viewer; it should be used clearly as a dramatic example of what should not be done; and the negative consequences of such violence should be demonstrated. There is much more to be done in this area, and our research is continuing, but I think we are definitely moving in the right direction.
problem testimony	In addition to the question of violence, we were concerned about the ideas young viewers were getting from the programs they watched. Recently, one of our consultants, Dr. William Hooks of the Bank Street College of Education, made a list of some of the qualities we would like to shine through our programs. It is keyed to the word "respect," and I would like to repeat it here:
repetition device	*respect for the individual;* *respect for differences;* *respect for religious beliefs and ethnic qualities;* *respect for all animal life and for the environment;* *respect for private and public property;* *respect for moral values;* *respect for the feelings and sensitivities of others;* *and, not least, respect for oneself.*
assertion	We hope all the programs our young viewers see can live up to this principle of respect. We take very seriously our responsibility for our younger viewers.
solution	But let me emphasize that ours is only a part of the overall responsibility for the effect that television has on our children. We in the television industry can control our programs and what happens to them right up to the point where they enter the home. But in the living room or the family room, control can be exercised only by parents. The most constructive use of television for children can come about only through the sharing of responsibility by broadcaster and parent.
support	Recently, the Roper Organization asked a national sample of parents with children under the age of 16 what sorts of rules they had for their children. As you'd expect, a sizable majority had strict rules about what their children ate, what time they went to bed on weeknights, when they did their homework (if they had homework), and knowing where they went when they left the house.
statistics assertion	But the Roper people also asked parents what sorts of rules they had about television viewing. And they found that only about two-fifths had rules about what programs their children were allowed to watch. Less than a third of those with children under the age of 12 have rules about letting children watch television after 9 P.M. in the evening. And those who do have such rules based them on the lateness of the hour, not on the kinds of programs which are on at that hour. We know, too, from other research, that most parents are not present when their children do the greatest part of their viewing.

What this appears to mean is that parents who take active charge of most of the elements of their children's upbringing allow a kind of anarchy to prevail where television viewing is concerned. To me, this is a cause for real concern. Children are unique creatures, with their own personal areas of knowledge and ignorance, their own needs and fears and insecurities. No television program, no matter how sensitively it is designed, can be guaranteed to affect all children in the same way.

A given television program may inform a child—or it may confuse him. It may delight a child—or it may disturb him. The difference is the degree of his parent's involvement. Eda LeShan, a noted expert in the field of child

psychology, tells the story of a mother whose marriage was collapsing. She thought she and her husband had shielded their problems from their 11-year-old son, until the day she and her son watched an ABC Afterschool Special dealing with divorce.

The mother reported that "as the program went on, Andy kept inching closer and closer to me. I put my arm around him and suddenly realized his whole body was trembling. It was a terrible shock. I realized that he had known all along what was going on, was terrified, and that my husband and I should have discussed it with him a long time before. That program kicked off the most honest and important conversation I'd ever had with my child." We can all wonder what effect the program would have had on the child if his mother hadn't been there.

That's an extreme example, but a revealing one. Let me offer a different one, from a study conducted at the University of Texas not long ago. An episode of a television program was shown in which playing hooky was involved. With one group of preschoolers, a teacher commented during the show that "that boy is in trouble. He did not go to school when he was supposed to. He was playing hooky, and that is bad." The other group didn't get that comment. Before and after the show, both groups were asked

whether they thought playing hooky was all right. For the boys, the percentage of those who thought playing hooky was a bad idea increased 75 percent among those who heard the teacher's comment; it decreased among those who didn't. For the girls, the number improved 120 percent among those who heard the comment, and 80 percent among those who didn't.

Based on observations of this sort, the Texas study concluded that "parents are the single most important contributor to a child's development. Furthermore, while most parents believe they are in hopeless conflict with the ever-present television, the project's results indicate parents can directly and easily moderate the influence of television. The results indicate that

parents should not let the television become a surrogate parent. Instead, parents should watch television with their child and talk about the programs."

Problem

Eda LeShan put the same thought very succinctly: "No [television] program can seriously damage a child in any way if a concerned and loving adult shares the experience and uses it as an opportunity to talk about feelings."

Solution

So much for the problem. How is it to be solved? To begin with, I do not believe that parents are thoughtless, selfish creatures who have abandoned their children to the television set—any more than I believe that television is a vicious electronic monster programmed to corrupt the youth of America. I do think, though, that there are a good many parents who are still learning how to cope with the presence of the television set in their home, who—not knowing quite what to do about it—do nothing at all about it.

ethos

For that reason, we have tried to draw together from our outside consultants—people like Dr. Melvin Heller, an eminent child psychiatrist at Temple University, and the people at the Bank Street College of Education—a few suggestions for parents to help them deal with their children and their television set. They may sound a little obvious, but they can make a difference.

solutions
assertions
clarification

First suggestion: Know what your children watch. See the programs for yourself, and read about them as well. Not every program is suitable for every child of every age, especially late at night when we offer programs designed for more mature audiences. All the television networks provide advisory notices when the subject matter of a program may be unsuitable for younger viewers, but the final decision must rest with the parents, who know their children best. It is imperative that parents make those decisions actively, not by default. And it's useful, too, if children know the standards by which their parents select programs for viewing.

clarification

Second suggestion: Watch television with your children. No, this does not mean watch every program with your children; there's absolutely no harm in their watching television while you snatch an extra hour's sleep on Saturday morning. But do try to watch some of the things your children watch, in the morning and the afternoon as well as the evening. That is the only way to know how they react, as well as what they are reacting to.

clarification

Third suggestion: Comment on the things you see with your children. When you read stories to your children at bedtime, you probably comment on the things you are reading. Even the smallest remarks, such as "gee, that was scary, wasn't it?" can make a difference in the effect an episode has on your children.

clarification

clarification

Fourth suggestion: Use your family television viewing as a basis for conversations. Many families find serious discussion difficult during their children's growing-up years; communication about personal feelings and experiences is sometimes almost nonexistent. But those feelings can often be unlocked and those experiences shared, if parents will use similar situations seen on television to initiate dialogue with their children. And there are also a number of educators who have devised games and other techniques by which parents can use television to further their children's education.

ethos

And, finally, a fifth suggestion which does not come from our consultants, but from me: Let us know what you think of the programs you watch with your children. It is an unfortunate truth that exceptional programs, for children as well as for adults, cost more than routine programs. We do not begrudge the cost of exceptional programs for children, any more than we begrudge the cost of covering a presidential election or the Olympic Games, but we need to know when our efforts succeed.

Conclusion

repetition of main points

problem

Whether a child watches five hours of television a week, or 25, his viewing is an important part of his life. Knowing that imposes an awesome responsibility on all of us in the television industry, and we have committed ourselves in the strongest possible terms to live up to that responsibility. But the quality of our efforts can only be as good as the use to which they are put in the home. For parents who pay little or no attention to their children's television viewing, television is no more than an electronic babysitter, an informative and entertaining gadget whose value will vary from child to child in unpredictable—and sometimes undesirable—fashion. This we must try to avoid.

solution

On the other hand, for parents who grasp firmly their share of the responsibility, who actively involve themselves in their children's viewing experience, television can be—and will be—a significant and constructive contributor to the growth of the generation of young people that will take over where we, their parents, leave off. That is the goal all of us should work toward. At ABC, we are doing everything we can to reach that goal, and we hope all of you will share this responsibility with us.

Appendix C

Sample Student Outlines*

1. Title: The Role of Comic Books in American Society

  I. Introduction

    A. "Outside, the London nightlife is just beginning. Trafalgar Square is crammed with curious tourists, St. Martin's Lane bustling with anxious theatregoers. Inside, a lone woman makes a fateful decision. Is this what I've become? A thief? A scavenger? Heaven help me, I'm reduced to stealing food to live. Is this my curse for becoming the Spiderwoman?"

    B. Comic books are a part of every kid's and many adults' lives

    C. Comic books are a part of the media in the United States.

      1. As a medium, comic books reflect some of society's attitudes and values.

      2. Three comic books, *Red Sonja, Ms. Marvel,* and *Spiderwoman*, reflect our notions about women.

  II. Body

    A. Three comics are published by Marvel comics, but each has its own history.

      1. *Red Sonja* first appeared in 1975.

        a. The origin of Red Sonja is unclear.

        b. Red Sonja lives in the "Hyporian Age" in the distant past.

      2. *Ms. Marvel* was presented in January 1977.

        a. Ms. Marvel has amnesia and does not know her origins.

        b. Ms. Marvel is a superhero in the tradition of Superman.

      3. *Spiderwoman* is the newest of the female superheroes, with her first issue appearing in April 1978.

---

*These outlines were prepared by Debbie Smith of Southwest Texas State University and are reproduced with her permission.

440

        a. Jessica Drew (Spiderwoman) is half-spider, half-woman from another world.

        b. Spiderwoman is attempting to learn to live on Earth.

  B. Violence is an aspect of all three comics, but each deals with violence in a different way.

    1. *Red Sonja* is a graphically violent comic book.

        a. The only weapons Red Sonja uses are her blade and sword.

        b. Red Sonja kills for self-preservation and pay.

    2. Ms. Marvel fights violence in true superhero tradition.

        a. The violence in the comic is beyond the comprehension of mortal man.

        b. *Ms. Marvel* involves fantasy violence where no one is killed or seriously injured since they are super villains.

    3. Spiderwoman uses violence only for justifiable reasons.

        a. Spiderwoman fights for the good of society.

        b. In the first issue, she does not use her full power even against a criminal.

  C. Each of the three comics makes a statement about women.

    1. Red Sonja is considered the "she-devil with a sword."

        a. The comic does not deal with women's rights specifically since it is set in the distant past.

        b. Red Sonja fights her battles alone.

    2. It is obvious from the title *Ms. Marvel* that this comic has been influenced by the women's movement.

        a. Ms. Marvel's slogan is, "This female fights back."

        b. Carol Danvers (Ms. Marvel's alter identity) is the editor of a feminist magazine.

    3. Spiderwoman is learning how to deal with her identity while living on earth.

        a. The comic says, "To know her is to fear her."

        b. Spiderwoman is searching for her own identity.

III. Conclusion

  A. The comics present strong, independent women.

  B. Solo female superheroes, while not very real, do suggest a growing awareness of women.

  C. But perhaps the comics say it best: "Like the Valkyrie guards of Valhalla, she sweeps across the face of the earth, arms as widespread as an eagle's wings, eyes burning, jaw set, every sinew throbbing with battle anticipation . . . her name is her own, but for want of something better we may call her Marvel, Ms. Marvel, and because of her the world may never be the same."

2. Title: Crime and the Elderly

  I. Introduction

    A. A New York couple—Hans Kabel, 78, and his wife Emma, 76—were assaulted twice in less than two months.

B. The older people in our cities are viewed as victims or potential victims of criminals.
   1. Most are poor and unable to move.
   2. The elderly are living in fear in the cities.

II. Body
   A. Fear of a criminal attack is now the major concern of the elderly.
      1. New York City officials believe that there are 30 victims for every crime reported.
      2. Chicago demonstrates the plight of the elderly.
         a. On the South Side, the elderly are faced with gangs of potential assailants on the first of the month, when Social Security checks arrive.
         b. On the West Side, no one goes out after dark.
      3. Statistically, the elderly are not victimized more than any other age group, but the impact is more severe.
         a. Physical injury is greater for the elderly in an assault.
         b. Emotionally, elderly persons' lives are governed by fear of an attack.
   B. The assailants of the elderly are primarily young juvenile criminals.
      1. The crimes are called "crib jobs" because it is like taking candy from a baby.
         a. The youngsters usually operate in teams.
         b. The elderly are young criminals' ideal victims.
      2. The rights of juveniles are so well protected that it is almost impossible for there to be repercussions.
         a. About 75 percent of the juveniles apprehended have been arrested before.
         b. Prosecutors are prevented from revealing a juvenile's arrest record.
      3. Judges do not know if they are dealing with a first offender or a longtime criminal.
      4. A juvenile who had beaten and robbed an 82-year-old woman was released on a $500 bond even though he had 67 previous arrests, one for murder.
      5. Violent crime against the elderly is increasing.
         a. In Seattle, violent street crime has increased 18 percent.
         b. In New York, two 16-year-olds raped a 75-year-old woman.
         c. In Detroit, an 80-year-old woman was killed because she clung to her purse.
   C. Cities have started several programs to help solve the problem.
      1. Seattle engages policemen to serve as decoys.
      2. Chicago, Los Angeles, and New York have received federal funds to start self-help and victim assistance programs.
      3. San Francisco provides an escort service for the elderly.

      4. In Charleston, West Virginia, elderly residents call in to the police department each day.
      5. In some cities, high school students serve as escorts for the elderly.
   D. The best solution is to have more police patrolling the streets.
      1. New York City has done this in a few areas, and it has been very successful.
      2. It is the solution most often recommended by the elderly.
III. Conclusion
   A. Crimes against the elderly are significant and increasing.
   B. Solutions exist that can help solve the problem.
   C. Unfortunately there are also counterproductive solutions. The Kabels, the elderly couple mentioned at the beginning of the speech, used a counterproductive solution—dual suicide—saying they did not want to live in fear anymore.

3. **Title: Implications of Group Ownership in the Newspaper Industry**
   I.   Introduction
        A. In 1960, chains and conglomerates controlled 30 percent of the nation's newspapers and 46 percent of the readership.
        B. In 1977, chains and conglomerates controlled 59 percent of the newspapers and 71 percent of the readership.
        C. There has been a growing concern about the increasing group ownership of American newspapers.
   II. Body
        A. Increasing chain ownership is not viewed as threatening by some people.
           1. Chain ownership saves newspapers.
              a. Small newspapers that are going under are bought by large chains.
              b. The chains have more money to invest in the newspapers to keep them in business.
           2. The chains are improving the quality of the newspapers they buy.
              a. The chains hire more staff for the newspapers.
              b. The chains add additional news services.
           3. Some of the leading newspapers in the country, such as the *Washington Post* and *Los Angeles Times*, are owned by conglomerates.
        B. Chain ownership is perceived as destructive to the press in the United States.
           1. Chains are concerned with profits.
              a. Profits take precedence over quality
              b. Concern with profits conflicts with serving the public interest.
           2. Competition is necessary for a good press.
              a. Without competition an inferior product can be produced without challenge.

        b. With chain ownership there is no competition.

    3. Chains do not improve the quality of the newspapers.

        a. Papers tend to stay mediocre if bought by a chain.

        b. Outstanding newspapers have never been created by chains.

  C. Chain ownership threatens the free press.

    1. Chain ownership violates the intent of a strong, free press.

    2. Newspapers play a special role as sources of opinion and information that should not be controlled by a limited number of owners.

III. Conclusion

  A. Chain ownership has reached epidemic proportions.

  B. The trend is continuing at a fast rate.

  C. Something should be done to prevent domination of such an important source of public information as newspapers.

Glossary

Abstract Representing feelings or thoughts that cannot be sensed directly.

Accenting Use of gestures such as nods, blinks, squints, and shrugs to help emphasize or punctuate spoken words.

Acceptance Speech A speech designed for the acceptance of an honor or award.

Accuracy Precise use of words.

Achieved Role Position in society that is earned by individual accomplishment.

Action-Oriented Listener Listener who is task-oriented and prefers information to be presented in a logical, organized way.

Advertising Method of persuasion concerned with influencing people to buy, or to continue to buy, a product.

Affect Display Body change that conveys internal emotional states.

After-Dinner Speech In general, a form of entertainment speech intended to make the audience feel relaxed and comfortable.

All-Channel Network Communication network in which all positions send and receive messages to and from all other positions.

Alternating Monologue Unproductive communication in which each person knows the other is speaking but does not listen openly to what is being said.

Ambiguity Language difficulty caused when one symbol (word) has several different meanings.

Ambiguous Feedback Response that gives no indication that the message has been received positively or negatively.

Anecdote A brief story that relates to an important idea in the speech.

Appraisal Interview Designed to get and evaluate information about a worker's past performance and future potential.

Appropriateness Use of language style that is adapted to the occasion, audience, and type and purpose of the speech.

Articulation Process by which the voice is altered into recognizable speech sounds.

Ascribed Role Position in society based primarily on sex, age, kinship, and other factors that are out of a person's control.

Assessing Making judgments about a message and its importance to us.

Assimilation The process of incorporating some aspect of the environment into the whole set of mental functionings in order to make sense of what goes on around us.

Attending The initial step of the listening process. Involves focusing attention on a message.

Attitude Learned tendency to react positively or negatively to an object or situation.

Attraction Positive attitude, movement toward, or liking between two people.

Audience Analysis The act of acquainting yourself with the audience before giving a speech.

Authoritarian Leader Individual who directs

the group with goal-oriented behaviors and firm opinions about how to achieve group goals.

Automatic Processing Cognitive processes that yield behaviors that we have learned or rehearsed to the point that we no longer have to think when we are performing them.

Avoiding Relationship disintegration stage in which one or both parties act as though the other person does not exist.

Award Presentation A speech designed for the presentation of an honor or award.

Barrier Factor that causes incorrect meanings, or no meanings, to be communicated.

Belief Probability statements about the existence of things or statements about the relationships between an object and another quality or thing.

Biofeedback A form of external self-feedback used to control physiological processing.

Body Image A person's perception of his or her physical self.

Body Manipulator Movement originally associated with body functioning, but that has come to be used unconsciously and independently of bodily needs.

Body of a Speech Portion of the speech that elaborates and clarifies the main points for an audience.

Bonding Final stage of relationship development; usually signifies commitment through a formal contract.

Business Conference Small group within an organization that meets to disseminate information or develop solutions to current organizational problems.

Bypassing Situation in which people argue or reach an impasse when they are actually in agreement.

Casual Audience Small, heterogeneous group of people who gather at the same place for a short period of time.

Cause-and-Effect Pattern In a speech, a persuasive structure of organization that establishes a relationship between two events.

Chain Network Similar to the circle communication network, except that the members at each end of the chain send messages to and receive messages from only one position.

Chain-of-Events Pattern Informative organizational structure based on the development

of a series of steps, with each step dependent upon the previous one.

Change Agent One who is responsible for making policy and creating change.

Channel Means by which a message is communicated.

Chronological Pattern Informative pattern of organization that follows a subject through time.

Circle Network Communication network in which messages are sent to the left and right of a position, but not to other members in the group.

Circular Response Mutual feedback between speaker and audience that increases participation and strengthens the bonds between them.

Circumscribing Controlled disintegration stage with less total communication and expression of commitment.

Clarity The art of saying exactly what is meant, thus increasing audience comprehension.

Cognitive Processing Storage, retrieval, sorting, and assimilation of information.

Cohesion Degree to which group members identify themselves as a team.

Communication Apprehension Anxiety associated with the process of communication.

Comparison-Contrast Defining a word, idea, or concept by pointing out similarities and/or differences between it and something with which the audience is already familiar.

Complementary Relationship A relationship in which one person is more dominant and the other person is less so.

Complementing Messages Nonverbal messages that complete or accent explanations and/or descriptions.

Compliance/Dynamism Factor related to source credibility that reflects the amount of real or implicit power a speaker is perceived to have.

Concerted Audience Collected group of individuals with an active purpose and mutual interest without separation of labor or strict organization of authority.

Conclusion of Speech Final portion of speech, which summarizes and reinforces the speaker's point of view.

Concrete Symbolizing objects or events that

can be pointed to, touched, vicariously experienced, or directly experienced.

Conflict Management Means by which two or more people settle disputes or conflicts.

Conformity Acceptance of a group's norms.

Connotation Meanings beyond the objective reference of a word (abstract meaning).

Constitutive Rule A rule which defines what a given act (or behavior) should "count as" and allow us to decide what each others' behavior "means."

Content-Oriented Listener Listener who focuses easily on the content of a message and tends to critically evaluate all incoming information.

Context Circumstances that surround and give meaning to words and statements.

Control The dimension of interpersonal relationships that focuses on the distribution of power.

Coordinated Management of Meaning Theory of communication that focuses on how humans coordinate and manage meanings in everyday life.

Covert Stimuli External changes or actions received at the subconscious level.

Creativity Originality of thought and use of imagination.

Credibility-Centered Approach When a speaker comes to a public communication setting with the objective of demonstrating competence and trustworthiness.

Dampening Strategy used by listeners to calm a speaker when he or she is experiencing a negative emotional state.

Deception Cues Cues that suggest possible falsehood but do not tell what information is being withheld or falsified.

Decoding Act of interpreting a message.

Deductive Pattern Persuasive structure that applies a previously accepted generalization to a specific case.

Deductive Reasoning Moves from the general to the specific.

Defense Mechanism Method of resolving anxiety produced by intrapersonal conflict.

Defensive Attitudinal Function Function of attitudes expressed whenever we experience some form of personal anxiety or insecurity regarding the target in question.

Delivery Physical and vocal elements of a speaker's presentation.

Demassification Using channels of communication to reach highly specialized interest groups.

Democratic Leader Individual who guides rather than directs the group, leaving most decision making to the group itself.

Demography Statistical study of populations (age, sex, educational levels, etc.).

Denotation Objective reference of a word (its factual, concrete meaning).

Description Method of defining a word, idea, or concept.

Differentiating Relationship state characterized by increased interpersonal distance.

Diffusion of Information Manner in which the public learns about new events, products, and changes in policy, ideas, philosophies, and so forth.

Digging Strategy to help listeners discover underlying issues and concerns by reflecting on the emotions and thoughts of speakers.

Directive Interview Structured and planned interaction situation that is generally conducted by using a step-by-step outline or format of questions.

Discussion Group Group of three or more persons characterized by cooperation among members, face-to-face interaction, shared perceptions, and verbal and nonverbal communication.

Dogmatism Personality trait characterized by a closed mind and a reluctance to accept new ideas and opinions.

Downward Communication Information messages directed to subordinates within an organization.

Dyad Two people in close physical contact.

Early Childhood Period of language learning that takes place from approximately 24 to 48 months.

Economy Use of the right words in the most efficient manner.

Effortful Processing Occurs whenever we are required to process information consciously in order to complete an act.

Emblem Commonly recognized sign (usually a gesture) that communicates a message usually unrelated to an ongoing conversation.

Emotional Processing Nonlogical response of an organism to a stimulus.

Emotional Self Intrapersonal processing center associated with emotions.

Employment Interview Situation in which employers and applicants attempt to get pertinent information before making hiring decisions.

Encoding Process of generating and creating a message to be sent to a receiver.

Ends-Justifies-Means Approach When a speaker adopts the position that any available means of persuasion may be used as long as the result is honorable, just, or desirable.

Equal Time Rule Stations must give all political candidates the same amount of time under the same terms.

Esteem Needs Human desire for dignity, achievement, competence, and status.

Ethos Perception of the speaker by the audience (source credibility).

Eulogy Farewell speech that marks someone's death.

Evaluation Group Uses information from the fact-finding group to determine the scope of a problem and the priorities in finding a solution.

Exit Interview Situation designed to find out how an employee feels about the company, work environment, and job conditions after he or she has decided to leave the position.

Experiential-Schematic Attitudinal Function Function of attitudes that involves the general cognitive maps that we develop about a target object, issue, person, or group.

Experimenting The "do you know" period of interaction development.

Extended Example Illustration or story carried out to considerable length in order to clarify or emphasize a very important idea.

External Self-Feedback Part of a person's own message that is heard by the person.

External Stimuli Stimuli that originate in the environment outside of the human body.

Extrinsic Motivation Motivation that arises from an outside source (such as extra credit points).

Fact-Finding Group Type of problem-solving group that gathers as much information as possible about a particular issue or problem.

Fairness Doctrine All stations must provide time to discuss controversial issues and must encourage opposing viewpoints.

Farewell Speech Expresses regret about leaving and thanks those left behind.

Fear-Arousing Appeal Threat or scare tactic designed to persuade.

Feedback Response to a verbal or nonverbal message by a receiver.

Feedforward Anticipation of feedback from others.

Flexibility The ability to perform a variety of different tasks effectively and efficiently.

Focusing Taking responsibility for the success of communication by preparing oneself to listen.

Forewarning Information of the speaker's intent given prior to the speech.

Formal Communication Structured communication situation in which more attention is paid to both verbal and nonverbal messages.

Formal Communication Structure Rules, regulations, and procedures within an organization.

Formal Presentation The most structured form of organizational communication, in which responsibility is placed on one person to create interests and motivation to listen.

Forum Type of public discussion in which the audience actively participates in the discussion.

Functional Role Role that aids the group in accomplishing its objectives by keeping the discussion on course.

Functional Theory of Interpersonal Communication Theory that delineates three primary purposes of communication: linking, mentation, and regulation.

Gatekeeper Individual or organization that controls or influences a mass communication message.

Gender Role Behavior that is ascribed, defined, and encouraged by each society's culture to be appropriate for either males or females.

Gestalt Viewing an object or event as "a whole" rather than looking at its individual components.

Gesture Movement of the body that communicates messages to others.

Global Village Theory that the world is "smaller" than before due to advances in mass communication.

Group Any number of people with a common goal who interact with one another to accomplish the goal, recognize each other's existence, and see themselves as part of a group.

Habit Repetitive behavior so automatic that a person is unaware of it.

Hearing Physical act of receiving sounds.

Hierarchy of Human Needs Five basic human drives, as described by Maslow. They include physiological, safety, love, esteem, and self-actualization needs.

Homophily Degree to which two interacting individuals are similar in characteristics such as beliefs, values, education, social level, and so on.

Human Messages Messages that focus on the relational element of the organization and that are associated with and directed by the attitudes, values, preferences, likes, and dislikes of organizational members.

Humor A variable a persuasive speaker should consider.

Hypothetical Example An event or incident that could possibly occur but that did not really happen.

Identification An attempt to find security by forming a psychological bond with other persons or groups.

Illustration Use of verbal examples or visual aids to help clarify information.

Illustrator Body expression that accents or adds emphasis to a word or phrase, shows the direction of thought, points to an object or place, depicts spatial relationships, rhythms, or bodily actions, or demonstrates shape.

Imitative (Learned) Behavior The belief that interaction with other human beings is necessary for language development.

Immediacy Degree of liking or disliking for a person or task.

Impromptu Speech Presentation made on the spot without any preparation.

Increased Availability of Information A phenomenon that came about with the computer age.

Increasing Levels of Difficulty Pattern Informative organizational structure used to present complex topics clearly and logically.

Inductive Pattern Persuasive structure that presents several specific cases that serve as a basis for a generalization.

Inductive Reasoning Moves from the specific to the general.

Infancy Period of language learning that occurs from birth through approximately 12 months.

Informal Communication Relaxed communication situations in which speakers are free to be themselves.

Informal Communication Structure Interpersonal relations that develop among employees in addition to the formal communication structure.

Informal Network Messages sent haphazardly within an organization (grapevine, rumor, etc.).

Initiating Relationship development stage in which conscious and unconscious judgments are made about others.

Innateness Theory Belief that evolution is responsible for the ability to produce and use language.

Innovative Messages Messages that help an organization adapt to the changing environment; associated with projects, new products or services, planning sessions, focus groups, and brainstorming sessions.

Instinctive Component Consists primarily of internal bodily functions and all other physiological processes that are capable of functioning below our level of consciousness.

Instrumental Values Guidelines for living and on which we base our daily behavior.

Insulation Isolation of contradictory feelings and/or information.

Integrating Relationship stage when two persons agree to meet each other's expectations.

Intellectual Self Intrapersonal processing center associated with mental processes.

Intensifying Relationship stage when steps are taken to strengthen the bond between two persons by asking for and reciprocating favors.

Intensity Determines which stimuli individuals will attend to when bombarded by many different ones.

Intentional Communication Occurs when messages are sent- with specific goals in mind.

Interaction The sharing and communication of ideas and emotions with oneself or others.

Interaction with Empathy Communication that involves deep understanding between the participants, feeling their pain and sharing their joy.

Interaction with Feedback Communication situation in which there is give-and-take by both participants.

Interactive Listening A series of interrelated processes including attending, perceiving, interpreting, assessing, and responding.

Interference Any factor that negatively affects communication.

Intergroup Conflict Interaction that often benefits a group by increasing goal-oriented activity and causing members to value their work more highly.

Intermediary Messenger between the source and receiver.

Internal Self-Feedback Messages picked up through bone conduction, nerve endings, or muscular movement.

Internal Stimuli Stimuli that originate from within a human's body.

Interpersonal Communication Informal, spontaneous, loosely organized exchange of messages between two or more people to achieve some goal.

Interpreting Process of understanding the meaning of a message.

Interrupting Response Response that breaks into the words and thoughts of another person.

Interview Dyadic communication situation designed to get information for employers and applicants by asking and answering questions.

Intimacy The degree to which two people can uniquely meet one another's needs.

Intimate Distance Spatial zone of interaction stretching from actual contact (touching) to 18 inches.

Intragroup Conflict Interaction that often destroys a group by reducing cohesion, decreasing productivity, and causing members to discredit their achievements.

Intrapersonal Communication The sending and receiving of messages within an individual.

Intrinsic Motivation Motivation that arises from an internal source (such as desire to learn).

Introduction of a Speech First portion of a speech, which captures the audience's attention and prepares them for the rest of the speech.

Irrelevant Response Response that does not apply to the topic being discussed.

Kinesics Study of body movement.

Labeling Identifying an object, act, or person by name so that it may be referred to in communication.

Laissez-Faire Leader Individual who offers the group no direction and gives advice only when the group asks for it.

Language Communication of thoughts and emotions by means of a structured system of symbols (words).

Language Acquisition Device Innate device in humans that helps them sort out language and understand grammatical rules.

Larynx (Voice Box) Transforms vibrations of air to produce basic voice sounds.

Lateral (Horizontal) Communication Information messages between peers at the same hierarchical level.

Leader Any person who helps the group reach its goals.

Leadership Behavior that helps the group reach its goals.

Leakage Nonverbal behavior that implies that information is being given inadvertently.

Leveling Minimizing or omitting information from a message.

Linking Function The function of communication that allows a person to interact with his or her environment.

Listener The person receiving the message.

Listener Feedback Involves verbal and nonverbal responses to a message.

Listener Preferences Preferences developed for types of information and sources and that emerge as a function of socialization and reinforcement patterns.

Listening A process that involves hearing, attention, understanding, and remembering.

Listening Energy The energy needed to make conscious choices about to whom and what we will listen during the day.

Lively Quality Selection of words that leave a lasting impression.

Locus of Control Degree to which we perceive reinforcement either as contingent upon our own efforts or actions (internal locus of control) or as a result of forces beyond our control and due to chance, fate, or some other external force (external locus of control).

Logos Rational approach to persuasion based on logic and reasoning.

Long-Term Memory Permanent storage of information for future reference.

Maintenance Rule Functional role that is concerned with the feelings and emotional behavior of the group.

Manipulation Method of dominating and controlling others, frequently through skillful use of verbal and nonverbal communications.

Mass Communication Process by which messages are transmitted rapidly and inexpensively through some mechanical device to a large, diverse audience.

Maturity Differential stages of personal growth and behavior patterns.

Memory Storage of information that a person chooses to remember.

Mentation Function The function of communication that allows humans to conceptualize, remember, plan, and evaluate.

Message A sign or symbol that has meaning for both the sender and the receiver; the information to be communicated.

Moving Component Consists of automatic and effortful processing of information and the behaviors that result.

Need for Love Human need to give and receive affection, care, and concern.

Negative Feedback Response that indicates that a receiver has misunderstood a message.

Network Interconnected channels or lines of communication used in organizations to pass information from one person to another.

Networking The process of developing and using contacts for information, advice, and moral support.

Non-Allness Korzybski's law that states that a word cannot symbolize all of a thing.

Nondirective Interview Planned interaction situation in which freedom is given to participants in terms of how they ask questions and give responses.

Non-Identity Korzybski's law that states that a word is not the thing it represents.

Nonverbal Communication Involves using symbols other than spoken or written words in the communication process.

Normative/Identification Credibility factor that arises when a source is identified with a particular group that is important to the listener.

One-Down Message A message that relinquishes control in a relationship.

One-Sided Presentation Persuasive speech approach in which the speaker presents only the side of the issue he or she supports.

One-Up Message A message that exerts control in a relationship.

Open (Public) Discussion Group meeting conducted before an audience who listens and/or participates.

Operational Definition Defining or delineating a term by establishing the means by which it can/will be measured.

Opinion Positive or negative reaction to or statement of an attitude.

Opinion Leader Receiver of information from a change agent, who then disseminates it to the general public.

Oral Communication Messages that are transmitted aloud from one person to another.

Organization Collected group of individuals constructed and reconstructed to work for goals that could not be met by individuals acting alone.

Organizational Communication Focuses on ways to analyze and improve leadership ability, develop greater responsiveness to clients, create more efficient work environments, build effective self-management teams, and optimize the flow of information within organization and with their publics.

Organized Audience Group of listeners who are directed totally toward the speaker with strict labor and authority lines.

Overt Stimuli Internal or external changes or actions received at the conscious level.

Panel Type of open discussion in which a group of well-informed people exchange ideas before an audience.

Paralanguage Variations in the voice that give clues about emotional states, sex, age, status, etc.

Participative Management Management style that includes employees in management decisions.

Passive (Partially Oriented) Audience Captive listeners who have no choice but to listen to the speaker.

Pathos Approach to persuasion that appeals to the emotions.

People-Oriented Listener Listener who is primarily concerned with how his or her listening preferences influence relationships with other people.

Perceiving Use of one or more of the basic senses to receive verbal and nonverbal messages.

Personal Distance Spatial zone of interactions from 1½ to 4 feet, used for casual interactions.

Personal Interview Interaction conducted on a one-to-one basis with a person who has information or knowledge about the topic of your speech.

Phonation Process by which air is pushed through the vocal cords, which then vibrate to produce sound.

Physical Self Self associated with instinctive component, moving component, and body concept.

Physiological Needs Human drive or need to satisfy the desire for food, water, shelter, and sex.

Physiological Processing Subconscious and conscious physiological responses to internal stimuli.

Pitch Highness or lowness of vocal tones.

Platform Situation in which the audience participates in the exchange of information.

Polarization Point at which the audience members recognize their role as listeners and accept someone else as a speaker.

Policymaking Group Makes changes or takes actions after the evaluation group offers its recommendations.

Positive Feedback Response that indicates that the receiver has understood a message.

Prejudice Preformed judgments about a person, group, or thing.

Primacy Effect Arguments presented first in a speech tend to have persuasive effect.

Primary Group (Psyche Group) Collected group of individuals who function as a support system for its members.

Private (Closed) Discussion Group meeting held without an audience to listen or participate.

Problem-Solving Group Most often a private group that follows a logical, step-by-step procedure to find solutions to problems.

Problem-Solving Pattern/Problem–Solution Method Persuasive structure of organization based on a logical, step-by-step analysis of a particular problem.

Professional Worker characterized by commitment to his or her job.

Progression Arrangement of ideas in a logical order in a speech outline.

Projection Attributing personal traits, motives, or behaviors to others.

Proxemics Study of how people react to the space around them, how they use it, and how their use of space communicates information.

Public Communication Usually a one-way process in which one person addresses a group in a lecture or public speech.

Public Distance Spatial zone of interaction from 12 to over 25 feet, used in formal addresses or lectures.

Public Relations Method of persuasion concerned with promoting an image.

Public Speaking Communication situation in which one speaker directs a message to an audience.

Qualification/Expertness Component of credibility operating when listeners perceive a source has enough training, ability, and experience to merit belief.

Quality Circle A group of persons from three to ten in number who meet periodically to suggest ways of improving work life, increasing employee commitment, implementing suggested changes, and building attitudes geared toward problem prevention.

Rapport Development and maintenance of a positive relationship with an audience throughout a speech.

Rate Speed at which words are spoken.

Rationalization Attempt to justify personal failures or inadequacies.

Reaction Formation A defense mechanism by which an individual denies personally or socially unacceptable drives by reacting in the opposite direction.

Real Example An event or incident that actually happened.

Reasoning Process of thinking by which an individual arrives at conclusions.

Recall Reconstruction of information that has been stored.

Receiver Person who attends to the message of the communication process.

Recency Effect Arguments presented near the end of a speech tend to have persuasive effect.

Reception Process by which the body receives stimuli.

Recognition Awareness of familiar information based on previous experience.

Redirecting Strategy used by listeners to help a speaker get back on track from an inappropriate or lengthy digression.

Reference Group Group that gives a person a sense of identity and help in establishing personal attitudes and a value system.

Referent Actual object as it exists in reality.

Reflecting Strategy by which listeners test their understanding of or clarify messages.

Regulation and Policy Messages Messages that take the form of policy statements, organizational procedures, agendas, schedules, orders, and control measures that ensure that the organization will function properly; associated with formal and informal rules of the organization.

Regulative Rule A rule that tells us how we should behave in a given situation.

Regulators Body movements or expressions that control verbal communication.

Regulating Function The function of communication that allows us to regulate our own and others' behaviors.

Relational Communication Theory Theory that addresses interpersonal communication by examining the dimensions of relationships.

Repeating Nonverbal behavior that conveys the same message as the verbal message.

Repetition Means by which audience learning may be increased via the presentation of material in a recurring fashion.

Repression Keeping thoughts and feelings beneath the conscious level.

Resonance Variations in voice from a thin and quiet voice to a loud and booming voice. Also, movement of air through the mouth, nose, and throat, which gives amplification and richness to the voice.

Responding The completion of the communication process by the receiver through verbal and/or nonverbal feedback.

Retrieval Bringing back into conscious awareness information that previously has been stored in the brain.

Reward Appeal Persuasion that promises listeners personal gain or profit if they believe or behave in a desired manner.

Role Behavior a person performs to meet the expectations of others in different social settings.

Safety Needs Human need to feel secure, stable, and in control.

Safety/Trustworthiness Factor related to credibility that operates when a source is believed to be telling the truth.

Selected Audience Group of people collected together for a specific purpose.

Selective Perception Screening out a large number of stimuli to permit an individual to attend to just a few.

Self-Actualization Human need to reach one's fullest potential.

Self-Concept A person's attitude about and view of the self.

Self-Disclosure Process of revealing significant aspects of the self to others.

Self-Esteem Enduring evaluation of the self.

Self-Expressive Behaviors Behaviors that emerge when we use our attitudes as a vehicle for expressing values that are important to us.

Self-Feedback Perception of a person's own nervous system via muscular movements as the person hears himself or herself speak.

Self-Fulfilling Prophecy Positive or negative experiences that color the self-concept and create expectations that influence later behavior.

Self-Reflexiveness Korzybski's law that states that a word can refer both to something in the real world and to itself.

Self-Serving Role Counterproductive role that has a negative effect on a group's emotional climate as well as on its ability to reach its goal.

Semantic (Linguistic) Stereotyping Assuming automatic relationships between linguistic styles and personal traits.

Semantics Study of relationships between word symbols and their meanings.

Sense Subjective feelings about a symbol (word).

Sensory Storage Ability to hold some information for a fraction of a second after the stimulus disappears.

Series Transmission Communication through a number of individuals who act first as receivers and then as transmitters of messages.

Sharpening Magnifying some details of a message.

Short-Term Memory Process by which data are analyzed, identified, and simplified to be conveniently stored and handled.

Situation Ethics Approach When a speaker takes the position that consideration must be given to the nature of each situation before determining the "best" or "most loving" thing to do.

Small Group Communication Process involving three or more persons with a common goal and potential for interaction between members.

Social Distance Spatial zone of interaction from 4 to 12 feet, used by people meeting for the first time or by people conducting business.

Social Facilitation Influence of one audience member on another.

Social-Oriented Listener Listener who easily listens to sources of information that are charismatic and entertaining.

Social Roles A person's duties, skills, and norms defined by ascribed and achieved roles.

Social Utility Approach When a speaker determines which programs he or she should advocate based on perceptions of a particular group's needs.

Sorting Selection of the most relevant information from the brain's storehouse of knowledge.

Source Initiator of the communication process.

Spatial Pattern Informative organizational structure based on the relation of one part to others or to geographical progressions.

Speech to Convince Speech intended to get an audience to think, believe, or feel a certain way.

Speech to Entertain Informal speech designed to bring the audience pleasure.

Speech to Inform Speech designed to increase audience learning and comprehension.

Speech to Move an Audience to Action Persuasive speech that seeks some form of action on the part of the audience.

Speech to Persuade A deliberate attempt by one person to modify the attitudes, beliefs, or behavior of another person or group of people through communication.

Speech to Stimulate Speech intended to reaffirm or strengthen preexisting beliefs or feelings.

Speech to Welcome Presentation to a group, or to an individual, about to join an organization or attend a meeting.

Stagnating Relationship disintegration stage in which all efforts to communicate are abandoned.

Statistic A numerical fact or datum.

Stimuli Elements that cause a reaction in one or more of a person's senses.

Stimulus-Response Interaction Communication situation in which the speaker proceeds in a set manner, independent of responses made by the listener.

Style Individual selection, organization, and use of language.

Substituting Using nonverbal messages to take the place of words.

Survey Detailed gathering of information by questionnaire, observation, interview, etc.

Symbol Word or nonverbal sign used to represent objects, ideas, and feelings to others.

Symbolic Process Use of words as symbols to represent objects or concepts.

Symbolization Visual form of coordination, subordination, and progression of a speech outline.

Symmetrical Relationship A relationship in which partners often mirror each others' behavior.

Symposium Form of public discussion in which a group of experts presents its views, one speaker at a time.

System A unique entity, bond, or relationship

that is created, defined, and ultimately maintained through the process of communication.

Tangential Response Response that side-tracks a conversation.

Task Messages Messages that focus on the products, services, and activities of an organization.

Task-Oriented Role Functional role that is directly related to a group's goal.

Team Rewards and Recognition Team rather than individual efforts and results will be rewarded.

Tempo Rate of speech in a given amount of time.

Terminal Values Ultimate aim(s) toward which we work.

Terminating Final relationship disintegration stage, which may be either rapid or delayed.

Territoriality Possessive desire or ownership reaction to the space and objects around us.

Testimony Information derived from a direct witness to an event or from an expert in a particular field.

Thesis Statement Sentence that presents the specific purpose of a speech.

Thinking–Speaking Time Differential Listener's time to summarize and evaluate what has been said. (People think several times faster than others can talk.)

Threshold of Consciousness Boundary between conscious and unconscious awareness of stimuli.

Toddlerhood Period of language learning that takes place between approximately 12 and 24 months of age.

Tolerance of Ambiguity Ability to accept poorly defined and unclear situations.

Topical Pattern Informative organizational structure in which information is presented according to specific category or classification.

Tracking Encouraging others to continue talking until their message is complete.

Trait Quality that distinguishes one person from another.

Transition Statement that smoothly connects one idea to the next.

Transmission Process by which messages are sent from a source to a receiver.

Trust The responsible acceptance of the control dimension in a relationship; includes both trusting and trustworthy behaviors.

Trusting An admission of dependency on the part of persons involved.

Trustworthiness Acceptance of an obligation not to exploit control in an interpersonal relationship.

Turn-Denying Cues Cues that we use when we are listening, the speaker wants us to take a turn, and we do not wish to speak at that time.

Turn-Maintaining Cues Cues that are used when we are speaking and do not wish to yield the floor to the listener.

Turn-Requesting Cues Cues that are used when we want to take a conversational turn.

Turn-Yielding Cues Cues that tell the listener that we no longer wish to speak for the moment and want him or her to take a conversational turn.

Two-Sided Presentation Persuasive speech approach in which the speaker presents both sides of an issue.

Unintentional Communication Messages (usually nonverbal) that are sent without communicators being aware of them.

Unity Principle Need that humans have to maintain a unified conceptual system.

Upward Communication Information messages directed to superiors or those of higher status within an organization.

Vagueness Caused by the relative meaning of words that need more precision in usage.

Values Specific types of beliefs that form the core of our belief system.

Variable Compensation Idea that compensation for work will take the form of base pay, with few or no automatic annual increases, but more bonuses or incentive increases.

Verbal Communication Involves the use of symbols that have universal meanings for all involved in the communication process.

Visual Aid Anything (other than the speaker) that is used to get a message across to an audience.

Vocal Delivery Mechanics of vocalization, vocal characteristics, and pronunciation.

Vocal Quality Timbre of voice, which distinguishes one voice from another.

Voice Sounds or tones produced through phonation.

Volume Intensity or loudness of speech sounds.

Wheel Network Two-way communication network with all communication directed to and from a centralized position.

Word Structured system of symbols that when joined with other words create language.

Written Communication Primarily verbal messages conveyed in writing.

Y Network Communication network in which the central position does not communicate with one of the members.

Bibliography

AJZEN, I. (1989). Attitude structure and behavior. In A. R. Pratkanis, S. J. Breckler, and A. G. Greenwald, eds., *Attitude structure and function.* Hillsdale, N.J.: Lawrence Erlbaum Associates, 241–274.

ANDERSEN, K. E. (1989). The politics of ethics and the ethics of politics. *American Behavioral Scientist, 32*(4), 479–92.

ANDERSON, V. A. (1977). *Training the speaking voice* (3d ed.). New York: Oxford University Press.

ATKIN, C. (1983). Effects of realistic TV violence vs. fictional violence on aggression. *Journalism Quarterly, 60*(4), 615–21.

ATKINS, C. P. (1988). Perceptions of speakers with minimal eye contact: Implications for stutterers. *Journal of Fluency Disorders, 13,* 429–36.

BALES, R. F. (1970). *Personality and interpersonal behavior.* New York: Holt, Rinehart & Winston.

BALES, R. F., & COHEN, S. P. (1979). *SYMLOG: A system for the multiple level observation of groups.* New York: The Free Press.

BARKER, D. R., BARKER, L. L., & FITCH HAUSER, M. (1988). Origins, evolution, and development of a systems-based model of intrapersonal processes: A holistic view of man as information processor. In B. D. Ruben, ed., *Information and behavior,* vol. 2. New Brunswick, N.J.: Transaction, Inc.

BARKER, L. L., JOHNSON, P. M., & WATSON, K. W. (1991). The role of listening in managing interpersonal and group conflict. In *Listening in everyday life.* Ed. D. Borisoff and M. Purdy. New York: University Press of America, 139–62.

BARKER, L. L., WAHLERS, K. J., WATSON, K. W., & KIBLER, R. J. (1991). *Groups in process: An introduction to small group communication* (4th ed.). Englewood Cliffs, N.J.: Prentice Hall.

BAROL, B. (5 August 1985). He's on fire. *Newsweek,* 48–54.

BAXTER, J. S., MANSTEAD, A. S. R., STRADLING, S. G., CAMPBELL, K. A., REASON, J. T., & PARKER, D. (1990). Social facilitation and driver behavior. *British Journal of Psychology, 81,* 351–60.

BEATTY, M. J., BALFANTZ, G. L., & KUWABARA, A. Y. (1989). Trait-like qualities of selected variables assumed to be transient causes of performance state anxiety. *Communication Education, 38,* 277–89.

BEHNKE, R. R., SAWYER, C. R., & KING, P. E. (1987). The communication of public speaking anxiety. *Communication Education, 36,* 139.

BIBEN, M., SYMMES, D., & BERNHARDS, D. (1989). Contour variables in vocal communication between squirrel monkey mothers and infants. *Developmental Psychobiology, 22*(6), 617–31.

BIGGART, N. W., & HAMILTON, G. G. (1987). An

institutional theory of leadership. *The Journal of Applied Behavioral Science, 23*(4), 429–40.

BLACK, J. (1970). *How to get results from interviewing.* New York: McGraw-Hill.

BODAKEN, E. M., LASHBROOK, W. B., & CHAMPAGNE, M. (1971). Proana 5: A computerized technique for the analysis of small group interaction. *Western Speech, 25,* 112–15.

BOHANNON, J. N. III, MacWHINNEY, B., & SNOW, C. (1990). No negative evidence revisited: Beyond learnability or who has to prove what to whom. *Developmental Psychology, 26*(2), 221–26.

BOOTH-BUTTERFIELD, S. (1988). Instructional interventions for reducing situational anxiety and avoidance. *Communication Education, 37,* 214–23.

BOSTROM, R. N. (1983). *Persuasion.* Englewood Cliffs, N.J.: Prentice Hall.

BOYETT, J. H., & CONN, H. P. (1991). *Workplace 2000.* New York: Dutton.

BRADLEY, B. E. (1988). *Fundamentals of speech communication: The credibility of ideas* (5th ed.). Dubuque, Iowa: Wm. C. Brown.

BRILHART, J. K. (1986). *Effective group discussion.* Dubuque, Iowa: Wm. C. Brown.

BRILHART, J. K., BOURHIS, J. S., MILEY, B. R., & BERQUIST, C. A. (1992). *Practical public speaking.* New York: HarperCollins.

BRODER, S. N. (1987). Helping students with self-disclosure. *School Counselor, 34*(3), 182–87.

BURGOON, J. K., BIRK, T., & PFAU, M. (1990). Nonverbal behaviors, persuasion, and credibility. *Human Communication Research, 17*(1), 140–69.

CALTABIANO, M. L., & SMITHSON, M. (1983). Variables affecting the perception of self-disclosure appropriateness. *Journal of Social Psychology, 120,* 119–28.

CANARY, D. J., CUNNINGHAM, E. M., & CODY, M. J. (1988). Goal types, gender, and locus of control in managing interpersonal conflict. *Communication Research, 15*(4), 426–46.

CASPY, T., PELEG, E., SCHLAM, D., & GOLDBERG, J. (1988). Sedative and stimulative music effects: Differential effects on performance impairment following frustration. *Motivation and Emotion, 12*(2), 123–38.

CELANO, J., & SALZMAN, J. (1988). *Career-tracking:*
26 success shortcuts to the top. New York: Simon & Schuster.

CHANEY, R. H., GIVENS, C. A., AOKI, M. F., & GOMBINER, M. L. (1989). Pupillary responses in recognizing awareness in persons with profound mental retardation. *Perceptual and Motor Skills, 69,* 523–28.

CHENGHUAN, W., & SHAFFER, D. R. (1987). Susceptibility to persuasive appeals as a function of source credibility and prior experience with the attitude object. *Journal of Personality and Social Psychology, 52*(4), 677–88.

CHRISTEN, Y. (1991). *Sex differences: Modern biology and the unisex fallacy.* New Brunswick, N.J.: Transaction Publishers.

CLARK, A. J. (1974). An exploratory study of order effect in persuasive communication. *Southern Speech Communication Journal, 39,* 322–32.

CUMMINGS, H. W., LONG, L., & LEWIS, M. (1987). *Managing communication in organizations: An introduction* (2d ed). Dubuque, Iowa: Gorsuch-Scarisbrick.

DAMHORST, M. L., & PINAIRE REED, J. A. (1986). Clothing color value and facial expression: Effects on evaluations of female job applicants. *Social Behavior and Personality, 14*(1), 89–98.

DANCE, F. E. X., & LARSON, C. (1976). *The functions of human communication.* New York: Holt, Rinehart & Winston.

DEWEY, J. (1933). *How we think.* Boston: Heath.

DEWINE, S., & CASBOLT, D. (1983). Networking: External communication systems for female organizational members. *The Journal of Business Communication, 20*(2), 57–67.

EKMAN, P. (1988). Lying and nonverbal behavior: Theoretical issues and new findings. *Journal of Nonverbal Behavior, 12*(3), 163–75.

EKMAN, P., & FRIESEN, W. V. (1969). The repertoire of non-verbal behavior: Categories, origins, usage, and coding. *Semiotica, 1*(1), 49–98.

EKMAN, P., & FRIESEN, W. V. (1975). *Unmasking the face.* Englewood Cliffs, N.J.: Prentice Hall.

ELSEA, J. G. (1985). Strategies for effective presentations. *Personnel Journal, 64,* 9, 31–32.

FELDMAN, D. C. (1984). The development and enforcement of group norms. *Academy of Management Review, 9,* 47–53.

FIELD, H. S., & HOLLEY, W. H. (1976). Résumé preparation: An empirical study of personnel managers' perceptions. *The Vocational Guidance Quarterly* (March), 234.

FISHER, B. A. (1980). *Small group decision making: Communication and the group process* (2d ed.). New York: McGraw-Hill.

FUKADA, H. (1986). Psychological processes mediating persuasion-inhibiting effect of forewarning in fear-arousing communication. *Psychological Reports, 58*, 87–90.

GALST, J. P. (1980). Television food commercials and pro-nutritional public service announcements as determinants of young children's snack choices. *Child Development, 51*, 935–38.

GAMBLE, T. K., & GAMBLE, M. (1982). *Contacts: Communicating interpersonally.* New York: Random House.

GELLES-COLE, S. (ED.). (1985). *Letitia Baldrige's complete guide to executive manners.* New York: Rawson Associates.

GIAMMATEO, M., & GIAMMATEO, D. (1981). *Forces on leadership.* Reston, Va.: National Association of Secondary School Principals.

GOLDHABER, G. M. (1990). *Organizational communication* (5th ed.). Dubuque, Iowa: Wm. C. Brown.

HAGAFORS, R., & BREHMER, B. (1983). Does having to justify one's judgments change the nature of the judgment process? *Organizational Behavior and Human Performance, 31*, 223–32.

HAN, PYUNG. (1983). The informal organization you've got to live with. *Supervisory Management, 28*, 25–28.

HASKINS, J. B., & MILLER, M. M. (1984). The effects of bad news and good news on a newspaper's image. *Journalism Quarterly, 61*(1), 3–13, 65.

HAZLETON, V., CUPACH, W. R., & LISKA, J. (1986). Message style: An investigation of the perceived characteristics of persuasive messages. *Journal of Social Behavior and Personality, 1*(4), 565–74.

HESS, H. (1965). Attitude and pupil size. *Scientific American, 212*(4), 54.

HOLLIMAN, W. B., & ANDERSON, H. N. (1986). Proximity and student density as ecological variables in a college classroom. *Teaching of Psychology, 13*(4), 200–203.

HOLLINGWORTH, H. L. (1935). *The psychology of the audience.* New York: American Book.

HOMER, P. M., & KAHLE, L. R. (1988). A structural equation test of the value-attitude-behavior hierarchy. *Journal of Personality and Social Psychology, 54*(4), 638–46.

HORNSTEIN, G. A., & TRUESDELL, S. E. (1988). Development of intimate conversation in close relationships. *Journal of Social and Clinical Psychology, 7*(1), 49–64.

JANIS, I. L. (1982). *Victims of groupthink: A psychological study of foreign policy decisions and fiascos* (2d ed.). Boston: Houghton Mifflin.

KEREK, G. M. (1987). Can functions be measured? A new perspective on the functional approach to attitudes. *Social Psychology Quarterly, 50*(4), 285–303.

KIPNIS, D., SCHMIDT, S., PRICE, K., & STITT, C. (1981). Why do I like thee: Is it your performance or my orders? *Journal of Applied Psychology, 66*, 328.

KLEINKE, C. L. (1986). Gaze and eye contact: A research review. *Psychological Bulletin, 100*(1), 78–100.

KNAPP, M. L. (1984). *Interpersonal communication and human relationships.* Boston: Allyn & Bacon.

KORNBLUM, A. (December 1984). Stage fright in the executive suite. *Nation's Business, 72*, 56.

KRANTZ, J. (1990). Lessons from the field: An essay on the crisis of leadership in contemporary organizations. *The Journal of Applied Behavioral Science, 26*(1), 49–64.

KUBEY, R. W., & PELUSO, T. (1990). Emotional response as a cause of interpersonal news diffusion: The case of the space shuttle tragedy. *Journal of Broadcasting & Electronic Media, 34*(1), 69–76.

LAZOWSKI, L. E., & ANDERSEN, S. M. (1990). Self-disclosure and social perception: The impact of private, negative, and extreme communications. *Journal of Social Behavior and Personality, 5*(2), 131–54.

LEEDS, D. (1988). *PowerSpeak: The complete guide to persuasive public speaking and presenting.* New York: Prentice Hall Press.

LEWIN, K. (1947). Frontiers in group dynamics. *Human Relations, 1*, 5–41.

LITTLEJOHN, S. W. (1989). *Theories of human communication* (3d ed.). Belmont, Calif.: Wadsworth.

LUFT, J. (1984). *Group processes: Introduction to*

group dynamics (3d ed.). Palo Alto, Calif.: Mayfield Publishing Co.

LUFT, J. (1984). *Of human interaction.* Palo Alto, Calif.: National Press Books.

LYNN, R., HAMPSON, S., & AGAHI, E. (1989). Television violence and aggression: A genotype-environment, correlation and interaction theory. *Social Behavior and Personality, 17*(2), 143–64.

MAASS, A., SALVI, D., ARCURI, L., & SEMIN, G. (1989). Language use in intergroup contexts: The linguistic intergroup bias. *Journal of Personality and Social Psychology, 57*(6), 981–93.

MACLACHLAN, J. (1983–84). Making a message memorable and persuasive. *Journal of Advertising Research, 23*(6) 51–59.

MCCLELLAND, V. (1987). Mixed signals breed mistrust. *Personnel Journal, 66*(3), 26.

MARQUES, J. M., & YZERBYT, V. Y. (1988). The black sheep effect: Judgmental extremity towards ingroup members in inter- and intra-group situations. *European Journal of Social Psychology, 18,* 287–92.

MASLOW, A. H. (1970). *Motivation and personality* (2d ed.). New York: Harper & Row.

MASLOW, A. H., & MINTZ, N. L. (1956). Effects of esthetic surroundings. I. Initial effects of three esthetic conditions upon perceiving "energy" and "well-being" in faces. *Journal of Psychology, 41,* 247–54.

MATTHIESSEN, P. (1991). *In the spirit of Crazy Horse.* New York: Viking.

MEHRABIAN, A. (1981). *Silent messages* (2d ed.). Belmont, Calif.: Wadsworth.

MENDELSOHN, H. (1989). Socio-psychological construction and the mass communication effects dialectic. *Communication Research, 16*(6), 813–23.

MILLAR, F. E., & ROGERS, L. E. (1976). A relational approach to interpersonal communication. In G. Miller (ed.), *Explorations in interpersonal communication.* Beverly Hills, Calif.: Sage.

MILLARD, R. J., & STIMPSON, D. V. (1980). Enjoyment and productivity as a function of classroom seating location. *Perceptual Motor Skills, 50,* 439–44.

MOLLOY, J. T. (1985). *Molloy's live for success.* New York: Bantam Books.

MULAC, A., WIEMANN, J. M., WIDENMANN, S. J., & GIBSON, T. W. (1988). Male/female language

differences and effects in same-sex and mixed-sex dyads: The gender-linked language effect. *Communication Monographs, 55*(4), 315–35.

NASH, L. L. (1990). Ethics without the sermon. In W. M. Hoffman and J. M. Moore, *Business ethics: Readings and cases in corporate morality* (2d ed.). New York: McGraw-Hill.

NEIMEYER, R. A., & MITCHELL, K. A. (1988). Similarity and attraction: A longitudinal study. *Journal of Social and Personal Relationships, 5,* 131–48.

NICOLL, M. (1984). *Psychological commentaries on the teachings of Gurdjieff & Ouspensky,* vol. 3. Boulder, Colo.: Shambhala.

NIIT, T., & VALSINER, J. (1977). Recognition of facial expressions: An experimental investigation of Ekman's model. *Tartu Riikliku Ulikooli Toimetised: Trudy po Psikhologii, 429,* 85–107.

NORRIS, P. (1986). Biofeedback, voluntary control, and human potential. *Biofeedback and Self-Regulation, 11*(1), 1–19.

OUSPENSKY, P. D. (1974). *The psychology of man's possible evolution* (2d ed.). New York: Vintage Books.

PEARCE, W. B., & CONKLIN, F. (1971). Nonverbal vocalic communication and perceptions of a speaker. *Speech Monographs, 38,* 235–41.

PEARCE, W. B., & CRONEN, V. (1980). *Communication, action, and meaning.* New York: Praeger.

PEARL, D. (1984). Violence and aggression. *Society, 21,* 17–22.

PEMBER, D. R. (1983). *Mass media in America* (3d ed.). Chicago: Science Research Associates.

PIERCE, W. D. (1987). Which Coke is it? Social influence in the marketplace. *Psychological Reports, 60,* 279–86.

PRIZANT, B. M., & WETHERBY, A. M. (1990). Toward an integrated view of early language and communication development and socioemotional development. *Topics in Language Disorders, 10*(4), 1–16.

ROBBERSON, M. R., & ROGERS, R. W. (1988). Beyond fear appeals: Negative and positive persuasive appeals to health and self-esteem. *Journal of Applied Social Psychology, 18*(3), 277–87.

RODDY, B. L., & GARRAMONE, G. M. (1988). Appeals and strategies of negative political advertising. *Journal of Broadcasting & Electronic Media, 32*(4), 415–27.

ROSENKOETTER, L. I., HUSTON, A. C., & WRIGHT, J. C. (1990). Television and the moral judgment of the young child. *Journal of Applied Developmental Psychology, 11*, 123–37.

RULE, B. G., & FERGUSON, T. J. (1986). The effects of media violence on attitudes, emotions, and cognitions. *Journal of Social Issues, 42*(3), 29–50.

SALTER, C. A., & SALTER, C. D. (1982). Automobile color as a predictor of driving behavior. *Perceptual and Motor Skills, 55*, 383–86.

SCHEIN, V. E. (1985). Organizational realities: The politics of change. *Training and Development Journal, 39*, 37–41.

SCHULTZ, B., & ANDERSON, J. (1984). Training in the management of conflict: A communication theory perspective. *Small Group Behavior, 15*, 333–48.

SELLERS, D. E., & STACKS, D. W. (1990). Toward a hemispheric processing approach to communication competence. *Journal of Social Behavior and Personality, 5*(2), 45–59.

SMELTZER, L. R., & WATSON, K. W. (1986). Gender differences in verbal communication during negotiations. *Communication Research Reports*, 74–79.

SMITH, A. P. (1977). How to make sure your next résumé isn't an obituary. *Training* (May), 63–66.

SPARKS, G. G. (1986). Developmental differences in children's reports of fear induced by the mass media. *Child Study Journal, 16*(1), 55.

STANAT, K. W., & REARDON, P. (1977). *Job hunting secrets and tactics*. Milwaukee: Westwind Press.

STEELE, B. H., RUE, P., CLEMENT, L., & ZAMOSTNY, K. (1987). Quality circles: A corporate strategy applied in a student services setting. *Journal of College Student Personnel, 28*(2), 146–51.

STEIL, L. K., BARKER, L. L., & WATSON, K. W. (1983). *Effective listening: Key to your success.* Reading, Mass.: Addison-Wesley.

STEWART, C. J., & CASH, W. B. (1983). *Interviewing: Principles and practices* (3d ed.). Dubuque, Iowa: Wm. C. Brown.

SYPHER, B. D., & ZORN, T. E., JR. (1986). Communication-related abilities and upward mobility: A longitudinal investigation. *Human Communication Research, 12*(3), 420–31.

TAYLOR, M. S., & WALTHER, F. T. (1981). *The relationship of feedback dimensions to work attitudes and behavior: Process and practical implications.* Paper presented at the meeting of the Midwestern Academy of Management.

TESSER, A., & SHAFFER, D. R. (1990). Attitudes and attitude change. *Annual Review of Psychology, 41*, 479–523.

TOFFLER, A. (1981). *The new wave.* New York: Bantam Books.

VERDERBER, R. F. (1987). *Communicate.* Belmont, Calif.: Wadsworth.

WALLACH, G. (1990). Magic buries Celtics: Looking for a broader interpretation of language learning and literacy. *Topics in Language Disorders, 10*(2), 63–80.

WALTHER, F., & TAYLOR, S. (1983). An active feedback program can spark performance. *Personnel Administrator, 28*, 107, 109, 111, 147, 149.

WASS, H., RAUP, J. L., & SISLER, H. H. (1989). Adolescents and death on television: A follow-up study. *Death Studies, 13*, 161–73.

WATSON, K. W., & BARKER, L. L. (1990). *Interpersonal and relational communication.* Scottsdale, Ariz.: Gorsuch-Scarisbrick.

WATSON, K. W., & BARKER, L. L. (1991). *Presentation skills manual: A guide to effective oral presentations.* New Orleans, La.: Spectra, Inc.

WATSON, K. W., & BARKER, L. L. (1992). *Personal listening preference profile.* New Orleans, La.: Spectra, Inc.

WHAT TV DOES TO KIDS. (21 February 1977). *Newsweek*, 63–70.

WHETMORE, E. J. (1991). *Mediamerica* (4th ed.). Belmont, Calif.: Wadsworth.

Photo Credits

Chapter 1: Laima Druskis, xiv, Grant Le Duc/ Monkmeyer Press, 8; Robin Platzer/Images, 17 (left); John Schultz/Reuters/Bettmann, 17 (right); Mark Antman/The Image Works, 19. **Chapter 2:** Rhoda Sidney, 25; Shirley Zeiberg, 29; Ken Karp, 33, 42. **Chapter 3:** Joseph Schuyler/Stock, Boston, 49; Marc P. Anderson, 52; Ken Karp, 59; Larry Murphy/University of Texas at Austin, 70. **Chapter 4:** Arlene Collins/ Monkmeyer Press, 79; Laima Druskis, 86, 91, 97; George Bellrose/Stock, Boston, 92; United Nations, 96; Harriet Gans/The Image Works, 98; Marc P. Anderson, 100; Hugh Rogers/ Monkmeyer Press, 103; George Dole, 106. **Chapter 5:** Rhoda Sidney, 119; Jim Whitmer/ Stock, Boston, 122; Rhoda Sidney/Monkmeyer Press, 127; Laima Druskis, 129; University of Miami, Coral Gables, Florida, 130; Owen Franken/Stock, Boston, 131; George Dole, 137. **Chapter 6:** Miro Vintoniv/Stock, Boston, 148; Spencer Grant/Monkmeyer Press, 157; Barbara Alper/Stock, Boston, 161; Ken Karp, 164 (top three), 165; Steve & Mary Skjols/The Image Works, 164 (bottom left); AFL-CIO News, 164 (bottom right); Ray Ellis/Photo Researchers, 165 (top); Rick Kopstein/Monkmeyer Press, 165 (middle); Laima Druskis, 165 (bottom left and right); Elizabeth Crews/Stock, Boston, 169. **Chapter 7:** Rhoda Sidney, 184; Arend Van Dam, 186; United Nations, 190; Marc P. Ander-son, 205; NASA, 209. **Chapter 8:** Spencer Grant/Monkmeyer Press, 227; Laima Druskis, 230; NCR/Visual Resources, 235; Ken Karp, 240; David E. Dempster/Allyn & Bacon, 244; Jeffey Myers/Stock, Boston, 246; A.T.&T. Company Phone Center, 247, 248. **Chapter 9:** Michael Sargent/The White House, 253; Reuters/Bettman, 256, 259, 270; Michael Kagan/ Monkmeyer Press, 266; Ken Karp, 267; Lois Zenkel/Monkmeyer Press, 275; Stan Wakefield, 278; Mark Antman/The Image Works, 280. **Chapter 10:** Reuters/Bettmann, 289, 292; UPI/ Bettmann, 297, 299; New York Public Library Picture Collection, 301; AP/Wide World, 313. **Chapter 11:** Hewlett-Packard, 321; Laima Druskis, 327, 342; Mark & Evelyn Bonheim/ Woodfin Camp & Assoc., 328; UPI/Bettmann Newsphotos, 333; Rhoda Sidney, 335; Ken Karp, 353. **Chapter 12:** UPI/Bettman, 357; Thomas Hopker/Woodfin Camp & Assoc., 363; UPI/Bettmann, 368 (top and bottom left); AP/ Wide World, 368 (top right); Martin Benjamin/ The Image Works, 368 (bottom right); Laima Druskis, 369 (top left); AP/Wide World, 369 (top right); Beringer/Dratch/The Image Works, 369 (bottom left); UPI/Bettmann, 369 (bottom right). **Chapter 13:** Paul Conklin/Monkmeyer Press, 385; RCA, 388; Bob Daemmrich/Stock, Boston, 404, 407; Alan Carey/The Image Works, 409; Viewtron, 412.

463

Index

A

Abstract words, 34
Accenting, 83
Acceptance speech, 313
Accountability in outlines, 344–45
Accuracy of language, 378
Achieved roles, 238
Action-oriented listeners, 60
Active listener, 189–90
Adolescents, 124–28
Advertisers, influence of, 391
Advertising, 260, 311–12, 398
  employment, 427–28
Affect displays, 91
After-dinner speech, 313–14
Agahi, E., 402
Agenda, decision-making, 204–7
Ages of audience, 265
Aggression in children, 401–2
Aggressor, 191
AIDS, 306, 323
Ajzen, I., 304
Alcoholics Anonymous, 214, 277
Alice's Adventures in Wonderland
    (Carroll), 36
All-channel network, 213
Alternating monologue, 168–69
Ambiguity, 34
  tolerance of, 140
Ambiguous feedback, 13
American politics, 257
Amish people, 40
Analyzer, 189
Andersen, K.E., 403

Andersen, S.M., 156
Anderson, V.A., 372
Anderson, H.N., 102
Anderson, J., 210
Anecdotes, 347
Animal communication, 9–10
Aoki, M.F., 88
Appeal
  fear-arousing, 298–99
  reward, 298
Appearance, personal, 93–94
Appraisal interviews, 244
Appropriateness of language, 379
Architecture, 104–5
Arcuri, L., 39
Arguments
  one-sided vs. two-sided, 307
  primacy and recency in, 309–10
Aristotelian theories of persuasion,
      296–303
    ethos (source credibility), 257, 262,
      271, 299, 301–3, 358
    logos (reasoning), 262, 296–98, 299
    pathos (feeling), 262, 298–300
Aristotle, 255, 264, 296
Articulation, 372–73, 376
Ascribed roles, 128
Assessing level of listening, 54–55
Assimilation, 135, 238
Atkin, C., 401–2
Atkins, C.P., 371
Attending level of listening, 53–54
Attention
  faking of, 61–62
  sustaining, 291–92

Attitude(s), 138
    of audience, 270–73
    functions of, 305–7
    as predictors of behavior, 304
    about speeches, 362
    structure of, 303–4
Attraction, interpersonal, 160–61
Audience
    information exchange and,
        290–95
    interaction with speaker, 279–80
    methods of investigating, 273–74
    moving to action, 295
    size of, 277, 278–79
    speech delivery and, 363
    types of, 263–64, 274–78
        casual, 275
        concerted, 277
        organized, 278
        passive, 275–76
        selected, 276–77
Audience analysis, 263–73
    audience attitudes, 270–73
    checklist for, 281–82
    demographic analysis, 265–69
    psychological variables, 269
Authoritarian leaders, 196, 197
Authority, conformity and, 211
Automatic behaviors, 121
Avoiding stage of relationship
        disintegration, 166–67
Award presentation speech, 313
Awareness, intrapersonal
        communication and, 124–25

B

Bailey, F.L., 9
Baldrige, L., 80, 94
Bales, R.F., 214
Balfantz, G.L., 359
Barker, D.R., 121
Barker, L.L., 60, 64, 66, 121, 150, 181,
        281, 294
Barriers to communication, 14
Baxter, J.S., 280
Beatty, M.J., 359
Behavior(s)
    attitudes as predictors of, 304
    automatic, 121
    imitative, 29
    language and, 38–43
        linguistic stereotyping, 40–41
    learned, 29
    repetitious, 123
    voting, 399

Behnke, R.R., 360
Beliefs, 139, 269
Benefits of effective listening, 57–59
Berg, P., 230–31
Bernhards, D., 10
Biden, M., 10
Biggart, N.W., 196
Biofeedback, 136
Birdwhistell, R., 89
Birk, T., 370
Birmingham, S., 365
Black, J., 120, 418
"Black sheep" effect, 270
Blocker, 191
Bodaken, E.M., 214
Body image, 122
Body manipulators, 91–92
Body movements, 89–93, 366–67
Body of speech, 332–33
    arrangement of, 336–41
        for informative speeches, 336–38
        for persuasive speeches, 338–41
Bohannon, J.N., III, 30
Bolles, R., 427
Bonding
    of group members, 208
    during relationship development, 163
Booth-Butterfield, S., 362
Bostrom, R.N., 302
Bourhis, J.S., 310
Boyett, J.H., 229, 231, 232
Bradley, B.E., 257, 258, 259, 260
Brain wave activity, 135–36
Brehmer, B., 68
Brilhart, J.K., 201–3, 310
Broder, S.N., 156–57
Bulwer-Lytton, E., 121
Burgoon, J.K., 370
Bush, G., 280, 403
Business conferences, 246–47
Business teams, 231–32, 277
Bypassing, 186

C

Caltabiano, M.L., 157
Campaigns, political, 397, 403–4
Campbell, K.A., 280
Canary, D.J., 140
Carlyle, T., 155
Carlzon, J., 229
Carroll, L., 36
Carter, J., 364
Casbolt, D., 242
Cash, W.B., 243
Caspy, T., 107

Casual audiences, 275
Cause-and-effect speech pattern,
    340–41
Celano, J., 184–86
Ceremonial communication, 312–14
Chain network, 213
Chain-of-events speech pattern, 338
Challenger space shuttle disaster,
    55, 396
Champagne, M., 214
Chaney, R.H., 88
Change agent, 396
Channels of communication, 12–13,
    236–38
Chenghuan, W., 301
Childhood, early, 32
Children and television, 399–403,
    434–39
Chomsky, N., 29–30
Christen, Y., 268
Chronological speech pattern, 337, 342
Circle network, 212
Circular response, 280
Circumscribing stage of relationship
    disintegration, 166
"Civil War, The" (serial drama), 387
Clarification, 346–48
Clarity of language, 379
Clark, A.J., 310
Classrooms
    information exchange in, 295
    seating arrangements in, 100–103
Clement, L., 182
Clemons, C., 366
Climate, informative vs. persuasive
    communication and, 295–96
Closed discussion groups, 181
Clothing, 94–95
Coca-Cola Company, 302
Cody, M.J., 140
Cognitive processing, 134–35
Cohen, S.P., 214
Cohesion of small groups, 207–9
Coke Classic, 302
Cold calls, 429
Colors, 105–6
Commercials, 398, 402–3
Communication, 1–23
    animal, 9–10
    contexts of, 14–20
    defining, 3–4
    formal, 7–8
    human-computer, 6, 9
    informal, 8
    intentional, 8
    process elements of, 10–16
        barriers, 14
        channels, 12–13

context or situation, 14–15
    feedback, 13–14
    message, 12
    receiver/decoder, 13
    source/encoder, 11
    system, 15–16
reasons for studying, 2–4
unintentional, 9
verbal, 5–6
written, 6–7
Communication apprehension,
    359–62
Communication Inventory, 3, 4–5
Communication skills, 198
*Company Manners: An Insider Tells
    How to Succeed in the Real
    World of Corporate Protocol and
    Power Politics* (Wyse), 26
Comparison, clarification through,
    347–48
Compensation, variable, 232
Competer, 191
Complementary relationships, 152
Complementing, 82
Compliance, source credibility and, 303
Compromiser, 190
Computer-human communication, 6, 9
Computers, 411–12
Concerted audiences, 277
Conclusions, 310–11, 334–35
Concrete words, 34
Conferences, business, 246–47
Conferencing, computer, 411–12
Conflict
    in decision-making group, 209–10
    intergroup, 209
    interpersonal, management of,
        170–71
    intragroup, 209–10
    personality, 207
Conformity in decision-making group,
    210–12
Conklin, F., 110
Conn, H.P., 229, 231, 232
Connotation, 35
Consciousness, threshold of, 133
Conservation, energy, 50–51
Consonants, 372–73
Constitutive rules, 154
Content, public speaking and, 256
Content-oriented listeners, 60
Context, 14–20
    matching delivery and, 362–63
    nonverbal communication and,
        108–9
Contingency theory, 196
Contrast, clarification through,
    347–48

Control, locus of, 139–40
Control dimension of interpersonal
    relationships, 152
Coordinated management of meaning
    theory (CMM), 150, 153–55
Corporate etiquette, 80
Cosby, B., 302
Costs of ineffective listening, 56–57
Courtroom, 311
Covert stimuli, 133
Creativity
    of children, 400–401
    organizational, 229–30
Credibility, source (ethos), 257, 262,
    271, 299, 301–3, 358
Credibility-centered approach, 259–60
Crisis, conformity and degree of, 212
Cronen, V., 153–54, 155
C-SPAN cable channel, 406
Cues
    deception, 84
    regulating, 83
    social, 159
Cultural background, audience
    analysis and, 268–69
Cummings, H.W., 209
Cunningham, E.M., 140
Cupach, W.R., 291

D

Damhorst, M.L., 95
Dampening, 65–66
Dance, F.E.X., 151
Darwin, C., 86, 93
Debates, presidential, 390
Deceiving, 84–85
Decision-making groups, 199–213
    decision-making agenda, 204–7
    factors affecting performance of,
        207–13
        cohesion, 207–9
        communication networks, 212–13
        conflict, 210–12
        personality, 207
    kinds of topics or problems, 199–201
    reflective thinking in, 203–4
    research for discussion, 201–3
Decoder, 13
Deductive reasoning, 296–97
Deductive speech pattern, 339–40
Defense mechanisms, 141–42
Defensive function of attitudes, 305–6
Defensiveness, gestures of, 93
Definitions, clarification through,
    347–48
Delayed feedback, 388

Delivery, public speaking and, 256
Demassification, 410–12
Democratic leaders, 196, 197
Demographic analysis, 265–69
Denotation, 35
Description, 347
Desires, persuasion and, 300
Development of language, 28–32
    process of, 30–32
    theories of, 28–30
Dewey, J., 203–4
DeWine, S., 242
Diaphragm, 376
Dickinson, E., 141
Differentiating stage of relationship
    disintegration, 166
Difficulty, speech pattern of
    increasing, 338
Diffusion of information, 396–97
Digging, 65
Directive interview, 245
Director, television, 408
Discussion group, 181–83
Disintegration of relationship, 163–67
Displays, affect, 91
Distortion of messages, 238
Distractions in listening
    environment, 61
DNA recombinations, 230
Dodgson, C.L., 36
Dogmatism, 140
Dolphins, 10
Dominance, eye behavior and, 89
Downward communication,
    238–39, 240
Duchenne's smile, 84
Dukakis, M., 403
Durham, L., 422
Dyadic relationships. *See* Interpersonal
    communication
Dynamism, source credibility and, 303

E

Early childhood, 32
Economic gatekeeping, 390–91
Economy of language, 379
Education
    of audience, 265–66
    pronunciation and, 377
Effortful processing, 121–22
Ekman, P., 84, 86, 89
Electronic Information Exchange
    Service, 411–12
Electronic media, 329
Elsea, J.G., 85, 263–64, 271
Emblems, 90

Emergency, conformity and degree of, 212
Emerson, R.W., 158
Emotional appeal, 262
Emotional processing, 135
Emotional self, 122–23
Emotions revealed by facial expressions, 86–87
Empathy, 168, 169
Employment agencies, 428–29
Employment interview, 243–44
Encoder, 11
Ends-justify-the-means approach, 258
Energy, listening, 50–51
Entertainment, 262
   as goal of communication, 312–14
   from mass communication, 397
Environment
   informative vs. persuasive communication and, 295–96
   nonverbal communication and, 103, 104–8
     architecture and objects, 104–5
     colors, 105–6
     music, 107–8
     time, 106–7
   public communication and, 278–79
   voice quality and, 375
Equality, skills in, 198
Equal time rule, 390
Esteem needs, 131
Ethics, 257–61
   credibility-centered approach to, 259–60
   defined, 257
   ends-justify-the-means approach to, 258
   situation ethics, 258–59
   social utility approach, 258
Ethos (source credibility), 257, 262, 271, 299, 301–3, 358
Etiquette, corporate, 80
Eulogy, 314
Evaluation group, 182
Events, shaping of, 405
Evidence, use of, 308
Examples
   clarification through, 346–47
   as form of support, 348–49
Exchange of information, 261–62, 290–95
Exercises, voice, 375
Exit interviews, 244
Expediter, 189
Experience, self-concept and, 126–27
Experiential-schematic function of attitudes, 305

Experimenting stage of relationship development, 162
Expertness, source credibility and, 302
Expert testimony, 350
Extended example, 347
External self-feedback, 136
External stimuli, 132–33
Extrinsic motivation, 291
Eye behavior, 87–89
   eye contact, 88, 160, 365–66, 371

F

Face-to-face interaction, 181
Facial expressions, 85–87, 370
Facilitation, social, 280
Fact(s)
   concentrating on easy-to-remember, 63
   problems of, 200
Fact-finding group, 182
Fairness doctrine, 390
Farewell speech, 314
Farnsworth, T., 195
Fatigue, voice, 376
Fear-arousing appeal, 298–99
Fear (communication apprehension), 359–62
Federal Communications Commission (FCC), 389–90
Feedback, 13–14, 67–73
   ambiguous, 13
   defined, 67
   delayed, 388
   effective, 72–73
   effects of, 69–71
   functions of, 68–69
   interaction with, 169
   in interpersonal communication, 158–59
   in intrapersonal communication, 136
   listener, 68
   mutual, 279
   negative, 13
   positive, 13
   self-feedback, 67–68, 136
   in small groups, 184–86
Feedforward, 158–59
Feeling (pathos), 262, 298–300
Feeling statements, 159
Feldman, D.C., 187
Ferguson, T.J., 402
Field, H.S., 425
Film, 391–92

Fisher, B.A., 213
Fitch-Hauser, M., 121
Flexibility, organizational, 229
Focusing, 64
Forewarning, persuasion and, 308
Formal communication, 7–8
  in organizations, 235–36
  presentations, 247–48
Forum, 182
Freestanding networks, 242
Freud, S., 85
Friesen, W.V., 86, 89
Front person, 190
Fukada, H., 308
Functional communication theory,
    150, 151
Functional roles in small groups, 188–
    91

G

Galst, J.P., 403
Gamble, M., 158, 170, 171
Gamble, T.K., 158, 170, 171
Game leader, 189–90
Garramore, G.M., 397
Gatekeeper, 190
Gatekeeping, 389–91
Gaze, mutual, 89
Gelles-Cole, S., 80, 94
Gender roles, 128
Georgia Power, 233–34
Gestalt, 135–36
Gestures, 367–70
Giammatteo, D., 191–92, 198, 199
Giammatteo, M., 191–92, 198, 199
Gibson, T.W., 39, 40
Givens, C.A., 88
Global village, 387
Goals of communication, 289–319
  entertainment, ceremonial, and
      other special-occasion
      communication, 312–14
  eye behavior and, 89
  information exchange, 290–95
    audience participation, 294–95
    increasing audience learning
        through, 290–94
  persuasion, 295–312
    Aristotelian theories of, 296–303
    contemporary theories of,
        303–7
    informative vs. persuasive
        communication, 295–96
    situations for, 311–12
    techniques of, 307–11
Goldberg, J., 107
Goldhaber, G.M., 233, 239

Gombiner, M.L., 88
Government
  gatekeeping by, 389–90
  mass communication and, 406
Graham, B., 359
Grapevines, 239–40
Grasping stage of small group
    development, 172
Griffith, T., 395
Griping stage of small group
    development, 172
Groping stage of small group
    development, 172
Group(s), 179–80. See also Small
    groups
  defined, 179
  reference, 127–28
Group action stage of small group
    development, 172
Grouping stage of small group
    development, 172
Group membership, audience analysis
    and, 268
Group pressure, 210–12
Groupthink, 210

H

Habits, the self and, 123
Hagafors, R., 68
Hall, E.T., 97
Hamilton, G.G., 196
Hampson, S., 402
Han, P.E., 236
Hand signs, 8
Hanes Knitwear, 231–32
Harmonizer, 189–90
Haskins, J.B., 395
Hazleton, V., 291
Hearing, defined, 52
Hearst, P., 9, 17
Hell's Angels, 187
Hess, E.H., 88
Hierarchy of human needs, 129–31
HIV virus, 306, 323–24
Holley, W.H., 425
Holliman, W.B., 102
Hollingworth, H.L., 274–75
Homer, P.M., 300
Homophily, 396
Honesty during job interviews, 430–
    31
Horizontal communication, 239
Hornstein, G.A., 156
How to Find a Job (Larson), 427
How We Think (Dewey), 203–4
Human-computer communication, 6, 9
Humane Society, 214

Human messages, 233–34
Humor
   persuasion through, 309
   in special-occasion speeches, 314
Huston, A.C., 401
Hypothetical examples, 346–47

I

Idea person, 189
Ideas, effective development of, 291–93
Identification, 142, 303
Illustrations, 347
Illustrators, 90–91
Imitative behavior, 29
Immediacy, 236–37, 428
Impromptu speeches, 314, 371
Indentation in outlines, 345
Inductive reasoning, 297–98
Inductive speech pattern, 338–39
Industry gatekeeping, 389
Infancy, achievements during, 31
Informal communication, 8
Informal networks, 239–40
Informal organizational communication, 235–36
Information
   diffusion of, 396–97
   exchange of, 261–62, 290–95
   group decision making and, 202–3
   increased availability of, 231
   from mass communication, 394–97
   retrieval of, 134
   transmission of, 27–28
Information giver, 188
Information seeker, 188–89
Informative speech, 261–62, 290–95
   audience participation, 294–95
   body of, 332, 336–38
   conclusion of, 334
   increasing audience learning through, 290–94
   persuasive communication vs., 295–96
Ingham, H., 124
Initial benefit statement, 290
Initiating stage of relationship development, 162
Innateness theory, 28
Inner voice, 58
Innovative messages, 234
In Search of Excellence, 18
Instinctive component of physical self, 121
Instrumental values, 269
Insulation, 142

Integrating stage of relationship development, 163
Intellectual self, 123
Intelligence, conformity and, 211
Intensifying stage of relationship development, 163
Intensity of stimuli, 133
Intentional communication, 8
Intentions, 304
Interaction, 27
   with empathy, 169
   eye behavior and, 88
   face-to-face, 181
   with feedback, 169
   social, 168–69
   stimulus-response, 169
Interactive listening, 52
Interdependence, organizational, 230
Interference in intrapersonal communication, 137
Intergroup conflict, 209
Intermediary, 237
Internal self-feedback, 136
Internal stimuli, 132
Interpersonal communication, 15, 18, 147–75
   defined, 148
   dyadic vs. small group communication, 149–50
   interpersonal relationships, 161–71
      conflict management in, 170–71
      development phases, 162–63
      disintegration phases, 163–67
      levels of social interaction, 168–69
      types of, 167–68
   model of, 148–49
   theories of, 150–55
      coordinated management of meaning, 150, 153–55
      functional, 150, 151
      relational, 150, 151–53
   variables affecting, 155–61
      feedback and feedforward, 158–59
      interpersonal attraction, 160–61
      nonverbal behavior, 160
      self-disclosure, 156–57
      trust, 152–55, 158
Interpreting level of listening, 54
Interrupting responses, 71
Interview(s), 243–46
   job, 417–33
      frequently asked questions in, 431–32
      honesty during, 430–31
      post-analysis, 433

Interview(s) (*cont.*)
  responsibilities of interviewee,
    419–30
  responsibilities of interviewer,
    417–18
  personal, 274, 327
  as source of materials, 327–28
Intimacy dimension of interpersonal
    relationships, 153
Intimate distance, 97, 98
Intragroup conflict, 209–10
Intrapersonal communication, 18,
    119–45
  hierarchy of human needs, 129–31
  intrapersonal variables affecting
      communication, 137–42
    defense mechanisms, 141–42
    personality traits, 139–41
    personal orientation, 138–39
  process of, 132–37
    feedback, 136
    interference, 137
    processing, 134–36
    reception, 133
    stimuli and, 132–33
    transmission, 136
  the self and, 120–25
    awareness and, 124–25
    emotional self, 122–23
    habits and, 123
    intellectual self, 123
    physical self, 121–22
    unity principle of, 123–24
  self-concept, 125–29
    past experiences and, 126–27
    reference groups and, 127–28
    roles and, 128
Intrinsic motivation, 291
Introduction part of speech, 330–32
Invitation committee, 273
IQ, listening, 62
Iran-Contra scandal, 260, 406
Irrelevant responses, 71

J

Jackson, J., 377
Janis, I.L., 210
Jargon, 26
Jefferson, T., 179
Job interview, 417–33
  frequently asked questions in,
    431–32
  honesty during, 430–31
  post-analysis, 433
  responsibilities of interviewee,
    419–30

researching company, 429–30
  securing interviews, 427–29
  self-evaluation, 419–24
  written preparation, 424–27
  responsibilities of interviewer,
    417–18
Jobs, S., 230–31
Jobs '77 (Yeomans), 421
Job search. *See* Job interview
Johari Window, 124–25
Johnson, P.M., 64
Joker, 191
Jonson, B., 364

K

Kafka, F., 133
Kahle, L.R., 300
Katz, D., 348
Kennedy, J.F., 331, 365
Kerek, G.M., 305, 306
Ketteringham, J.M., 120
Kibler, R.J., 181
Kinesics, 89–93
King, M.L., Jr., 314
King, P.E., 360
King, Rodney, 394
Kipnis, D., 197
Kleinke, C.L., 87
Knapp, M.L., 162
Kornblum, A., 359
Korzybski's laws, 37–38
Krantz, J., 230
Kubey, R.W., 396
Kuwabara, A.Y., 359
Kuwait, 1990 invasion of, 258

L

Labeling, 27
Ladder, listening, 52–56, 63–66
Laissez-faire leaders, 196–97
Language, 27–47
  behavior and, 38–43
    linguistic stereotyping, 40–41
  defined, 5, 27
  development of, 28–32
    process of, 30–32
    theories of, 28–30
  effective, 41–43
  features of, 34–37
  functions of, 27–28
  meaning and, 32–33
    Korzybski's laws of, 37–38
Language acquisition devices (LADs),
    29–30

Larson, C.E., 151
Larson, D., 427
Larynx, 372
Lashbrook, W.B., 214
Lateral communication, 239
Lazarsfeld, P., 399
Lazowski, L.E., 156
Leader(s)
  defined, 193
  emergence of, 197–98
  game, 189–90
  opinion, 396–97
  skills of, 198–99
Leadership
  defined, 193
  of discussion group, 181
  of small groups, 192–99
    styles of, 196–97
    theoretical approaches to, 193–96
Leadership Assessment Questionnaire,
    193, 194–95
Leakage, 84
Learned behavior, 29
Learning
  motivation and, 291
  observational, 401
Lectern, 371
Leeds, D., 309
Lenneberg, E., 28
Lerbinger, O., 240
Letitia Baldrige's Complete Guide to
    Executive Manners, 80, 94–95
Leveling, 238
Lewin, K., 389
Lewis, M., 209
Linguistic stereotyping, 40–41
Linking function of interpersonal
    communication, 151
Liska, J., 291
Listener
  active, 189–90
  feedback from, 68
Listening, 49–66
  defining, 52
  energy conservation and, 50–51
  five-step approach to (listening
    ladder), 52–56, 63–66
    assessing, 54–55
    attending, 53–54
    interpreting, 54
    perceiving, 54
    responding, 55–56
  improving, 63–66
  interactive, 52
  poor habits of, 61–63
  preferences, 59–61
  reasons for, 56–59
  in small groups, 184–86

Listening energy, 50–51
Listening IQ, 62
Littlejohn, S.W., 269
Lively quality of language, 379
Locus of control, 139–40
Logos (reasoning), 262, 296–98, 299
Long, L., 209
Long-term memory, 134
Love, need for, 131
Luft, J., 124, 213
Lynn, R., 402

M

Maass, A., 39
McAuliffe, C., 55
McClelland, V., 228
McClure, J., 208
McGinniss, J., 404
MacLachlan, J., 290
McLuhan, M., 387, 400
MacWhinney, B., 30
Magazines, 411
Maintenance roles, 189–90
Management, participative, 232
"Management revolution," 18–19
Manipulation, 140
Manipulative relationships, 167
Manipulators, body, 91–92
Mannerisms, 63, 365
Manstead, A.S.R., 280
Marques, J.M., 270
Marriage, 163, 167–68
Marsden, C., 273
Masked smile, 84
Maslow, A.H., 105, 129–30
Mass communication, 19, 385–416
  advertising, 260, 311–12, 398
    employment, 427–28
  appearing on radio or television,
    406–10
    performing, 408–10
    stations and, 406–7
    television studio and, 407–8
  characteristics of, 387–91
    delayed feedback, 388
    gatekeeping, 389–91
  effects of, 399–406
    children and TV, 399–403,
      434–39
    on government, 406
    political campaigns, 397, 403–4
    sex stereotyping, 404–5
    shaping of events, 405
  functions of, 394–97
    entertainment, 397
    information, 394–97

Mass communication (*cont.*)
  persuasion, 397
  future of, 410–12
  media for, 391–94
    film, 391–92
    radio, 393
    recording, 392–93
    television, 393–94
  overview of, 386–87
  public relations, 398–99
Mass media sources, 274
Matthiessen, P., 258
Maturity, 141
Meaning
  coordinated management of, 150,
    153–55
  language and, 32–33
    Korzybski's laws, 37–38
  sharing of, 149
Media, electronic, 329
Media for mass communication,
    391–94
  film, 391–92
  radio, 393
  recording, 392–93
  television, 393–94
Mehrabian, A., 236
Memorizing speeches, 361
Memory, 134
Mendelsohn, H., 395
Mentation function of interpersonal
    communication, 151
Message(s), 12
  controlling, 152
  distortion of, 238
  immediacy of, 236–37
  mixed, 228
  organizational, 233–34
Miley, B.R., 310
Millar, F.E., 152
Millard, R.J., 102
Miller, G.R., 16
Miller, M.M., 395
Mintz, N.L., 105
Mitchell, K.A., 160
Mixed messages, 228
Molloy, J.T., 2
Momentary interests, 276
Moments of Truth (Carlzon), 229
Money lost to ineffective listening, 56
Monologue, alternating, 168–69
Monopolizer, 191
Moods, colors and, 105–6
"Motherese," 10
Motivation, increased learning and, 291
Moving component of physical self, 121
Mulac, A., 39, 40
Murrow, E.R., 403

Music, 107–8
Mutual feedback, 279
Mutual gaze, 89
Muzak Corporation, 107

N

Naisbitt, J., 388
Nash, L.L., 261
National Organization for Women
    (NOW), 277
Needs, hierarchy of, 129–31
Negative feedback, 13
Negative reinforcement, 109
Neimeyer, R.A., 160
Networking, 242
Networks
  in decision-making group, 212–13
  organizational, 238–40
New Coke, 302
News media, 394–97, 411
Newspapers, 395, 411
Nicoll, M., 123
Night and Day (Woolf), 349
Niit, T., 87
Non-allness, Korzybski's law of, 37–38
Nondirective interview, 245–46
Non-identity, Korzybski's law of, 37
Nonverbal communication, 5–6,
    79–117, 363
  awareness of, 108–10
  clothing, 94–95
  environmental factors, 103, 104–8
    architecture and objects, 104–5
    colors, 105–6
    music, 107–8
    time, 106–7
  eye behavior, 87–89
    eye contact, 88, 160, 365–66, 371
  facial expressions, 85–87, 370
  functions of, 81–85
    accenting, 83
      complementing, 82
      deceiving/revealing, 84–85
      regulating, 82–83
      repeating, 81
      substituting, 81–82
  interpersonal communication
    and, 160
  kinesics and body movement, 89–
    93, 366–67
  paralanguage, 102–3
  personal appearance, 93–94
  proxemics, 97–102
    seating arrangements, 99–102
    spatial zones, 97–98
    territoriality, 98–99

smell and taste, 104
touching, 95–96, 160
Normativeness, source credibility
   and, 303
Norms of small groups, 187–88
Norris, P., 136
North, O., 377, 406
Note cards, 371

O

Objects, nonverbal communication
   and, 104–5
Observational learning, 401
Occupations of audience, 267
Office politics, 241–42
One-down messages, 152
100 Careers: How to Pick the One That's
   Best for You (Durham), 422
One-sided vs. two-sided arguments, 307
One-up messages, 152
Open discussion groups, 181–82
Openness, gestures of, 93
Operational definition, 348
Opinion giver, 188
Opinion leaders, 396–97
Opinions, 139
Opinion seeker, 188–89
Oral communication, 6. *See also* Public
   communication
Orators, street, 275
Organization
   of information, 291
   of speeches, 361
Organizational communication,
   18–19, 227–51
   business conferences, 246–47
   channels of, 236–38
   formal and informal, 235–36
   formal presentations, 247–48
   interviews, 243–46
   networks of, 238–40
Organizational skills, 198
Organizations
   characteristics of, 229–32
   defined, 228–29
   professionalism and, 240–43
   secret words of (jargon), 26
   types of messages sent in, 233–34
Organized audiences, 278
Orientation, personal, 138–39
Ouspensky, P.D., 121
Outlines, speech, 341–46
   accountability in, 344–45
   inclusion of points in, 345
   logical progression in, 346
   sample, 440–44

simplicity in, 343–44
underscoring relationships in,
   345–46
use of symbols and indentation
   in, 345
Overt stimuli, 132–33

P

Panel, 181–82
Paralanguage, 102–3
Paraphrasing, 159
Parker, D., 280
Partially oriented audiences, 275–76
Participative management, 232
Passive audiences, 275–76
Pathos (feeling), 262, 298–300
PBS, 395–96
Pearce, W.B., 110, 153–54, 155
Pearl, D., 401
Peleg, E., 107
Peluso, T., 396
Pember, D.R., 405
People-oriented listeners, 60
Perceiving level of listening, 54
Perception, selective, 133
Perelson, B., 399
Performance
   of decision-making groups, 207–13
   feedback and, 69–71
Personal appearance, 93–94, 243
Personal behavior, skills of, 198
Personal distance, 97, 99
Personal interviews, 274, 327
Personality
   decision-making groups and, 207
   style and, 37
   susceptibility to group pressure
     and, 211
Personality conflict, 207
Personality traits, 139–41
Personal mannerisms, criticism of, 63
Personal orientation, 138–39
Persuasion, 262
   degrees of, 295
   by mass communication, 397
Persuasive (rhetorical) principles, 257
Persuasive speech, 295–312
   Aristotelian theories of, 296–303
     ethos (source credibility), 257, 262,
      271, 299, 301–3, 358
     logos (reasoning), 262, 296–98,
      299
     pathos (feeling), 262, 298–300
   body of, 332–33, 336–41
   conclusion of, 334
   contemporary theories of, 303–7

Persuasive speech (*cont.*)
  informative communication vs.,
      295–96
  situations for, 311–12
  techniques of, 307–11
Pfau, M., 370
Phonation, 372, 376
Physical delivery, 366–71
  eye contact, 371
  facial expression, 370
  gestures, 367–70
  lectern and note cards, 371
  posture and body movements,
      366–67
Physical involvement in speech, 361
Physical self, 121–22
Physiological needs, 130
Physiological processing, 135–36
Pierce, W.D., 302
Pinaire Reed, J.A., 95
Pitch, 102, 373–74
Placement offices, 428
Platform format, 294
Polarization, 279–80
Policy, problems of, 201
Policymaking group, 182
Policy messages, 233
Political campaigns, 397, 403–4
Politics
  American, 257
  office, 241–42
Polls, public opinion, 274
Positive feedback, 13
Posture, 92–93, 366–67
PowerSpeak (Leeds), 309
Practicing speech delivery, 360–61
Preferences, listening, 59–61
Prejudices, 139
Presentation(s). *See also* Public
      communication; Speech(es)
  formal, 247–48
  one-sided vs. two-sided, 307
Presidential debates, 390
Pressure, group, 210–12
Price, K., 197
Price, W., 265
Primacy organization, 309–10
Primary (psyche) group, 180–81
Printed material, 329
Print medium, 411
Private discussion groups, 181
Private vs. public self, 124–25
Prizant, B.M., 31–32
Problem definition, decision making
      and, 204
Problem-solution method, 341
Problem-solving group, 182–83. *See
      also* Decision-making groups

Processing
  effortful, 121–22
  in intrapersonal communication,
      134–36
Producer, television, 408
Professionalism, 240–43
Professionals, defined, 241
Progression in outlines, 346
Projection, 142
Pronunciation, 376–77
Prophecy, self-fulfilling, 126
Proxemics, 97–102
  seating arrangements, 99–102
  spatial zones, 97–98
  territoriality, 98–99
Psyche (primary) group, 180–81
Psychological needs, 300
Psychological variables in audience
      analysis, 269
Public Broadcasting Service (PBS),
      395–96
Public communication, 18, 255–87.
      See also Speech(es)
  audience analysis, 263–73
    audience attitudes, 270–73
    checklist for, 281–82
    demographic analysis, 265–69
    psychological variables, 269
  audience types, 263–64, 274–78
    casual, 275
    concerted, 277
    organized, 278
    passive, 275–76
    selected, 276–77
  defined, 255
  environment's effects on, 278–79
  ethical responsibility and, 257–61
    credibility-centered approach,
        259–60
    defined, 257
    ends-justify-the-means approach,
        258
    situation ethics, 258–59
    social utility approach, 258
  methods of investigating audience,
      273–74
  overview of, 255–56
  purposes of, 261–62
  speaker-audience interaction,
      279–80
Public discussion groups, 181–82
Public distance, 97
Public health issues, 299
Public opinion polls and surveys, 274
Public relations, 398–99
Public relations person, 190
Public service announcements (PSAs),
      pro-nutritional, 403

Public speaking. *See* Public
communication; Speech(es)
Public vs. private self, 124–25
Pupil size, 88
Purpose
audience attitude toward speaker's,
272–73
discussion group and, 181
interpersonal vs. group
communication and, 149

Q

Qualifications, source credibility
and, 302
Quality
of speaker's voice, 103
vocal, 375
Quality circles, 182–83
Quantum Leap (TV show), 391
Questions
asking, 159
in interviews, 431–32
Quotations, 326

R

Radio, 387, 393. *See also* Mass
communication
advertising on, 398
appearing on, 406–10
specialization of, 411
Ramirez, C., 138
Ranganath Nayak, P., 120
Rapport, speech delivery and, 365–66
Rate of speech, 374–75
Rather, D., 377
Rationalization, 141–42
Raup, J.L., 402
Reaction formation, 142
Reagan, R., 278
Real examples, 346–47
Reardon, P., 427
Reason, J.T., 280
Reasoning (logos), 262, 296–98, 299
deductive, 296–97
inductive, 297–98
Recall, 134
Receiver, 13
Recency effect, 309–10
Reception, 133
Recognition, 134, 231
Recording, 392–93
Redirecting, 66
Reference groups, 127–28
Referent, 33
Reflecting, 65

Reflective thinking, 203–4
Regulating, 82–83
Regulation messages, 233
Regulative rules, 154
Regulators, 91
Regulatory function of interpersonal
communication, 151
Reinforcement, negative, 109
Relational communication theory, 150,
151–53
Relationships
interpersonal, 161–71
conflict management in, 170–71
development phases, 162–63
disintegration phases, 163–67
levels of social interaction,
168–69
types of, 167–68
lost, due to ineffective listening, 57
Repeating, 81
Repetitious behaviors, 123, 293
Repression, 142
Research
for group decision making, 201–3
on hiring company, 429–30
Resonance, 102, 372
Responding level of listening, 55–56
Response(s)
circular, 280
feedback, 71
informative vs. persuasive
communication and, 296
Resúmé, 424–27
Retrieval of information, 134
Revealing, 84–85
Reward appeal, 298
Rewards, team, 231
Rhetorical (persuasive) principles, 257
Robberson, M.R., 298
Roddy, B.L., 397
Rogers, C., 198
Rogers, L.E., 152
Rogers, R.W., 298
Rogers, W., 276
Rokeach, M., 269
Role(s)
self-concept and, 128
in small groups, functional, 188–91
Ropp, Robert de, 67
Rosenkoetter, L.I., 401
Rue, P., 182
Rule, B.G., 402

S

Safety, source credibility and, 303
Safety needs, 130

Sales, 311–12
  effective listening and increased, 57
Salter, C.A., 105–6
Salter, C.D., 105–6
Salvi, D., 39
Salzman, J., 184–86
Sarnoff, D., 400
Sawyer, C.R., 360
Scandinavian Airlines (SAS), 229
Scare tactics, 300
Schanck, R.L., 348
Schein, V.E., 241–42
Schlam, D., 107
Schmidt, S., 197
Schultz, B., 210
Seating arrangements, 99–102
Secondary interests, 276
Secret words (jargon), 26
Selected audiences, 276–77
Selective perception, 133
Self, 120–25
  awareness and, 124–25
  emotional, 122–23
  habits and, 123
  intellectual, 123
  physical, 121–22
  private vs. public, 124–25
  unity principle of, 123–24
Self-actualization needs, 130, 131
Self-concept, 125–29
  past experiences and, 126–27
  reference groups and, 127–28
  roles and, 128
Self-confidence, conformity and, 211
Self-disclosure, 156–57
Self-esteem, 141
Self-evaluation, 419–24
Self-examination, skills of, 198
Self-expressive function of
    attitudes, 308
Self-feedback, 67–68, 136
Self-fulfilling prophecy, 126
Self-help groups, 179
Self-reflexiveness, Korzybski's law of, 38
Self-serving roles, 191
Sellers, D.E., 135
Selling of the President, The
    (McGinniss), 404
Semantics, 32–33
Semantic stereotyping, 40–41
Semin, G., 39
Sense, 33
Sensory storage, 134
Series transmissions, 237–38
Sex differences
  in language patterns, 39–40
  in status, 160
Sex of audience, 267–68

Sex stereotyping, 93, 404–5
Shaffer, D.R., 300, 301, 303, 305–7
Shakespeare, W., 102, 366
Sharpening, 238
Short-term memory, 134
Signs, hand, 8
Simplicity in outlines, 343–44
Sisler, H.H., 402
Sitting positions, 93
Situation, 14–15
Situation ethics, 258–59
Skills, leadership, 198–99
Small group communication, 18
  dyadic communication vs., 149–50
  interpersonal communication
      vs., 149
Small group discussion, 246–47
Small groups, 177–225
  analyzing interaction in, 213–16
  decision-making groups, 199–213
    cohesion of, 207–9
    communication networks in,
        212–13
    conflict in, 210–12
    decision-making agenda, 204–7
    kinds of topics or problems,
        199–201
    personalities and, 207
    reflective thinking in, 203–4
    research for discussion, 201–3
  defined, 180
  development of, 191–92
  functional roles in, 188–91
  leadership of, 192–99
    emergence of leaders, 197–98
    skills of effective leaders, 198–99
    styles of, 196–97
    theoretical approaches to, 193–96
  norms of, 187–88
  overview of, 178–79
  participating in, 183–86
    bypassing, 186
    listening and feedback, 184–86
    responsibilities of, 183
    speaking, 183–84
Smell, 104
Smeltzer, L.R., 71
Smiling, 84
Smith, A.P., 424
Smith, D., 440
Smith, Kline and French Laboratories
    (SK&F), 120
Smithson, M., 157
Snow, C., 30
Social approval, conformity and, 211
Social cues, 159
Social distance, 97
Social facilitation, 280

Social interaction, 168–69
Social roles, 128
Social utility approach, 258
Socioeconomic statuses of
    audience, 266
Solutions, decision-making agenda
    and, 206–7
Sorting, 134–35
Source, 11
Source credibility (ethos), 257, 262,
    271, 299, 301–3, 358
Source materials for speech, 326–29
Sparks, G.G., 400
Spatial speech pattern, 337–38
Spatial zones, 97–98
Speaker. *See also* Speech(es)
    audience attitudes toward, 270–71
    credibility of, 271
    criticism of, 63
    voice quality of, 103
Speaker-audience interaction, 279–80
Speaking in small groups, 183–84
Special-occasion communication, 312–
    14
Special pleader, 191
Speech(es), 321–55. *See also*
        Informative speech; Persuasive
        speech
    attitude about, 362
    to entertain, 262
    gathering source materials for,
        326–29
    impromptu, 371
    memorizing, 361
    organization of, 361
    outlining, 341–46
        accountability in, 344–45
        inclusion of points in, 345
        logical progression in, 346
        sample of, 440–44
        simplicity in, 343–44
        underscoring relationships in,
            345–46
        use of symbols and indentation
            in, 345
    parts of, 329–36
        body, 332–33, 336–41
        conclusion, 334–35
        introduction, 330–32
        transitions, 335–36, 337
    physical involvement in, 361
    rehearsing for, 360–61
    sample, 434–39
    special-occasion, 312–14
    supporting material for, 346–50
        clarification, 346–48
        support, 348–50
        testimony, 350

topic of, 323–26
    involvement with, 361–62
    narrowing, 325–26
    selecting, 323–24
Speech delivery, 357–83
    communication apprehension,
        359–62
    ethos and, 358
    physical, 366–71
        eye contact, 371
        facial expression, 370
        gestures, 367–70
        lectern and note cards, 371
        posture and body movements,
            366–67
    principles of, 362–66
        appropriate presentation style,
            363–65, 377–79
        establishing rapport, 365–66
        looking natural, 362, 365
        matching delivery and context,
            362–63
    style, 377–79
    vocal, 372–77
        factors influencing voice, 375
        improving vocalization, 375–76
        mechanics of vocalization, 372–73
        pronunciation, 376–77
        vocal characteristics, 373–75
Speech tension (communication
    apprehension), 359–62
Sponsors, TV network, 390–91
Springsteen, B., 366
Stacks, D.W., 135
Stage fright (communication
    apprehension), 359–62
Stagnating stage of relationship
    disintegration, 166
Stanat, K.W., 427
"Standard American speech," 377
Statement(s)
    feeling, 159
    initial benefit, 290
    thesis, 331–32
Stations, radio, 406–7
Statistics, 349–50
Status differences related to sex, 160
Steele, B.H., 182
Steil, L.K., 66
Stereotypes
    linguistic, 40–41
    nonverbal communication and,
        109–10
    sex, 93, 404–5
Stewart, C.J., 243
Stimpson, D.V., 102
Stimulation, persuasion through,
    295

Stimuli
   intensity of, 133
   intrapersonal communication and,
      132–33
Stimulus-response interaction,
   169
Stitt, C., 197
Storage, sensory, 134
Stradling, S.G., 280
Street orators, 275
Stress, effective listening and
      reduction of, 57–59
Studios, television, 407–8
Style(s)
   criticism of, 63
   leadership, 196–97
   meaning and, 35–37
   of presentation, 363–65, 377–79
Subject, audience attitudes toward,
      271–72
Submissiveness, eye behavior and,
      89
Substituting, 81–82
Super Bowl, 405
Supporting material, 346–50
   clarification, 346–48
   support, 348–50
   testimony, 350
Surveys, 274, 328
Symbolic process, 33
Symbols, 12, 33
   outline, 345
Symmes, D., 10
Symmetrical relationships, 152
Symposium, 182
Sypher, B.D., 228
System, communication, 15–16

T

Tagamet, 120
"Talking down," 363–64, 365
Tangential responses, 71
Task messages, 233
Task-oriented roles, 188–89
Taste, 104
Taylor, S., 69–71
Team rewards and recognition, 231
Teams, business, 231–32, 277
Teleconferencing, video, 247
Television, 393–94. See also Mass
      communication
   advertising on, 398
   appearing on, 406–10
   children and, 399–403, 434–39
   commercials on, 402–3

network sponsors, 390–91
   political campaigns and, 403–4
   specialization of, 411
   violence on, 401–2
Tempo, 102
Tension, speech (communication
      apprehension), 359–62
Terminal values, 269
Termination of relationship, 167
Territoriality, 98–99
Tesser, A., 300, 303, 305–7
Testimony, 350
Thesis statement, 331–32
Thinking, reflective, 203–4
Thinking-speaking time differential,
      63
Thomas, C., 255, 256
Threshold of consciousness, 133
Thriving on Chaos, 18
Through the Looking Glass (Carroll), 36
Time
   listening and, 56, 57
   nonverbal communication and,
      106–7
   thinking-speaking differential in, 63
Time-oriented listeners, 60–61
Toddlerhood, 31–32
Toffler, A., 410–11, 412
Tolerance of ambiguity, 140
Topic(s)
   for group decision making,
      199–201
   limiting the, 204–5
   of speech, 323–26, 361–62
      narrowing, 325–26
      selecting, 323–24
Topical speech pattern, 336–37
Touching, 95–96, 160
Tracking, 64
Traits, personality, 139–41
Transitions in speech, 335–36, 337
Transmission(s)
   of information, 27–28
   in intrapersonal communication,
      136
   series, 237–38
Trial bonding, 163
Tritten, L., 394
Truesdell, S.E., 156
Trust dimension of interpersonal
      relationships, 152–55, 158
Trustworthiness, 153, 303
Turn-denying cues, 83
Turn-maintaining cues, 83
Turn-requesting cues, 83
Turn-yielding cues, 83
Two-sided vs. one-sided
      arguments, 307

U

Unintentional communication, 9
Unity principle, 123–24
Upward communication, 239, 240

V

Vagueness, 34–35
Valsiner, J., 87
Value(s), 138
    audience analysis and, 269
    emotional appeal to, 300
    instrumental, 269
    problems of, 200–201
    terminal, 269
Variable compensation, 232
Verbal communication, 5–6
Verderber, R.F., 189, 190, 191
Video teleconferencing, 247
Village, global, 387
Violence on television, 401–2
Visual aids, 248, 292, 293–94, 335
Vocal delivery, 372–77
    factors influencing voice, 375
    improving vocalization, 375–76
    mechanics of vocalization, 372–73
    pronunciation, 376–77
    vocal characteristics, 373–75
Vocal quality, 375
Voice, 372
    exercises for, 375
    inner, 58
    variations in (paralanguage), 102–3
Voice box, 372
Voice fatigue, 376
Volume, 374
Voting behavior, 399
Vowels, 373

W

Wahlers, K.J., 181
Wallach, G., 6–7, 30
Walther, F., 69–71

Want ads, 427–28
Wass, H., 402
Watson, K.W., 60, 64, 71, 150, 181, 294
Watson, W., 66
Wavelengths, communication, 14
Welcoming speech, 312–13
Wetherby, A.M., 31–32
Wexner, L.B., 105
What Color Is Your Parachute?
    (Bolles), 427
Wheel network, 213
Whetmor, E.J., 394, 395
Whistler, J.M., 332
Widenmann, S.J., 39, 40
Wiemann, J.M., 39, 40
Wiseman, G., 281
Withdrawer, 191
Woolf, V., 349
Words
    abstract, 34
    concrete, 34
    defined, 27
    precise use of, 378
    secret (jargon), 26
Wright, J.C., 401
Written communication, 6–7
Wyse, L., 26

X

Xerox Corporation, 290

Y

Yeomans, W.N., 421
Y network, 213
Yzerbyt, V.Y., 270

Z

Zamostny, K., 182
Zorn, T.E., Jr., 228